BEHAVIOUR THERAPY

BEHAVIOUR THERAPY
Techniques, Research and Applications

S P K Jena

SAGE Los Angeles • London • New Delhi • Singapore
www.sagepublications.com

First published in 2008 by

 SAGE Publications India Pvt Ltd
B1/I-1, Mohan Cooperative Industrial Area
Mathura Road, New Delhi 110 044, India
www.sagepub.in

SAGE Publications Inc
2455 Teller Road
Thousand Oaks, California 91320, USA

SAGE Publications Ltd
1 Oliver's Yard
55 City Road
London EC1Y 1SP, United Kingdom

SAGE Publications Asia-Pacific Pte Ltd
33 Pekin Street
#02-01 Far East Square
Singapore 048763

Published by Vivek Mehra for SAGE Publications India Pvt Ltd, typeset in 10/12 pt Times New Roman by Star Compugraphics Private Limited, Delhi and printed at Chaman Enterprises, New Delhi.

Library of Congress Cataloging-in-Publication Data

Jena, S P K, 1960–
 Behaviour therapy : techniques, research and applications/S P K Jena.
   p. cm.
 Includes bibliographical references and index.
 1. Behaviour therapy.   I. Title
   [DNLM: 1. Behaviour Therapy.   WM 425 J51b 2008]

RC489.B4J46   616.89'142—dc22   2008   2007047661

ISBN: 978-0-7619-3624-4 (HB)   978-81-7829-788-0 (India-HB)

The SAGE Team: Sugata Ghosh, Vikas Jain, Amrita Saha and Trinankur Banerjee

*To the clients, their families with whom I have had the
opportunity to work and explore, who have guided my thinking
about the practice and science of behaviour therapy*

Contents

II. TECHNIQUES OF BEHAVIOUR THERAPY

III. RESEARCH AND PRACTISE

List of Figures

Preface

In the last quarter of the century, the empirical and clinical applications of behaviour therapy have witnessed explosive growth. This has transformed it from the state of a therapeutic dealing with problems of individual nature to a social movement to facilitate social change, and from cure to prevention. Our understanding of many themes of behaviour therapy has advanced considerably beyond what we knew a few years ago. Its empirical approach, demonstrable theoretical foundations and expanding applications are responsible for this fascinating development.

Shaping of a progressive society depends not only on the material resources it has but also on the skills that people possess. Thus, shaping of human skills is recognised as an area of great concern in today's world. How well we modify human behaviour to maximise his/her potential is an issue of considerable significance. Helping people learn new patterns of effective responding, eliminating the ineffective ones and, thereby, improving the quality of life are among the broadest goals of behaviour therapy. In this context, behaviour therapy which is also known as applied behaviour analysis has made substantial contribution.

In this volume, attempt has been made to bring out the fundamental principles and some of the exciting research and applications in the field. I am acutely aware of the fact that a single volume would not be sufficient to incorporate the wide range of issues addressed by behaviour therapists. I have tried to present a concise view of the different facets of this rapidly expanding field. Although primarily addressed to the professionals engaged in behavioural intervention, I hope that it will benefit a wide range of readers; even those having no background knowledge of behavioural psychology.

The book is comprised of nineteen chapters, which are placed in three sections: I—Foundations, Developmental issues and Assessment, II—Techniques of Behaviour Therapy, and III—Research and Practice. The first section is comprised of five chapters. The first chapter provides a historical account of behaviour therapy, outlining its definition, scope and fundamental assumptions. Here, an attempt has been made to trace out the historical account of behaviour therapy from the dawn of human civilisation until the present times. In this context, various approaches that have influenced the growth of behaviour therapy have been discussed. Radical behaviourism, cognitive behaviourism and modern systematic eclecticism are considered as three distinct approaches within the field of behaviour therapy. The second chapter is devoted to the conceptual issues. This chapter is considered important for understanding the basic principles that guide the practice of behaviour therapy. Basic concepts like reinforcement, punishment, extinction and stimulus control have been introduced briefly before elaborating on their applications. These concepts have been elaborated in the second section of the book. The third chapter is intended to explore the psychobiological foundations of behaviour therapy. The issues like functional autonomy of learned responses, arousal theory and conditionability, and functional reorganisation of the brain are discussed in the context of behaviour therapy. The developmental perspective of behaviour therapy is the theme of the fourth chapter. It focuses on a distinctive approach to the childhood behavioural problems—a perspective which the adult-oriented therapist sometimes loses sight of. The rationale for special treatment of children as clients and the pitfalls of fitting the adult-oriented approach to children are discussed along with key issues like learning at different stages of development, the young child's preparedness to learn and self-control. The purpose is to sensitise the readers about intricacies of child behaviour therapy.

The assessment data are generally considered indispensable for evaluating the progress of behaviour change. Therefore, the fifth chapter is designed to explain the meaning of behavioural diagnosis. It is contrasted with the traditional medical diagnosis of mental disorders. Apart from the fundamental differences between these two approaches, it discusses the mental disorders in the light of learning paradigm. Methods of behavioural observation, assessment of behaviour in group setting, observer training and methods of assessing inter-observer reliability are among the other aspects that have been covered in this chapter. The idea is to provide a scientific orientation to examine the target behaviour that a practitioner wishes to modify.

The second section of the book—Techniques of Behaviour Therapy—is the largest section of this volume. It is comprised of eleven chapters—6 to 16. It contains discussions on a wide range of behavioural and cognitive-behavioural techniques used to increase desirable behaviour, developing new behaviours and eliminating undesirable behaviour. Chapter 6—on increasing desirable behaviour—explains procedures for effective use of reinforcement and explains the conditions that enhance their effectiveness. In the next chapter, attempt is made to familiarise readers with techniques that are used for developing behaviours not available in the response repertoire. The techniques include stimulus control, shaping, chaining, prompting and fading. Examples and case studies are provided to facilitate their application. The subsequent chapters in this section deal with techniques of modelling. Its rationale, processes involved and applications in various types of behaviour disorders have been explored. The subsequent chapter for this section deals with aversive methods of response elimination. Types of aversive stimuli, determinants of effective punishment, its side effects, predictors of positive outcome and ethical issues have also been explained to provide a comprehensive view of punishment as a technique of intervention. The side-effects are particularly focused on to ensure ethical use of the technique. The next chapter deals with non-aversive procedures such as extinction, differential reinforcement, time-out and response cost. Exposure procedures that eliminate maladaptive response through production of anxiety, also known as anxiety-producing techniques for response elimination, are discussed in chapter 11. The techniques included are flooding, implosion and aversion relief. At the end of the chapter ethical issues have been discussed. Special techniques like relaxation, desensitisation, restricted environmental stimulation therapy, eye movement desensitisation reprocessing and covert conditioning procedures have been covered in this section as well. The last chapter of this section deals with various techniques of cognitive-behaviour therapy which is considered to be the most recent trend in behaviour therapy.

Conducting scientific research is a very important step in the progress of behaviour therapy. A therapist should be well conversant with research methods. Therefore, the third and last section of this book is devoted to research related issues. It is comprised of three chapters, from 17 to 19. The 17th chapter is a discourse on methodological issues. Various research designs, including group as well as single-case designs, have been discussed with special emphasis on their application and limitations. Chapter 18—on evidence-based approach to behaviour therapy—attempts to sensitise the readers about the need of research-based practice. It includes issues like theory-driven vs. diagnosis-based protocol approach, efficacy research, transportability, dissemination of information and system evaluation.

Use of behavioural technology for human service without ethical considerations always entails the danger of abuse. In this context, issues like informed consent, confidentiality, harms and benefits as well as respect for human dignity in behavioural treatment are considered in the last chapter which is on ethical issues. This chapter provides a guideline for ethical practice of behaviour therapy. Readers are advised to adhere to such ethics while selecting and applying behaviour therapy techniques to their clients.

Behaviour therapy contains much more than what is written in this volume. The idea was to present a comprehensive view of the field to the readers. The volumes of previous published work on behaviour therapy explicate and demonstrate that it can serve as an effective treatment modality for a large variety of disorders. The procedures of treatment are simple; therefore, apart from the students of behavioural sciences, it can be easily learned by parents, family members and other care-givers under the guidance of an experienced behaviour therapist. From this angle, I hope this text would be helpful not only to a wide range of professionals working in the field of health-care, education and rehabilitation, but also to common people. A series of sample forms have been provided at the end of the book to facilitate systematic application and recording of behavioural procedures with individual clients. Although I am acutely aware that some gaps do exist in this volume which are rather inevitable, the material is arranged in such a manner that the parts make up a meaningful whole.

S P K Jena

Acknowledgements

A number of persons, including colleagues and students, have provided me the intellectual impetus to work on this book. Their discussions have benefited me enormously. I owe much to them and sincerely acknowledge their help. My chief debts are due to Haripad Mishra and V. Kumaraiah, former professors of Clinical Psychology at NIMHANS, Bangalore and R.G. Sharma at Central Institute of Psychiatry, Ranchi, who have inspired me immensely and shaped my ideas during my early years of internship and doctoral research on clinical psychology. I would also like to acknowledge the help extended to me by the librarians of the University of Delhi and the National Medical Library, New Delhi, in consulting the current literature on the subject. I extend my gratitude to SAGE, New Delhi for careful review and acceptance of this manuscipt for publication. In fact, the reviewer's observations served as a 'third eye' to see the manuscipt from the reader's angle.

My wife Manisha and son Mrunmoy have been enduring resources for me throughout. I thankfully acknowledge them for tolerating my compulsiveness and preoccupation for bringing out this book.

New Delhi   S P K Jena

PART I
FOUNDATIONS, DEVELOPMENTAL ISSUES AND ASSESSMENT

1

The Philosophical and Historical Foundations

Human behaviour is a fascinating subject. Its splendid variation, unimaginable complexity and magnificent responsiveness to the changing environment have attracted scholars for ages. The scientific study of behaviour perhaps started in those cradles of civilisation, where land was rich, the division of labour was highly specialised and people were secured. Perhaps it provided ideal conditions for people to observe themselves and others closely to explore the intricacies of human behaviour. Gardner Murphy, one of the historians of psychology, estimated that it might have happened in India, China and Greece around 500 BC (Murphy 1973). Since then, the study of human behaviour has evolved a great deal. Innovative ideas and new approaches have kept enriching our understanding of human behaviour. In this context, behaviourism emerged as a distinct trend and has continued to influence generations of scholars. Today's behaviour analysts are more concerned with predictive and descriptive problems rather than the epistemological ones.

Behaviour therapy emerged as a technology of behaviour change in the 1930s and is considered an important milestone in the development of psychology as a behavioural science. Its adherence to principles of learning distinguishes it from other approaches to behaviour change. It includes all those procedures, which are derived from or at least consistent with the findings of experimental psychology, particularly in the field of learning (Chesser 1970). Its primary focus is on the present behaviour, therefore, it is considered as a 'here-and-now' approach. Empiricism is its guiding principle. Behaviour therapy has been playing a significant role in alleviating human miseries.

Effective learning is one of the key processes, which is involved in shaping intelligent behaviour. Throughout the life span, the individual's behavioural ecology keeps unfolding opportunities for new learning. Formation of civil societies and progressive nations of the modern world are the products of newer forms of learning. Therefore, the role of learning is so critical. However, people learn not only through direct interactions with the environment that constitutes the present but also from experiences and knowledge bases that constitute their past. A closer look at our social behaviour would reveal that every society attempts to reinforce good behaviours and discourages the unproductive, undesirable and destructive ones. The extent of programming these contingencies defines social development. Environment that is not adequately engineered to support adaptive responding through consistent contingencies of reinforcement (as well as punishment), tends to establish weak, fragile and pathological behavioural tendencies. Such unprogrammed and chaotic contingencies may lead to deviance. Crime, violence, delinquency and mental disorders are some of its consequences. Shaping of the individual and collective responses requires scientific understanding of the functional relationship between behaviour and its consequences, that is, how environment responds to a given behaviour.

Increasing dissatisfaction with the traditional models of psychopathology, such as psychoanalysis or humanistic-existentialism, and their questionable theoretical validity and practical ineffectiveness created a fertile ground for the development of behaviourism. In this context, behaviour therapy emerged as a powerful movement in conceptualising the treatment of behaviour pathology. It has influenced not only the contemporary practice of clinical psychology, social work, and other human services but also revolutionised our current understanding of psychopathology of human behaviour. Introduction of sophisticated techniques of observation and analysis has expanded our understanding in many unexplored areas of human behaviour.

Methods of unparalleled effectiveness have been developed through experiments in laboratory and natural environment. Behaviour analysts' prime concern is to analyse the behaviour-environment relationship and reprogramme the interaction in a manner that facilitates development and sustains desirable responding. Apart from problems of personal concern for people, they respond to many pressing problems of the society. We believe that this methodologically exacting and effective profile will continue to influence the human service scenario in a significant manner for decades to come.

THE TERMINOLOGY AND BASIC ASSUMPTIONS

In contemporary scientific literature, terms like 'behaviour therapy', 'behaviour modification' and 'applied behaviour analysis' are often used interchangeably; although there are finer paradigmatic differences in conceptualisation of the analysis of behaviour in terms of cause-and-effect relationship. Here, paradigm refers to the constellation of beliefs, values, techniques, and so on, shared by the members of the scientific community (Kuhn 1970). The behaviour analysts primarily focus on the environmental variables that include the antecedents (A), behaviour (B) and its consequences (C), popularly known as the A-B-C paradigm, or 'three-term contingency'. Modern behaviour therapists have expanded it to include the organismic variable (O) also. It is symbolically stated as the 'A-O-B-C paradigm' (Paniagua and Baer 1981).

Although some critics like Graziano and Mooney (1984) conceptualised behaviour therapy as a pathology-linked and adult-oriented approach confined to clinical applications only, its methods are equally applicable to clinical problems as well as enhancement of normal adaptive functions, including prevention, education and rehabilitation. The term 'therapy' is used in an ameliorative sense. Paradigmatically, it is a stronger approach than behaviour modification or behaviour analysis due to its broader theoretical base. Common features of all the above are: (i) adherence to learning principles as mediating process for behaviour change, and (ii) empiricism as the method of analysis.

However, some authors view behaviour therapy as an 'atheoretical' approach (Kazdin 1982). Therefore, it is presumed that its techniques can be researched without a distinctive underlying theory. In that case, apart from being a science, it is viewed as a technology that is conceptualised as scientific knowledge used in practical ways. Innovations in behaviour therapy combine knowledge derived both from experimental as well as applied analysis of behaviour. The behavioural techniques are the ways in which this knowledge and special skills are applied for changing human behaviour. Thus, it is seen both as science as well as technology.

Although, there is no clear practical advantage in understanding a behaviour disorder theoretically, it is necessary to develop new treatment techniques on sound theoretical basis. This is not because it helps in alleviating the problem behaviour but to understand why one technique is more effective or ineffective as compared to others. Theoretical principles would provide the basis for explaining the success of a technique. Thus, it would even facilitate new developments of techniques by predicting their effectiveness. Hence, behaviour therapy is not just a bundle of divergent techniques. It is the systematic use of that body of knowledge, which is derived from the application of experimental methods in psychology and its closely related disciplines (Yates 1970).

Learning theories alone does not provide adequate foundation to the current development of behaviour therapy. Modern behaviour therapists incorporate knowledge from diverse disciplines. Therefore, it has attained an eclectic quality. Based on these observations, one may make the following assumptions about behaviour therapy:

1. Behaviour therapy is an empirical approach.
2. Most behaviour is learned and therefore, can be unlearned.
3. Maladaptive behaviours are learned in the same manner as the adaptive ones.
4. Historical account of development of problem behaviour is less relevant than the present ones.
5. Behaviour therapy rejects the assumptions of traditional trait theory (Eysenck 1959).

The methods used in behaviour therapy are tailored and adapted to the situation and the individual client. The same behaviours may have quite different learning histories; therefore, they require different treatments too. Thus, individualised behaviour analysis is considered as a prerequisite for behavioural intervention.

In the earlier stages of its development, behaviour therapy was fulfilling its promises. However, its ideology was diluted in due course of time. Similarly, its scope has increased enormously. Apart from treatment, it is now used for prevention of abnormal behaviour. In order to do so it makes use of the controlled experimental studies.

Present day behaviour therapists rely on the principles of experimental psychology instead of learning theories alone. The approach includes elements of social learning, cognition and other principles of perception, motivation and observations drawn from other biological sciences. Therefore, it is now considered as a broad-spectrum approach.

HISTORICAL PERSPECTIVE

We believe that behaviour therapy has a long past but a short history. Glimpses of its guiding principles have been found in the Vedic tradition of treatment and in the writings of Upanishads, the most ancient literature of the world (Singh and Oberhummer 1980). Many Buddhist treatments of *klesha* (psychological stress) have close similarity with modern techniques of behaviour modification. De Silva (1984) illustrated several cases from *Vatamiga Jataka*. One of those cases was that of Sanjaya, who could successfully alleviate the fear of an antelope and bring it up to the king's palace. The animal's fear for human beings was reduced by feeding it with honeyed grass. The technique used had striking similarity with the technique of systematic desensitisation. However, these antecedents neither have been reported systematically, nor based on any scientific principle. Therefore, these literatures do not constitute scientific schools but cults concerned with faith rather than facts. There is more of mysticism and metaphysics than empiricism. Therefore, this is viewed as 'historical precursors' of behaviour therapy rather than its 'history' (Kazdin 1978).

Behaviourism as an active philosophy of human behaviour is a product of the 20th century. A related technology did not appear before the third quarter of the century (Skinner 1979). The roots of behaviour therapy lie in the behaviourism of John. B. Watson. Highlighting the role of learning in shaping behaviour, he said, 'Give me a dozen healthy infants... and I'll guarantee to take any one at random and train him to become... doctor, lawyer, artist, merchant, chief and yes, even beggar man and thief' (Watson 1924: 82). Although, this radical perspective of behaviourism has been debated seriously, at large, his radical approach heralded a new era of optimism, inspiring generations of scholars.

The classic experimental work on behaviour therapy originated in laboratory experimentation of Bekhterew (1912) in the former Soviet Union. The scientific optimism attached to behaviour change was then closely connected with explorations in the field of conditioning of animal behaviour. Although as early as 1920, Watson and Rayner demonstrated experimental induction and elimination of fear in a young child, the scope of behaviour modification was much restricted until Pavlov (1927) developed the classical conditioning theory. He conducted a series of experiments on animals. It broadened the base of behavioural explanations of psychopathology. He explained that conditionability is the function of the strength, that is the excitability of the nervous system. Behaviour problems were considered as the consequences of disorders in two basic central processes—excitation and inhibition. These are adversely affected when there is either (i) intense stimulation, (ii) increased delay between conditional and unconditional stimulus, and (iii) simultaneous occurrence of positively and negatively conditioned stimuli.

During 1930s, various childhood problems were being successfully treated with behaviour therapy, such as tics (Dunlap 1932), stuttering (Moore 1938), and enuresis (Morgan and Whitmer 1939; Mowrer and Mowrer 1938). Warren and Brown (1943) directed behavioural analysis to the learning of young normal children. Fuller (1949), and Ferster and DeMyer (1961) tried to apply behaviour analysis to young autistic children.

The next observable trend in child behaviour therapy was the development of special techniques that enabled teachers, parents and childcare workers to apply behaviour therapy procedures in their own settings. Reviewing almost hundred such studies in child behaviour therapy, Gelfand and Hartmann (1968) observed inherent methodological problems in many of them; many of which failed to meet the required experimental controls. A small number of controlled studies demonstrated the power and efficiency of behavioural approaches. Increasing numbers of clinicians, educators, parents and paraprofessionals have been turning to behaviour therapy for treatment of childhood behaviour disorders. This popularity has been attributed to several reasons. The first of which is the changing mode of scientific thought in psychology and other clinical sciences (Kuhn 1962), characterised by a shift in emphasis from theoretical orientation to pure empiricism.

Krasner (1971) traced out three distinct origins of behaviour therapy. The first was that of Lindsley, Skinner and Solomon's (1953) work that used the term 'behaviour therapy'. They applied operant conditioning techniques to hospitalised clients. Second, in 1958 when Joseph Wolpe, developed the concept of 'reciprocal inhibition' as a procedure for dealing with maladaptive autonomic responses like anxiety, by following Pavlovian and Hullian models of conditioning. The idea was crystallised in his book entitled *Psychotherapy by Reciprocal Inhibition*. Third, when Lazarus (1958) used the term 'behaviour therapy' referring to the application of objective techniques designed to inhibit neurotic patterns. In order to offset the psychoanalytic tradition and to legitimise behavioural intervention as an essential part of effective clinical practice, he also introduced the term 'behaviour therapist' into the scientific and professional literature (Lazarus 1981). About a year later in 1959, Eysenck defined it as 'a method of treatment derived from modern learning theory'. He extended Pavlov's basic concept of types of nervous system to a two-dimensional theory of personality. Through experimental works, he explained learning efficiency, that is conditionability as a function of the personality type such as introversion and extraversion.

An individual's conditionability determines the prognosis of behaviour change (Figure 1.1). The introverts are more readily conditionable than the extraverts. This is due to the reason that the former group has an easily excitable nervous system than the latter. Based on this observation, Eysenck (1959) attempted to explain an individual's susceptibility to certain categories of mental disorders. Certain client variables, such as premorbid personality, age, presence of anxiety, depression, rigidity (Sahoo, Gillis & Mishra 2002), phobia, neuroticism, conditionability (Mukhopadhyaya, Dutta and Sanyal 1998; Sahoo, Gillis & Mishra 1999; Slade 1974) and exaggerated responsibility (Rachman 1993) are predictors of good outcome in behaviour therapy.

FIGURE 1.1
Conditionability as a Function of Behavioural Types

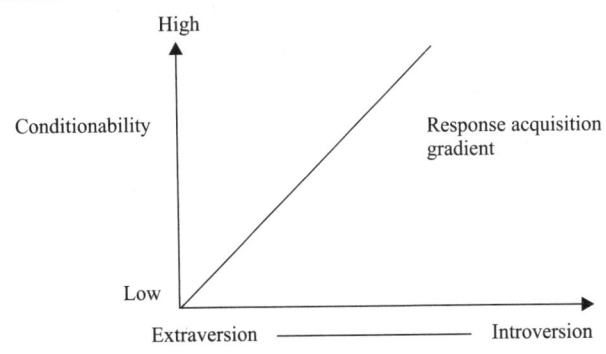

Eysenck's (1979) later account of behaviour encompassed a broad functional approach that included not only the history of reinforcement (Skinner 1953) or drive reduction (Thorndike 1911; Hull 1943) but also supplemented it with recognition of genetic determinants and biological substrate. Based on his empirical work, Eysenck (1959), proposed the following assumptions of behaviour therapy: (i) Behaviour therapy is based on consistent, properly defined theory, leading to testable deductions. (ii) Its principles are derived from experimental studies specially designed to test basic theories and deductions made there from. (iii) Symptoms are considered as maladaptive behaviours. (iv) They are acquired through faulty learning. (v) The individual differences in conditionability and autonomic liability as well as accidental environmental circumstances account for the difference in learning. (vi) All treatments of neurotic disorders are concerned with the habits present; historical development, is largely irrelevant. (vii) Cures are achieved by treating the symptom itself, that is by extinguishing maladaptive conditional responses and establishing desirable conditional responses. (viii) Interpretations, even if not completely subjective and erroneous, are irrelevant. (ix) Symptomatic treatment leads to permanent recovery, provided autonomic as well as skeletal surplus conditional responses are extinguished. (x) Personal relations are not essential for cures of neurotic disorders, although they may be useful in certain circumstances.

However, the learning principles which provided basis for most behaviour therapy work, were those derived primarily from operant conditioning model of B.F. Skinner. His contribution has been catalytic in its impact on clinical and educational settings.

Radical Behaviourism

The most spectacular development that emerged in the traditional thinking of the causation of behaviour was that of Skinner's (1953) radical behaviourism, in which behaviour itself was assigned the importance of the determinant of the future behaviour and the conventionally used terms were redefined operationally. The triggering action of the environment and its effect on the organism, together compose a 'reflex'. Skinner stated that a reflex is possible even in the decapitated body. Therefore the classical stimulus-response model to explain human behaviour is never convincing. '...because something like an inner man had to be invented. We must take into account what the environment does to an organism not only before but also after it responds' (Skinner 1971: 23). The issue of voluntary behaviour occupied a central position in his writing. Most voluntary behaviours 'operate' on the environment to produce a 'consequence'. In this sense, this form of learning is termed as 'operant'. The relationship between behaviour and its consequences or contingencies is important in determining the appearance or disappearance of the behaviour, irrespective of the fact whether it is performed in a planned manner (as done in behaviour therapy) or not (were left to chance).

The organism must first perceive the state variable, such as drive or need state, that makes a response effective in controlling other responses (Figure 1.2). Two types of controlling stimuli trigger a response. Repeated responding helps in discriminating certain stimuli from the rest of the stimulus setting in which the response takes place. These are termed as 'constant stimuli'. They themselves do not elicit any response, though they set occasions for a response to occur. The responses are shaped through re-inforcement and punishment.

FIGURE 1.2
Operant Conditioning Model

Controlling Stimuli	State Variable	Reinforcing Events
Constant Stimuli (SS^c)	Organismic Condition	Differential Reinforcement
Discriminating Stimuli (S^D-S^Δ)	RESPONSE $\longrightarrow$	(S^R-S^O)
		Programming

There are a number of criticisms of the operant conditioning model. Skinner's emphasis on operant conditioning as an important behavioural process is sometimes interpreted as a denial of other influences on behaviour. This may not be correct. The extent to which behaviour can be modified by operant conditioning is limited by constitutional and genetic factors (Seligman 1970). Restriction of the study of behaviour to directly observable public behaviours alone, excludes important cognitive events. Skinner (1963) however, explained that no entity or process which has any explanatory force, is to be rejected on the ground that it is subjective or mental. If it has an important role to play in influencing human behaviour, it is well under the scope of experimental analysis of behaviour. An adequate science of behaviour must consider what happens under the skin of the organism as a part of the behaviour itself. Physiology is considered as a 'bridge' between the past environment and the present behaviour. However, unlike some S–O–R formulations (e.g. Eysenck 1979), radical behaviourism assigns no special causal or explanatory status to physiological processes. Socially oriented approach added a new dimension to the physiological and radical bases of behaviour change. It explained psychological functioning in terms of continuous reciprocal interaction between personal and environmental experience. Except some behaviour, like rudimentary reflexes, most behaviour is learned by observing others, or even through verbal explanations and imaginations of the acts. Acquisition of a response by the observer is determined by its consequences on the model. This is illustrated in Figure 1.3. Broken lines in the diagram indicate the observer's vicarious imitation by observing the effects of a stimulus event on the model (M). If the consequences are positive (C^+), the chance of imitation will increase, when negative (C^-) it will decrease.

Recently, the cognitive variables have also been recognised as important mediating factors in behaviour change. Therefore, they have been incorporated into the base animalistic S–R processes. In spite of the fact that there are several recent innovations in the field of behaviour modification, operant conditioning has remained the most widely accepted approach in understanding behaviour problems. This is probably because of its efficacy and simplistic formulations.

Like all technologies, its practical effectiveness has overridden the theoretical dogma. Many present-day behaviour therapy techniques may be considered only as a lip service to their behaviouristic origin. The links between fundamental and applied research seem to be strained (Dave 1981).

FIGURE 1.3
Social Learning Model

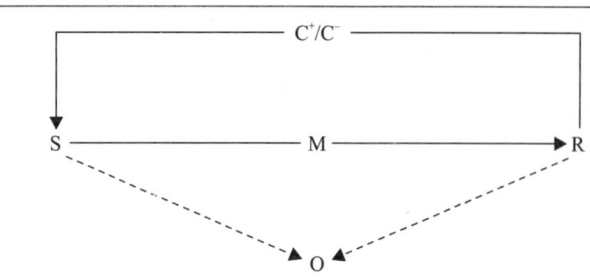

Cognitive Behaviourism

During the 1970s, there was a perceptible tilt towards cognitive-behavioural orientation. There was an increasing emphasis on the role of cognition in behaviour disorders. Behaviour therapists were increasingly concerned about the role of effect in the genesis as well as the treatment of behaviour disorders. They explored the clinical implications of emotional states on behaviour change. Rachman and Wilson (1980: 289) for instance, suggested, 'we should aim to expand behaviour modification to include affect modification'. They predicted that use of affect is the new direction that behaviour therapy will take in the 1980s. Recent expansion of the behavioural models has been focused on external as well as internal mediation processes. As compared to radical behaviourism, more emphasis is given on training general cognitive styles such as coping and problem solving by teaching what-to-think and how-to-think strategies. In recent years, self-control training to foster generalisation of the learned behaviour has gone beyond therapeutic setting.

Skinner, (1938) viewed 'self-control' as a process or response sequence which an individual makes to control another response. The former was labeled as *controlling response* and the latter as *controlled response*. The controlling responses are maintained by the individual through operant self-reinforcement, that is, by administration of reward by the individual himself following controlling responses. It forms the basis of self-control. Experimental foundation of self-instruction as a self-control technique dates back to Luria (1961) and Vygotsky's (1962) work conducted in the erstwhile Soviet Union. They proposed a theory of developmental interaction of verbal and nonverbal behaviour. Both emphasised on the self-regulatory aspect of a child's speech. Explaining the critical difference between the position of Luria and Vygotsky, Zivin (1979: 32) stated, 'For Luria, the children are talking to control themselves; for Vygotsky, they are thinking and talking, and talk happens to affect behaviour.' The child's verbalisation gradually comes to control behaviour as the child progresses in age. Self-control develops in three stages:

Stage 1: Another person's instruction controls child's behaviour.
Stage 2: Child's self-instruction controls his behaviour.
Stage 3: Child's covert self-instruction controls his covert behaviour.

These developmental sequences of a thought process have been kept as basic guidelines for many forms of self-instruction programme, generally called 'think aloud' programme (Meichenbaum 1975).

The cognition-based programmes and packages typically consist of procedures, which are conventional behaviour strategies, such as rehearsal, modeling, feedback, contingency management programme and cognitive training. Self-instructional training is one of the principal methods of cognitive behaviour therapy. It is primarily focused on training covert statement (thought processes), which guides behaviour. Meichenbaum (1977) suggested a self-instructional programme for children, which consisted of the following steps:

(1) *Cognitive modelling*: A model engages in competent behaviour while speaking aloud the covert statements (thoughts) that guide behaviour.
(2) *Imitation*: The child imitates and performs the same behaviour. The model directs him by asking questions and prompts the verbalisations of the previously modelled verbalised thought process.
(3) *Cognitive-motor execution:* The child himself performs the same behaviour while speaking aloud the questions and instructions modelled previously.
(4) *Fading of Self-instruction:* He whispers the same questions and instructions that are competing to guide activities while engaging in the behaviour.
(5) *Independent Performance:* Finally, the child engages in behaviour while guiding his activities through sub-vocal speech, that is, thinking. The instructions consist of four basic performance-enhancing skills such as (i) identification of problem, (ii) focusing attention on task and guiding behaviour to produce a solution, (iii) feedback to sustain appropriate behaviour, and (iv) performance evaluation and correction of errors with consistent practice of the instruction gets abbreviated and automatic.

Another variety of self-instructional training was 'Think Aloud Programme' (TAP). This was primarily based on the work of Meichenbaum and Goodman (1971), and Shure and Spivack (1974). The therapist in a TAP models for verbalisation of his own cognitive-behaviour and lets the children develop his their own solutions. The therapist encourages the client to verbalise his own thoughts in order to help him examine the latter's rationality. Finally, the procedure is faded out as the child learns the task. The core of TAP is the use of self-guiding speech in problem solving through games. Bash and Camp (1986) suggested that the programme can also be adopted for a group by using written language, although it is applicable only in small groups. It has almost parallel steps like that of Meichenbaum and Goodman (1971). The initial stage devoted to the development of an organised approach to the problem consists of four questions: (i) *What is my problem? or What am I supposed to do?* (ii) *How can I do it? or What is my plan?* (iii) *Am I using the plan?* and (iv) *How did I do?* The programme teaches the children to address these questions to themselves, which helps them correct their plans of action. Self-evaluation is an important aspect of this programme, which is based on several criteria like completing the task, effort made, efficiency in following the plan and neatness in performance. Following adequate performance, cognitive tasks of increasing difficulty are introduced by the therapist through modelling. For controlling impulsivity and altering negative emotions, they develop certain teaching strategies. These strategies consist of the following steps: identifying the need for reorganising a particular emotion, showing facial expression that characterises the emotion, labeling and defining the emotion, providing personal examples, restating definition, showing different pictures that might have provoked the emotion, and instructing about things a person can do to lessen or intensify the emotion.

In order to facilitate self-instructional training, many authors have attempted to introduce problem-solving games as task materials. Measures of cognitive disturbances including impulsivity, inattention or poor self-control are taken through psychological tests like Matching Familiar Figures test (MFF) or Self-Control Rating Scale (SCRS) (Kendall and Wilcox 1979).

Now a wide range of cognitive behavioural techniques are available to deal with different behaviour disorders. Rational Emotive Therapy (Ellis 1957, 1962, 1977), Stress Inoculation Technique (Novaco 1975, 1978), the Turtle Technique (Schneider 1974) are some of them. A large number of empirical studies on clinical and non-clinical population reaffirm the role of cognitive factors in behaviour change. Training in 'thinking before acting' is the core component of this approach. However, in spite of encouraging progress in the field, a number of questions are yet to be answered. Effects of context of training, its relation to the level of cognitive development and its generalisation in natural setting are some of the crucial issues.

Systematic Eclecticism

A related development that requires to be documented here is the emergence of what Lazarus termed as 'broad spectrum' behaviour therapy (1971) and the 'doctrine of technical eclecticism'. In this approach, the emphasis on jargons used in classical or operant conditioning, as well as the overemphasis on 'techniques' was ignored. The introduction of additional cognitive techniques attempted to free behavioural intervention from the narrowband stimulus–response formulations of behaviour therapy that prevailed as a major influence on behavioural sciences. Lazarus (1981) termed this approach as multi-modal behaviour therapy. It dissected human personality and modes of behaviour into affect, sensation, imagery, cognition, interpersonal and biological modalities. Difficulties within any modality influence the others. These 'firing orders' are assumed as variable. Multi-modal therapy, in this sense attends to specific problems of a given modality as well as to the interaction between one modality and six others. Leiberman (1978) proposed a revised definition of behaviour, placing it at a multi-modal level. He included four groups of behaviour: (i) overt and instrumental acts, (ii) social interactions, (iii) private events, and (iv) physiological events which are dependent on the biological substrate as well as the environment. The treatment techniques are derived not only from the principles of learning and empirically derived relationship between behaviour and its environmental antecedents and consequences, but also from eclecticism, serendipity and creativity. The treatment techniques would take into consideration the individual's environment, behavioural ecology, as well as the biological substrate.

After observing the emergence of divergent groups of methodology, and clinical practice in behaviour therapy, it is felt that no single theoretical formulation is sufficient in itself to treat divergent groups of behavioural problems that individuals exhibit at different levels of their functioning. A word of caution was put by Eysenck (1971). He figuratively stated that, the new approach should not be 'a mish-mash of theories, a hugger-mugger of procedures, a galimatry of therapies, and charivaria of activities having no proper rationale and incapable of being tested or evaluated' (p. 67). The logic for new synthesis of the available theoretical propositions may be that, in clinical areas it has been found that rigid adherence to a particular school has receded into minority. Practitioners who employ a diverse range of theories and methods have replaced them (Lazarus 1971). The hard-earned principles derived from years of animal and human experimentation can never be overlooked. They should form guidelines for intended behaviour change. In this context, serendipitous and creative findings in individual cases may serve to add new principles of behaviour and prevent the behavioural approach from enshrinement to any given cult of behaviourism.

Irrespective of its theoretical basis, from a broader perspective, behaviour therapy (and behavioural medicine) has three functions: prevention, treatment, and consultation. It is viewed as an attempt to alter behaviour that contributes to the progression of a disorder before it reaches a pathological state (prevention) or modify the course of disease/behaviour disorder once it has occurred (treatment); or to support medical intervention by providing the client with behaviour that allows him to cooperate more fully with the treatment protocol (adherence), or by assisting medical health providers in application of their science (consultation) (Hollandsworth 1986). The scope of behaviour therapy is expanding constantly, with its application to various aspects of human behaviour both in health and disease.

2

Conceptual Issues

Behaviour therapy is firmly embedded in the philosophy of behaviourism and more concerned with control and prediction of behaviour rather than understanding of mind. Although learning foundation forms the core approach, the multiple shades and brands of therapeutic techniques practiced today pose some fundamental questions regarding the basis of behaviour therapy. Looking at the deviations and new areas of venture, some critics like Locke (1971) were pressed to the question: is behaviour therapy always behaviouristic? Take for instance Wolpe's systematic desensitisation procedure. Is the technique entirely behaviouristic? Such questions require to be explained in the backdrop of how behaviour therapists themselves interpret behaviourism. Eysenck (1972) distinguished three kinds of behaviourism: metaphysical (radical), methodological and analytical. He pointed out that ignoring this distinction would make disputes about behaviourism merely disputes about words. The metaphysical or radical behaviouristic view is that the mind or mental events do not exist at all. Analytical or logical behaviourism is of the view that all mental events can be translated into behaviour or behavioural dispositions. Mind whether it exists or not cannot be studied scientifically unless mental events are stated in operational terms. Most behaviour therapists consider them as 'effects' instead of 'causes' of behaviour. There are sound methodological reasons for not treating them as independent variables. Methodological behaviourists spoke about private events that served as stimuli as well as (covert) responses. Skinner stated that it is wrong on the part of behaviour therapists to consider self-descriptive statements of people to be correct, in the same way as psychoanalysts did not. However, in spite of the limitation of its authenticity and accuracy of such statements, a therapist, at best, learns about the personal history by asking how his client 'feels'. Inferences about mental states like 'depression', 'pleasure' or 'pain' are indicated by behavioural responses (e.g. verbal reports and behavioural signs). Similarly, use of mentalistic terms like 'imagery' (imagined scenes), 'sexual fantasy' or 'irrational beliefs' are not entirely inconsistent with behaviourism from the methodological or logical behaviouristic angle as long as they are not used as independent variables, whether in case of systematic desensitisation or cognitive behavioural interventions.

In a reply to his critics, Skinner (1988: 212) stated, '...traditional expressions referring to mental events, I regard as surrogates of histories of reinforcement. Thus, for me, the bonafide subjects are: not thought, but what is happening as one thinks and the history of reinforcement responsible for it; not beliefs, but behaviours with respect to controlling stimuli and the histories responsible for that control; not perception, but the current control exercised by the stimuli as a result of earlier contingencies of reinforcement, and so on'. This statement reflects the subtle difference between radical behaviourism and methodological behaviourism, and perhaps the rest of the behaviouristic approaches. Whether behaviour is overt or covert, it serves certain functions as an independent variable itself. The current practice of behaviour therapy is converged not only on modifying behaviour through external agents in the individual's social environment but also enhancing the functional role of behaviour in modifying itself. Now, it is necessary to understand the functional role that behaviour plays in modifying itself.

How behaviour occurs and what effects it produces on the environment are the two crucial questions that relate to the role of behaviour, both as an independent and a dependent variable, that is, the cause as well as the effect of another behaviour. Behaviour analysts examine behaviour carefully by using principles of learning. The experimental analysis of behaviour exemplified by works of Pavlov, Thorndike, Hull and Skinner offered a broad philosophical base for behaviour therapy. Instead of attributing the causes of behaviour to unobservable events and the events that occur below the skin, behaviourists have attempted to define the causes operationally. The mentalistic and physiological concepts were explained in terms of their corresponding operations. The concrete criteria for their applicability were denoted in their definitions. Skinner argued that psychologists need not be concerned about the locus of private events in the nervous system. Objecting to the use of mentalistic and teleological terms, he stated, 'A science of behaviour... must not take over without careful consideration of the schemes which underlie popular speech' (Skinner 1950, 1953: 7) as the terms used in popular speech are not always convenient in dealing with the data.

In applied behaviour analysis, human organism is considered as an active agent of change and a source of causal variable. A response occurs and it effects a change in the environment. Such events determine the probability of future shape and occurrence of the response. Therefore, it is logically assumed that careful manipulation of the environmental contingencies will facilitate durable change in the behaviour. Skinner explained three classes of events that affect the probability of a response; (i) the earlier response, that is a single occurrence of the response, (ii) antecedent events which occurred prior to the critical response, and (iii) consequences, that is, events that occur following a response. This interaction is termed as 'three-term contingency'. The entire behaviour-analytic framework rests on this simplistic analysis of the behavioural events, that is, the cause and effect relationship. Before we proceed into the discourse on techniques of behaviour therapy, a brief discussion is necessary to clarify these concepts.

ANTECEDENTS

Antecedents include the setting events (constant stimuli SS) and the discriminative stimuli (S^D) that trigger a response. Setting events are those relatively nondiscriminated aspects of the environment that initiate behaviour, or rather set the occasion for the behaviour to occur, and not necessarily produce it.

Discriminating stimuli are those which have a discriminative function, that is, in presence of which certain responses are reinforced or punished and thereby 'discriminated' from the background events of the rest of the environment (stimuli in presence of which the response is either not reinforced or punished). The latter is termed as S^Δ. For instance, a dark night (SS) may set a stage for fear to occur, but fluttering of a nocturnal bird may act as a discriminative stimulus (S^D) to cause fear in a child. However, recently these expressions like S^D, S^Δ or SS have lost grounds to expressions like S^+ (positive stimulus) and S^- (negative stimulus) (Catania 1992) or S^0 (neutral stimulus).

Skinner (1938) explained that the experimental analysis of behaviour employs two types of responses: (i) the Pavlovian (classical), and (ii) the Skinnerian (operant). This was challenged by Konorski and Miller (1937). They questioned the operations involved and whether one paradigm could be reduced to another. In a series of papers (Miller and Carmona 1967; Brown and Jenkins 1968), it was claimed that automatic responses are controlled by respondent procedures, whereas somatic responses are controlled by respondent procedures. Catania (1971) attempted to resolve this issue by offering a fourfold classification of the stimulus and response (S-R) relationship, which exhausts the logical possibilities: R-R, S-R, R-S and S-S. In the above scheme of relationships between stimulus and response, the R-R relationship indicates the relationship between responses in the process of classification of responses and determining their hierarchical positions; the S-R pair indicates which stimuli of the environment can be manipulated to elicit or control behaviour, that is, how the environment controls the behaviour; the R-S unit indicates how behaviour is controlled by its consequences, and lastly the S-S unit indicates the experimental operations and properties of the environment. All these four units of paired relationships were reduced to three dimensions: elicitation (stimulus) dimension, environmental effect dimension (S-R) and discriminative control (S:R). The *elicitation* dimension was further classified into three sections: aversive, neutral and appetitive. The *environmental effect* dimension indicates effects of a stimulus on the environment, which can be divided into three sections based on whether a stimulus has the capacity to increase or decrease behaviour, or makes no change in it. The *discriminative* dimension shows the relationship between a discriminative stimulus S^D and discriminative control R:S.

CONSEQUENCES

Operant behaviour is purposive and voluntary that can be modified by its consequences. Consequences are the effects that behaviour produces on the environment. The effect is considered as 'reinforcing' if it increases the probability or tendency of reoccurrence of the same behaviour and 'punishing', if it decreases the same. The former groups of events or stimuli are called reinforcers and the latter are known as punishers. The process of response decrement because of non-reinforcement is called extinction. Both, reinforcing and punishing consequences have been further classified as positive or negative, depending on whether it happens through presentation or withdrawal of certain stimuli or events following a response. Accordingly, operationally four groups of events can be conceptualised as consequences: (i) positive reinforcement, (ii) negative reinforcement, (iii) positive punishment, and (iv) negative punishment. This is illustrated in Figure 2.1.

FIGURE 2.1
Types of Reinforcement

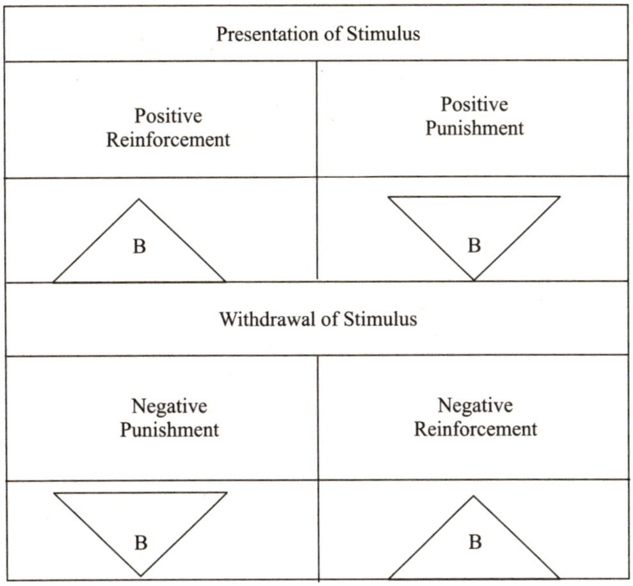

Presentation of Stimulus	
Positive Reinforcement	Positive Punishment
B	B
Withdrawal of Stimulus	
Negative Punishment	Negative Reinforcement
B	B

If in the presence of a stimulus, a behaviour is reinforced and in presence of other stimulus, the response is *not* reinforced or even punished, the former stimulus tends to exert control over the occurrence of subsequent behaviour. The higher the number of such occurrences, the stronger would be the stimulus control. Hence, these stimulus events simultaneously teach the organism to discriminate such relevant stimuli from the irrelevant ones. As stated earlier, there are two forms of reinforcement: positive and negative. A *positive reinforcement* makes an action; it follows more probable by its occurrence. Actions like praise, appreciation, or positive attention increases the probability of occurrence of adaptive responding (e.g working on academic tasks, grooming or on-seat behaviour of children, when they are made contingent on these behaviours). On the other hand, a *negative reinforcement* makes the action it follows more probable in its termination or non-occurrence (Fantino and Logan 1979). For instance, in the absence of the class-teacher, the classroom's disruptive behaviour increases or threat of switching off television may increase study behaviour of a young child.

There is a strong tendency to use terms like negative reinforcement and punishment interchangeably. This is because both involve aversive events (Yulevich and Axelord 1983). Some authors (e.g. Michael 1975) advocated that such finer distinction should in fact be dropped, since the lay vocabulary includes only dichotomous distinction of events taking place in the natural environment, simply as 'good' or 'bad'. The science of behaviour too needs a way of identifying such events. The good things may be generally termed as *reinforcers* and the bad things as *punishers*. One set of terms is operationally tied to a strengthening effect and the other to a weakening effect. Thus, the distinction between two types of reinforcement (and punishment) based upon the distinction between presentation and removal can simply be dropped. Whether an event, say for instance, smiling will act as a reinforcer or a punisher would depend on the learning history of the individual.

STIMULUS CONTROL

In day-to-day life, a galaxy of stimuli control human behaviour. Under certain stimulus conditions, a response may occur more frequently than in other conditions. These stimuli literally 'prompt' the individual how to behave or when to behave. For example, the shape and size of a water tap attached to a washbasin 'prompts' how to make use of it; a switch 'teaches' a user how to turn it on or off; and a chair; 'tells' us, how to shape the posture in order to sit on it comfortably. In the above examples, being able to get water from a tap, operating an electrical appliance, and sitting comfortably on a chair are some of the responses that are frequently associated with the above stimuli, respectively. Like these reinforcing stimuli, there are many stimuli that yield highly probable painful responses. For instance, touching a live wire, stepping on a sharp object, interacting with a nagging boss, and wearing thin clothes in a chilly winter night could be punishing experiences. People tend to avoid them. These stimuli, serve as stimulus control for avoidance response. Throughout the lifetime many such stimuli including people, situations and objects acquire controlling effects on our behaviour. In fact, the unique personality character-istics that people have, indicate unique stimulus controls. The *rate* of emission of response is a common behavioural measure of stimulus control. The higher the degree of stimulus control, the higher is the chance and rate of emission of a response.

Even for the same stimulus, a specific dimension of it may serve as stimulus control, whereas the others may not. Activities such as repeated verbal instruction, and enhancing the perceptual attributes (e.g. shape, size, colour etc.) of the stimulus, may make the stimulus object more attractive and discriminating. It helps in developing better stimulus control. Behaviour therapy is primarily devoted to develop appropriate stimulus controls that make behaviours more predictable in a given stimulus condition.

In summary, stimulus control indicates the extent to which the value of an antecedent stimulus determines the probability of the occurrence of a conditioned response (Terrace 1966). Much abnormal behaviour may be seen as the outcome of either poor, excessive or inappropriate stimulus controls. The practice of behaviour therapy could be seen as an attempt to establish appropriate stimulus control. Therefore, in order to conduct therapy, the clinician has to identify the sources of stimulus control or modify the existing ones to determine the desired occurrence of a critical behaviour.

GENERALISATION AND DISCRIMINATION

Many stimulus classes, which include sets of similar or related stimuli, too exert similar control over the behaviour as the actual conditioned stimulus. Certain responses become more probable than other responses when a member of the stimulus control is present. Even other stimuli present in the same environment may also come to exert similar control over the acquired response as that of the original one because of their association. A child, who is afraid of his mathematics teacher due to punishment may show avoidance response by being absent from his class, if punishment is too severe. Depending on the frequency and intensity of consequences, the response may be elicited by other members of this stimulus class. Thus, *generalisation* occurs when a class of stimuli serves as stimulus control. In a simplistic manner, Becker, Engelmann and Thomas (1975) put like this: 'When an individual responds in presence of a new stimulus in the same way as to a previously taught stimulus having some of the same characteristics, the event is called stimulus generalisation' (p. 145). For example, if a child has learned to read the letter 'A' and pronounces it correctly, he is expected to read it in the same way even if some variations occur in the size or shape of the letter as '*A*', 'A' or '*A*'. This example is given in the context of teaching. In general, responses learned in a specific setting or stimulus condition, if transferred to similar situations in the natural environment, is called generalisation of a learned response. An individual requires not only generalising a newly acquired response, but also discriminating between appropriate and inappropriate stimuli. Failure to do so leads to several behavioural abnormalities. Anxiety reactions may occur due to discrimination failure.

The other meaning of generalisation is the transfer of a learned behaviour to natural environment. On many occasions, we notice that responses learned in the clinical or educational setting are not transferred to the natural environment. For instance, parents often report that their child performs well in school but does not perform in a similar manner in the home environment or vice versa. This is a problem of generalisation.

A discriminative stimulus (S^D) sets the occasion for the occurrence of a conditioned operant. Even the stimuli associated with the S^D come to acquire similar capacity to elicit such responses. The former is called *discriminative* function (Skinner 1938; Keller and Schoenfeld 1950) and the latter as *generalisation* function. When there are two traditionally used terms like generalisation and discrimination for the same phenomena, why is there a need of another term, 'stimulus control'? The above two terms describe the processes of learning whereas the latter is an empirical function (Brown 1965; Prokasy and Hall 1963). An alcohol addict, for instance may resort to excessive drinking simply after the sight of an empty alcohol bottle or even looking at the pegs. A child avoids talking and disturbing others in the classroom in presence of a punitive class teacher. Fetishists initially use objects such as undergarments, shoes, hair or perfumes associated with the opposite sex for sexual arousal. Then it becomes a stable conditioned response. Rachman (1966) experimentally demonstrated the creation of a mild fetishist in laboratory condition. A photograph of a female's boot was repeatedly shown with sexually stimulating female nudes. Later on, the subjects showed sexual arousal as measured by increase in the penile volume when only the picture of boots was presented. In therapeutic setting, the client is reinforced for his desirable responses to certain stimuli, while either ignoring or even punishing him for undesirable responding. It must also be noted that stimulus control implies only the eliciting and discriminative function, not the primary and secondary reinforcement functions (Terrace 1966).

In clinical condition like phobia, excessive fear is often reported by the client for specific stimuli. This may be due to inappropriate stimulus control. Objects, places or situations that normally do not arouse fearful reactions come to be perceived as threatening or fearsome due to conditioning. The counter conditioning (systematic desensitisation) procedures are used to develop an antagonistic form of coping response by altering the stimulus control. Providing pleasant stimulation in actual or imagined conditions helps the client in developing appropriate stimulus control. In fact, this is the principal objective of most behaviour modification techniques. Let us take another example. While teaching language to young children, coloured pictures of objects (flash cards), gestures or actual objects are often used. When the subject is reinforced (S^+) for using the corresponding word for a stimulus (e.g. 'a' for 'Apple') and provided the reinforcement ('Very Good'), the response is strengthened. On the other hand, the subject is even punished for not responding correctly (S^-). Both these consequences strengthen stimulus control. In fact, every technique of behaviour modification involves these two fundamental processes: discrimination and generalisation. Stimulus control is their empirical consequence. It is observed in the modified behaviour.

When there is no clearly identifiable stimulus event preceding the behaviour, it appears peculiar, magical or abnormal. Much abnormal behaviour may be explained as forms of inappropriate stimulus control. A schizophrenic's self-talk, a client suffering from pica (eating inedible stuff), or a paedophile's perverted sexual attractions towards children, are some of the examples. Behaviours that fail to either occur or are exhibited poorly may be due to poor stimulus control. This is generally manifested as skill deficits. A large group of behaviours of retarded individuals may fall in this category. Behaviour analysis becomes more complex when one particular aspect of the event or the entire event comes to represent another and starts acting as a stimulus control. In this situation, repeated behavioural observations and experimental manipulations of the variables help in identifying the stimuli that actually controls the behaviour. Thus, establishing appropriate stimulus control is one of the major goals of behaviour therapy.

What separated Skinner from the modern cognitivists was his reluctance to acknowledge these representations. He considered the search for such unobservable events as a regression to mentalism. However, the later behaviourists advocated that the study of representations could be regarded profitably as an extension of the study of stimulus control only (Terrace 1982).

APPLICATIONS

Stimulus control has been used extensively in many areas of behavioural intervention. Two fundamental steps are involved in developing stimulus control. The first step is *selective attention* and the second is *differential reinforcement*. For focusing attention on a target task (stimulus) at the outset, it is required to reduce all irrelevant stimuli. Specification of the setting and time, reducing the source of distractions such as noise, glare of the light, or even irrelevant stimuli and movement, helps in creating a congenial environment for learning. When the target behaviour starts occurring, it requires to be reinforced at a different rate than before, so that it can be adequately discriminated and learned. Use of differential reinforcement techniques have been discussed in Chapter 10.

By developing good stimulus control, a wide number of behaviours can be improved. Poor studying, for example, is a common behaviour problem among many students. Even if a student intends to study, he is distracted by other events in the environment such as watching TV, listening to stereo, gossiping and socialising with people, playing, daydreaming or engaging in other pleasurable activities. This is a specific instance of poor stimulus control. Looking at these problems among students, Fox (1962) devised a stimulus control programme for college students. He collected a weekly schedule of the activities and found out one hour when the student was free each day. The student was instructed to: (i) study the most difficult subject everyday at that time and place, (ii) take only relevant study materials, (iii) not use the room at other times, and (iv) if bored, he had to read one more page and leave the place immediately. Initially the students found it difficult to study for long at the new setting, they would leave the room before the scheduled time. Gradually there was an increase in the study period. The students could now concentrate on their studies for the entire one-hour period. At this point of time, the student was asked to study in a different location, for one hour daily at a specified time. The student was instructed to leave the room immediately if he engaged in any behaviour other than studying; for example daydreaming. Even in case they wished to spend more than the specified time on studying, they were allowed to do so but not in the special room.

The students demonstrated considerable improvement in their grade points. During the treatment, they were also given training in another technique called SQ3R (survey, question, read, recite and review). Although it was difficult to assess whether the positive effect was due to stimulus control or SQ3R, Fox reported that knowing even the best method of studying would have done little good if the student never found time or place to put them into practice. Therefore, it was assumed that the positive effects were largely due to the use of stimulus control technique.

Insomnia is another problem in which the role of stimulus control technique is suggested. Although a small group may have medical problems causing insomnia, most insomniacs have the problem of poor stimulus control. Instead of sleeping, they keep thinking about the day's events or doing some other work. The bed and associated stimuli which should set the occasion for sleeping fail to do so. Interestingly, these people sleep comfortably in other settings. On the other hand, those who have developed good stimulus control sleep well at their homes but find it difficult to fall asleep when they are in other situations such as a hotel room or another person's place. Bootzin (1972) treated a man who would lie on the bed for several hours thinking about every day problems before falling asleep with the television on. The client was instructed not to go to the bed until he felt sleepy. Whenever he found difficulty in sleeping, he would go to another room and do whatever he liked to do. He would not return to the bed.

This treatment has been used for many insomniacs effectively (Bootzin and Nicassio 1978). There were two principal elements involved in this procedure. First, creating adequate need for sleep by preventing the client from sleeping; staying engaged in any behaviour other than sleeping in one's bed is an important issue. He is not allowed to go to bed, if he is not sleepy. It helped the client to discriminate sleep from non-sleep activities and set the occasion for sleep, increasing the chance of falling asleep on the bed. Second, he is not allowed to do anything other than sleeping on the bed in order to reduce association of bed with non-sleep activities (e.g. daydreaming or thinking about the days events). As we stated earlier, two fundamental processes involved in stimulus control technique are *discrimination* and *differential reinforcement*. As a first step, the client should learn to discriminate desirable behaviour from the undesirable ones and eliminate the undesirable ones. This would facilitate attending to the desirable ones. Reinforcement of desirable behaviour in terms of attention, time allocation, and administering various forms of reinforcement would facilitate it to occur.

Occasionally certain behaviours are acquired due to the learner's inadvertent attention to an irrelevant stimulus in the learning situation. Subsequently, it develops into unintentional stimulus control. As a result, the acquired behaviour occurs only in the presence of these stimuli and not otherwise. For instance, young children demonstrate appropriate social behaviour only in the presence of parents or teachers who had taught them the behaviour and not otherwise. In order to reduce the probability of such context-bound responses, special attention is required to fade out the trainer and other controlling variables from the learning environment. This issue had been carefully examined by Rincover and Koegel (1975) while studying autistic children. They found that out of 10 children, six showed generalisation of acquired responses whereas four did not. Careful observation indicated that they were selectively attending to a stimulus in the original environment, which was incidentally present in the treatment setting of the classroom. When this stimulus was introduced to a new situation, the behaviour was generalised. Generalisation of a learned behaviour is affected due to the learner's attention to such inadvertent stimuli; when they are not present the behaviour does not occur. Hence the treatment fails to generalise to other situations. On the other hand, some superstitious (irrational) behaviour may appear to be out of context when one finds it difficult to identify the antecedent stimulus triggering them (e.g. hallucinatory behaviour, self-talk and stereotyped behaviours). Thus, the behaviour appears to be magical or 'abnormal'.

Stimulus control has wide application in behaviour therapy, particularly in programmed instruction in a classroom setting and in the treatment of many clinical conditions. Identifying stimulus controls for behaviours in the natural environment and developing a desirable relationship of a stimulus with the target behaviour is the fundamental task involved in behaviour therapy. The central issue involved in this process is analysing, planning, and structuring the physical environment. The contingencies are designed in such a manner that they will modify behaviour in a predictable direction. The 'Skinner box' used for animal learning is the prototype of programmed environment that can facilitate the emission of desirable responses. In his book *Walden II*, Skinner (1948) expanded this idea of operant conditioning and explained that shaping of human behaviour would shape a better future for the humankind.

3

Psychobiological Basis of Behaviour Therapy

Behaviour therapy is not an amalgamation of a large number of techniques. Roots of many of its techniques are embedded in the functioning of the nervous system itself. Pavlov's (1927) work on the conditioning of 'psychic salivation' was the first attempt and a paradigmatic shift that explained learning in terms of physiological principles. It paved the way for the development of modern behaviour therapy. Therefore, it is considered as a turning point. Thereafter, growing and sustained effort has been made to explain the techniques of behaviour therapy in terms of psychophysiological events. Rachman (1986) euphemistically stated, 'behaviour therapy cannot survive without its physiological base, if at all; it will perhaps be a scrawny, interesting orphan among many clamorous competitors'. Understanding the relationship between learning and its psychobiological consequences is essential for its growth. Otherwise, behaviour therapy may degenerate into simply a bag of techniques. Despite the fact that it grew out of research in the physiology of the nervous system, little attempt had been made to look for the physiological events associated with behaviour change. Applied behaviour analysis has distanced itself and had attempted to ignore the physiological bases of behaviour change altogether.

In the past there have been many attempts to translate clinical phenomena into a terminology that would be acceptable to behavioural psychologists (Dollard and Miller 1950; Shoben 1949). Even now, there has been growing effort to explain behaviour change in terms of physiological events. For example, a large group of techniques in behaviour therapy, like autogenic training, relaxation, systematic desensitisation and biofeedback, is used to reduce the reactivity of the autonomic nervous system that exacerbates the disease process.

Behaviour disorders have been explained by using a wide range of biological concepts such as arousal, Central Nervous System dysfunction, brain damage, genetic predispositions or neurochemical imbalances and so on. Any such biological explanation of behaviour disorders without consideration of the learning histories would be incomplete or rather misleading for the reason that most pathological behaviours are shaped and sustained by the environment. Conversely, a functional explanation overlooking the biological substrates that mediate the manifestation of behaviour would be equally erroneous. For any meaningful experimental analysis of behaviour, understanding of both these angles is essential.

BEHAVIOURAL 'MARKERS'

It has been increasingly realised that behaviour itself is a determining factor in causation, maintenance, as well as prevention of many disorders. For instance, the predominant habits or personality traits, such as extreme introversion and extraversion may lead to certain specific health-related problems. Their manipulation through behaviour therapy techniques can promote health. Many psycho-physiological disorders are linked with dominant behavioural characteristics of the individual. For instance, people with Type A behaviour, characterised predominantly by hostile and competitive behaviour, are prone to coronary heart diseases. Similarly, Breznitz (in, Siegel 1988) demonstrated that psychological events like positive and negative expectations have opposite effects on cortisol and prolactine level in blood that are known to activate the immune system. The significant role that emotions play in a wide range of other psychosomatic disorders such as cancer, has been explored by some investigators (e.g. LeShan 1977). In a study of functional pain, Nathawat and Gupta (2000) reported that people suffering from functional pain scored significantly higher on somatic anxiety, psychic anxiety, psychasthenia, muscular tension and detachment. Conversely, we hypothesise that behavioural intervention, in order to modify these behavioural markers, will reduce an individual's vulnerability to disease. If a stressor can activate a pathological gene, a stress-free environment conducive for health promoting behaviour can inhibit the same.

Traditionally, behaviour therapists have been most concerned with deriving clinical procedures from learning theories and applying them to problems of human behaviour. There is a need for broadening the base of behaviour therapy in view of the current challenges posed by other contemporary approaches to treatment of behaviour disorders. Exploring its psychobiological basis would facilitate better understanding of the *process* of change. For instance, the associated changes that take place in terms of neural transmission, electrical activity of the brain and neurochemistry during behaviour therapy may have important bearing on predicting the extent of behaviour change. What changes take place before, during and after the application of behaviour therapy techniques—particularly in anticipation, discrimination, or generalisation—are worth exploring. This approach would not rob behaviour therapy of its essential characteristics rather it would strengthen and expand its base.

Presently, a wide range of precise electrophysiological, biomechanical and biochemical techniques are available with exquisite computer-assisted data processing systems to aid the investigator. Behavioural telemetry provides excellent opportunity to record a client's behaviour during behaviour therapy sessions. However, one of the most difficult challenges is to differentiate the behavioural processes involved in acquisition, generalisation and discrimination of response by using biological parameters. Although reductionism would not be the final answer to many daunting questions of behaviour therapy, the search for an organic explanation of behaviour change would expand our understanding of the mediating variables that operate within the process of change.

STIMULUS COMPLEX AND FUNCTIONAL AUTONOMY

The response tendencies are largely determined by stimulus characteristics, such as intensity, continuity, as well as environmental contingencies, that is, the schedule by which a specific stimulus is presented or withdrawn. The most formidable task for the behaviour therapist is to 'programme' the operation of these contingencies in such a manner that it would facilitate occurrence of a desired response.

In this context, the role of instructions is much more complex than what is traditionally thought of. The words spoken or written to the clients acquire symbolic value because of their association with a wide range of events in the life of the individual. They tend to evoke complex responses acting upon an abstract representational system. Platanov (1959) termed it as the 'second signaling system'. For instance, the word 'chalk' represents the real one when it is written or spoken to another individual. By association with various real stimuli of the first signaling system, a word becomes part of a real and significant system. Finally it constitutes the basis of a system that mediates several complex behaviours. Later, it acts as an abstraction from reality, forming our entire thinking process. The image of objects or actions expressed in words replaces their concrete effect. Due to higher order conditioning, the same stimuli elicit a quite different form of response than before. At times, they appear to be so much out-of place that they are labeled as 'psychotic' (e.g. hallucinations and delusions). When certain responses are elicited automatically under specific situations (e.g. in isolation, in presence of significant people or objects or environment like in class or office room), during psycho-physiological states (e.g. under trance, fear, rage), and even at specific time or season of a year (e.g. winter), behavioural diagnosis becomes a challenging task. The symptoms appear to be complex, until such specific conditions are identified.

EARLY TRAUMA

A lot of importance is attached by some authors to the early traumatic experience that causes behavioural disturbance in the later stages of life. Stimuli associated with the trauma or having similarity with them may lead to certain pathological behaviours. These behaviours cannot be studied meaningfully by focusing on the immediate environment alone. In order to understand them early learning history requires to be probed more intensively than what is done in a traditional 'here-and-now' approach. In this context, the therapist's words serve as an important vehicle to unearth these traumatic early experiences.

CONDITIONABILITY

Clients, even with the same type of behaviour problems, may have completely different learning histories. Not all of them are equally conditionable. Pavlov (1928) observed that conditionability of an organism depends on the strength of its nervous system (i.e. its reactivity to stimuli). Those with 'weak' nervous system are relatively more conditionable than the ones with stronger nervous system. He explained that 'neurotic' breakdown occurs under five different conditions: (i) use of intense aversive stimuli, (ii) increased delay between the presentation of signal (conditioned stimulus) and food (unconditional stimulus), (iii) induction of a difficult response for discrimination between two conditioned stimuli,

(iv) continuous alternation of positive and negative stimuli for the same task, and (v) physical stress. Eysenck (1955, 1958) extended Pavlov's basic concepts about types of nervous system to a two-dimensional theory of personality and psychopathology. He explained extraversion and introversion in terms of the functional status of the reticular activating system (RAS) that facilitates or inhibits learning. Introverts have chronic and long-term arousal, therefore are more conditionable than the extraverts who have short-staying arousal. This is often described as 'Eysenck's demon'. The arousal theory of conditionability has generated a plethora of research in explaining response tendencies of people suffering from various types of psychopathology.

Pavlov's early work on conditioned reflex laid the renaissance in psychobiology of learning. His concept of excitation and inhibition as fundamental mechanism of CNS activation are considered as one of the best abstractions about CNS. Excitation was described as any change in the general level of central activity, which showed itself as measurable increase in conditional reflex, and inhibition was described as any change, which manifests itself in decreasing conditional reflex.

REINFORCEMENT

It is the core behavioural process, which facilitates interaction between environment and organism and considered as the key issue in facilitating behaviour change. Although there is a correspondence between the reinforcement process and drive reduction, such causal relationship does not exist always. Two aspects of reinforcement can be distinguished: (i) drive reduction, and (ii) affective and motivational aspect. A behaviour therapist should carefully look into these two aspects while undertaking reinforcement sampling, listing out the reinforcers in consultation with the client and significant people and choosing the most appropriate reinforcers. Berlyne (1960) used the term 'arousal jag' referring to the external source of reinforcement which does not satisfy any need state but causes arousal; for instance, roller coaster rides, horror films or infants tossed in air. They seem to increase the drive state instead of meeting them. The pattern of neural responses activated by many stimuli may also elicit pleasurable sensation. Emphasising on this aspect of stimulation, Pfaffmann (1960) pointed out that, there is increasing evidence to establish that 'sensory stimulation divorced from its need or drive reducing concomitant may function as a reinforcer in its own right' (p. 254). Young (1948) distinguished between 'appetite' (i.e. dietary) and 'enjoyment' (i.e. motivational) aspects of food as a reinforcer. These two can be distinguished experimentally. The former is the delayed after-effect whereas the latter is the immediate effect. Considerable evidence now exists to establish the fact that the reinforcement process does not always depend upon the 'feedback' from the physiological consequences of behaviour (Valenstein 1966). In spite of drive reduction, a stimulus may not act as a reinforcer. For instance, a bitter tasting food may tend to act more as a punisher than a reinforcer. Thus, the motivational aspect of a reinforcer is more important than the drive reduction aspect. Brain stimulation studies (e.g., Olds and Milner 1954) have demonstrated that reinforcement can be produced by activating certain neural structures. This has seriously weakened drive reduction theories. Even the 'pleasing' aspect of the reinforcer can be detected at the sensory response level. These observations expand our understanding of the effects of reinforcement on the client's response pattern. A behaviour therapist should attend to both 'motivational' and 'appetitive' aspects of the reinforcement in order to make them more effective. The former has more immediate effect than the latter.

In Hull's (1952) formulation,

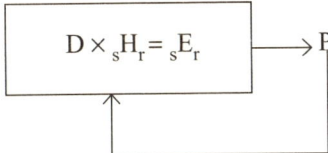

$$D \times {}_sH_r = {}_sE_r \longrightarrow P$$

He assumed that, all changes in the organism's reaction potential (sEr) due to reinforcement (drive reduction) were inaccessible to direct observation. Here, P (performance) refers to the observable aspect of sEr. The recent psychophysiological studies have thrown more light on the inaccessible aspect of sEr.

A number of investigators (e.g. Shvets 1958 and Morrell 1960) have reported perceptible shifts in the steady potential (SP) obtained from the cortex during the acquisition phase of conditioning experiments. It may be equated with arousal, activation, or excitation response involving the cortex. This is consistent with Hull's (1952) formulation.

COGNITIVE MAP, BRAIN INJURY AND 'DIASCHISIS'

Human brain is an extremely complex mechanism that helps in adaptation of the individual to the complex demands of life. Brain injury causes disorganisation of planned activities, that is, the 'cognitive map'. Until the 1960s it was believed that destroyed nerve cells do not regenerate, therefore functions lost cannot be restored. However, Hughling Jackson (1979) stated that symptoms of brain damage do not necessarily reveal the function of the damaged tissue; rather it reflects more accurately, what the remaining areas of the brain can do after an injury. Luria (1963, 1980) offered a conceptual framework to the current neuropsychological and behavioural rehabilitation of people with brain injury (Christensen, Caetano and Rasmussen 1969). Behavioural rehabilitation programmes for brain-injured people helps in functional reorganisation. The clients are trained to perform much behaviour through other channels by reorganising the residual behavioural assets (e.g. Weniger et al. 1980). The process specific approach to neuropsychological rehabilitation suggests that a group of tasks which target the same component of a particular cognitive or behavioural process, is administered systematically and repeatedly in a hierarchical order (Sohlberg and Mateer 1989). The method is identical to the shaping procedure of operant conditioning.

In 1914, von Monakow distinguished a special form of temporary disturbance of function caused by local brain damage called 'diaschisis'. This is caused by excessively strong stimulus that inactivates areas which are far away from the actual site of the lesion. Even the areas situated symmetrically in the opposite hemisphere belonging to the same functional system may be temporarily affected. The shock raises the threshold of excitability. The 'diaschisis' or temporary inactivation is explained as a form of parabiotic or protective inhibition (Pavlov 1949). This can be overcome through retraining. The underlying process is called 'deblocking', or facilitation of the synaptic conduction (Grashchenkov 1946). It explains that behaviour therapy can play a significant role in the restoration of brain function.

4

Developmental Perspective

Behaviour therapy procedures have been demonstrated to be particularly relevant and efficacious in the treatment of childhood behaviour disorders. Many behavioural strategies developed in laboratory setting have been successfully applied to a variety of childhood behaviour disorders in natural settings. Scientific application of learning theory to childhood behaviour disorders appeared as early as the 1920s. A major antecedent of behaviour therapy was Watson and Rayner's (1920) pioneering work on the conditioning of an 11-month old infant, Albert. It successfully demonstrated the acquisition and extinction of fear in children. It was a landmark in the history of behaviour therapy, and treatment of phobia in particular. It influenced later developments in child behaviour therapy. In 1924, Mary Cover Jones used counter conditioning technique in the treatment of a 3-year old child Peter, using feeding as a competing response. Similar findings were obtained by other investigators (Gregman 1934; English 1929; Holmes 1939).

Behaviour therapy holds considerable potential for prevention of behaviour problems at later stages of life too. In order to implement effective intervention programme, a behaviour therapist should acquaint himself/herself with the developmental factors that influence therapy. This is for the reason that shaping of a technology of behaviour-change can proceed faster if contact with the relevant basic research in behavioural development across the life span is established. Developmental researchers have contributed significantly to the practice of psychological treatments including behaviour therapy. Development of the capacity to control physiological states (e.g. hunger, physical distress, bowel and bladder control) by appropriate responding, self-soothing ability, establishment of routines, modulation and co-ordination of motor activity, even the capacity to focus attention or derive meaning from the events that occur in the environment, play the central role in determining the efficacy of behaviour therapy.

CHILD AS A CLIENT

Once it was believed that childhood behaviour disorders represented 'downward extensions' of adult disorders (Phillips, Draguns and Bartlett 1975). Thorpe and Olson (1990) termed this approach as 'adultomorphism'. Child behaviour disorders require to be understood as unique in their own right. Children cannot be treated as 'miniature adults'. Their behaviour problems cannot be understood without a reference to the developmental and social context. Formulation of childhood behaviour problems is multifactorial. At different stages of development, different factors come to play significant roles in an individual's life. In spite of their similarities with adults, children are functionally different from them. They are not only smaller and less physically and mentally coordinated, they have less life experience too. They construe the world differently than adults do (Harris and Ferrari 1983).

Although children's behaviour often looks funny and humorous or, at times, seemingly disorganised and unstable, they are rule-governed and lawful. The immense complexity and its dynamic qualities claim closer scientific scrutiny. These peculiarities and deviant patterns of responses pose a wide variety of empirical questions to explore.

IDENTIFYING DYSFUNCTION

Childhood is a period of rapid behavioural change. Child behaviour changes are faster than adult behaviour, and therefore, their diagnosis and classification have always posed problems for the clinician. Unlike adults, who normally reach the plateaus in many respects of development, children continually experience major changes in biological, cognitive, social and emotional spheres. A child's behaviour is not only fluid, but the differences in response patterns between infants, toddlers, preschoolers, elementary school children and adolescents are as great as their similarities.

Adult psychopathology is often marked by a decline from the attained level of functioning, whereas child problems often involve failure to develop. It can be best conceptualised as 'normal development gone awry' (Wenar 1982). At different stages of life, the child is exposed to different demands, rules and expectations. They are evaluated by multiple circumstances within a short span of life (e.g., home, neighbourhood, daycare centre, prenursery, nursery, primary or secondary schools). At different stretches of time, a child's associates and environmental agents get him to behave in a particular fashion, not as he wants to do. This is termed as 'environmental force unit' (EFU) (Schoggen 1963). These EFUs bring significant variation in child behaviour. At times, when the child starts resisting the environmental force, even normal behaviour is considered as deviant. Therefore it requires great care to make treatment decisions.

Some behaviour problems are relatively common to some degree as a part of normative development. Therefore, one of the major challenges to treatment is the qualitative and quantitative characteristics of behaviour that are either maladaptive or within the normative range for the period of development (Kazdin and Weisz 2003). Moreover, not every child grows in a normal and secured environment against the backdrop of which the child's behaviour is generally evaluated. Some of them grow amidst disadvantaged or crippling environmental conditions such as utter poverty, insecurity or disturbed interpersonal relationship. Under these conditions, a behaviour therapist has to be cautious in choosing targets of intervention. Selection of behavioural techniques for intervention requires careful consideration. Great deal of therapeutic effort is required to be directed towards modification of agents which maintain or elicit undesirable responses.

There are certain behaviour problems which are specific to childhood and rarely noticed among adults. Behaviours like enuresis, nail biting, thumb sucking, body rocking and hyperactivity are more common among children than in adults. Kagan (1971) puts forth the notion of 'discontinuity' in the developmental trends in children and adults. New organisation of behaviour does wipe out the old ones.

LEARNING AND DEVELOPMENTAL PROGRESSION

Many therapists ignore the uniqueness of a child as a client, considering that children learn in the same way as adults do. Therefore, same principles of learning are applicable for both children and adults. Although this proposition is well accepted by some radical behaviourists, there are subtle differences in child and adult learning. Many investigators have considered age as an important predictor of therapeutic outcome. Here, the chronological age should not be interpreted as a generic predictor of therapeutic success; rather the biological and psychological changes accompanying the aging process are important. For example, Sahoo, Gillis and Mishra (2002) reported that age is one of the most sensitive indicators of the outcome of behaviour therapy for people suffering from obsessive-compulsive disorders.

Here, we would address the issue of behavioural transformation from childhood to adulthood in the context of intervention. The reflexes and organised instrumental or voluntary acts are not distinct categories of responses, rather different levels of transformation. The voluntary responses are more advanced 'mediated' responses. In stimulus–response theory, a 'mediator' is a cue-producing response that controls further responding through the associative function of the cue produced (Reese and Porges 1976). During the course of development, the simple reflexive (S–R) bonds are transformed into extended S-r_m-s_m-R bonds (Goss 1961) through higher order conditioning. Here S is the initial stimulus, that elicits the mediating response (r) producing a cue or mediating stimulus (s_m), which finally produces a terminal response (R). When either the initial stimulus (S) fails to produce a mediating response (r_m), or the cue produced by the mediating response (r_m) fails to produce a terminal response (R), mediational failures occur. The first form of failure is labeled as 'production deficiency' and the second as 'mediational deficiency' (Flavell, Beach and Chinsky 1966). Both types of 'inefficiencies' (Reese and Porges 1976) are more common in children than in adults. During the course of development, cognitive processes begin to replace the reflexive ones. By the time, the child reaches 5–7 years of age, learning is primarily cognitive. The transition may be noted appearing distinctively (Kendler 1962; Reese 1962; White 1965).

PREPAREDNESS

The human infant is born with certain operating instruments (i.e. the body) and with certain predispositions to respond in a characteristic manner. These responses are more or less appropriate to his environment (Seligmn 1970). At the same time, he is innately prepared to respond to some stimuli (conditional stimuli) more effectively than others do. These stimuli are considered more 'associable' than others. Preparedness is the organism's predisposed subtle ability to link certain stimulus contingencies. He is prepared either by evolution or by maturation to respond to them more readily than other stimuli. For example, 3–5 year olds exhibit fearful reaction to a wide variety of stimuli like insects, animals or darkness, which is not found earlier. These responses are partly influenced by their relative helplessness as well as their unpreparedness to respond. Developmental progression is indicated by a shift from such simple reactions to more cognitively mediated learning of fear and anxiety. Fear of supernatural beings, such as ghosts, or demons are found to be more prominent at these stages than at the earlier or later stages of development. Emergence of comprehensible language brings a sea-change in the learning process. Speech acts a mediator for higher-order conditioning. Mere verbal descriptions can help visualise the scene at later stages of development.

COGNITIVE DEVELOPMENTAL LEVEL AND TREATMENT OUTCOME

Many researchers (Borden, Brown, Wynne and Schleser 1987; Schleser, Cohen, Meyers and Rodick 1984; Schleser, Meyers and Cohen 1981) have suggested that measures of cognitive development level act as a moderator of cognitive behaviour therapy. Impact of self-instructional training is greater in children functioning at higher levels of cognitive development. Cognitively sophisticated children are in a better position to systematically apply problem-solving strategies and employ recursive thought processes (Forehand and Eierson 1993).

CAPACITY TO USE IMAGERY

Due to relative developmental immaturity and limited life experience, children's ability to imagine and visualise scenes, is poorer than an adult's. In many cognitive behavioural approaches where these skills are needed, children fail to perform well. Thus, adult models of therapy should not be imposed on children. For instance, the research till date on systematic desensitisation indicates that in its pure form this technique has not been successful in reducing phobia in children. Many studies that report success are often based on case reports lacking scientific rigour (Hatzenbuehler and Schroeder 1978). Reporting on the age sensitivity to imagery, Strosahl and Ascough (1981) stated that there is no definite answer to it. However, in another study by Purkel and Bornstein (1980) reported that the 9-year olds could make effective use of the imagery, whereas children of lower age group failed to do so. Therefore, while generating complex images, a therapist should ascertain by exploring whether the child is at all able to visualise them and make use of them.

SELF-CONTROL

Initiation of Motor Acts

Initiation of motor acts through speech is an important achievement during childhood. Wide ranges of cognitive behavioural therapies are based on the client's capacity for regulating their own behaviour through self-instruction. Luria (1969) observed that in the earlier years of language usage (before 3 years of age), children's speech has no self-regulatory function. Therefore, logically they cannot benefit from cognitive self-instruction training. In the period between 3, and 4.5 years or 5 years, an adult's verbalisation can initiate motor acts. Towards the end of this period they can attend to the meaning of self-instruction and inhibit as well as initiate actions according to self-instruction. Therefore tasks like praising themselves, self-evaluation of performance or inhibiting one's own behaviour are difficult for children to perform prior to this age.

Self-prohibitive Rule

Different types of self-instruction (self-verbalisation) have different effects on children. Their age is also an important determinant. In a study conducted on first and second grade children, it was found that although they did equally well in reducing their deviant behaviour by self-instruction, when a self-prohibitive rule was introduced, only the second graders showed reduction in disruptive behaviour. The first grader could do it after directing their attention to permissible alternative activity (Sawin and Parke 1979). Older children show more improvement when they are given less concrete and more generalised instruction (Kendall and Wilcox 1980). Toddlers show more self-control when they are given verbal command than an abstract signal like a buzzer (Birch 1966). These observations have a bearing on designing therapeutic programmes for children.

ADAPTATION OF TECHNIQUES

In the view of developmental progression, the instructional procedure and methods of introducing training tasks make substantial difference to the treatment outcome. Developing a working relationship with children is much different from adults. They require a different language in order to be comprehensible. Therefore, the language requires to be moulded according to the level of their development. Developmental researches also reveal that the same words may have altogether different meaning for the children. They use them differently than adults (Spinetta 1974; Buckley Simeonsson and Monson 1979; Brodzinsky et al. 1981). Inclusion of play-like substitute actions for young children enhances acceptability, hence adding to the effectiveness of therapy. A clinician must be sensitive to these issues. Appropriateness of certain techniques depends on the level of development. The child's level of cognitive development, for instance, decides the appropriateness of specific cognitive behavioural therapies. Madders (1987) suggested a number of special relaxation techniques for young children, such as 'fighting fingers', 'floating fingers', 'body flop', 'my secret picture', and other group techniques like 'iron man/woman', 'rocking the dummy', 'shoulder shove', 'turning the turtle', tormentor' or 'calm down' for children in middle childhood (7–12). Under stress, even adults often 'regress' to the earlier stage of associative learning. White (1965) reported, 'The stressed adult might revert to more sophisticated version of the associative system, which young children also favour' (p. 216). Under these conditions behavioural techniques require careful modification. There are certain techniques which are developmentally sensitive. For example, researchers who conduct intervention with young children in the age group of 4–8 years often report success by using techniques such as videotape modelling or life-size puppets rather than strict cognitive approaches (Eyberg et al. 1998). Most children have difficulty in distinguishing emotions. Therefore, age should be considered while addressing motivational issues (Piacentini and Bergman 2001). Sometimes drawings, cartoons and pictures used in media such as television or films may be more useful than those created by the therapist.

TREATMENT DECISIONS

A crucial issue while working with children is to make treatment decisions. One has to make careful scrutiny whether it is the child who requires professional help or the family members who often refer him/her for treatment. On certain occasions, the adult's request for help is considered as a sufficient reason to intervene. In case of children, the decision is taken by parents and other family members; therefore it is crucial to determine the source of the child's problem. Sometimes even parents do not know that the problem lies with the family instead of the child. Thus, the clinician should see whether the target behaviour is normal under a given situation or not. Some investigators have attempted to provide norms for a wide spectrum of frequently occurring behavioural disorders among children (MacFarlane, Allen and Honzik 1954).

However, the therapist develops an internal set of norms for child behaviour through his experience either by watching his own children grow or referring to the developmental norms. The clinical information processing is largely influenced by these factors. Distortions may occur if he fully relies on the information of the parents or caretakers alone, for the reason that their observation or narration may have different goals than the therapist's. The child's report about significant family members is also considered as a valuable source of information. It helps the behaviour therapist to navigate through the information and decide the target of treatment.

RECOMMENDATIONS

1. The therapist must stay current with the developmental literature by making himself/herself conversant with the recent works published in scientific journals on child development, particularly clinical issues within developmental context and training programmes. It should also be cautioned that developmental research may not *always* be useful in guiding the treatment of individuals, because the group trends that emerge in developmental research may not apply to a specific case (Weisz and Hawley 2002).
2. Developmentally sensitive techniques should be used with children. For example, researches have shown that young children (ages 4–8) suffering from conduct disorder benefit better from videotape modelling and use of life-size toys than strict cognitive approaches (Eberg, Schuhmann and Rey 1998).
3. In the treatment of older children the therapist should think multi-systematically considering the child's context (Forehand and Eierson 1993; Henggler, Schoenwald, Borduin, Rowland and Cunningham 1998; Kazdin 1979; Reid 1993). In this context, the involvement of parents, teachers and peers is important.

4. The therapist should keep in mind the future developmental milestones as well as possible behavioural exacerbations at certain points of the developmental period. He should also consider that similar psychopathology may arise due to various causes. This is called *equifinality*. This issue has been discussed by Cicchetti and Rogosch (2002), and Shirk, Talmi and Olds (2000).

5. The armamentaria of therapeutic tools for children should include the treatment techniques, which are supported empirically. Instead of using these methods rigidly, defined set of age-appropriate therapeutic techniques should be used. This may involve different treatment delivery models as well. Drawing a parallel between treatment for psychological symptoms and physical symptoms, Kazdin (1997) suggested six such models, which vary with respect to dosage, the number of systems targeted, and the degree to which the treatment is continuous. Like diabetes, some require continuous care and monitoring whereas others may require care only when the symptoms exacerbate like that of dental problems. 'Booster' sessions may be required from time to time for some children in order to reinforce the continuing treatment.

5

Behavioural Assessment and Diagnosis

In behaviour therapy, assessment and diagnosis are closely linked issues in behaviour therapy. Diagnosis of a disorder generally determines its etiology, and assessment determines the cause and effect relationship. Thus, it precedes treatment. When the diagnosis is provisional, treatment is provided on trial basis in order to establish the functional relationship between behaviour and the immediate environment. In the field of medicine, diagnosis is a process of classification of the nature of a disorder through examination of the symptoms. A diagnostic system from this angle provides a scheme of classification for disorders along the line of etiology, symptoms or prognosis. Based on the approach to diagnosis, the relative focus of the treatment also differs. Diagnostic systems that are based on etiology share the assumption that common etiological factors lead to similar symptoms, and therefore would respond to similar treatments. Instead of analysing the finer variations of behaviour in different situations, it is considered logical to put them under a single label. For instance, instead of describing various types of excessive checking, cleaning or washing behaviour, it is convenient to put them under a single diagnostic category like 'obsessive compulsive disorder'. Such a scheme of classification economises the clinician's effort to analyse and treat these problems as separate behavioural disorders. Extensive correlation analyses of symptoms yield symptom clusters called 'syndromes'. Many classification systems reflect the psychometric tradition of test construction. R.B. Cattell, for instance, vividly explained the use of factor-analytic approach while constructing the '16 Personality Factors Questionnaire' to assess personality traits of people. Similar psychometric statistical tradition is reflected in major psychiatric diagnostic systems. If the symptoms are occurring frequently under different situations, they are believed to be independent of the stimulus condition. A broad distinction of 'organic' and 'non-organic' disorders, for instance, is based on such etiologic considerations. Certain classification systems may be based on the manner in which a client will react to treatment, irrespective of the current behaviour or past history (Kanfer and Saslow 1969). In many cases where the diagnosis is uncertain due to the complexity of symptoms, response to different forms of intervention may help in determining the diagnosis.

A medical diagnostic system evolves from a clinician's observations, who notes the occurrence of some behaviour with regularity, and then categorises them. The cross-cultural validity is determined through extensive research. The Diagnostic and Statistical Manual of Mental Disorders (DSM-IV, APA 1993), International Classification of Diseases (ICD-10, WHO 1993), Feighner's Criteria (Feighner et al. 1972) or its expansion, Research Diagnostic Criteria (Spitzer, Endicott and Robbins 1978) are some of the standard diagnostic systems prevalent in psychiatry. Most of them have their relative advantages and limitations. Despite the use of global rating of psychological stressors and the client's highest level of functioning during the past year, most of these diagnostic systems rely heavily on clinical judgment and categorise individuals in terms of broadly defined illnesses (McLemore and Benjamin 1979). Several criticisms of DSM were brought out by Begelman (1976). He pointed out that: (i) DSM relies excessively on the medical model of abnormal behaviour, (ii) it facilitates stigmatisation of individuals, (iii) theoretical notions employed for diagnosis are debatable, (iv) it has poor or low validity and reliability, (v) this diagnostic system has little relevance in assessing the treatment effects and future prediction of behaviour, (vi) one may also note that such diagnostic systems dehumanise client–therapist relationship, (vii) there is poor consistency in categorical grouping, (viii) arbitrary decision rules promote biases, and (ix) it also promotes homogeneity among people having same clinical labels. The criticism of most psychiatric classification systems focuses around four issues: internal consistency, explicitness, precision and reliability (Kanfer and Saslow 1969). The medical model is not sensitive to socio-psychological and interpersonal problems (McReynolds 1979). A disease condition implies some kind of tissue damage, destruction or injury. Many diagnoses provided in psychiatric diagnostic systems in this sense do not match the above criteria. There is an underlying assumption that behaviours are correlated and are consistent in each individual. No matter how extensive the psychiatric diagnostic system is, it does not go beyond labeling. The adverse consequences are many; therefore, these are considered closed systems.

Behavioural disturbances are not manifested as single disturbance but with multiple associated problems. This constellation of problems varies with a particular disorder so widely that the traditional psychiatric classificatory systems, including a multiaxial system may not provide the best understanding as in other organic disorders. For instance, an individual suffering from obsessive compulsive disorder may exhibit symptoms of affective disorders too. Co-occurrence of a variety of behavioural disturbances along with core disturbance is quite frequent. It questions the validity of diagnostic labeling. Further, the concept of syndrome is not necessarily associated with disease model. It can be empirically described in terms of general behaviour disorder (Kazdin 1983).

BEHAVIOURAL DIAGNOSIS

In the field of psychological disorders, there is a general misconception that clinical diagnosis is primarily the responsibility of the psychiatrist, while research and evaluation are the domains of psychologists (Nathan 1984). However, clinical psychologists are also equally equipped to make a behavioural diagnosis and screen out cases in order to carry out intervention programme or make referrals for further investigation. Thus, fitting the classification of behavioural dysfunction to medical diagnosis is not well founded. Behavioural diagnosis is primarily a process of identifying those environmental antecedents, which determine the occurrence of problem behaviour. Apart from classification, it helps in determining the direction of treatment. Diagnosis is an active process, involved in the entire course of interview, assessment and intervention. The primary function of behavioural diagnosis is formulation of inferences regarding the causation of behaviour. Simultaneously, it helps in eliminating those variables, which play little functional role in influencing the target behaviour. This process requires a distinct orientation. Behaviour analysis occupies a special position in explaining the functional role of the behaviour under analysis. It not only facilitates closer analysis of the environmental and organismic variables that influence behaviour, but also explains the behavioural effects on the environment. In this sense, it is also called functional analysis. Its link with behavioural treatment is remarkably close. Such diagnostic process makes space for scientific reasoning before treatment. The client who is referred for specific behaviour problem is not the target for treatment, alone. Others who control the contingencies of reinforcement and punishment maintaining this behaviour are also brought under the purview of the comprehensive treatment programme. The contributing factors to behaviour problems are many. As a wide variety of factors influence human behaviour, the diagnostic process is required to be 'necessarily' elaborate. Although, it starts with some basic hypotheses concerning the disorder, the diagnostic process continues throughout behaviour analysis.

Kanfer and Saslow (1969) provided an elaborate system of behavioural diagnosis. The system proposed a seven-stage analysis for conducting behavioural diagnosis.

Initial Analysis of Problem Situation

This is the first stage of analysis. It deals with prioritisation of target behaviours and the study of situations that elicit and sustain the target behaviour. The undesirable behaviour is classified under three broad groups, as either the behavioural excesses or deficits or under inappropriate stimulus control. The behavioural assets that include client's abilities, efficiencies or skilled behaviours are also systematically explored in the treatment.

Clarification of Problem Situation

Clarification of problem situation helps explain how the problem behaviour is perceived by those who are affected and how the significant others would respond to the treatment.

Motivational Analysis

Motivational analysis includes analysis of the reinforcement and punishment history that maintain problematic behaviour of the client. It also includes identification of major dispensers of reinforcement and punishment in the natural setting.

Developmental Analysis

This analysis helps to trace out the course of development of the index behaviour, including associated physical disorders, biological deviations and limitations. Sociological change is also considered under developmental analysis. It has an important bearing on treatment. It includes socio-cultural background, ethnic affiliation, and peer group influences.

Analysis of Self-control

Empirical analysis of self-control of the client provides an idea about the client's ability to control problematic behaviour and his dependency on the significant others, and whether punishment has been able to control the problematic behaviours. Whether the client has been able to avoid those situations that elicit such behaviour and has the capacity to use self-control in the situations where it is desired, are important issues. The behaviour analyst examines whether there is a correspondence between the verbalised report of self-control and actual exercise of control. Others' observation in the social environment is also shared to determine the client's self-control. It helps in exploring the possibility of using his self-control in therapy.

Analysis of Social Relationships

Behaviour of the people in the client's environment who significantly influence his behaviour through reinforcement and punishment are important. Their mutual expectations and roles in treatment are carefully analysed.

Analysis of the Social-cultural-physical Environment

The extent to which behaviour is perceived to be problematic or abnormal under a specific socio-cultural setting determines the selection of treatment modalities. The behaviours, which are well accepted in the family, neighbourhood, peer group or in the occupational settings, are not considered for treatment until the individual reports personal distress. The differential support, tolerance, antagonistic response to the target behaviour and acceptance of psychological treatment by the family members are focused in this analysis. Thus, behaviour analytic approach has a broader scope than the pathology-linked medical approach to treatment.

A wide range of instruments is used by behaviour analysts for behaviour analysis, assessment, formulation of treatment strategies and evaluation. Wolpe's (1969) 'Life History Questionnaire', and Lazarus' 'Multimodal Life History Questionnaire' (Lazarus 1980) are some of the examples. The present author has devised a 'Behavioural History Form for Adults' (BHFA) for behaviour analysis and intervention for use by behaviour therapists (Appendix-1). The BHFA has 10 different dimensions. It is designed to obtain information on the events that contribute to the present problems of the client. This form is filled-in at different stages of intervention. Once at the initial case history taking stage; second, prior to intervention; and the third and final entry is made after intervention. A 'Child Behaviour History Form' is used particularly for children (Appendix-2). Separate forms called 'Behaviour Therapy Forms' (A: Behaviour Analysis, and B: Record Treatment Sessions; Appendices 3–4) are designed for detailed behaviour analysis and intervention. These forms may be used along with BHFA.

BEHAVIOURAL ASSESSMENT

Defining Behaviour

For conducting a formal behavioural assessment, the target behaviour requires to be identified from a stream of other behaviours and then defined. In most situations the client himself reports about the behaviour that causes distress to him or in which he seeks further improvement. When the numbers of such behaviours are too many, the client is usually asked to put them in the order of priority for intervention. The process is called 'prioritisation'. These behaviours require to be objectively defined. A vague, subjective or incomplete definition of behaviour poses considerable difficulty in scientific communication, assessment, as well as intervention.

Some generally described target behaviours (molar behaviours) actually consist of a number of component behaviours (molecular behaviours), often called behavioural categories. Description of these categories helps the observer to make an accurate and reliable observation. Second, it helps in isolating the effects of intervention on different components of the target behaviour. For example, target behaviour such as aggression may be constituted of such categories like physical assault (PA), verbal aggression (VA), hostile gesture (HG) and property destruction (PD).

Checklists

In order to identify the problem behaviours in different areas of functioning, many researchers have developed comprehensive checklists. These instruments are used almost like menu cards in a restaurant, in order to identify problem behaviours quickly for intervention. These checklists are filled out by the client himself. The advantage of using checklists is that it provides an opportunity to the client to assess his behavioural adequacy in different areas of functioning. Many areas, which might not have been either thought of by the client or difficult to explore during the interview by the behaviour analyst, may be easily identified through checklists. Problem specific survey schedules are also developed by some authors in order to make detailed assessment like the 'Fear Survey Schedule' (Wolpe and Lang 1964). In this schedule, the client is required to rate a series of objects and experiences in terms of their fear-provoking potential. Similarly, the 'Cues for Tension and Anxiety Schedule', developed by Cautela (1973) is used to identify the cues that arouse tension and anxiety in specific ways (e.g. palpitation, tension in neck muscles, tingling sensation in the limbs). These problem specific survey schedules are generally used after an initial behavioural interview. The major advantage of this method is that it taps many cognitive variables, which maintain the problematic behaviour. These variables cannot be assessed otherwise.

Self-assessment

Evaluation of change in the severity or intensity of behaviour by the client himself is a crucial aspect of evaluating the effectiveness of intervention. In recent cognitive orientation in behaviour therapy, such assessment procedures have added a new dimension to interpretation of the genesis as well as the change of behaviour. However, self-report is an indirect method of assessment. Therefore, it does suffer from some disadvantages concerning its reliability. In view of this, direct behavioural observation is used as both an alternative as well as additional measure along with self-report.

Direct Behavioural Observation

For implementing a behavioural intervention programme, direct behavioural observation is an important prerequisite. Observational methods gained popularity in the domain of behaviour therapy of children in the 1920s and onwards. Direct behavioural observation is considered as one of the 'greatest contributions', the 'hallmark', and the '*sine qua non*', of behaviour modification (Johnson and Bolstad 1973; Haynes 1978). As compared to other assessment procedures, it is more consistent with behaviourism's epistemological emphasis on observable behaviour and the assumptions of environmental causality (e.g. Goldfried and Kent 1972; Haynes 1978). It helps precisely to identify how environmental contingencies elicit or influence certain behaviour. Data are delineated to gather information primarily from the motoric response modality. This approach followed logically from the theoretical assumption of applied behaviour analysis, that directly observable behaviour is the only appropriate domain for empirical study. Behaviour therapists have little interest in the personality of a client. Behavioural assessment is based on the idea that people tend to exhibit certain behaviours in specific situations because of certain reinforcing contingencies and not because of their personality 'traits' as such. A client's actions, thoughts and feelings in actual situations are assessed in the context of the setting events. Hence, frequency, rate and duration measures of the behaviours of interest were considered important, although existence of organismic conditions and affective-cognitive states of the individual were also acknowledged. Recently the scope of direct behaviour intervention has broadened even further to incorporate large-scale social systems like schools, work setting or socio-cultural influences on behaviour. For the evaluation of change, in many therapeutic programmes, psychometric testing and rating scales are also used before and after the treatment. Though such assessments are advantageous in terms of economy of time and effort, their relationship to actual behaviour is often uncertain. They may not reflect the real change in behaviour (Barkley and Cunningham 1978). Although, behavioural observation procedures are time consuming, they have the advantage of dealing with actual behaviour under study, not the presumed ones. In this approach, diagnosis is not treated as a separate entity but is a part of the ongoing process of intervention. The aim is not just to diagnose and label the problem behaviour but also to examine the effects of intervention. For their closer relation to treatment, attention is now shifted to direct behavioural observation. Hypothesis testing is the basic function of behavioural assessment. A well planned behavioural assessment leads to specification of the intervention method. It is a continuous activity, which occurs throughout the programme. Therapy without assessment is meaningless as we are not concerned with the subjective feeling of well being but also observable positive change in behaviour.

METHODS OF OBSERVATION

Systematic observation involves three interrelated activities: selection, provocation, and recording and encoding of behaviour in the context of a particular setting (Weick 1968). Selection refers to identification of a target response from a stream of behaviours. It requires not only a precise definition in order to distinguish target behaviour from other behaviours, but also a good amount of training for the observer to perform this activity in an actual setting. In order to perform this function, an armchair description of behaviour is not sufficient. Observation has to be conducted repeatedly in situations that elicit such behaviour. Therefore, the individual under observation is required to be placed in actual settings where the target behaviour occurs. Exceptions are those behaviours that are harmful for the individual himself or for others, (e.g. self-injurious behaviour or violent and antisocial acts like arson or fire-setting). Recording is the most significant aspect of behavioural assessment. Substantial amount of time is spent by behaviour therapists in designing appropriate method of recording procedures in order to implement them in a natural setting. Recording procedures are largely influenced by the ongoing stream of behaviour. The recording procedure has to be changed with change in the occurrences of the behaviour.

There is a large variety of behavioural observation methods. However, only the principal ones are discussed in this chapter. That includes event recording, duration recording, latency recording, interval sampling, realtime sampling and intensity recording.

Event Recording

This is one of the simplest methods of recording. The number of occurrences of the behaviour is recorded by counting them. Using a writing device the observer may tally the number of occurrences of certain behaviour on a recording sheet or use mechanical devices like wrist counters used by golfers, an electronic tally counter, a calculator or a computer. Apart from the conventional clipboards, wrist tally boards encased in a plastic holder on a watchband, stickers attached to a desk or a wristwatch may also be used for convenient recording. To make it more unobtrusive, small objects like beads or paper clips can also be transferred from one hand (or container) to the other. However, when the target behaviour occurs at a very high rate, or continuously for a long duration, event recording will be a rather an inappropriate method.

Recording the *rate* of occurrence of the behaviour makes the observation data more meaningful for behaviour analysis. Frequent occurrence of a response in one situation than in the other implies that different contingencies of reinforcement or punishment are operating in these situations. Event recording is more useful for discrete behavioural events. However, it provides only a rough estimate of the response. Figure 5.1 provides a sample data sheet for event recording.

Duration Recording

The time for which the client engages in any behaviour is recorded by taking the duration of such behaviours into account. This method is used when there is a clear-cut beginning and ending of a response. Two types of duration recording may be used: (i) Duration per occurrence, and (ii) Total duration recording. The 'duration per occurrence' recording requires noting down the duration of each occurrence of the behaviour during a specified observation period. Therefore, both frequency and duration of the behaviour are recorded automatically. Stopwatch is one of the most convenient devices to record the duration of a behaviour. At the onset of the behaviour, the stopwatch is started and stopped when the behaviour ceases to occur. Observer resets his stopwatch after recording each of its occurrences. A sample form of duration recording is provided in Figure 5.2.

'Total duration recording' requires the observer to record the total time an individual is engaged in a given behaviour. This is also termed as 'continuous real time recording'. This kind of data is useful for

FIGURE 5.1
Sample Event Recording Form

EVENT RECORDING FORM

Participant_____ Observer_____ Date_____ Behaviour_____

Period of Observation: from _____ to _____Setting/Condition_____

OBSERVATION	TALLY	FREQUENCY
Observation 1		
Observation 2		
Observation 3		
Observation 4		
Observation 5		
Total		

FIGURE 5.2
Sample Latency and Duration Recording Form

LATENCY AND DURATION RECORDING FORM

Participant_____ Observer_____ Date_____ Behaviour_____

Period of Observation: from _____ to _____Setting/Condition_____

RESPONSE	LATENCY/DURATION	RESPONSE	LATENCY/DURATION
1._____		6._____	
2._____		7._____	
3._____		8._____	
4._____		9._____	
5._____		10._____	

Total :   Average :

time allocation and preference studies, where the amount of time engaged in a specific behaviour by the client during the observation period is recorded. Each onset and termination of behaviour is cumulatively recorded. The cumulative total is calculated in terms of percentage by using a simple formula:

$$\frac{\text{Total duration of target response}}{\text{Duration of observation period in specific setting}} \times 100$$

The observer is not required to reset the instrument after each recording. If behaviour endurance (i.e. continuity of a behaviour) is the major consideration, then total duration recording may be sufficient (Tawney and Gast 1984). It provides the most precise temporal structure of a response, such as the pattern of occurrence, torque, bouts, inter-response times and cyclic variation data (Rojahn and Schroeder 1983).

There are many behaviours which may not occur during a fixed period during which an individual is under routine observation. They occur occasionally at critical moments and are to be recorded as and when they occur. The period of occurrence is considered as a 'critical' period and the method of recording is called 'critical event sampling'. The observer is required to record this behaviour only in these critical periods. Follingstad, Sullivann and Hayenes (1978) used this method to record critical communication of a dissatisfied marital couple using a tape recorder with condenser microphone. Their verbal interactions were coded after they were instructed to activate the recorder during all arguments and disagreements over a two-week baseline period. In another experiment, McCommon and Palotai (1978) used tape recorders to record the interactions of a 7-year old girl in the car while travelling from a day-care centre to home. The time was specified as 'problematic'. They were also instructed to switch-on the tape recorder during any situation they felt constituted an antecedent to a tantrum.

Electronic and mechanical devices are now increasingly used in behavioural assessment. A review of the current state of this practice would require a separate chapter. Here, we would restrict the discussion to specific content. Event recorders are used to record the frequency as well as duration of behaviours more reliably than individual observers do. Baker and Whitehead (1972) developed a remote controlled apparatus, which consisted of eight miniature push buttons that enabled the behaviour analyst to record the frequency and duration of eight different behaviours simultaneously. A sample recording form is provided in Figure 5.3. It allows the observer to be stationed in a natural setting. He presses the push button as long as the behaviour occurrs.

Similar instruments were also used by Heimstra and Davis (1962), and Hanf (1973). A 20-pen event recorder was developed by Gardner et al. (1968) to record the frequency as well as the duration of a specified social interaction of a schizophrenic child with his parents and therapist. The duration of behaviour is computed by using the following formula:

Duration = Length of response/Paper speed = 4 cm/4 cm (per second) = 1 second

The length of the response as well as the speed per second can be measured by using a ruler. Pearson's product moment correlation can be used for calculating the reliability of observation made by two observers observing the same behaviour. Lovaas and his associates (1968) trained pairs of observers over several hours of practice to record certain target behaviours using event recorders. A light was activated each time there was a disagreement between the observers.

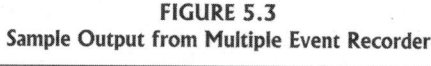

FIGURE 5.3
Sample Output from Multiple Event Recorder

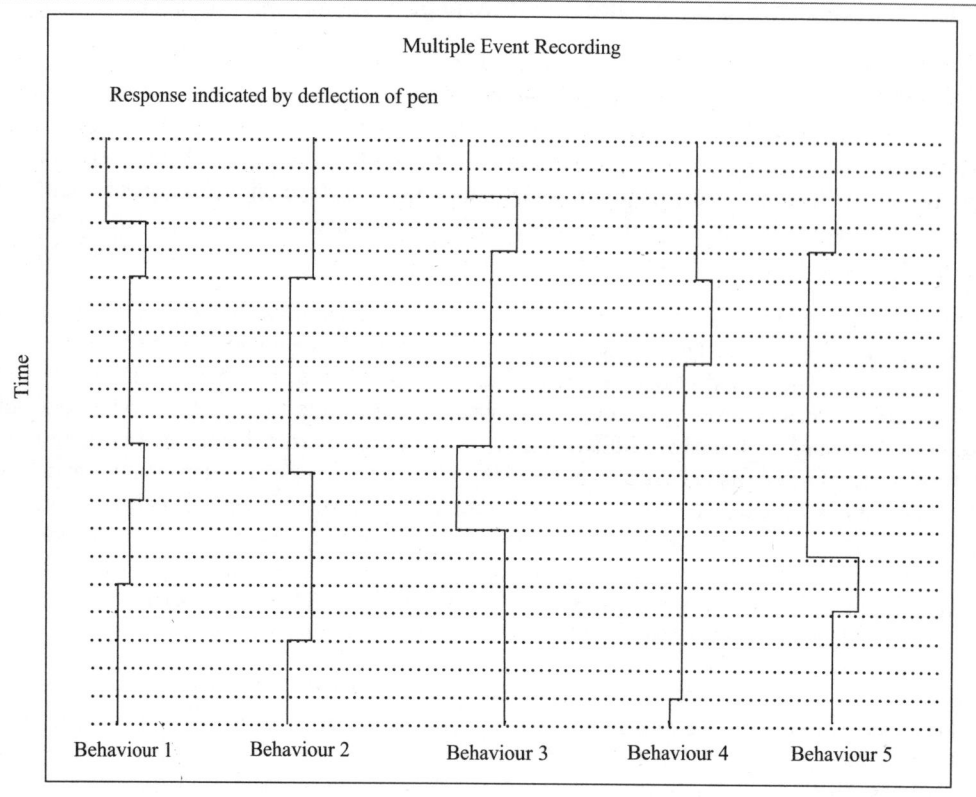

Latency Recording

The temporal gap between the presentation of a stimulus and the onset of a response is called latency. Latency recording is required when the immediacy of response initiation is the target of intervention that is, the response initiation is either delayed or too fast. For instance, many people with retardation exhibit delayed response to instruction or signal given to them for certain activity. Conversely, people with anxiety disorders and attention deficit with hyperactivity disorder (ADHD) respond too quickly to many stimulus conditions; sometimes they start responding even before completion of the instruction or presentation of a signal. Latency recording may be useful where reaction time is a significant aspect of human performance. In the field of human engineering, training of athletes or military personnel, response latency is an important determinant of performance. Even ordinary people who wish to speed up their specific activity require enhancing their response latency. A mechanical or electronic stopwatch can be used as a useful device for recording response latency. The timer is started immediately after cessation of a stimulus and stopped immediately at the initiation of a response in order to measure the latency.

Interval Sampling

Recording a target behaviour at predetermined discrete time intervals is termed as interval sampling. The interval may range from a few seconds to few hours. It provides opportunity for an intensive analysis of moment-to-moment changes in behaviour. This is probably the most frequently used measurement system in behaviour therapy. In general, a standard observation session (30–40 minutes duration) is divided into equal observation intervals of 5–20 mintutes. The observer first scans the behaviour in each interval and then records the occurrence of the target behaviour on an observation sheet.

There are three types of interval sampling methods: (i) whole interval sampling, (ii) partial interval sampling, and (iii) event-within-interval sampling. In whole interval sampling, the behaviour under study is present during the entire interval. In partial interval sampling, it must be present for some proportion of the interval before it is recorded. In event-within-interval sampling, the observer records the number of times the behaviour occurs within an interval event sampling.

Real-time Sampling

Observing a participant continuously for a prolonged period, say 30–45 minutes may not be feasible always. Further, this may involve a good deal of monotony as well. Due to this, an observer may find difficulty in continuously attending to a specific response. This may cause 'observer drift' and add to observation error. When recording of multiple responses or a single response of a number of participants are involved, continuous observation system poses considerable difficulty.

Under the above circumstances, (momentary) time sampling (Figure 5.4) is suggested as the most appropriate observation method. Here 'moment' means, 'for a few seconds'. Instead of observing the presence or absence of behaviour in each interval, the observer may take samples of such observation from time to time during the entire observation period. The observer occasionally checks whether the behaviour is occurring or not. Momentary time sampling requires the response to be recorded even if it appears shortly during the interval. The length of occurrence is not the criteria of recording. It simply indicates whether the response is at all present or absent during an observation interval. The length of interval is usually 5–15 seconds only. Saudargas and Zanolli (1990) suggested that at short intervals (15 seconds) momentary time sampling is quite accurate.

When data is summarised from interval recording procedure, it is presented in terms of percentage of occurrence. The disadvantage of this method of recording is that, the observer apparently loses the actual time of onset, frequency and duration of occurrence of the target response.

Intensity Recording

Intensity is defined as the magnitude, acuteness, amplitude, strength, or force of a response; and clinically, the severity of a response. Some behaviours are considered as problematic because of its intensity; for instance, loudness of voice, severity of anxiety, fear, or depression. Except at a very low or very high level of intensity, virtually all responses to a changing level of stimulation can be rated by

FIGURE 5.4
Sample Interval Recording Form

INTERVAL RECORDING AND MOMENTARY TIME SAMPLING RECORD FORM

Participant_____Observer_____Date_____ Observation Time: From _____ to _____

Setting/Condition_____ Behaviour _____ Description _____

1'				2'				3'				4'				5'			
15"	15"	15"	15"	15"	15"	15"	15"	15"	15"	15"	15"	15"	15"	15"	15"	15"	15"	15"	15"

6'				7'				8'				9'				10'			

11'				12'				13'				14'				15'			

16'				17'				18'				19'				20'			

21'				22'				23'				24'				25'			

26'				27'				28'				29'				30'			

using semantic differential scales (e.g. self-reports). In order to measure intensity (amplitude) of various psycho-physiological signals is transduced through mechanical and electronic devices (EEG, GSR, ECG or EMG) in order to understand their intensity as well as the duration.

ASSESSING GROUP BEHAVIOUR

Behaviour analysts have also included assessment of groups in a variety of institutional and social settings; for example, in classrooms, hospitals and in other natural settings. Once the problem behaviour is identified, the behaviour analysts attempt to find out how many people in the group or in the selected sample exhibit such behaviour. In an attempt to reduce the speed of vehicles on highways, Van Houten, Nau and Marini (1980) used unobtrusively placed radar system to find out those drivers who crossed the speed limit. The prevalence of use of seat belts among elementary school children was studied by Sowers-Hoag, Thyer and Bailey (1987). They recorded the percentage of children who used seat belts as the baseline for the study. Assessment of groups of subjects at a time has been used most frequently in classrooms. Instead of focusing on one student, many investigators have attempted to conduct behavioural observation for more subjects in classroom settings. Barrish, Saunders and Wolf (1969); Harris, and Sherman (1973); and McAllister, Stachowiak, Baer and Conderman (1969) developed relatively simple observation instruments for observers to record attentive and disruptive behaviours in the classroom set-up. The subject-sampling instruments facilitate random observation of each subject in the sample, so that each will have an equal chance of being observed for the same period. Kazdin and Klock (1973) conducted sampling and recording of attending behaviours of 12 children who were retarded, in 15 seconds intervals. The observations were conducted in a fixed order until each subject was observed for 20 intervals. In another study, randomised observation techniques have been used in group setting by several authors. For example, Broden et al. (1970) used this technique for assessing attending behaviour of two children sitting in adjacent benches. Hall, Panyan, Rabon and Broden (1968) conducted observation of 30 children simultaneously. Thomas, Becker and Armstrong (1968) also used subject-sampling procedures. They used randomised blocks of 5–10 second interval samples to study disruptive behaviour of 10 children in a classroom. Occurrence of any of the five disruptive behaviours was scored in any interval. Each child was observed twice in a 20-minute observation period for a total observation of 100 seconds per child. 'Planned Activity Check' (PLACHECK) (Figure 5.5) was used by Doke and Risley (1972). In this method, a group of individuals engaged in a specified behaviour are observed at a time. A group of individuals is observed at the end of the specified time. They authored this method while studying group participation of young children.

It is required that the observational instrument and method of observation be standardised so that they are able to differentiate between untreated clinical groups and controls. Some authors suggested that collection of observational data on normal individuals could also be used to evaluate the degree to which the treatment normalises behaviour (e.g. Gittleman, Abicoff, Pollack, Klein, Katz and Matters 1980; Loney, Weissenberger, Woolson and Lichty 1979; Walker and Hops 1976).

FIGURE 5.5
PLACHECK Record Form

CLASSROOM BEHAVIOUR		
Observer_____ Date_____ Time: From_____ to_____ Setting_____		
Target Behaviours		
OS (Out of Seat) PA (Physical Aggression) VA (Verbal Aggression)	TO (Talking Out) LA (Looking Around) NM (Noise-making)	BR (Body Rocking) PL(Play) SL (Sleep)
Interval	Child	Behaviours
1	___	OS PA VA TO LA NM BR PL SL
2	___	OS PA VA TO LA NM BR PL SL
3	___	OS PA VA TO LA NM BR PL SL
4	___	OS PA VA TO LA NM BR PL SL
5	___	OS PA VA TO LA NM BR PL SL

A focal individual sampling method (Altman 1974) was used in group setting to record all occurrences of specified behaviours during a sample period for each subject. The order of observation for each sampled subject was determined by a random list, so that each subject had an equal probability of being observed at a given time. The length of each focal sample is usually about one minute, during which all the target behaviours are recorded.

OBSERVER TRAINING

The data collected by a treatment-blind observer provide objective information. These are independent of potentially biased ratings and judgments made by those involved in therapeutic efforts. When involved in observation, a therapist cannot be aware of the events, which will be apparent to a detached observer. Sometimes such awareness may be low for the simple reason that the intervention activities are habitual. That leads to poor reliability. Therefore, in order to assess the impact of treatment effects objectively, the observers are required to be trained.

Analogue Assessment

Training observers in a natural setting where the behaviour under study occurs is a costly affair. It consumes a good deal of time and effort, at times disturbing the natural occurrence of the behaviour itself. In order to reduce the cost of training, analogous environment is created. A variety of such analogues has been considered.

Paper-and-pencil Analogue

It is required of the observer to either write or verbally describe how he would record the target behaviour in a specific sample environment. He may be provided with a wide range of narrated 'natural' environments along with a detailed description of behaviour and setting. He is asked to report how to record the target behaviour either in different situations, presented on cards or on a piece of paper. Multiple choice questions are used to assess the observer's efficiency. In case open-ended questions are to be put, there should be standardised methods of evaluation. Even verbal analogue method can be used to elicit the observer's knowledge of the observation methods to be used in an actual setting. The major drawback of this method is that even if the observer is excellent in demonstrating his knowledge of the techniques and methods, he may not be able to translate the knowledge into actual skills required in actual setting. This can be used as an adjunct to other procedures of observer training.

Audio-visual Analogue

It requires audio-visual presentation of the target behaviour to the observer. The respondent records this behaviour on a data sheet. An attempt is made that the audio-visual recording takes into account the actual behaviour and the natural setting in which it occurs. A narrator explains the technique of observation.

Guided examples are provided for practice. Multiple observers can be trained simultaneously by using this procedure. Another advantage is that, the same set of behaviour can be presented repeatedly until the observer acquires the criterion level of skills. Inter-rater reliability checks can help in standardising the methods of recording. 'Picture-in-picture' (PIP) technique can be used in making simultaneous presentation of the observer's behaviour along with the sample behaviour under study. These videotapes can be used by the observer himself as a feedback for his own performance during observation. This is considered as one of the most effective methods of observer training, as it provides an opportunity for comparing observation skills of different observers for the same index behaviour. The facial expressions, body movement and many other features that cannot be observed carefully during a single observation can also be carefully studied through repeated display. Although, a wide range of target behaviours have been recorded, like social skills (Conger and Keane 1981), and used as a method for training behavioural observers, it may prove to be expensive when observer's competence is to be developed for recording a variety of behaviours. Lack of flexibility in the procedure is one of its major drawbacks.

Enactment and Roleplay Analogue

Live enactment of the index behaviour by an 'actor' in either clinical or natural setting is used for training the observer. The actions of the actor closely resemble that of the actual client. The advantage of this method is that it provides opportunity to record identical behaviour in a simulated setting. Many situational and subject-related variables that cannot be presented through audiovisual methods can be easily presented through this method. Further, there is a better scope for changing the complexity of observed behaviour, matching it to the observer's skill. For most enactment, a formal scoring system is used. The main constraint is that some natural environments and target behaviours are very difficult to reconstruct or may be quite expensive to do so.

OBSERVER AGREEMENT

Inter-observer agreement is a method of reporting reliability of observations. It plays a crucial role in advancement of behaviour analysis. Instead of taking a single measure of reliability, repeated observer agreement is obtained before, during and after the intervention. It helps in defining the target behaviours, provide taxonomic distinctions between different behaviours, shape the observation procedure and finally help in objectively evaluating effectiveness of an intervention programme. Without reliable data, the behaviour analysts would not be in a position to say whether the change in behaviour is due to intervention or that it is a normal variation in the behaviour. Thus, inter-observer agreement data allows drawing meaningful conclusion. Two or more observers are engaged to observe the same behaviour simultaneously and reliability checks are made from time to time.

Methods of Computing Inter-observer Agreement

There are number of different methods of computing inter-observer agreement. They are determined by (i) the dimension of behaviour measured, (ii) the number of observers used for recording, (iii) the method of recording itself, and (iv) the meaning of 'agreement' or 'disagreement' used in a specific context. Some principal methods of inter-observer agreement are discussed here.

Frequency Ratio

When comparisons are made between two observers' independently recorded behaviour, this method is used. Although it is most suitable for frequency (event) recording, particularly when there is no temporal limit to the frequency of response, that is, free operant behaviour, it can also be used for latency, duration, as well as interval recording. Inter-observer reliability is calculated by dividing the smaller total by the larger and multiplying by 100 that is (smaller total /larger total) × 100.

For instance, if an observer observes behaviour in 20 intervals and another observer observes the same in 18 intervals the frequency ratio will be 18/20 × 100 = 90 per cent. The drawback of this method is that only the occurrence of the behaviour is taken into account, non-occurrence of the behaviour remains unscored, as a result of which the accuracy is low.

Point-by-point Agreement

In case of interval recording and momentary time sampling, where both occurrence as well as non-occurrence of the target behaviour are taken into account, this method aims at computing whether there is an agreement on each instance. Here, agreement means instances in which both observers agree in recording the behaviour whether it occurs or not. This means agreement for both, occurrence as well as non-occurrence of the target behaviour. Disagreement means that one observer recorded the behaviour as occurring and the other, as not occurring. The inter-observer agreement is calculated by dividing the number of agreement intervals (AI) by total number of agreements (AI) plus disagreement intervals (DI) multiplying by 100 that is (AI)/(AI + DI) × 100 = % agreement.

A time-sample recording sheet for computing inter-observer agreement percentage is provided in the Figure 5.6.

The inter-observer agreement method discussed above for interval recording is also called the interval-by-interval method (Hawkins and Dotson 1975). In this method, all observation intervals are counted for assessing inter-observer agreement. There are two variations of this method: scored interval (S-I) method

FIGURE 5.6
Inter-observer Agreement Scoring Form

Intervals	1	2	3	4	5	6	7	8	9	10	11	12	13	14	15	16	17	18	19	20
Observer 1	√	√	√	X	√	X	√	√	√	√	X	X	X	√	X	X	√	√	√	X
Observer 2	√	√	X	X	√	√	√	√	X	√	X	X	X	√	X	√	√	√	√	√

Presence of behaviour (√)   Absence of behaviour (X)
Inter-observer agreement : AI/(AI + DI) × 100 = % agreement i.e. (15/20) × 100 = 75 %

and unscored interval (U-I) method. The first method requires the agreement to be computed by taking only those intervals for which, both the observers have scored for occurrences of the target behaviour. Whereas, the second method requires that all intervals in which both the observers have recorded non-occurrence of behaviour be counted for computing inter-observer agreement. All these computational methods yield different agreements; therefore the behaviour analyst should also specify the procedure while reporting agreement data. In behaviour therapy, conventionally, agreement percentage between 80–100 per cent is considered as high level of reliability.

The percent agreement is used most often as an index of inter-observer agreement. The reason is that it is easy to compute. However, it has been criticised on the ground that the value of its statistics may be inflated when the target behaviours occur at extreme rates. Very high or very low frequency behaviours may have high chance level of agreement (Johnson and Bolstad 1973). Second, it treats the degree of inter-observer agreement as an all-or-none phenomenon, and therefore, insensitive to partial or incomplete agreements (Mitchell 1979). In order to overcome these drawbacks, alternatively coefficients have been considered (Tinsley and Weiss 1975). This may be called as 'correlation method'.

Correlation Method

Pearson's product moment correlation (r) is often used for checking inter-observer agreement. Reliability checks are conducted at specific intervals in order to find the levels of agreement of two independent observers observing the same behaviour. The agreement is calculated using the following formula:

$$r = \frac{N\sum XY - (\sum X)(\sum Y)}{\sqrt{\left[N\sum X^2 - (\sum X)^2\right]\left[N\sum Y^2 - (\sum Y)^2\right]}}$$

where, X = scores of observer A, Y = scores of observer B, XY = cross product scores and N = total number of checks, that is, the days or number of times the scores of the observers are checked. The correlation coefficient ranges from –1 to +1. 'Chance' agreement can be used as an additional check on the reliability of observation. The formula for calculating chance agreement for occurrences may be stated as follows:

$$\frac{O_A \text{ for agreement} \times O_B \text{ for agreement}}{(\text{Total number intervals checked})^2} \times 100$$

For example, if in 100 observations, observer A records occurrences of a behaviour for 80 times and observer B for 70 times, as per the above formula, the chance of agreement for occurrences is $[(80 \times 70)/100^2] \times 100 = 56$ per cent. Similar formula can be used to calculate the chance of agreement for non-occurrences. In this case, it is $[(20 \times 30)/100^2] \times 100 = 6$ per cent. The rule of the thumb is that, agreement on occurrences is calculated only when the behaviour occurs in relatively few intervals, that is, the rate of occurrence is low. When the occurrences of behaviour are relatively high, the agreement can be computed by taking the agreement on non-occurrence into consideration. In some cases, the rate of response varies over time. In this case, overall weightage may be given for occurrence and non-occurrence intervals (Harris and Lahey 1978).

Some researchers prefer to use proportions for assessing inter-observer reliability. Here, it should be made clear that inter-observer reliability should not be confused with observer agreement percentage. The experimenter may use the split-half or alternative intervals for computation of inter-observer reliability. He may take both the odd and even numbered observations into account, or the first and second halves of the observation. Apart from the computational method used, inter-observer agreement is influenced by many other factors. For example, during the initial as well as the concluding stages of observation, the accuracy is poorer than what is obtained during the middle phase of the observation. The accuracy increases with experience as well as training. Similarly, when the observers are aware that spot checks are going to be conducted, they record behaviours more accurately (Romanczyk et al. 1973). Other variables, which contribute to the inter-rater agreement are incomplete instruction, or ambiguity of response definition and language used for describing the rating procedure.

PART II
TECHNIQUES OF BEHAVIOUR THERAPY

6

Reinforcing Desirable Responding

NATURE OF REINFORCEMENT

Reinforcement plays a vital role in strengthening and maintaining most of our behaviours in day-to-day life. In a way, the living organism's survival and behavioural processes are closely linked with the delivery of reinforcement. Conversely, a prolonged history of loss of reinforcement may cause syndromes like depression. Loss of reinforcement very early in life may arrest adaptive behaviours leading to mental retardation. Particularly, when the environment is dull, unstimulating, unvaried and social interactions are highly restricted it creates a situation of severely deficient reinforcement. It weakens the strength of much adaptive behaviour. If it occurs at an early stage of life when the brain structures are highly plastic, it may lead to extensive retardation in adaptive responding. This condition is often seen as mental retardation. This has been well documented by several investigators. Curtiss (1977), for example, provided a moving account of the case history of a girl called Genie who was confined to a room from the time she was 20 months old until she was 13 years. During daytime, her father used to confine her on a potty chair on which she could only move her limbs. During nights, she used to be put in a sleeping bag and restrained to a straightjacket. People noticed her only after she escaped with her partially blind mother and was treated in a hospital. Her mental age was only at 1 year level. Although there were developments in certain functions with intensive training, she never used pronouns, could never speak a sentence nor could ask questions. Possibly her left hemisphere was atrophied.

Behavioural models of retardation focus on the adverse reinforcement and punishment history of the client during the early stage of developmental period (Bijou 1963). Some parents even wish to see their children hopeless and dependent on them that reduce their chance to be independent in day-to-day activities (Campbell 1973). Poor or intermittent reinforcement for adaptive responding during developmental period may have devastating effect as seen in case of Genie. Therefore, we often find a large number of children with mental retardation are from isolated communities, poor families or from orphanages that fail to provide stimulating (reinforcing) environment for these children.

The foods that we eat, the air that we breathe, the temperatures that we need to survive are all different types of reinforcers available either in continuous or intermittent schedules. When their contingencies are disrupted, it threatens our survival. Even some life threatening ritualistic acts are backed by their immediate sensory and social consequences, which act as reinforcers, like social attention. Quality of life is the consequence of the quality of reinforcers that people get from their environment. The power structure in society is determined by distribution and controls of reinforcers. In a broader sense, reinforcement is linked with the survival, development and extinction of organisms. Therefore, its role is crucial in understanding human behaviour.

Certain responses produce automatic reinforcement and sustain on their own, such as autonomic responses (e.g. respiration and cardiac activity) and voluntary responses (e.g. reading a novel, watching a television or driving a car). These responses keep occurring spontaneously, whereas there are large varieties of responses, which do not occur so spontaneously or in desired quality or quantity. Under these situations, one requires to 'programme' the environment in such a manner that their occurrence would be more probable. Here a distinction should be made between the act or operation called reinforcement, and the stimulus that is called the reinforcer, although at times, it is difficult to distinguish between the two. In the next section, we have discussed different types of reinforcers.

Reinforcement refers to those consequences of behaviour, which increase the probability of its occurrence and decrease it in its absence. Accordingly, there are two varieties of reinforcement. The first variety of reinforcement is called positive reinforcement, and the second is called negative reinforcement. Skinner (1971: 7) categorically stated, 'The kind of consequences which increase the rate of a response are positive or negative depending on whether they reinforce when they appear or disappear.'

In technical literature, the term 'reinforcement' is used in place of 'reward' in order to avoid the teleological undertone inherent in the popular usage of the term 'reward'. Reward suggests compensation for behaving in a given way, whereas reinforcement simply designates the act of strengthening of a response. This fine distinction, in fact, reflects the finer difference between a mentalistic and behaviouristic approach to human behaviour. The definition of reinforcer has its basis in its effect on behaviour; a reward, on the other hand, is used to indicate a subjective state leading to pleasant or satisfying sensations. Second, while the definition of reinforcer is always in terms of measurable stimulus or measurable behaviour of the individual, the definition of reward is not (Ayllon and Azrin 1968: 57–58). Reinforcers set the occasion for behaviour to occur. At the same time, these also influence the relative probabilities of different behaviour available in the response repertoire. When a chocolate is presented to a child after homework, the most probable response that may be reinforced is homework; but it will depend on the drive state as well as the reinforcement history of this behaviour. There are no absolute classes of reinforcers (Premack 1959, 1965). In order to know why a stimulus event will act as a reinforcer, one must look into the learning history as well as evolution of species.

The evolutionary changes that occurred in animal species were due to the changes in their natural selection of behaviours. Those behaviours which were successful in improving the chances of their survival, such as catching a prey or escaping from a predator, were shaped and strengthened due to consequent reinforcement. The chances of success determined their future probability and failures weakened them. In this process, some behaviours became relatively permanent and crystallised and acquired 'trait-like' characters, called 'species-specific' behaviours. Those which were inconsequential, painful, caused distress, disease or death, declined in strength, thereby increasing their chances of extinction. Now, those species, which exhibited ineffective defensive and predatory behaviours, or were unable to face the adverse natural condition, got extinct. Precisely, the reinforcing and punishing consequences played a key role in the process of evolution. Thus, apart from the present consequences, the previous evolutionary history, determine the present choice of reinforcers, and of course, the actions that we chose to attain them.

In order to explain the occurrence and non-occurrence of a response, analysis of its consequences is important. Everett (1981) used reinforcement theory in order to explain why people prefer driving a car to using public transport. Car driving was observed to be facilitated by many reinforcers such as short travelling time, prestige, arrival/departure flexibility, exhilaration, privacy, route selection, cargo capacity, predictability and delayed costs. These reinforcers outnumber the punishers like congestion, gas/fuel and maintenance cost. Mass transit facility is facilitated by very few reinforcers like freedom of car ownership responsibilities or making friends. Whereas, it is adversely affected by a large number of punishers such as exposure to weather, discomfort, noise, dirt, surly personnel, long walks to stops, immediate costs, unpredictability, minimum cargo capacity, minimum route selection, crowdedness, minimum arrival/departure flexibility, low prestige and long travel time. Behavioural analysis has important bearing on shaping government policies on many social issues, such as selective taxation, benefits and concessions, apart from travel behaviour.

TYPES OF REINFORCERS

Certain standard things such as food, drinks, rest or warmth act as reinforcers, because they have been doing so in the past by satisfying some basic needs. These are called unconditional (primary) reinforcers (S^R). They gain their power from the phylogenetic history. Nevertheless, there are large groups of reinforcers, which are learned or conditional. One must find them out from the particular person's preferences and actual observations. Conditional (secondary) reinforcers (S^r) are learned (e.g. attention, praise, tokens, money or a gift). Their reinforcing property lies in their prior pairing with other primary reinforcers. Since individual learning history plays an important role in search of reinforcers, it is essential that the reinforcer should be matched to individual's preference. An object, which is highly reinforcing for one individual may be rather unattractive for another. Therefore, reinforcers should be matched with the individual preferences and based on careful observation. In order to do so, a reinforcer menu may be prepared by the therapist taking a list of possible reinforcers and asking the subject to select some of them. While doing so, the therapist must see whether such reinforcers are effective in behaviour change. This can also be examined by watching if the absence of a specific reinforcer decreases the target behaviour. Its effectiveness must be demonstrated. While doing so, one has to see that ethical guidelines should be observed. For instance, an individual cannot be deprived of food for testing its reinforcing quality.

The sources of reinforcement are mostly embedded in the social nexus of the individual. Careful behaviour analysis is required to identify and programme them effectively in the clients' natural environment. One must also note that while reinforcing clients, the role of intrinsic reinforcers should not be undermined. In fact, after increasing behaviour, our ultimate goal is to maintain it without extrinsic reinforcers. In the following section, some of the widely used reinforcers in behaviour therapy are discussed.

Edibles

Food is a basic biological requirement for survival. Therefore it acts as a powerful reinforcer. Particularly for children, edibles are attractive reinforcers because of their limited experience with other forms of reinforcers. Under deprived conditions its reinforcing effect is much more conspicuous. Use of a variety of edibles increases their effectiveness. Moreover, repeated use of the same kind of edible reinforcers would decrease its effectiveness. In order to increase the effectiveness of edible reinforcers, Kazdin (1975) suggested the following guidelines: (i) Edibles should be delivered in small quantity at any one point of time, (ii) they should be altered from time to time to prevent satiation, (iii) the same edibles may be distributed over a period of time to maintain the performance, (iv) substitution of the edibles to tokens prevents onset of satiation, (v) increment in the criterion of responses for which reinforcement is delivered would also prevent early satiation, (vi) development of other conditioned reinforcers like attention, praise and the like helps in maintaining the reinforcing effect, and (vii) the individual under treatment should himself choose his own edible reinforcers.

However, the therapist should attempt to use reinforcers which are natural. This will increase the effectiveness and help in generalisation. A therapist should consider the physical health of the client while using or recommending edible reinforcers, as specific types of food may aggravate certain disorders.

Activity

Preferred activities serve as reinforcers for a wide range of desirable behaviour. While using an activity as a reinforcer, one must see that the activity must be enjoyed by the participant as 'fun', and not as a burden or responsibility. Activities like watching a preferred television serial, riding a bicycle or a car, free play, reading a story or a comic book and acting as the class monitor may be used as activity reinforcers for children. In a group contingency management programme, Packard (1970) used such activities like using a private study booth, typewriter, time in school gym and playing a piano as activity reinforcers for kindergarten children, and third, fifth and sixth grade levels in a public school for improving attention in their classrooms. Jacobs (1970) used release time and recreation programme effectively for teaching reading skills to the rural and economically deprived fourth grade slow learner children. Similarly, Brook and Snow (1972) used time to read and build puppets for improving academic skills of a 9-year-old low achiever in a classroom setting. In an earlier study, Schmidt and Ulrich (1969) examined the effects of group contingent events such as extra time added to the gym period, two minute break to talk, sharpen pencils upon classroom noise of low middle and middle-class children. These activity reinforcers improved their quiet behaviour and reduced classroom noise. Chadwick and Day (1971) used a systematic reinforcement programme that included field trips including fishing, boating, swimming, parties, and trips to a farm, a bank, a hospital, and even a pet shop for improving the academic performance of underachievers in the age group 8–12 years. Walker and Buckley (1972) also used field trips, cartoon films, class parties, and trips to special school events like basket ball games for improving the academic performance of elementary school children. They attempted to examine their generalisation and maintenance effects across time and settings. Campbell and Sulzer (1971) suggested a wide range of activities as reinforcers for retarded people. The reinforcing activities may include things like extra swimming time or game during recess period, more library time, getting more snacks during break, and so on. Sulzer and Mayers (1972) suggested many such activities for children between 3–12 years of age like:

- blowing up a balloon and letting it go
- jumping down from a high place into the arms of adults
- playing with a typewriter
- watching a train go round the track
- running equipment like string toys and light switches
- listening to one's own voice on a tape recorder
- building up and knocking down blocks
- pushing around an adult in a swivelling chair (on which the seat turns around without moving the base)
- pulling another person in a wagon
- looking out from a window
- playing short games (e.g. puzzles, joining dots)
- blowing bubbles (e.g. soap or gum)
- reading a comic book
- painting with water on the black board
- pouring water through a funnel from one container into another
- cutting with scissors
- modelling with clay
- throwing a ball
- climbing a ladder
- turning on a flashlight
- sitting on an adult's lap
- looking at projected slides
- listening to a short recording
- watching a short film (view master, film strips)
- walking around in high heels
- wearing funny hats
- carrying a purse or a briefcase
- popping a balloon or a paper bag
- stringing beads
- playing with a magnet
- singing or listening to a song
- performing before a group (e.g. singing a song, reciting a poem, doing a dance, stunt, or a trick)
- blowing out a matchstick
- combing one's own or an adult's hair
- looking into a mirror
- playing an instrument (e.g. drum, whistle, piano, and the like)
- using the playground equipment
- drawing and colouring
- being hugged, kissed, patted, swung around, turned around in swivel chair, pushed on a swing or a merry-go-round, or pulled in a wagon.

Many more activities may be introduced as reinforcers for children. Children themselves may be asked to list out reinforcing activities in order to identify their preferred activities easily. In a study, Broden and his associates (Broden et al. 1970) asked the 7 and 8 grade exceptional children (children with retardation, reading and speech difficulties, delinquency etc.) to choose reinforcing activities from a list of such activities prepared by the students themselves.

Premack's Principle

Using a highly probable response for relatively reinforcing another, low probable response is termed as Premack's principle. In a series of laboratory experiments, Premack (1959, 1965) found that when participants were allowed to choose reinforcers for their responses, they chose the high frequency activities instead of the ones, which were performed at lower rates. He gave the children free access to candy and pinball machines. They chose the latter as they preferred activity. Later on, he used the high frequency behaviour (working on the pinball machine) as a reinforcer for the low frequency behaviour (eating candy). Thus, it proved the hypothesis that a response that occurs at higher frequency serves as a reinforcer for the low frequency behaviour. Researchers (Homme et al. 1963; Long and Williams 1973; Medland and Stachnik 1972; Osborne 1969; Wilson and Williams 1973; Winett and Vachon 1974) used free time activities and recess for reinforcing various classroom behaviours of school children. Topic sequencing was also used as a variant of this technique, in which the most preferred topics are used as reinforcers for certain target behaviours. However, as reported earlier in all cases a reinforcing activity need not be necessarily a high frequency activity or any socially acceptable activity in order to act as a reinforcer. Simple activities that are preferred by the individual and considered pleasurable may act as effective reinforcers.

Attention

The most easily dispensable reinforcers are the social reinforcers such as attention, praise or encouragement. Smiles or approach of significant family members or a class teacher may serve as effective social reinforcers. Overtime, the association between adult attention, approach, even simply their physical proximity during the delivery of primary reinforcers like food, drinks, comforts or warmth, make attention a powerful reinforcer.

In a classic study, Brackbill (1958) examined the effects of adult attention as a powerful reinforcer for smiling responses in three and four-and-half month old infants. The rates of smiling increased as an adult attended them by smiling and picking them up. The infants' smiling rate was directly related to the ratio of social reinforcement and increased smiling. The more the smiles that were required in order to obtain the reinforcement, the more the infant smiled. The reinforcing consequences are also more resistant to satiation effect. In fact, much maladaptive behaviour is a result of positive attention. In most situations, maladaptive behaviour draws more attention than the adaptive ones (Repp 1983). Some revealing experiments were conducted by some investigators on school children during the 1960s and 70s. In these experiments, it was observed that teachers gave more attention to non-task behaviour than to the classroom appropriate behaviour of disruptive children (e.g. Hall et al. 1968;

Patterson et al. 1973). Walker and Buckley (1970) reported that 70 per cent of the teacher's attention was devoted to problem children and only 23 per cent was devoted to non-problem children. Out of the total attention given to the problem children, 89 per cent was contingent upon problematic behaviour and only 11 per cent for classroom appropriate behaviour. Several studies have indicated the effectiveness of teacher-attention in increasing the study behaviour of students in regular schools (Hall et al. 1968; Hall et al. 1968). For some children, any adult attention is reinforcing. Talking to the deviant child following his disruptive act, trying to 'understand' him and suggesting other activities may have paradoxical effects, increasing deviant behaviour. Even some forms of critical comments do strengthen certain disruptive behaviour (Madsen et al. 1967). At the initial stage, approval of task-appropriate behaviour by positive attention at times, increases the inappropriate behaviour. However, at a later stage, with successive trials this may help in discriminating between appropriate and inappropriate responses.

Tokens

Tokens are secondary reinforcers, which can be exchanged for other primary or backups reinforcers. Plastic chips, stars, coins, paper currency or cards with specific denominations are some of the examples. A reinforcement system, which is based on delivery of tokens is referred to as 'token economy' (Kazdin 1977). Tokens earned for particular behaviour can purchase backup reinforcers ranging from consumables to preferred activities and privileges. Tokens earned for specific target behaviour can be spent for different things within a defined therapeutic environment, or may be saved for future purchases. Tokens can also be withdrawn, contingent on maladaptive behaviour or due to non-occurrence of desirable behaviour. This is effectively used with school children in a classroom setting, juvenile delinquents in prisons and psychotic patients in a ward setting.

Social reinforcers (e.g. praise, touch, attention and smile) are the most easily available reinforcers. A review of research conducted indicates that some people are less responsive to social reinforcers (Patterson et al. 1968; Wahler 1967). In such circumstances, primary and other forms of reinforcers act more effectively than social reinforcers. One may first start with primary reinforcers combining it with social reinforcers, and gradually fading out the primary reinforcers, so that the response keeps getting reinforced with socially reinforcers alone. Later on, this may be faded out to maintain the behaviour independently.

SCHEDULES OF REINFORCEMENT

A reinforcer as such does not have the capacity to strengthen a response unless it is used consistently after the target response. This arrangement of reinforcements is called schedule of reinforcement. In other words, it is 'the rule followed by the environment ... in determining which among the many occurrences of responses will be reinforced' (Reynolds 1968: 60). At the initial stage of teaching a response, continuous reinforcement is more effective than intermittent ones. Towards the final stage of learning, the reinforcement is faded out and made intermittent. An intermittent reinforcement schedule simulates reinforcement for the behaviour in a natural setting. An interval schedule is based on the interval between the emitted response and the delivery of the reinforcer, whereas ratio schedule is based on the frequency of responses emitted by the participant, after which the reinforcers are delivered. These two schedules may further be divided into two: fixed and variable, depending on whether the reinforcer is delivered for either a fixed or a variable number, or duration of responses. Accordingly, if we combine all these, there are four basic schedules of reinforcement: (i) fixed interval (FI), (ii) variable interval (VI), (iii) fixed ratio (FR), and (iv) variable ratio (VR) schedules. Continuous reinforcement schedule (CRF) is the most powerful schedule to increase desirable responding. In this schedule, every correct response is reinforced. However, for the maintenance of behaviour continuous schedule should be converted to an intermittent schedule.

In order to increase the attending behaviour of a 9 and a half-year-old child, Walker and Buckley (1968) used a reinforcement contingency condition where the child's attending behaviour was reinforced in a variable interval (VI) schedule after reaching a criterion of 30, 60, 120, 240, 480 and 600 seconds. Because of this increasing variable interval schedule of reinforcement, the child's attending behaviour increased from an average of 33 per cent to 93 per cent after 15 sessions of training.

AUTOMATIC REINFORCEMENT

Not all forms of reinforcers are programmed by the social environment of the client. Some reinforcing consequences occur automatically. For instance, body rocking provides visual and vestibular stimulation that serve as reinforcers whenever a response occurs. These sensory consequences are consistently and automatically paired with each episode of body rocking, which maintain the response. A wide variety of reinforcers is considered as automatic reinforcers such as pain attenuation (Cataldo and Harris 1982), production of endogenous opiates (Sandman et al. 1990) or sensory and perceptual reinforcement (Lovaas et al. 1987). When responses are maintained by such operant mechanisms independent of social environment (Vaughan and Michael 1982; Vollmer 1994), they become resistant to change. Such automatic and continuous reinforcement contingencies seem to maintain much aberrant behaviour. A careful behaviour analysis is required to identify the automatic reinforcers and carry out effective treatment programme.

Case Study

Salzinger et al. (1965) demonstrated the use of different levels of fixed ratio (FR) schedule to increase speech output of a speech deficient child with hyperactivity, occasional trembling and convulsions (IQ 32), temper tantrums and self-injurious behaviour. His vocal responses were restricted to a variety of vowels, constant sound that varies in pitch intensity and duration. He spoke only a single word 'cocooning' appropriately at home.

The behavioural treatment was conducted over a period of nine months almost daily for 256 sessions. During the first 195 sessions, he used reinforcement (S^r) contingencies in operation. In the next 61 sessions, he introduced various verbal and non-verbal responses to the response repertoire in order to attain stimulus control.

In the first phase (1–2), that is, two sessions, attempt was made to establish the experimenter as a source of reinforcement by providing S^rs such as candy, peanuts, spoonfuls of soda.

In the second phase (3–82), that is, 80 sessions, fixed ratio (FR) schedule of reinforcement was used where only the name of the particular S^r was spoken to the child whenever it was delivered. For instance, the E (experimenter) said 'candy' when it was presented to him. The C (client) often produced continuous vocalisations punctuated by one or more stress. Initially the C was provided S^r in FR 1:1 schedule for (i) extended continuous vocalisations for some sessions in order to enhance the chance of getting S^r, then for (ii) stresses on specific sounds, and finally for (iii) short discrete words. Undesirable sounds such as spitting noises or animal-like screeches were not reinforced at all.

The next 12 sessions (83–104) were devoted to (i) fading of the previous pattern of reinforcement (i.e. FR continued and increased up to 1:50 and (ii) continuous reinforcement (FR 1:1) with E's (experimenter) repetition of the word spoken and candy for words and close approximations to words whenever they occurred.

Repetition of words and candy were provided only for words or close approximation of words in FR 1:1 schedule in next nine sessions (105–113).

The next 29 sessions (114–142) were devoted to discrimination training. Familiar objects like a book and several stuffed animal toys were introduced for this purpose. These objects had no discriminative control on the verbal responses of the client. Now they served as discriminative stimuli (S^Ds), in presence of which if the child spontaneously utters the appropriate word for which he was reinforced and in absence of these objects if the word occurred the response is not reinforced (S^Δ).

The S^D and S^Δ period was of five to 10 minutes duration and the length of each session was between 30 to 50 minutes.

During the next 36 sessions (143–178), this critical interval was reduced to three minutes only. The toys served as secondary reinforcers. The reinforcement was contingent on the predetermined latency period. The S^D was first presented with the client's first word. If no word was emitted within three minutes, it was removed from the experimental room. Thus, the minimum requirement for the child's keeping the toy was one word in every three minutes. Towards the end of these sessions, (170–78) the critical interval was reduced to two minutes only. Reinforcement for verbal responses consisted of candy, repetition of the word or handing of the toy.

In the concluding sessions (179–95), the client was required to identify one out of four toys and bring it to the E (experimenter) upon verbal command. In earlier sessions, the client was requested to prove one toy for a predetermined number of times (usually five) and switch to another toy if he did not comply. Now, if the client failed the E handed him the appropriate one, returned to his place and asked him to bring the toy to him across the room. If the child still fails to do so, the E added another command: 'That's right. Now, bring the _____over here'. If he picked up the wrong toy, E said, 'No, that's your _____. I want you to bring me the _____'.

The procedure not only enhanced the rate of verbal responding but also reduced undesirable responding like making animal-like screaming, and hyperactivity.

REINFORCER SAMPLING

Selection of appropriate reinforcers for increasing desirable responses is called reinforcer sampling. There are many objects, situations or people about which individuals may not have any prior experience. However, even if they have some idea, they do not know how to react in a certain condition, where a specific response has to be emitted. Under such circumstances, when their reinforcing properties are not known, reinforcement sampling is required in order to select appropriate reinforcers. Sulzer and Mayers (1977) gave examples of roller coaster or water skis. Initially people are 'scared stiff' when they stand on a ski or ride a roller coaster, but gradually get habituated and enjoy them as reinforcing activities. Similarly, Holz et al. (1963) reported how in mental hospitals the patients are persuaded to try certain forms of reinforcers like certain foods. Later, they work to get these reinforcers. Ayllon and Azrin (1968), suggested that before using an event or stimulus as a reinforcer, sampling of the reinforcer is required in the actual situation in which it is to be used. For reinforcer sampling, a client is provided with a sample or small portion of a reinforcer in order to examine its effectiveness in increasing desirable responding. If it does, the event is repeated, and the reinforcer is used or purchased for the client. Reinforcer sampling may be used as a special case of response priming that elicits early steps of a response chain as well.

In a token economy programme Sulzer et al. (1973) borrowed some excellent films for children from a university library. The films were run free of cost until it was exciting. At this point, the projector was turned off. The students were asked if they would like to purchase with points and see the remaining part of the film. All students wanted to do so. This reinforcing contingency was used for motivating them to perform well academically.

Reinforcer sampling is particularly useful when it is difficult to identify appropriate reinforcers for the client and/or when the client is not in a position to convey his preferences; for example, children with retardation, autism or adults with schizophrenia.

EFFECTS OF REINFORCEMENT ON THE THERAPIST

It should also be noted that reinforcement not only influences the responding of the client, but also changes the therapist's behaviour. Behaviour control is not a one-way affair and that counter controls are asserted by the client. The reinforcing behaviour of the therapist is also reinforced when desirable changes start occurring in the client's behaviour. He selectively learns those special skills that are most effective in changing behaviour. The therapist should be in a position to counter the outer control in order to act as a good therapist (Krasner 1963). Due to repeated reinforcement for positive behaviours, client himself is likely to act as a stimulus control eliciting reinforcing behaviour in the therapist. The situation appears to be analogous with 'counter-transference' in psychoanalysis.

7

Developing New Behaviour

Teaching new behaviour is one of the major objectives of behaviour therapy. Lack of motivation, inadequate reinforcement, unavailability of basic skills required for performing a behaviour, or inability to organise the responses in the required sequence are some of the main reasons for which people fail to acquire new behaviours. For instance, a child with developmental disabilities may have considerable difficulty in acquiring new behaviour. Earlier, we discussed various forms of reinforcers and the effective ways in which they can be delivered in order to increase the already existing responses. Now, we would focus on how to develop new behaviour which is not present in the response repertoire at all, or not meaningfully organised in a proper sequence. The techniques, which are frequently used, include shaping, chaining, prompting or cuing, and fading.

SHAPING

Many responses are adequately reinforced and maintained by naturally occurring contingencies of reinforcement in the natural environment. These behaviours continue to survive as long as they are instrumental in making desirable changes. A newborn, for instance, who has a limited response repertoire uses elementary verbal responses like crying, babbling or cooing to draw attention from people. Later, these responses are shaped into fluent articulation and eventually transform into spontaneous speech. Many other new responses are acquired in this manner. Chances of drive reduction, sensory stimulation or relief from the discomfort are some of the reinforcing events that sustain the process. It paves the way for behavioural development. Directionality in developmental sequence emerges because of auto shaping. General responses become more specific, gross behaviour becomes finer and precise, non-purposive responses become more purposive and goal directed. A rich and interactive environment helps in speeding up behavioural development. The process is called auto shaping. Both, instrumental learning and maturational process play significant roles in it.

However, not all behaviours are learned like this, through naturally occurring contingencies of reinforcement, and some people even have poor capability to benefit from such naturally occurring contingencies. Here comes the role of a human mediator (a teacher, therapist or an instructor), who 'programmes' these contingencies in order to set the occasion for occurrence of more effective forms of behaviour and 'tailors' the environment to facilitate its occurrence. This process is called shaping. In other words, shaping is a procedure by which new behaviours are learned by systematically reinforcing successive approximations toward a terminal behaviour. Thus, two fundamental procedures are involved in shaping; the presentation of prompts and then refining the successively approximate response. Gradual altering of stimulus characteristics (prompts) to facilitate appropriate responding is called stimulus shaping, whereas refining the response is called response shaping.

Stimulus Shaping

In this procedure, a specific property of the stimulus is gradually modified to facilitate transfer of skills. This is also referred to as within-stimulus prompting (Schreibman 1975; Wolfe and Cuvo 1978). Progressive change in the stimuli is used to produce changes in spatial topography of the response as well. Progressive alteration of the stimulus properties that already controlled responding leads to gradual alteration in the response required, until the terminal performance is achieved. Throughout the training, the correct choice is reinforced (Huhuenin et al. 1983). At the initial stage, the therapist attempts to emphasise the distinctive aspect of a training stimulus. In other conditions, new structural features are added to the existing stimulus and errorless performance is reinforced until the terminal stimulus is responded to correctly. Constant reinforcement of the correct response brings the behaviour under instructional control.

Wikings et al. (1974) used stimulus shaping to train a 10-year-old boy with retardation to drink from a cup. The child was able to drink from a spoon but not from a cup. The authors took a series of steps to transform the shape of spoon into a cup, at each stage reinforcing the child's drinking behaviour. It continued until he could drink from the cup, the terminal stimulus. This kind of stimulus shaping has implications for teaching a wide range of adaptive skills to people with disabilities, even to normal people whose specific responses require generalisation or transfer to other stimuli.

One of the earliest laboratory experiments on stimulus shaping was conducted by Sidman and Stoddard (1967) on retarded and normal children. In the experimental condition, the participants sat facing a display panel containing nine response keys arranged in 3×3 matrix. The correct choices were reinforced with automatic delivery of token and candies. The participants were first reinforced for selecting the key that projected a circle, from among the keys that contained relatively flat ellipses. As the training advanced, the vertical height of the ellipses was increased while the circle remained constant. Selection of the key that projected the circle was constantly reinforced. Finally, the participants were able to make very finer distinction between a circle and an ellipse. In another experiment Stoddard and Gerovac (1981) used stimulus shaping to teach a complex motor skill to individuals with profound mental retardation. The stimulus shaping procedure used in their study was different from discrimination learning, where the response remains invariant. Here, progressive change in the stimulus condition was made in order to produce a change in the spatial topography of response. In this study, severely and profoundly retarded children were taught how to insert a token into the proper slot of a machine that automatically delivered edibles. A series of graded steps were used to teach this skill. It started with touching a token that projected slightly from the illuminated slot that leads to reinforcement. Then, reinforcement was made available for putting a coin dangled by a string from the slot at increasing distances. Finally, the token remained in the tray from which the participants had to pick them up and insert into the slot. Stimulus shaping has extensive applications in preparing adapted appliances for the disabled, as also in designing better living environment for people, where analysis of body movement, postures and the range of responses have immense significance.

The main disadvantage of the shaping procedure is that it is a time consuming process. The therapist has to wait until the appropriate response appears under a given stimulus condition. Further, the progress is not linear in the sense that the individual does not proceed from one behaviour to the next in a continuous, uninterrupted flow. It is often erratic, and therefore consumes considerable time (Cooper, Heron et al. 1987). Since most of these responses are not reflexes, the therapist cannot elicit them directly. Once the client does make the response, it comes under the control of reinforcement contingency. Then he speeds up this process by shaping. Certain complex behaviour would require years to teach, as they are not very frequent and one has to wait until an approximate response occurs. For some behaviour, it is almost impossible to expect an approximate response to occur. Even for the relatively simple ones, the therapist must be well trained. He should be vigilant enough to detect the minute changes in behaviour to reinforce it as it occurs. The reason is that, the next behaviour cannot be reliably determined. Shaping is an art, which requires skills and ingenuity (Tsoi and Yule 1987). As Gelfand and Hartman (1975) put it, the art of shaping is to 'think small'. When a desired approximation occurs, the therapist has to immediately deliver a powerful reinforcer; otherwise, the therapist may keep reinforcing an incorrect response. Initially, every such topographically approximate response is reinforced to retain it in the response repertoire.

Skinner and Krakower (1968) used shaping, fading, immediate feedback and differential reinforcement in order to teach handwriting. Immediate differential reinforcement was provided for target responses (drawing shapes of letters successively closer to writing), by gradually attenuating the controlling stimuli (the letters those are traced) by fading out portions of the letter in order to enhance the skills of independent writing. A special ink and chemical treatment of the paper was used to provide immediate feedback (reinforcement). The pen makes black marks when the letter was properly formed. It turns the paper orange when the pen moves away from the prescribed pattern. Thus, the child gets an immediate feedback. The procedure was effective in teaching writing skills.

Response Shaping

Response shaping is the process by which responses that have some resemblance to the terminal response are systematically and differentially reinforced. Here, 'differential' reinforcement means reinforcing only one member of a compatible response class while not reinforcing the incompatible ones. Gradual development of new behaviour by repeatedly reinforcing minor improvement of steps toward that behaviour is an essential operation involved in shaping (Panyan 1980). Every minor step of progress is carefully identified and reinforced as it appears. This systematic reinforcement of the finer changes in behaviour helps the client to progress in a specific direction. The process of reinforcement continues until the criterion response is acquired. It enables him to discriminate between the responses, which are relevant, and those, which are not. Gradual development of new behaviour is fostered through differential reinforcement, reinforcing only one member of the response class while not reinforcing others (which have already been learned). It helps the client to make 'response differentiation', providing a 'road map' to progress towards the terminal response. Fleece et al. (1981) used operant shaping procedure to improve voice volume in two developmentally disabled children. The voice volume was measured on a 20 point scale, where 0 indicated inaudible voice volume; 10 indicated normal volume, and 20 indicated a screaming level. Recitation of a nursery rhyme was used as the experimental task. A voice-activated relay devise was used for recording. The voice volume activated a light display. The intensity of light varied according to the voice volume. Increase in the voice volume increased the intensity of light. At the initial stage of the experiment, even low voice was activating the light. As against this, at a later stage higher voice volume was required to activate the light. The procedure was effective in enhancing the speech volume of the children in 20 sessions. Follow up assessments conducted at one month and four month intervals indicated maintenance of the treatment effects. A classic study was conducted by Isaacs et al. (1960) on a catatonic client who had not spoken for 19 years. Even constant encouragement by the ward staff did not bring any change in his behaviour. When it was observed by a psychologist that the client made little lip movement when a packet of chewing gum dropped, it was used as a re-inforcer to strengthen his lip movement, which was a prerequisite for speech. When lip movement was established through reinforcement, the therapist switched over to the next behaviour; only movement associated with sound emission was reinforced, not the lip movement. It helped him to discriminate between non-speech lip movement and speech related lip movements. In a similar manner, the client's utterance of guttural sounds and vocalisations were differentially reinforced, until he uttered the word 'gum' and then requested, 'gum please'. Subsequently, he started speaking to the psychologist, the ward staff and revealed his identity and background. In this study, initially the psychologist had to wait for the response to be emitted, which was time-consuming. Therefore, at a later stage, after the sixth session, he used verbal statement like 'say, gum'. Otherwise, it would have required sufficiently large number of trials. In order to enhance the effectiveness of shaping, other techniques like verbal prompts and physical guidance or modelling are also used. Wolf et al. (1964) used shaping to teach wearing eyeglasses to a three-and-half year old autistic child. Following an eye operation to remove both his lenses, it was necessary to preserve his vision. The child resisted strongly throwing temper tantrums, banging his head, slapping his face and pulling his hair. The therapist introduced an empty spectacle frame just before the launch time. He was reinforced with more food as he held the frames for longer and longer period. Then reinforcement was contingent only on holding them closer to the face in correct orientation. Once he reliably placed them on the face, he was provided with other reinforcers too, in order to retain and strengthen the response. Thereafter, this practice was generalised to other settings successfully.

Cooper et al. (1987) attempted to distinguish between two types of response shaping, based on *across* and *within* response topographies. For shaping responses across topographies, the therapist selects a number of the constituent responses and keeps differentially reinforcing them until the terminal response. Whereas, for shaping within response topographies, he does it for different dimensions of the same target behaviour, such as frequency, duration and intensity.

CHAINING

Before proceeding to the procedural details of chaining, we must make a distinction between shaping and chaining. The fundamental difference between shaping and chaining is that shaping is used to develop new behaviours, whereas chaining is usually used to develop a sequence of behaviours using responses that approach the terminal goal (Kazdin 1975). In shaping, the responses are allowed to occur spontaneously and naturally. Any behaviour approximate to the desired one is reinforced whenever it appears; whereas in chaining, there is a deliberate effort on the part of the instructor to conduct task analysis and arrange the tasks in specific order (first-to-last or last-to-first manner). There is a specific direction involved in chaining.

All behaviours are not discrete reflexive responses like that of an eye blink or salivation. Most of them are constituted of a number of constituent skills, which are organised in a specific sequence. All of them have complex stimulus controls. Sometimes people fail to perform certain tasks for the very fact that even if the required behaviours exist in the response repertoire, they fail to organise these responses in a desired sequence. Under this circumstance, chaining can be used effectively as a procedure to sequence the sub-skills that constitute a complex skill. This is an instructional procedure, used to teach complex skills or tasks that are made up of several individual discrete components which must occur in a specific sequence for the skill to be correctly performed (Rehfeldt 2002).

At the outset, it is required that the complex task be divided into a series of teachable sub-tasks. Then, they are sequentially linked (chained) to teach complex skills. The sequence of responses is considered as 'chains'. A careful task analysis is required to identify the chains. Chaining is done step by step. After teaching one sub-skill in the chain, the therapist links it to the next. Verbal feedback provided after the performance at each response in the chain facilitates acquisition of the response. Along with the movement from one chain to the other, the client comes across new stimuli. Introduction of these new response-produced stimuli serve as discriminative stimuli (S^D) for eliciting new responses. Thus, the discriminative stimuli produced at each stage of chaining are ultimately paired with completion of response; thus keep acting as conditioned stimuli. Problem occurs when the therapist attempts to proceed when the previous step is not well established or the jump to the next step is too big. In that case, intermediate steps are to be determined by finer task analysis. Chaining of sub-tasks can be performed in either forward or backward manner.

Task Analysis

As stated earlier, task analysis is a fundamental requirement for chaining. The main purpose of task analysis is to identify each discriminative stimulus (S^D) and response (R) in the chain of behaviours for performing a complex task. For instance, a task like toothbrushing for a young child may be analysed into the following components: (i) Picking up the toothbrush, (ii) turning on the water tap on the wash basin, (iii) washing the toothbrush, (iv) putting toothpaste on the brush, (v) putting the brush in the mouth, and moving the brush back and forth across the mouth, (vi) rinsing the mouth, and (vii) rinsing the brush. Each chain involves one or more discriminating stimuli and one or more responses as shown below:

S^D_1 (toothbrush) $\longrightarrow$ R_1 (picking up and grasping)
S^D_2 (water tap) $\longrightarrow$ R_2 (turning on the tap)
S^D_3 (running water) $\longrightarrow$ R_3 (washing the toothbrush)
S^D_4 (wet toothbrush, tooth paste) $\longrightarrow$ R_4 (putting paste on the brush)
S^D_5 (paste on the brush) $\longrightarrow$ R_5 (movement of the brush)
S^D_6 (sensation in the mouth) $\longrightarrow$ R_6 (rinsing the mouth)
S^D_7 (dirty brush) $\longrightarrow$ R_7 (rinsing the brush)

In auto shaping, the individual automatically links these behavioural chains through their natural positive consequences. In case of shaping, any of this correctly performed behaviour is reinforced by a therapist; whereas, in chaining the therapist determines the sequence (forward or backward) apart from reinforcing the required response systematically.

Task analysis can be performed in four different ways: (i) Visualising the steps required by an individual to complete a target task, (ii) asking a skilled individual to identify the steps, (iii) looking at the performance of a skilled person while performing the task, and (iv) the therapist himself performing the task. Each of these methods has its advantages and disadvantages.

Forward Chaining

Forward chaining is a procedure in which a complex behaviour is taught in steps beginning with the first link in the chain to the end. The basic purpose is to establish a series of stimulus–response chains through reinforcement ($S^D \longrightarrow R \longrightarrow S^+$). At each stage, one or a group of discriminating stimuli is brought under stimulus control through reinforcement. Each higher stage of learning requires mastery of the previous ones. The first chain is taught until there is no prompt, and then it is linked with the second. In this manner, the therapist proceeds from first to the last in a cumulative sequence. The step at which the client has difficulty may be broken to smaller steps. Forward chaining is used when more efficient methods of training like verbal instruction, modelling cannot be used. For instance, Panyan (1980) used the following steps of forward chaining to teach a complex skill like riding a bicycle to children: (i) Getting on the cycle, (ii) pushing pedal on the cycle, (iii) moving and steering on the cycle, and (iv) starting, moving, steering and stopping. Wilson et al. (1984) used forward chaining to teach family-style dining skills to institutionalised people with profound mental retardation. The behavioural chains included the following components:

1. Hold a bowl with both hands
2. Place the bowl within one inch of the plate
3. Grasp a serving spoon
4. Grasp the bowl with one hand, without hand in food while spoon is in bowl
5. Serve food on the plate
6. Replace the spoon
7. Grasp the bowl with both hands
8. Pick up the bowl
9. Place in neighbour's hand or place within six inches of neighbour's plate.

FIGURE 7.1
Stimulus Prompt

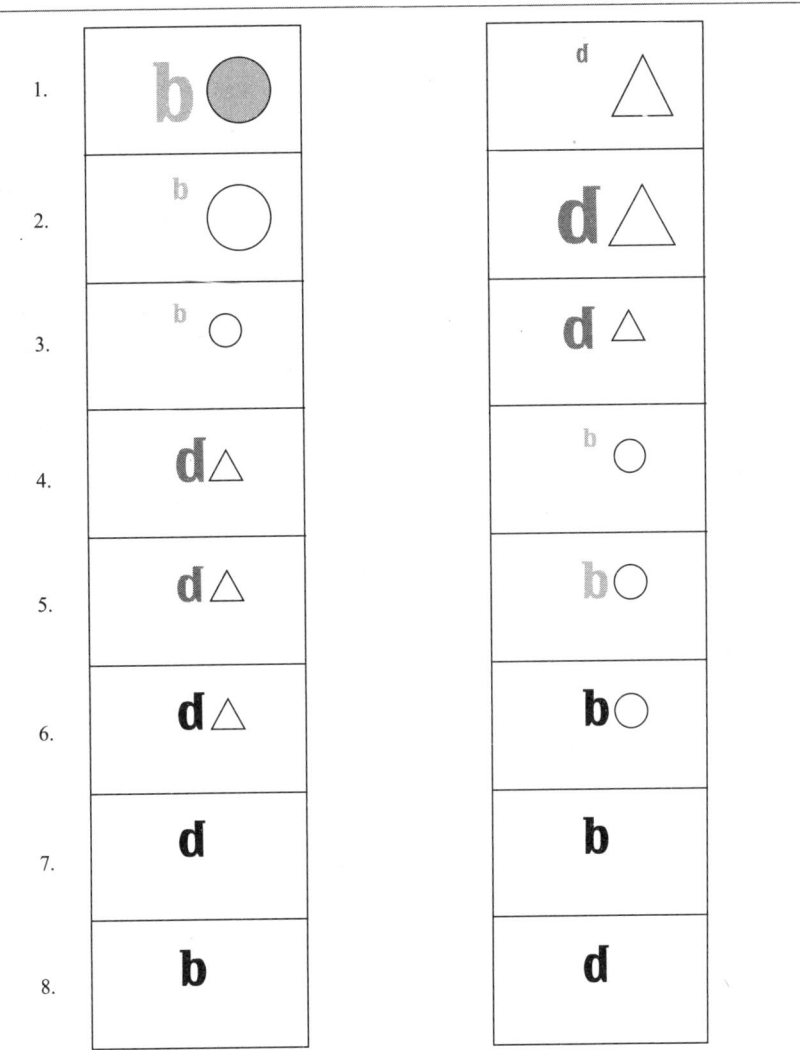

Horner (1971) excellently demonstrated the use of forward chaining in teaching the use of crutches to a child with mental retardation and spina bifida. The behaviour, which was more difficult was introduced gradually. Particularly, people with intellectual disability require the steps to be clearly described in order to acquire new skills. Thompson et al. (1982) taught laundry skills to individuals with developmental disabilities, using 47 responses grouped into seven major components. While using forward chaining, other procedures like prompting and fading were also used until the participant could demonstrate the skill without any assistance.

Backward Chaining

Some skills are taught better through backward chaining, in which the behavioural chains are taught in a backward fashion starting with the last link in the chain. This method has a theoretical advantage over forward chaining, as terminal reinforcement is made available much earlier and more frequently. Terminal reinforcement means the reinforcement that is provided after completion of the entire task; that is, the last behaviour in the chain. It serves as a secondary reinforcer for the steps performed prior to that. On the contrary, in forward chaining, terminal reinforcement is available only after performing all the steps successfully.

Backward chaining has been used successfully by several behaviour therapists. This techique has been used both, with children as well as adults to teach various self-help skills such as feeding, drinking, self-grooming, toileting, teeth brushing, socialisation, and traveling (Woods and Teng 2002). In an experiment, Hagopian et al. (1996) used backward chaining along with other methods to teach drinking water from a cup to a 12-year old boy with autism and mental retardation. The client was completely refusing to drink liquid. At the initial stage, a baseline of drinking behaviour was obtained and the task analysed. Then, the client was taught in three distinct steps as: (i) bringing the cup of water to mouth, (ii) taking water into mouth, and (iii) swallowing it. For backward chaining, first the child was reinforced by being allowed to engage in preferred activities for 90 seconds when he swallowed the water after being prompted to do so. In the second step, he was reinforced for drinking a small amount of water from a syringe. In the third step, he drank a small amount of water from a cup. This procedure helped the child to drink increasing quantity of water. Gruber et al. (1979) used this technique with four institutionalised profoundly mentally retarded children to teach travelling from their residence to school. Ash and Holding (1990) also used backward chaining for children with difficulty in learning music. The intervention was successful in teaching musical notes on an electric piano. Spooner and Spooner (1984) identified the following five major dependent variables associated with efficacy of backward chaining:

(1) Number of successful performance of the entire chain, that is, time to trainer-determined criterion;
(2) Number of incorrect responses in the entire chain;
(3) Number of correct responses;
(4) Rate of correct responses in a given period of time; and
(5) Rate of incorrect responses during a given period of time.

Similar procedure was used for teaching other self-help skills to retarded people by Minge and Ball (1967). Young (1987, cited in Wood and Teng 2002) used the procedure to teach articulation of words to two children who had problems of misarticulating. They frequently omitted weak syllables or consonants while speaking. During the treatment, they were required to say the last part of the word first correctly, (e.g. 'key') before saying the complete word (e.g. 'monkey'). Effectiveness of chaining depends on the accuracy of task analysis, proper sequencing of the steps as well as the reinforcement provided for each step.

PROMPTING AND FADING

Prompting and fading are two closely linked procedures, therefore discussed as a single procedure. If the former involves providing discriminative stimuli to facilitate learning of new skills, the latter involves the procedures of gradual withdrawal of these discriminating stimuli or assistance in order to sustain desirable behaviour in the natural environment. A prompt is a stimulus or event that makes the response more probable. Prompting is a method of providing assistance, cues or signals to elicit desired responding. Two types of prompts are frequently used: stimulus prompts and response prompts.

Stimulus Prompts

A stimulus prompt is a cue that facilitates a desired response. Some particular aspect of the actual stimulus or a signal is provided to the client in order to facilitate a complete response. Various types of stimulus prompts have been used to promote acquisition of new skills, such as verbal, visual and gestural prompts. For instance, in order to facilitate listening of a message in a crowded railway station, a cue signal is emitted before the announcement on the public address system. The cue signal acts as a prompt for auditory attention. Prompts act as discriminative stimuli (Foxx 1982). While teaching alphabets to young children, dotted lines are provided as visual prompts to join them and write alphabets. Lip movements are used to elicit correct verbal responses from language deficient individuals. Sometimes one form of a prompt is converted to another form depending on the situation and the stage of learning. For instance, manual gestures are used frequently, replacing verbal instruction for eliciting a wide range of responses at advanced stages of training.

Response Prompts

Response prompt is also called physical guidance, in which the client is physically assisted by the therapist to perform a response. Different types of response prompts are used by therapists and trainers, such as increasing assistance, decreasing assistance, graduated guidance, and delayed guidance (Billingsley and Romer 1983; Demchak 1990). Increasing assistance is used when the client fails to follow the usual instruction to perform an activity. The prompts are arranged from least-to-most intrusive order. The therapist moves from lesser to greater degree of assistance. This form of assistance is required when the client fails to respond within specific response latency, for instance within 15–20 seconds after the instruction. The therapist gives elaborate instructions with manual prompts. Progressively intrusive manual guidance may be given along with instructions, if he still fails to perform the task. Likewise, the trainer has to keep extending and elaborating the instructions until the response is performed. Then the prompts are gradually faded out. Decreasing assistance is provided in a most-to-least intrusive manner. In case, there is any error in performance, the training starts again from the previous level of prompts. These are the two fundamental procedures of prompting which are associated with other formal procedures. Zieler and Zervey (1968) demonstrated successful use of manual prompting in teaching feeding skills to a retarded girl. At the initial stage, the therapist manually guided the client through the various steps of eating. Then, gradually released her hand, fading out the prompts. Manual guidance is used most frequently as a form of prompt to teach new skills.

Another method, graduated guidance procedures for instance, makes use of these fundamental procedures. Only minimum amount of assistance, which is needed for completion of the task, is provided. The amount is gradually reduced as the sessions of trials proceed. This has been detailed in the subsequent section. Delayed prompting involves gradual increase in the time delay between the cue and the prompt. This can be used as a potentially effective method of fading (Touchette 1971).

Fading is the reversal of prompting procedure, in the sense that in the former technique assistance and cues are presented to elicit the response in a specific context, whereas in fading, they are gradually withdrawn, as the behaviour reaches a criterion level of success, so that it can occur independently without assistance. There are two basic procedural variations in the use of fading procedure; the first is based on fading of assisting response of the trainer and the second is the fading of certain properties of the training stimulus, so that the acquired response would sustain in the natural setting. The former is called response fading (i.e. fading of response prompts) and the latter, stimulus fading (i.e. fading of stimulus prompts).

Response Fading

Response fading involves systematic withdrawal of therapist's assistance. Most response fading procedures are arranged in the most-to-least prompt fading sequence. The therapist starts with the most intrusive assistance to the least. With increasing independence, the level of assistance is reduced, until the client achieves complete independence. Some authors consider it as graduated guidance. Foxx and Azrin (1973) discussed two procedures of graduated guidance: (i) shadowing and (ii) spatial fading. Shadowing involves physical movement of the therapist with the learner, holding or assisting him while performing a response. Gradually, the assistance is reduced as the client reaches the criterion level of independent performance. For example, for teaching how to ride a bicycle, the therapist may assist the client by holding his shoulder and walking along his side while riding. Gradually, he reduces this assistance as the client learns to acquire better balance and control. The assistance is completely withdrawn as he learns to ride independently. In spatial fading, the therapist provides assistance for completion of each unit of the task (sub-task), like holding the handle only, and moves on to the other tasks as he learns to perform it satisfactorily.

Stimulus Fading

Operationally, stimulus fading may be defined as the gradual removal of stimulus prompts, or artificially introduced discriminative stimuli for successful maintenance of a response in the natural environment. At the initial stage of learning, prompts facilitate the occurrence of a response. As the behaviour starts appearing without a prompt, such discriminative cues are gradually withdrawn by reducing their frequency or intensity, so that finally the behaviour appears spontaneously. This procedure helps to bring the target behaviour under the control of environmental stimuli, so that it will sustain with no or little error. Schreibman (1975), and Wolfe and Cuvo (1978) used extra stimulus prompting for discrimination learning of autistic and retarded children. The technique involved presenting two stimuli simultaneously, one of which had already exerted control over the behaviour (stimulus control) and the other (training stimulus) which had not developed such control. The training stimulus remains unaltered during the training period, while the added stimulus prompt is progressively decreased in magnitude until it is finally eliminated. For example, while teaching two-letter discrimination task, the configuration of the training stimulus (e.g. shaded background) that acted as stimulus control, is faded out by thinning out the background shade, while the other training stimulus is presented simultaneously without additional prompts. As the probability of correct discriminating response increases, both the training stimuli are presented in their actual form without the above stimulus prompts. For teaching stimulus discrimination, along with colour, shape and size of the stimulus can also be systematically varied and additional stimulus prompts may be faded out gradually. For example, for teaching the students to discriminate between two similar letters 'b' and 'd' (Figure 7.1), initially the size as well as shade of these two letters may be varied significantly so that they will be clearly distinguished. In order to make this discrimination more perceptible, geometrical forms may also be introduced. Here, a circle is presented along with the letter 'b', while a triangle with letter 'd' (Figure 7.1).

These techniques have greatly expanded applications in teaching new behaviours. Their applications are most frequently reported in the training of developmentally disabled people. Prompting has been used for treatment of various other psychological and behavioural disorders such as autism (Labbe and Williamson 1984) and academic behaviour (Kneedler and Hallihan 1981).

Demchak (1990) reviewed the fading and prompting procedures used by various investigators in the development of new skills. Effectiveness of prompting and fading largely depends on the response topography, the criterion of performance and the reinforcement available for the responses. Slow process of fading the prompts makes the client 'prompt dependent'. It slows down the process of skill acquisition. On the other hand, when fading process is too fast, it may increase the number of errors. In that case, training may revert to the previous steps. The following guidelines may be used in order to make fading effective:

1. *Positioning*: While training the client, competing responses (such as effort to balance oneself, unsteadiness, eyestrain, awkward positioning of learning materials) that interfere with the learning process should be avoided or minimised by providing a stable and comfortable body position.
2. *Attention prompts*: When the client fails to attend to a task, a signal may be used and his head and hands may be directed towards the materials or activity provided. Sometimes manual guidance may be required to do so.
3. *Instruction*: Instructions to be given to the client should proceed from general to specific ones.
4. *Contingency*: The learner must be clearly informed about the criterion performance and the specific reinforcement to be provided.
5. *Reinforcement*: The reinforcers should be non-interrupting and short-lasting ones, such as praise, backstroking and should be provided continuously. Long-duration reinforcement should only be provided for completion of the entire sequence of responses.

8

Modelling and Observational Learning

After classical and operant conditioning, observational learning is considered as the 'third force' in behaviour therapy. If people had to learn all behaviour through direct exposure to the actual situation as in classical or operant conditioning, this would severely restrict our behavioural development. In some circumstances, it may even prove to be quite dangerous; our survival itself would be at stake. A person need not necessarily have the experience of an accident in order to learn safe driving. One may easily and quickly learn from others' experiences too. Social learning or learning by observing others is considered as a higher form of learning. It does not require one to be present in the actual situation. By watching, listening and even reading consequences of others' actions we learn (as well as unlearn) much behaviour. In fact, most part of our organised behaviours is acquired in this manner.

The capacity of observing and imitating other peoples' behaviour is found to be present very early in life. A large variety of human behaviour is acquired through observation only. People also avoid those behaviours, which they find as causing discomfort to others.

In laboratory experiments with infrahuman species such as cats, dogs, birds and chimpanzees, imitative behaviour has been studied extensively since the 1960s (e.g. Hall 1963; Riopelle 1967; Simmel et al. 1968). In an earlier study, Masserman (1943) induced experimental neurosis in cats and used social imitation as a method of treatment for the same. When the frightened cat was placed with the non-frightened ones and was fed there, the cat recovered from the neurosis. Imitative behaviour in human beings was being studied extensively by Bandura and Wlaters (1963), and Miller and Dollard (1941).

RATIONALE

If direct methods of behaviour therapy like shaping, prompting, and reinforcement or punishment alone were to be used, without demonstration of complex skills, acquisition of new behaviours would be extremely time-consuming. Some behaviour may take years to learn. Learning such behaviours is facilitated significantly through modelling techniques. The therapist should demonstrate it to the client and instruct him/her to reproduce and consequate them appropriately.

Observation of the effects of reward and punishment on others' behaviour plays a key role in this act of copying behaviour, what is precisely called imitation. Successful accomplishment of a critical behaviour itself serves as reinforcement. However, overtly reinforced behaviours are more likely to be imitated than those which are not. The social cues associated with actual positive or negative consequences moderate the probability of imitation. People imitate even inappropriate behaviours when they observe such behaviour in other people getting social approval. Conversely, vicarious punishment reduces the chance of imitation.

Technically speaking, modelling procedure brings a person under a different kind of stimulus control, that is, instead of being controlled by one's own experience, the individual is under the control of discriminative stimuli of other people's behaviour. Once this is accomplished, these stimuli are used to alter his/her future behaviour. The person learns to attend to other people as sources of information. Hereafter, there will be 'no trial learning'. From this perspective, observational learning may be considered as an advanced form of learning. It explicates an intelligent form of adaptation.

MODELLING

An observer may learn much new and complex behaviour by merely matching a model's performance. A model may be either a live or a symbolic one. A live model may include individuals (e.g. a peer, parent, teacher, a religious *guru* or an authority figure), performing the behaviour in reality, whereas a symbolic model may be a character in a novel, cartoon, film, or a television serial. They may serve as models, under specific circumstances for specific behaviours. What determines their acceptance or non-acceptance as models again depends on a large number of variables. The psychological and physical characteristics of the model, situational variables, and consequences of their behaviour are some of the important ones. An act of imitation involves sequential coding of the events through mental representations, such as thoughts, images or memory. Again, behaviour learned through imitation may not necessarily be performed by an individual in a given situation. The expectancy of reinforcement and similarity of the performance environment with that of the learning environment would determine the probability of demonstrating a learned response.

Vicarious Contingencies

The degree to which action of a model would be imitated by an observer depends on the outcome it yields. Exposure to contingencies between critical response class and a reinforcer, such as appreciation or social approval can serve as effective reinforcing stimuli for the observer. The process is called vicarious reinforcement and similar procedure that is used for decreasing the chances of imitation of a critical response is called vicarious punishment.

Lewis and Duncan (1958) suggested that reinforcement for the client is mediated by arousal of an anticipatory goal response, cued off by a model's behaviour. Some authors find it difficult to distinguish vicarious reinforcement from direct reinforcement (e.g. Berger 1962). In modelling exercises, if specific instruction is given to the observer, reinforcement can be mediated. This is because of the anticipation of consequences for his/herown behaviour, after observing the model's behaviour.

Kanfer and Saslow (1965) stated that under appropriate motivational conditions, the administration of reinforcement to a member of the group might be as effective in changing the behaviour of an observing subject as direct reinforcement. The basic mechanism involved in this process of imitation is identification. Similarity is one of the bases of identification.

Modelling has some unique advantages over operant conditioning procedures. Situations where apparently there is no eliciting stimulus for the desired response, modelling is considered as the best procedure to teach a new behaviour. The discriminative cues provided by the social models while exhibiting the critical behaviour promote behavioural change. Even if the subject exhibits some approximations of the critical response, modelling techniques can considerably shorten the time required for learning. In fact, there are many situations where observational learning is the only method of learning.

PARTICIPANT MODELLING

In participant modelling procedure, the client is first required to observe a live model who is performing a behaviour. Then he is guided by the model progressively participating and performing the behaviour until the entire response is reproduced by him/her. Finally, the model's assistance is completely withdrawn to ensure that the client independently performs the task. Generally, participant modelling is more effective than covert modelling procedures that help the client to learn behaviour by reading, listening or watching the model on television or film. Like systematic desensitisation, the model gradually exposes the client to the critical task, so that the client finally performs this task on his own without the help of the model.

EFFECTS OF MODELLING

Modelling has a number of effects. Bandura (1971) identified three main effects:

1. Observational Learning Effect

Elements of behaviours, which are already present in the individual's response repertoire, are organised to form new behaviours. This is demonstrated most clearly when the model demonstrates a new behaviour that the observer has not yet learned. The latest response components are organised from common behavioural elements without recourse to the laborious process of shaping.

2. Inhibitory–Disinhibitory Effect

Behavioural restraints and disinhibition are largely determined by the observed punishing and reinforcing consequences of that behaviour, respectively. For example punishment given for undesirable behaviour in a group setting like a classroom may suppress, restrain or inhibit such behaviour in other children, whereas watching someone getting praised or reinforced for desirable responding may facilitate or disinhibit such behaviour in the observer. When the observer observes decrement of behaviour of the model, he inhibits his own behaviours, which are of identical nature. On the contrary, disinhibitory effect occurs when the observer finds that the model performs behaviour without experiencing any distress, discomfort or negative consequence, it tends to disinhibit the observer's restrained behaviour.

3. Response Facilitation Effect

Social behaviour of people has an inherent facilitation effect. When one or more individuals engage in a specific behaviour, the observer may tend to engage in the same response class. Thus, social activities have cuing and response facilitating function.

MODELLING PROCESS

Modelling involves certain sub-processes that include Attention process, Retention process, Motor reproduction process, and Reinforcement and Motivational process. Exposure of the modelled act to the observer is not sufficient for acquisition of modelled behaviour. The therapist has to look into the basic processes involved.

Attention Process

Selective and discriminative attention is a requisite condition for observational learning. It broadens the client's intellectual and social competencies. As stated earlier, modelling has a discriminative or cue function because of which the modelled behaviour becomes a prominent target for the observer to respond to. This cue function is closely associated with the individual's attentive processes such as selection of stimuli, discrimination and matching. The information presented by the model contains a wide range of stimuli, out of which certain relevant cues (information) play the role of S^D in order to elicit attention. The colour, size, shape, texture and loudness are some of the variables, which can enhance the attentive process. A skilled model attempts to carefully vary them in order to sustain attention of the observer. A young child who fails to benefit from identifying the normal alphabets written in the textbook may show better attention if the usual alphabets are presented in a rather bigger size, adding more colour, light and texture. While modelling his writing skills, he/she has to demonstrate the style of holding the writing material, the slant of the hand, its position with reference to the margin, or outline of the paper. An effort to distinguish these cues helps the observer imitate the behaviour more accurately than the condition where these cues are not properly distinguished. It also teaches the client which cues are to be followed and which are to be ignored. For developing language function in autistic children exhibiting withdrawal and stereotyped behaviour, Lovaas (1966) used several methods. These methods included sitting face-to-face with the client so that he cannot ignore the responses being modelled. The client was not allowed to withdraw from the therapeutic task by physically restraining him from turning away. Addressing the child sharply or repeatedly asking him to look into the therapist's eyes in order to establish eye-to-eye contact, or even mild slapping on the thighs, were used as some of the methods. The child's attention to modelling cues was enhanced by reinforcing him with food, affection and social approval. Breaking the complex terminal behaviour into smaller components enhances client attention; on the contrary, complex tasks that have high chances of failure jeopardise the attention process.

Retention Process

The modelled behaviour has to be retained in a symbolic form in order to be used after the observation. In order to make the client retain the learned social behaviour, attention has to be focused on the modelled behaviour. Bandura (1971) reported that observational learning involves two representational processes for the imitated behaviour to occur in the absence of the modelled act. These processes are: (i) imaginal and (ii) verbal. Imaginal elements include the images of activities, individuals and other objects used during modelling. The verbal representational system includes the instructions and verbal symbols, such as words that represent objects, situations and people. Most cognitive processes that regulate imitation are verbal rather than visual or auditory. Subjects who actively code, rehearse and engage in organising the coded information about the modelling stimuli into verbal and imaginal representations achieve better retention than those who passively observe or engage in symbolic activities. The latter impedes stimulus transformation processes (Bandura et al. 1966; Gerst 1969). Modelled activities may be presented from low level of difficulty to higher level of difficulty. At the same time, the model should shift the stimulus control from concrete objects to speech and see that the client is able to perform the task in his absence.

Motor Reproduction Process

The symbolic representation of the modelling phenomenon is utilised in overt performances when the observer displays imitated behaviour. Under conditions where the individual is guided by an external model through a series of instructions enacting response sequences, he acts on external cues, whereas in case of delayed imitation, the cues are symbolic. At the motor level, the responses are produced by previously learned components representing relatively complicated compounds of responses. The basic components of behaviour are not learned by the observer, yet they may be taught through modelling. Demonstration as well as prompting helps the observer imitate a task properly. Physical limitations, internal as well as observable cues like hesitation, previous unrewarding experience, at times, restrict the enactment of a modelled behaviour.

When the behaviour is a highly coordinated motor skill, failure may occur due to inadequate attention to subtle motor responses involved in the compound skill. Under these circumstances, the observer requires more focused demonstration and task analysis.

Motivational Process

Even after adequate acquisition of a modelled behaviour, execution of the response may not occur due to unfavourable incentives, criticism or punishment. Reinforcement not only regulates the overt expression of the modelled act, but also exerts selective control over the types of modelling cues. Selective retention and coding are shaped through reinforcement. In case of a difficulty in executing the motor skills, the therapist has to identify the sub-system in which the dysfunction resides.

Many behaviour disorders are complicated by disturbances of basic psychological functioning that affect learning. Schizophrenia, autism, mental retardation are some of the examples. Due to attention deficit, poor social skills or other repetitive forms of behaviours, people fail to learn from observation. When demands are imposed on them, they keep evading (Lovaas 1966; Colby 1967). However, when this is ignored, they start responding with appropriate behaviour (Risley and Wolf 1967).

MODELLING IN RELATION TO OTHER THERAPIES

Modelling is used as a component in many other forms of therapies. Kelly's 'fixed role therapy' (Kelly 1955) is almost exclusively based on modelling principles. A fixed role therapist, at the initial stage makes a personality sketch of the client, which can be enacted by him, as if he is the person portrayed in the sketched role. For example, a passive/inactive person is assigned an assertive and active role. These roles are normally in contrast to their customary mode of response. The client is asked to experimentally experience such a role for weeks , before its permanent adoption. The client is only told that he is adopting the role on a trial basis and it is not going to be a new character. Such experimentation and role simulation is essential before making a sweeping change in the lifestyle of the individual. Bandura (1971) suggested that role prescription may have only limited value as the person knows how to do it under a variety of settings. Kelly's approach may be used on alternate days followed by rehearsal of the prescribed role in everyday events. The therapist himself may act a role model to teach the new response to be adopted by the client. The experiences are discussed in detail whether the client adopts the role on permanent basis or not. If he likes the role, behavioural rehearsal may continue as long as necessary, until spontaneous and skilled performance occurs.

Psychodrama (Moreno 1958), behavioural rehearsal (Lazarus 1966; Wolpe and Lazarus 1966) and role-play (Corsisni and Putzey 1987) are the other approaches to psychotherapy, where modelling techniques are frequently used.

APPLICATIONS

Modelling has been used extensively in the treatment of a wide variety of behaviour disorders such as social skill deficits, phobias, linguistic skills, obesity and many more. Modelling based interventions are the most commonly used procedures to eliminate fears. Unlike desensitisation, modelling procedures have been effective with individuals across ages. Bandura et al. (1969) conducted a study on a sample of snake phobic volunteers allocating them to different experimental conditions. A behavioural avoidance test similar to the one used by Lang and Lazovik (1963) was used to assess the subjects' fear level. They were also required to rate their attitude towards snakes on several dimensions and completed a general survey questionnaire on specific fears. They were exposed to different treatment conditions, such as: (i) symbolic modelling, (ii) participant modelling, (iii) systematic desensitisation, and (iv) no-treatment control. The symbolic modelling subjects were shown a film showing people dealing with snakes. Progressively more challenging encounters with snakes were displayed in the film. They were asked to relax during the film presentation. They also controlled the anxiety level produced by the filmed material by stopping and reversing the film wherever necessary.

McFall and his colleagues (McFall and Marston 1970; McFall and Lillesand 1971; McFall and Twentyman 1973) conducted a series of studies using modelling to improve assertiveness in people. Lack of social skills is not always the problem in poor assertive behaviour. Inhibitory and discouraging self-statements may be the core problem in many such people (Schwartz and Gottman 1976). Thus, instead of modelling assertive behaviour, these individuals' self-statements require to be modified. A model can demonstrate appropriate self-statements in these situations. In a study on assertive training, Thorpe (1975) successfully used modelling procedure for modifying self-statements through cognitive restructuring. Covert modelling was used as a procedure of intervention by Harris and Johnson (1983) to treat 63 test-anxious students. Five experimental conditions that included test–retest group, received no-treatment, whereas the two main treatment groups received two different covert modelling treatments (one group attempted to develop a non-academic imagery of acting competently, whereas the other group imagined personal academic success). Two groups received relaxation training in addition to the other procedure for the group. The test–retest group was found to have performed worst. Their grade points declined while all other groups improved. However, the group with the non-academic imagery performed better.

Sarason and Ganzer (1967) made use of modelling procedures to develop vocational and interpersonal skills in delinquents. Coping with authority figures, negative peer interaction, responding to vocational demands and self-control were some of the target behaviours. Performance of the experimental group was better than the no-treatment matched control group, after using modelling as a technique of intervention.

Poor attention to environmental stimuli leads to poor social learning. Therefore, some clinical groups with attention problems labelled as 'autistic', 'retarded', 'hyperactive' and 'schizophrenic' show poor imitation of social behaviour. For example, Rogers et al. (2003) conducted a study on imitation performance in toddlers with autism and those with other developmental disorders and found that children with autism were more impaired in overall imitation abilities, which included oral–facial imitation, and imitation of actions or objects, than other children. However, systematic training may improve their imitation. Lovaas in a series of studies (1966, 1968, 1977) demonstrated the effectiveness of verbal imitation training in developing psycholinguistic skills in autistic children. The training programme consisted of the following steps:

Step 1. Reinforcing all vocalisations of the client irrespective of their function.
Step 2. Reinforcing them only within a predetermined time interval (normally between five to six seconds) after the therapist makes a sound.
Step 3. Reinforcing only those sounds that approximate, that is, imitate the therapist's emitted sound during the time interval.
Step 4. Introduction of new sounds randomly along with the learned ones.

For example, if the client has learned to imitate a sound 'oo' a new sound 'ee' may be introduced. Verbal imitation is taught through use of several increasingly fine discriminations (Lovaas et al. 1966). Verbal imitation training for autistic children is a highly time-consuming process. Hundreds of hours are required before the child produces speech. Lovaas used additional techniques like manual prompting (holding child's lips together to help him pronounce words like 'mm') and visual cues (like making a circular shape of the mouth while saying 'oo').

Some investigators (e.g Bricker and Bricker 1970; Sloane et al. 1968) have even suggested that verbal imitation programme should start with motor imitations. The training programme may start with simple motor imitations like clapping, standing or moving and then these general imitative skills ('generalised imitation') may be transformed into verbal imitation skills. However, supportive evidence for such hypothesis is poor (Guess et al. 1972). Other investigators still consider general imitation skill to be crucial for effective verbal imitation (Risley et al. 1972).

Sherman (1965), and Wilson and Walters (1966) made systematic use of modelling procedures for the treatment of debilitating behaviours of people suffering from psychosis. It can be used as an effective procedure to treat a number of social skill problems that ordinary people encounter in their day-to-day life. However, in spite of its efficacy, surprisingly little work has been conducted on this clinical population. Bandura (1971) attributed this vacuum to the strong adherence by behaviour therapists to the operant conditioning model alone.

9

Aversive Procedures

Human beings have evolved in such a way that they can be controlled by punishment. This biological vulnerability has made punishment an effective method of suppressing behaviour. A wide variety of punishment methods has been used to reduce inappropriate behaviours. It may range from simple verbal reprimands to capital punishment. The law of the land determines the extent of its application. Behaviour therapists, however, make use of milder forms of punishment under informed consent of the client and under due ethical considerations. The present chapter focuses on punishment within the purview of behaviour therapy.

In behaviour therapy literature, punishment refers to those consequences of behaviour that reduce the future probability of its occurrence (Azrin and Holz 1966). Punishment involves either presentation of an aversive event or withdrawal of a reinforcing consequence. Hulse et al. (1975) stated that, a response is punished when some painful stimulation or the threat of such stimulation is made contingent upon the response. However, painful experience itself does not explain if punishment has occurred. There are three reasons for not treating experience of unpleasantness as punishment: (i) if an event is experienced as painful or unpleasant it may not necessarily lead to decrease in target behaviour, (ii) one may not be in a position to perceive the unpleasantness of an event, which decelerates behaviour (e.g. withdrawal of sensory reinforcement), and (iii) there are individual differences in responding to the aversive events too. Suppressing effects of an event on behaviour is the key indicator of punishment. Therefore, without referring to this, a definition of punishment would be incomplete.

In behaviour therapy, punishment must be reasonable, appropriate and as less intrusive as possible, as its purpose is to control behaviour and not inflict either pain or discomfort. This is how it is distinguished from torture or physical abuse. Sometimes the term 'aversion therapy' is used to refer to the clinical application of aversive stimuli for treatment of behaviour disorders.

TYPES OF PUNISHMENT

Description of two types of aversive events is embedded in its definition itself. One type of punishment suppresses a response by contingent application of certain aversive events, (e.g. reprimand, warning or aversive stimulation). These events are broadly stated as 'punishment by application'. The second type of punishment involves contingent withdrawal of certain rewarding consequences. The individual is deprived of previously earned privileges or possessions, cessation or interruption of an ongoing pleasurable activity or the pleasant outcome of ongoing behaviour, contingent upon a response. This is often termed as 'punishment by withdrawal'. For instance, in token economy programme, when tokens earned for good behaviour are withdrawn for undesirable behaviour, the technique is called response cost.

THEORIES

Although it is a common observation that punishment decreases behaviour, there are several theories to explain why it does so. This suppressive effect is explained, both through conditioning theories as well as social learning paradigms. In classical conditioning, punishment is used as an unconditional stimulus. Repeated pairing of aversive stimuli with an undesirable behaviour reduces the occurrence of that behaviour. As a result of this pairing, the responses are unlearned. The character of aversive stimuli is such that they cause either pain or discomfort to the individual. Being associated with certain responses consistently, these aversive stimuli weaken their strength. This theory explains response decrement as a direct function of punishment (Thorndike 1911), often called single-factor theory or negative law of effect. Dinsmoor (1954, 1955, 1977) proposed an avoidance theory of punishment. He stated that every response consists of a chain of behaviour. When the terminal response is punished, the earlier behaviour in this chain begins to generate fear. In order to avoid fear the organism disrupts this chain and engages in other behaviour. However, the avoidance theory does not explain elimination of the punished behaviour, although it explains why one engages in other behaviour. Thus, the function of punishment is to increase other behaviour, whereas single-factor theory considers that reinforcement and punishment are direct opposites. Covert, visceral and cognitive responses do occur in the presence of stimuli that elicit deviant response. Therefore, pairing them with shock prevents the response to occur. Almost all studies on aversive procedures indicate that higher the intensity of aversive stimulation, greater is the chance of reduction of punished response.

Avoidance theory of punishment is difficult to test because it postulates that punished behaviour is controlled by unobservable factors like fear and sensory feedback received from each behaviour chain (Rachlin and Herrenstein 1969). Some psychologists (e.g. Mazur 1986) considered this hardly as a disproof of avoidance theory. Using mathematical analysis of both the above theories and empirical studies, DeVilliers (1977, 1980) and Farley (1980) explained that although these two theories make almost similar prediction about response decrement, mathematically the two-factor theory is incorrect. Viewed from the operant conditioning paradigm, aversive consequences are programmed by the therapist to evoke escape and avoidance responses. A response decreases simply because it produces a punisher almost all the time it occurs in a laboratory or natural setting. Consequently, the client actively engages in those behaviours, which help in avoiding aversive consequence of another response. Therefore, this is a 'response-dependent' active process and not simply a 'stimulus-dependent' event.

RATIONALE

There is burgeoning literature that reports on the effective use of milder forms of punishment in reducing severe behaviour problems. It has established its credibility as a method of treatment. Otherwise also, aversive contingencies are part of our day-to-day life. For example, naturally occurring punishments, such as fatigue, pain, discomfort and disease shape people's health sustaining behaviour through out their life span. Therefore, such events have survival value that promotes desirable responding. Our preference for nutritious food, daily exercise or maintaining hygiene depicting health sustaining behaviour is one of the examples. Road accidents and fines imposed for violating traffic rules modify our driving behaviour. The pain of falling 'teaches' the young child how to walk straight. Such numerous aversive contingencies in day-to-day life help people develop adaptive skills. Human survival itself is closely linked with the skills of avoiding punishment.

USES AND ABUSES

Punishment is one of the quickest methods of response elimination; therefore it tends to be widely abused too. Uninformed, uneducated and powerful individuals and groups are rather prone to abuse punishment. There are numerous instances in human history. Political abuses of punishment have occurred almost in every country. Inhuman treatment of Jews in the Nazi concentration camps in Germany was one of the worst examples of torture. The labour camps and prisons in the Gulag archipelago in the erstwhile Soviet Union are notoriously known for unethical psychiatric abuse of punishment against the political dissidents in the form of interning in psychiatric hospitals, administering several shots of drugs to tranquilizes them, creating irreversible side effects (Plyushch 1979). Many of them were loosely diagnosed as 'schizophrenic'. The diagnoses were based on the criminal case-files and reports of the nurses rather than interviews or symptomatology. They were treated by freely administering tranquilisers, truth serum and lumbar punctures. Tranquilisers and antidepressants (e.g. sulphazin) which induce extreme discomfort, high fever, elevated blood pressure, joint inflammations, stomach cramps and intense pain were administered to the dissidents as punishment, deliberately withholding the corrective drugs, so that such side-effects became permanent features. These psychiatrists were a little better than the Nazi concentration camp doctors were, as they masked their mendacity, deception and manipulation with professional affability. Nekipelov (1980) in his book *Institute of Fools* meticulously documented his personal experience at Serbsky Psychiatric Hospital. The most recent reports and photographs of sadistic and despicable criminal abuses of Iraqi prisoners by the US and British forces have hit the headlines of most international newspapers. Such observations, sensational reports and horrific historical accounts of abuse of punishment have sometimes led to condemnation of the aversive procedures altogether, as methods of treatment. Some authors even over-generalise and equate punishment of any form with cruelty, irrespective of their degree, although the clinical use of punishment is restricted to its mild forms only.

Historically, corporal punishment has been a part of the disciplining practice of parents and teachers for children. Bitensky (1998) reported that in spite of the fact that many countries have adopted policies to prevent corporal punishment for young children (e.g. Austria, Croatia, Cyprus, Denmark, Finland, Israel, Italy, Latvia, Norway and Sweden), it is still used very frequently. For instance, a recent survey on use of punishment for children reported that about 94 per cent American parents use spanking by the time children are 3–4 years old (Straus and Stewart 1999).

We believe that empirical research and adequate understanding of its effects will facilitate its controlled therapeutic use. As much as possible, punishment is avoided by behaviour therapists for the fact that they wish to ensure comfort and happiness of the client. It should be used only under the following conditions: (i) when other reductive techniques fail to decrease the undesirable behaviour, (ii) when the sources of reinforcement are difficult to identify and isolate, and (iii) when a client's behaviour is violent, and has the potential to cause injury to the individual himself and others.

AVERSIVE STIMULI

A wide variety of aversive stimuli has been used by therapists in the treatment of behaviour disorders. In this section, we shall discuss the use of those punishment procedures, which are being empirically studied. Reprimands (O'Leary et al. 1970), foul smell of aromatic ammonia (Tanner and Zeiler 1975), nauseating drugs (e.g. emetine), physical punishment like slaps on the thighs (Bucher and Lovaas 1968; Koegel and Covert 1972), aversive tickling (Greene and Hoats 1971) mild electric shocks (Baumeister and Forehand 1972), lemon juice (Sajwaj et al. 1974), citric acid (Mayhew and Harris 1979), water spray (Bailey et al. 1983), and aversive music (Greene et al. 1970) are some of the aversive stimuli used in behaviour therapy. Conditioned taste aversion research on animals has triggered a number of studies on chemical aversion with alcoholism and nicotine dependence. These observations have lent support to the proposition that nausea paired with the taste of alcohol can produce stable conditioned aversion and subsequent abstinence from alcohol or tobacco (Baker and Brandon 1988; Cannon et al. 1986).

Scolding, reprimand or warnings are the most frequently used non-corporal punishment. O'Leary et al. (1970) attempted to examine the effects of public and private reprimands on classroom disruptive behaviour of second graders. They observed that the manner in which the reprimand is given, determines its effectiveness. Many teachers use loud reprimands for disruptive children. This is heard not only by the disruptive child but also by others. This type of traditional practice of public reprimand was compared with a soft reprimand in which a teacher goes closer to the target child and reprimands him privately. Soft and private reprimand was found to be more effective than loud public reprimand.

Stronger forms of punishment are used for severe forms of disruptive behaviours. Many clients with retardation, autism or schizophrenia exhibit a variety of self-injurious behaviour such as head-banging, self-biting, face slapping and eye poking. In extreme cases, contingent physical restraint is also used for treatment.

Electric shock is used as a punisher in many behaviour modification programmes. It can be measured accurately and can be presented at low levels without causing damage to the tissue. This is also termed as 'faradic aversion'. Most therapists allow their subjects set the shock intensity at a level, which is unpleasant, but tolerable. Electric shock is administered in association with the stimulus that triggers a deviant response. Sometimes it is used in the first stage of conditioning and thereafter associated with the deviant response (e.g. sexual arousal in presence of inappropriate stimuli). Electric shocks are response interfering; therefore the limbs used by the client for executing an escape or avoidance response should not be shocked. For example, if the hand or palm has to be used, shock may be administered on the thighs. Marshall (1985) suggested that in order to avoid possible tissue damage due to inadvertent administration of high amperage shock, number 6 ignition batteries might also be used. The advantage is that, it permits an increase in the shock intensity (voltage) while holding the amplitude constant at a negligible level.

In a significant study, McGuire and Vallance (1964) used a technique of self-administered shock with smokers, alcoholics and sexual perverts. The clients themselves determined the shock level and administered it on themselves. This was also adjusted during the session. The treatment was moderately effective. Wolpe (1965) used self-administered shock for treatment of a client with drug addiction. The client was instructed to administer the electric shock whenever the craving arose. The apparatus used for this treatment was earlier developed by McGuire and Vallance (1961) originally to administer shocks to monkeys. The apparatus was fitted into a 6 inches square and 2 inches deep box.

Electrical aversion was found to be effective in treatment of sexual deviance, particularly in paraphilias like fetishism (Rachman 1961; Kushner 1965; Marks and Gelder 1967), transvestism (Blackmore et al. 1963), paedophilia (Bancroft et al. 1966) and homosexuality (Max 1935).

Lemon juice was used effectively as a punisher, in order to reduce rumination in a six month old infant (Sajwaj, Libet and Agras 1974). The infant was admitted to a hospital for failure to gain weight, which was associated with constant rumination. Few minutes after being served milk, this girl used to start ruminating for about 20–40 minutes until the milk was completely evacuated from the stomach. At the time of treatment, the infant's mouth used to be filled with lemon juice following every vigorous tongue movement that led to rumination. The client recovered from this life-threatening disorder after 16 feedings of lemon juice punishment. These results were replicated with individuals with mental retardation by Becker, Turner and Sajwaj (1978). The investigators used lemon juice with a 36-month old retarded girl. Lip smacking was observed as a precursor to rumination. They administered lemon juice contingent on occurrence of lip smacking. Although a 6-month follow-up indicated reduction in the rate of rumination, there was an increase in rumination after the initial reduction in rate of rumination. This increase was explained by the authors as the effect of losing aversive property of lemon juice.

Marholin et al. (1984) highlighted individual differences in responding to lemon juice while controlling ruminative vomiting in two children with profound mental retardation. With one case, the programme was quite effective and suppression was maintained over a period of nine months. In the second case, the lemon juice was initially effective, but there was recovery of ruminative vomiting after sometime. When the aversive stimulus was changed to Tabasco sauce, the response decreased again and it was maintained for about a month.

There are certain aversive cognitive stimuli such as imaginal situations, activities that elicit discomfort, fear or anxiety. Repeated association of these aversive stimuli with maladaptive behaviour weakens the latter's strength of occurrence. The prior reinforcement history, kind, degree and schedule of administration of aversive consequences determine their effectiveness.

DETERMINANTS OF EFFECTIVE PUNISHMENT

As stated earlier, the effects of aversive stimulus depend on the schedule, intensity and duration of aversive event, and the degree of reinforcement (pleasure) derived from the maladaptive target response. Generally, response contingent punishment is more effective than delayed punishment. Much undesirable behaviour is complex. They consist of an elaborate chain of responses. Early administration of punishment to the initial chain of the response sequence prevents the occurrences of terminal behaviour. The reason is that the occurrence of each response in the response chain that proceeds towards the terminal behaviour, is reinforcing. Punishment of the initial chain of response disrupts this progression. Thus, punishment can be made more effective by administering at an early stage of the response sequence (Kazdin 2001).

The unconditioned punishers such as physical punishment, shock and loud noise are considered more effective when compared to conditioned punishers. The response suppression effects of conditioned punishers like scolding, criticism and fines are acquired from their previous learning experiences. Thus, their effects are weaker than the natural or primary punishers are. They undergo the process of adaptation and extinction faster than primary punishers. However, the effects of such punishers can be maintained and enhanced by: (i) pairing with primary punishers intermittently, and (ii) introducing a variety of punishers before the suppressive effect is extinguished.

It is generally believed that greater the intensity of punishment, greater is its suppressive effect. For instance, Azrin and Holz (1966) found that a shock of greater intensity suppressed behaviour quicker than a low intensity shock. However, other laboratory experiments and applied research on punishment do not seem to support this finding. For instance, intense sound of a buzzer, loud reprimands, threats or shouts do not necessarily decrease the target responses more effectively. Similar observations were made by extending the time-out period (Hobbs et al. 1978) or by increasing response cost in the form of fines (Kazdin 1972). Reinforcing the alternative behaviour, while punishing the target ones make punishment more discernible. Both the components are used in the technique called overcorrection.

GENERALISATION OF TREATMENT

Catania (1992) stated that aversion therapy is not to be taken seriously as a technique for changing behaviour because it suppresses responding only temporarily. Other researchers have also repeatedly demonstrated poor generalisation of its suppressive effects to the post-therapy environment. This may be due to restricted stimulus control. Since punishment involves distressing or painful experience, the clients are more vigilant to this event and quickly learn to identify the source and agents administering aversive stimulus. He becomes more skilled in discriminating between the presence and absence of an aversive stimulus (e.g. Lovaas and Newsom 1976; Yeakel et al. 1970) and settings (Rincover and Cushing 1981; Corte et al. 1971; Lovaas and Simmons 1969) in which it is administered and also identifying the setting in which the punitive contingency is not operative.

Some investigators have attempted to identify the conditions, which improve the effectiveness of punishment. Azrin and Holz (1966), for instance, reported that punishers of low intensity gradually become ineffective after many presentations. Whereas a single or few aversive stimuli of high intensity may suppress a response for days, months or even for the lifetime or the recovery is so slow that it is difficult to notice (Catania 1992). Instead of observing the rate or immediacy of response suppression, the therapist should carefully focus on the rate of recovery of the targeted conditional response. Strengthening of the avoidance response itself suppresses the previously conditioned responses. Observations have revealed that the contingency of an aversive event is more important than simply the delivery of an aversive stimulus. The effect is weaker in conditions in which aversive events are independent of the conditioned target response, as compared to conditions where the event is response-dependent (Azrin 1956).

In order to promote generalisation beyond treatment setting, Rincover and Cushing (1981) conducted a study. The authors attempted to associate naturally occurring stimulus with punishment. The subjects were children who exhibited severe head banging. The natural stimulus was the absence of a protective helmet to prevent head banging. Punishment was administered only when the helmet was not used by the children. Initially, the criterion was only 1–5 minutes of absence of the helmet. Later, when the discrimination training decreased head banging, the criterion was increased to longer and longer periods of absence of the protective helmet in the classroom setting. Follow-ups conducted at 6, 12 and 24 months did not indicate any relapse. This was one of the clearly demonstrated cases in which the researchers made systematic attempt to generalise treatment effects of punishment in a natural setting.

EFFECTS OF PUNISHMENT

In the preceding sections, the discussion was focused on the controlled clinical use of punishment. In this context, empirical studies that demonstrated positive behaviour changes have been cited. Most laboratory studies have indicated that punishment helps in securing short-term immediate compliance (e.g. Newsom, Flavell and Rincover 1983). Although many people use it for such short-term goals, its long-term objective is to initiate discipline and promote development of internal control (Grolnick, Deci and Ryan 1997; Hoffman 1983; Kohlberg 1969; Lepper 1983; Piaget 1932). Punishment helps in moral internalisation as the individual learns to take over the values and attitudes of the society as one's own. As a result, socially appropriate behaviour is motivated internally and not by extrinsic factors (Grusec and Goodnow 1994).

Conditioned Emotional Response

Negative side effects of punishment increase with its intensity. Conditioned emotional response (CER) is one of the principal side effects of punishment. When a neutral stimulus is associated with punishment, it acquires the ability to elicit conditioned fear, which in turn functions to suppress the ongoing behaviour.

Severe punishment may cause extensive behavioural inhibition of responses, both preceding and following the critical response. Due to punishment, the next inappropriate behaviour in the hierarchy may appear (Rimm and Masters 1979). Bandura (1969) also pointed out that punishment may result in maladaptive conditioned anxiety, leading to a generalised suppression of socially desirable patterns of behaviour and avoidance of the punishing agents or the situation in which punishment occurred. For instance, severe punishment for poor scholastic performance may cause school avoidance (truancy) among children. In order to prevent such spill-over effect, alternative adaptive behaviours require to be reinforced.

Aggression

One who administers punishment acts as a role model of aggressive behaviour too. This may be imitated by the client who receives the punishment. Aversive stimulation causes counter-aggression. It may lead to aggressive acting-out, temper tantrums, an attack on the less powerful victims or property destruction. A child severely punished by an adult may not react against the adult directly, but may displace his anger by attacking a child younger to him or a peer. Thus, punishment predicts and promotes aggressive behaviour (Aronfreed 1969; Bandura and Walters 1959; Eron et al. 1971; Walters and Grusec 1977). Use of punishment early in life legitimises many forms of violence in later life (White and Straus 1981). Use of punishment sets a coercive cycle of aversive behaviour that reverberates with each attempt of punitive control (Dishion and Patterson 1999; Patterson et al. 1992). Attribution theorists explained that punishment promotes hostile attribution, making the client hyper-vigilant to aggressive cues. Consequently, it produces violent behaviour (Dodge et al. 1986).

Habituation

Habituation is considered as one of the worst negative side effects of punishment. Due to repeated presentation of aversive stimulus, not only the associated situations and people acquire secondary aversive qualities, but also the suppressive effect of the aversive stimulus habituates in due course of time. The client requires higher degree of punishment to have the same suppressive effect. The avoidance reaction declines with exposure to punishment. The individual becomes 'thick-skinned' or less responsive to punishment. For instance, a dehumanised prison system, implementing unreasonable punishment, may become the breeding grounds for hardened criminals; school administration imposing frequent punishment becomes ineffective in shaping discipline. The effect of punishment is the quickest of all methods of response suppression. Therefore, the therapist who has already used punishment earlier is more likely to use it again and there is a high chance of generalising such a practice to other unacceptable behaviours. Thus, it should be used as a last-resort method; only when other alternative methods fail to change the behaviour. In order to avoid or at least minimise the negative effects, punishment should be used as an adjunct to other reinforcement methods.

PREDICTORS OF POSITIVE OUTCOME

There are some positive predictors of aversion therapy, such as higher social class, good pre-treatment adjustment and availability of alternative adaptive behaviour (Rachman and Tisdale 1969). In a study on alcoholics, Lemere and Vogtlin (1950) reported that thousands of alcoholics who performed better after aversion therapy were from the upper socio-economic status. The success was closely associated with pre-treatment adjustment. This observation was reported by MacCulloch and Feldman (1967) while treating homosexuals. Since aversion therapy literally creates a vacuum, several authors have suggested that it should be accompanied with reinforcement of alternative adaptive behaviour in order to enhance its positive effects. Rachman and Tisdale (1969) believed that every human being is physiologically unique to create new responses in almost all new situations; when they fail to do so either by themselves or through the therapist, they look for another therapist. At this stage, they resort to aversion therapy. Thus, it should be considered as a last-resort treatment and should be used only when positive methods fail to bring any desirable change in the response.

ETHICAL ISSUES

Punishment is undoubtedly one of the most effective methods of immediate behaviour suppression. The effects are often magical and lasting. The higher the intensity of punishment, the quicker and longer is the effect. However, its negative side effects are equally stronger. Therefore, this has remained as one of the most abused methods and therefore, a matter of ethical concern, too. The ethics of punishment are determined primarily by its purpose, intensity and duration. For instance, incapacitation is one of the primitive purposes of punishment. The individual is punished so that he/she will not be in a position to perform a punished response again. Many forms of cruel corporal punishment like flogging in public view, stoning, ampu-tation of limbs or castrating are still prevalent in some societies. Another variety of punishment is aimed at compensation, where the individual is required to compensate his/her wrongdoings with fines, loss of property and so on. The history of civilisation is a continuous story of the abuse of power. Harsh punishments like imprisonment, torture, deprivation of property and execution have been used as powerful control techniques. This has reduced the individuals' freedom of choice. Freedom from torture and cruel treatment is one of the fundamental rights of every individual. Ethical and moral sanctions are revoked when punishment is used as cruelty or disrespects human dignity.

In this context, ethics refer to the standards of behaviour that are developed by a culture to promote survival of the culture (Skinner 1971, 1973) and the humankind at large. Moreover, it reinforces adaptive behaviour and also requires the development of a mechanism for punishing bad behaviour in order to strengthen as well as sustain the former. Like all scientific technology, punishment also entails some ethical principles. It would be a great tragedy if this technology were somehow used to harm humanity. Therefore, conscientious application of punishment is vital in developing an effective technology of behaviour change.

The extent to which people can be free to make choices have been critically examined by philosophers, scientists and theologists (e.g Skinner 1953a; Hospers 1961; Novak 1973). Certain people restrict the democratic rights of others indulging in violence and antisocial behaviours or restrict their own access to an enriched and stimulating environment (e.g. self-injurious, stereotyped behaviour). In order to enhance their access to better environment, such behaviours are required to be suppressed, if necessary, by punishment. At this point, it is important to decide how much punishment is desirable and whether methods other than punishment are available.

Even if one asks for punishment, it cannot be administered for ethical reasons. The greatest ethical concern has been voiced by the gay liberation organisations pertaining to the issue of homosexuality. Many homosexuals who look for painful treatment to shift their sexual orientation are actually believed to be seeking to punish themselves for the behaviour of the prejudiced society. Some behaviour therapists have even been accused by this group of impeding acceptance of homosexuality as a legitimate lifestyle (Silverstein 1972).

As discussed earlier, punishment should be used sparingly and for clearly defined behaviours. Use of fines as response cost for inadequate behaviour is preferred to physical punishment and time-out. Even while using fines, there is a need for adding training contingencies that teach how to accept fines relatively non-emotionally and non-aggressively. For use of punishment as a component of treatment, informed consent must be taken. For people with mental retardation or severe psychiatric disorders, the consent about acceptance of the treatment is generally taken from the legal guardians.

Much of the applied research on punishment is derived from problematic or ineffective behaviour of people. Suppression of these behaviours is consistent with the democratic value. It suggests that, within limits people should freely pursue their own objectives and at the same time should have protection against oppression too (Kazdin 1978). Therefore, standards of clinical practice of aversive procedures have been outlined by professional bodies. For instance, the Ethical Issues in Human Services have been explicitly outlined and adopted by Association for Advancement of Behaviour Therapy on 22 May 1977. In 1988, in its journal *Behaviour Analyst,* American Psychological Association (APA) published a statement of client's rights (Van Houten et al. 1988). Regarding selection of treatment, it is stated that the behaviour therapist should use the most effective, empirically validated methods with the least discomfort and least negative side effects. Therefore, they should use least intrusive and restrictive interventions wherever possible. Interventions based on positive reinforcement should be considered first. However, this does not mean that aversive procedures should never be used. Sometimes it may not be in the interest of the client to use slow-acting procedures, if available research indicates that aversive treatment would be more effective. Van Houten et al. (1988: 114) stated, 'In some cases, the client's right to effective treatment may indicate the immediate use of quicker-acting but temporarily more restrictive procedure.'

LaVigna and Donnellan (1986) argued that many professionals who make treatment decisions involving the use of punishment do so because they are unaware of the non-aversive treatment methods. Professional ignorance is not the only reason; some authors imply even darker reasons like discrimination of the client, or even fanaticism as the reason (e.g. Guess et al. 1986). However, these reasons do not seem to be convincing. In spite of legal sanctions and unpopularity of punishment as a method of treatment, parents, teachers, police and law-makers often use punishment universally. What could be the reason? This could be just due to the fact that effects of punishment are immediate and dramatic. Apprehension that some behaviours may lead to more dangerous ones also influence the decision-making. People's attitude about the behaviour itself plays a significant role. For example, punishment is used more frequently for those behaviours, which are believed to be resistant to change or those which do not simply respond to non-aversive treatment. Apart from that, many clients and their family members, and society at large require timely as well as magical treatment. Under these circumstances, behavior controlling authorities tend to use punishment. It is part of an individual's natural contingencies that shape and evolve behaviour. Thus, it is a part of our reality. A young child who learns to walk, learns about incorrect stepping not only from correct stepping but also from falling that hurts and injures him. Thus, punishment is an inseparable part of reality. People learn to avoid aversive conditions like sickness, pain and disease in order to enjoy a healthy and peaceful life. Thus, punishment has an important position in human adaptation. One cannot ignore these realities. It sensitises the client about the harmful effects of a mal-adaptive responding. In this sense, punishment has its own significance. However, this is no justification for using it as the sole method of behaviour control.

McGee et al. (1987: 24) suggested 'gentle teaching' method as an alternative to punishment, for persons with mental retardation. This method was based upon unconditional positive regard, bonding, human interaction and an anti-authoritarian attitude on the part of the therapist. In order to validate this method, he reported data of 73 people with developmental disability exhibiting self-injurious behaviour. They reported 86.3 per cent reduction in the self-injurious behaviour. However, there was no baseline data to evaluate the effectiveness of this gentle teaching method. These authors advocated a total rejection of punishment procedures on the ground that they are 'calculated, deliberate assault on human dignity'.

The society's perception and acceptance of a technology of punishment is determined by the extent to which it is used. Despite the potential efficacy of aversion therapy (e.g. Lovaas et al. 1965; Tate and Baroff 1966; Risley 1968), biases against use of punishment as a behaviour therapy technique is so much that it is given a separate name altogether, like passive avoidance (Catania 1992), that is, the paradigm in which an organism is taught to passively withhold a response to avoid punishment. There are considerable legal and ethical issues concerning the use of certain forms of corporal punishment like shock, slap and so on. (e.g. Lovaas and Newsom 1976; Romanczyk 1976). Therefore, more socially acceptable aversive stimuli like aromatic ammonia (Tanner and Zeiler 1975), facial screening (Lutzker 1978), citric acid (Mayhew and Harris 1979) and vinegar (Rincover and Cushing 1981) are used by behaviour therapists.

The society shies away from the use of a formal punishment programme for complex reasons. The major reason is its association with cruelty and inhuman treatment, production of unnecessary pain, and its association with the primitive methods of treatment of mentally ill in psychiatric institutions. Consequently, it has acquired a negative connotation (Whitman et al. 1983). In order to change this misconception, there is a need for more empirical research to examine its long-term effects by comparing with other non-punitive methods of intervention (e.g. extinction, differential reinforcement or overcorrection). At the same time, the ethical guidelines are to be followed more stringently to avoid its misuse. In behaviour therapy, punishment has the same significance as that of an injection causing mild pain, irritating medicine, a bitter tasting pill, or a surgery that combats against a dreaded disease. The stigma concerning use of punishment can be dispelled by its ethical use and through public education.

CONCLUSION

Usually punishment is recommended in situations, where supporting and reinforcing contingencies are difficult to be controlled because it is difficult to identify and isolate them, when the behaviour has achieved a state of functional autonomy (controlled by cognitive cues) or when higher order conditioning makes the reinforcers too obscure to detect. Under these circumstances, it becomes difficult to remove the reinforcer to decrease behaviour. Second, when behaviour is uncontrollable by other forms of non-aversive techniques, and third, when it is potentially harmful.

In classrooms, homes and in institutional settings, use of punishment is more frequent in comparison to reinforcement, as it is less expensive, easy to administer, and has a dramatic and immediate effect on the behaviour. Because of its quick suppressive effect on inappropriate behaviour, it is used more frequently than other alternative methods. Lack of understanding about the contingencies that maintain a behaviour in a social setting frequently leads to use of punishment; therefore, the significant people in the client's immediate environment are required to be educated about the analysis of inappropriate behaviour.

In spite of the large scale and effective application of punishment as a technique of behaviour change, its use particularly with children, has been challenged seriously on ethical grounds. Objections have also been raised for its negative side effects. Aggressive behaviour of the punisher generates counter aggression in children. Therefore, it should be sparingly used. When children are unable to exhibit counter-aggression against punitive adults, they 'displace' the same to other less powerful victims like peers or younger children. At times, it leads to destructive behaviour. These punitive agents serve as models for future aggression (Bandura, 1969). Conditioned avoidance responses may have 'spill-over' effects suppressing other adaptive responses. Punishment only teaches what not to do but does not teach new behaviour. It does nothing to remove the original source of aversive stimulation. Therefore, it is a rule of the thumb that punishment should be used as a 'last-resort treatment', only after other forms of reductive techniques like differential reinforcement, extinction or time out has been tried out and found to be ineffective (Bucher and Lovaas 1968). Clinically, the overall effects of punishment do not appear to be sufficiently positive to warrant its use as a primary intervention modality (Millan and Kolko 1985). It is to be used only when positive reinforcement techniques are ineffective in modifying the target behaviour (Risley 1968). Behaviour therapists should pay careful attention to the legal and ethical safeguards required for such a hazardous undertaking.

10

Non-aversive Procedures

Application of aversive stimuli used for response elimination has a number of undesirable effects; therefore, its application is restricted. Behaviour therapists feel more comfortable in using relatively less aversive methods of response elimination because these are more acceptable to the clients. The present chapter is devoted to description and use of non-aversive procedures of response elimination.

EXTINCTION

Gradual reduction of a behaviour following removal of the reinforcing event is generally termed as extinction. It is a procedure by which response-maintaining reinforcers are no longer made available following the occurrence of a critical response. As most undesirable behaviours are maintained by their reinforcing consequences, extinction is often used as a technique for weakening or eliminating them. Removal of the reinforcing stimuli produced by the response disrupts the contingency between the target behaviour and reinforcement, therefore results in response diminution. It reverses the developmental process in learning. On the contrary, much abnormal behaviour occurs as a manifestation of the extinction phenomenon. Mental (developmental) retardation is an example. Lack of reinforcement for adaptive behaviours during the early developmental period may cause severe retardation. Some behaviours drop out from the response repertoire almost permanently due to lack of reinforcement. Therefore, early stimulation (reinforcement) plays a significant role in retaining, developing and maintaining adaptive responses.

Undesirable behaviours are maintained by many reinforcing consequences. Some of them are conditioned reinforcers (S^r). In spite of the fact that the original reinforcing event is absent, they continue to maintain the undesirable behaviour. Identification of every source of reinforcement in the individual's behavioural ecology is virtually impossible although repeated observation and functional analysis would help in detecting many of them.

In our day-to-day lives, there are many examples of extinction. When a class teacher asks a question in the classroom and expects the students to raise their hand, some students do raise their hands but wave them or make noise to draw attention of the teacher. In this case, if the teacher asks only those students who quietly raise their hands to answer the question and ignores the ones who make noise, she places the undesirable responding under extinction. A husband ignoring the nagging of his wife, a psychotherapist ignoring irrelevant talk of a client, or a director ignoring untimely visitors to office beyond visiting hours are the examples of extinction in practice.

Applications

In a classic study, Etzel and Gewirtz (1967) used extinction paradigm to control crying behaviour of two very young infants. One was six and another was twenty weeks old. The study was conducted in the well-baby unit of a children's hospital. The investigators observed that both the infants cried three times than that of other infants and the staff would try to quiet these two infants by holding and soothing them. In order to study the effects of adult attention, they delivered contingent attention, that is, a two second smile coupled with a soft word and gentle nod toward the child contingent on responses which were incompatible with crying. For one child, smiling alone was reinforced, and for another, smiling with eye-contact was reinforced. Whenever the child cried, attention was immediately withdrawn and the experimenter showed a neutral face. In seven 15-minutes sessions daily, the rates of crying decreased dramatically and there was as much as a four fold increase in smiles. Etzel and Gewirtz gave a beautiful account of the response of one of the infants, Anthony showed during the extinction phase, 'Anthony would look at E again and smile, receive no reinforcement, wrinkle up his face as if to cry but without vocalizing, look at E again and smile and so on.'

Williams (1959) demonstrated the effectiveness of extinction procedure with a 2-year-old child who exhibited severe tantrums. This is considered as another classic study on extinction. Due to sickness, the parents had to deliver constant attention to this child in the first 18 months of his life. During bedtime, he would throw severe tantrums, for which the parents had to attend to him until he fell asleep. In order to eliminate tantrums they were instructed to put him on the bed, leave him and close the room. On the first night, tantrums continued for 45 minutes. After seventh night, it decreased to 0. The behaviour was inadvertently reinstated because of his aunt's attention. After another week of treatment, the tantrums again reduced to 0. A similar method was used successfully by Kakkar (1972) with a 2-year-old girl who threw tantrums on being taken to school. Extinction has been used as an effective method of treatment for various other behaviours such as throwing glasses (Wolf, Risley and Mees 1964), classroom disruptive behaviour (Thomas et. al. 1969; Zimmerman and Zimmerman 1962; O'Leary and Becker 1967). In an innovative experiment, Wilson and Hopkins (1973) introduced an automated popular music as a reinforcer for quiet classroom behaviour. The music was automatically switched on when the classroom noise was below a level of 70 decibels and was turned off when it rose above this level. It brought a dramatic reduction in the noise level in the classroom.

Factors Affecting Effectiveness of Extinction

Skinner (1938) stated that if extinction is used with maximum effectiveness, its results could be enduring. The undesirable behaviours rarely occur following the extinction programme. Several factors influence the effectiveness of this technique. The length of treatment is an important issue. Extinction is a slow procedure. In this respect, the role of the schedule of previous reinforcement, that is, reinforcement history is quite critical. It includes the frequency, intensity, duration and schedule of previous reinforcement. Responses that are reinforced for a long time are more resistant to extinction. Availability of reinforcement for alternative undesirable behaviour during the procedure would decrease the strength of extinction.

Extinction is often found to be less effective in controlling undesirable behaviour of individuals with retardation. The reason is that they already live in a deprived environment where the chances of reinforcement of adaptive responding are quite low. While explaining about retarded behaviour, Bijou (1963) stated how poor reinforcement and extinction play a significant role in delaying progressive change in behaviour. Some parents tend to provide very little or no reinforcement for independent behaviour, either due to anxiety or simply because they want to see them passive and dependent. For example, a child who has difficulty in communication is not encouraged to communicate in social situations, as the speech is incomprehensible. As a result, the child fails to develop adequate speech or does not emit verbal responses to communicate. Thus, independent behaviour gradually extinguishes, and passivity and dependence dominate the response repertoire.

Even awareness about the fact that a given response is no longer going to be reinforced influences the extinction process. At the early stage of extinction, there may be a temporary increase in the frequency of target behaviour. The individual may exhibit target behaviour more frequently than before, to 'test-out' whether the previously occurring contingency of reinforcement is in operation or not. For example, a disruptive child may engage in increased disruptive behaviour (e.g. crying, throwing tantrums) in the same way as a man repeatedly tries out an electrical switch when it no longer helps in activating an electrical instrument. These responses appear frequently or with higher intensity before they are finally extinguished and dropped. This temporary phenomenon is called extinction burst. These responses may be viewed as frustration responses. Their probability of occurrence is dependent on the prior schedule of reinforcement maintaining the target behaviour. Appearance of high frequency undesirable responding during this phase makes extinction a hazardous procedure. In order to make it successful there should be 100 per cent continuous non-reinforcement during extinction. A mere thinning of the schedule would make the response resistant to extinction as intermittent reinforcement runs the risk of strengthening the response. Parents, caretakers and other mediators should be counselled and trained to handle these situations. They have to continue to withdraw the response generated reinforcing consequences and wait patiently until the extinction burst is over, and uniformly adhere to the extinction procedure. Failure to do so would enhance the probability of the occurrence of the critical behaviour.

Appearance of alternative undesirable behaviour available at a lower level of response hierarchy under such circumstances is not rare. Instead of making noise, a child may engage in aggressive behaviour. The latter behaviour may even entirely replace the former. This is called symptom substitution. This undesirable effect may be suppressed by using punishment. Spontaneous recovery of the extinguished undesirable response may occur days, months, or even years after its initial extinction. It may appear just to disappear again. Therefore, it need not be considered as a programme failure. Very often, the behaviour change agents are not in a position to programme the social environment to maintain a complete extinction schedule. Therefore, it is crucial to strengthen an appropriate response incompatible with the extinguished one. Precisely speaking, a simultaneous reinforcement schedule should be maintained along with the extinction schedule.

Nature of inappropriate behaviour is another determinant of the success of these procedures. Although extinction procedure is applicable for a wide range of behaviours, its use is clearly contraindicated when the individual is engaged in aggressive, destructive behaviour and life-threatening behaviour such as self-injury. In most situations, undesirable behaviours are maintained by a good number of reinforcing events in the environment. It is difficult to identify all of them. Therefore, removal of only one source of reinforcement may not be sufficient to suppress the target behaviour. This is another limitation of extinction procedure (Madsen et al. 1968). In order to make extinction effective, it should be combined with reinforcement for desirable responding too. The technique is termed as differential reinforcement.

DIFFERENTIAL REINFORCEMENT

Differential reinforcement refers to the implementation of two clearly different degrees of reinforcement for two behaviours, one of which is to be replaced by the other. Depending on the type and rate of response(s) to be suppressed by reinforcing others, it may be placed under four operational categories: (i) differential reinforcement of other behaviour or '0' rate behaviour, (ii) differential reinforcement of low rate behaviour, (iii) differential reinforcement of incompatible behaviour, and (iv) differential reinforcement of alternate behaviour. In all the above varieties of differential reinforcement techniques, one or the other adaptive behaviours are reinforced while extinguishing the undesirable ones. These applications of differential rates of reinforcement of one or more desirable responding facilitate and strengthen the extinction process for the undesirable ones.

Differential Reinforcement of Other Behaviour or '0' Rate Behaviour (DRO)

DRO is used for reinforcing non-occurrence (i.e. '0' rate of occurrence) of target behaviour. The purpose is to eliminate a specific behaviour. The client is permitted to emit any behaviour other than the target behaviour (Repp 1983), which is placed on extinction. Reinforcement is delivered, if the target behaviour does not occur at all for a specific period (Reynolds 1968). Knight and McKenzie (1974) used DRO schedule for reducing thumb-sucking in three children. Due to this habit, two of them suffered from dental problems. During the baseline condition the experimenter kept reinforcing these children by reading an interesting book to them irrespective of whether they were thumb-sucking or not. During intervention, the experimenter stopped reading whenever the clients started sucking their thumbs. Reading was resumed only when the response was terminated. This procedure eliminated thumb-sucking in all the three children. Drabman and Spitalnik (1973) used the technique in special classroom setting to reduce disruptive behaviour (e.g. inappropriate noise, playing, turning around, touching, out-of-seat and vocalisations) of two children with retardation. In baseline condition, these disruptive behaviours were recorded. A moderately retarded male was employed as a teaching assistant. Either the teacher or the teaching assistant determined the criterion for receiving edible reinforcement (candy). Although the criterion was subjective, it was based on absence of disruptive behaviour. The two disruptive children showed decline in the target behaviour. In one case, the disruptions declined from 1.4 to 0.6 per 20-second interval while in the other case it declined from 1.1 to 0.4 incidents per 20-second interval.

Sulzer and Mayers (1977) discussed a 'quasi-DRO' schedule called 'momentary DRO'. The schedule requires ignoring undesired behaviour appearing within a defined interval and reinforcing its non-occurrences only at the moment of the termination of the specified interval. The requirement of 'momentary DRO' is less stringent; therefore, it is less effective than pure DRO schedule. DRO schedule is used for complete suppression of behaviour.

Differential Reinforcement of Low Rate Behaviour (DRL)

The DRL schedule is designed to decrease a behaviour to an acceptable level (Repp 1983). DRL schedule is used for the behaviour that is inappropriate only because it occurs at too high a rate. This schedule is arranged in intermediate steps of easily achievable criterion. The goal of this schedule is to stabilise behaviour at a lower rate of occurrence to prevent it from being excessive. The undesirable behaviour is tolerated as long as it does not interfere with others' freedom or privacy.

Deitz and Repp (1973) used the procedure to reduce talking-out behaviour of children with mental retardation in a special classroom setting. Edible reinforcers (candies) were used to reinforce non-occurrence of disruptive talking-out behaviour of 10 trainable children in a special classroom setting. After a baseline recording of talking-out behaviour, the treatment was implemented. Each child received two pieces of candies if the class made five or less talk-outs in a 50-minutes session. The treatment reduced the disruptive behaviour from an average of 32.7 to 3.1 per 50-minutes period. The return to baseline condition showed 27.2 talk-outs. Deitz and Repp also experimented on free time as a reinforcer for absence of talking-out, which is a cheaper alternative to edible reinforcers. They made free time of five minutes contingent on reinforcing decline in incidents of talk-out to three or less per 50-minute period. It reduced inappropriate verbalisation from an average of 5.7 to less than one incidence per session.

This approach is almost like changing a criterion design where the treatment goals change from time to time. There are three different methods of programming DRL schedule, which are based on the following criterion: (i) inter-response time or spaced responding, (ii) full session method, and (iii) interval method. In inter-response-time method, the goal is to produce a low, stable rate of responding. A response is reinforced only when it occurs after a criterion time following the prior response. Full session method requires the reinforcement to be delivered only when the response is below a limit for the whole session. Interval method is a variation of full session method. In this method, the session is broken into a number of intervals and reinforcement is delivered at the end of each interval, if a response is below certain level for that interval (Repp 1983). DRL programme may be viewed as a shaping procedure that utilises a changing criterion design (Hartmann and Hall 1976). The unique property of DRL schedule is that the procedure itself can be designed as an evaluation programme, involving step-wise chain from baseline level to acceptable levels of responding. It precludes the necessity of reversal phase or extended baselines (Repp 1983). The major drawback of a DRL schedule is that it cannot be used for those behaviours which are violent or self-injurious.

Differential Reinforcement of Incompatible Behaviour (DRI)

DRI schedule requires reinforcing those responses, which are topographically incompatible with the undesired target response. This means that the presence of one type of behaviour should eliminate the possibility of another type. Both cannot occur together. For example, if the purpose is to eliminate stereotyped hand flapping of an individual, by ignoring this behaviour he may be reinforced for engaging in incompatible activities like drawing, paper cutting or desirable play activities in which the same hand is used. A similar procedure was used by Twardosz and Sajwaj (1972) to reduce hyperactivity by enhancing sitting behaviour of a child.

In the DRI schedule, an attempt is made to increase the incompatible desired responding to such a degree that the inappropriate response does not occur at all. While attempting to record both the behaviours, the therapist only reinforces the incompatible desired responding, either in intervals or a ratio schedule. A few guidelines may be helpful for programming a DRI schedule. The target behaviour is one, which can occur across several settings in order to help in generalisation. A rule of thumb is that one should begin with a schedule in which the subject is frequently reinforced for an appropriate response.

Differential Reinforcement of Alternative Behaviour (DRA)

DRA is also a reinforcement-related reductive procedure like DRI but does not require the target behaviour to be incompatible with inappropriate behaviour. In a DRA schedule, the target behaviour to be reinforced need not be topographically incompatible. It may be any desirable alternative behaviour. For example, a disruptive child may be reinforced for his punctuality and ignored for his disruptive responses. Zlutnick et al. (1975) used a similar procedure in conjunction with physical guidance to reduce seizure-like behaviour in a 17-year-old boy with mental retardation. The boy was guided at the onset of a seizure-like behaviour to make an alternative response and then reinforced for this response. Although the authors describe the procedure as 'DRO', it fits into the DRA paradigm. An A-B-A-B experimental design was used to assess the effectiveness of this treatment programme. The procedure was effective in reducing seizure-like behaviour. DRA has been used extensively for modification of undesirable behaviour in classroom settings. Most of these alternative behaviours are task-oriented activities.

PUNISHMENT BY WITHDRAWAL

The two non-aversive response elimination techniques, time-out and response cost are considered as punishment by withdrawal (Van Houten 1983). These procedures are used extensively for children in educational settings.

Time-out

As we discussed in the previous section, it is not always possible to identify all the sources of re-inforcement that maintain undesirable responses, and remove them to decelerate the response. There are reinforcers in the social environment that cannot be removed even if one wants to do so. Under such conditions, time-out is used as an effective procedure. Time-out is one of the fundamental forms of punishment in which following an inappropriate behaviour, the client is required to spend a brief period of time in a relatively less reinforcing environment than the original one where the behaviour occurred earlier. In order to do that, the person himself is removed from the positively reinforcing condition upon inappropriate behaviour or denied access to the environment in which he has received positive reinforcement previously (Gardner 1971; Drabman and Spitalnik 1973). It is the time in which positive reinforcers are no longer made available (Leitenberg 1965). Various forms of time-out have been reported in clinical and experimental literature, such as social isolation or room time-out (Wolf et al. 1964), delayed time-out (Ramp et al. 1971), chair time-out (Hamilton et al. 1967; LeBlanc et al. 1973; Barkley 1997).

Brantner and Doherty (1983) classified time-out into three groups of operation: (i) isolation time-out, (ii) exclusionary time-out, and (iii) non-exclusionary time-out. In isolation time-out, the client is taken to a solitary and non-reinforcing area, where the behaviour of the client can be monitored. Wetzel et al. (1966) used social isolation as a time-out procedure to reduce temper tantrums in a 6-year-old boy. They gave an initial warning to the boy, followed by social isolation until the tantrum ceased for at least a 3-minutes period. Within one month the tantrums reduced to 0 level. Success of social isolation. Room time-out has prompted some investigators to develop a folding and portable time-out room. Harris et al. (1974) developed one such time-out room consisting of a three-panel screen, which is commercially available. In exclusionary time-out, the individual is not allowed to participate in the ongoing reinforcing activity; for example, taking the child to a quiet corner in a public place or classroom. In non-exclusionary time-out, the individual's participation in reinforcing the activity is restricted but he is not removed from the setting.

Brantner and Doherty discussed three further variations of non-exclusionary time-out: (a) contingent observation, (b) removal of reinforcing materials, (c) moving away from the client. The contingent observation procedure is used to prevent the client from participating in ongoing activities but allows him to watch others being reinforced for their good behaviour. This is a form of chair time-out, usually performed in a group setting. The moment a child engages in the critical behaviour, he is told about his wrong behaviour and what the appropriate behaviour should be, and is then separated from the group to observe other children. It facilitates acquisition of good behaviour through observation. The second form of non-exclusionary time-out requires removal of the reinforcing agent or objects that strengthen undesirable responding. Switching off a TV programme, or contingent removal of the toy objects when the client engages in disruptive behaviour are few examples. This can also be done in a substantial way by stopping all reinforcing activities until the client engages himself in the desired behaviour. All possible forms of reinforcers are removed to control behaviour. The technique is popularly called 'stop-the-world'. For example, a hyperactive child may be told, 'nothing will be provided to you until you stop moving out of your chair' and all reinforcing events like attention, recess, and verbal interaction of peers and the teacher will stop till he engages in the on-seat behaviour. Although it requires tremendous amount of effort to stop all possible sources of reinforcement, it is an effective method. Initially it may take more time to suppress the response, but with training, the delay will decline the target response substantially. However, the technique is difficult to exercise in classroom environment.

In an experiment with children who were mentally retarded, Plummer et al. (1977) removed the play materials and asked the teacher to turn away when aggressive-disruptive behaviours were emitted by the children. Although the method was effective with some other children, it was not so with these children. Foxx and Shapiro (1978) developed a procedure called 'time-out ribbon' for non-exclusionary time-out. The study was conducted on five children with mental retardation in a special education classroom. All of them wore a coloured ribbon indicating that they were eligible to receive the teacher's attention while participating in the group activity. During this period, the children received snacks and praise every few minutes. If they misbehaved, the ribbon was removed, and the teacher's attention and participation in activities ceased for a period of three minutes. The procedure was found to be effective in reducing disruptive behaviour. Such time-out procedure can be effective provided the disruptive behaviour during the time-out period is tolerated or backed up with additional exclusionary time-out.

How Long should the Time-out be?

Varied time-out intervals have been used by investigators that range from two minutes (Bostow and Bailey 1969) to three hours (Burchard and Tyler 1965). There is no general prescription for limiting the length of time-out period to make it effective. Some researchers have attempted to study the function of the length of the time-out period in elimination of certain responses. In a systematic study, Burchard and Barrera (1972) found greater suppression of response with 30-minutes than 5-minutes time-out. However, other investigators like Kendall et al. (1975) observed the reverse results. Freeman et al. (1976) compared effects of 1-hour and 3-minutes seclusion time-out, and the requirement that the child should be quiet for 15-minutes. Both long and short periods of time-out were ineffective, whereas the third requirement produced dramatic effect in the suppression of disruptive behaviour. In many instances, brief periods of time-out were found to be as effective as long periods of time-out. Thus, the results are inconclusive about the duration of time-out. The period of appropriate behaviour should be preconditioned to the release from time-out for its best effect. It encourages emission of appropriate behaviour along with suppression of inappropriate ones. Age and level of maturation of the client are obviously important considerations for determining the length of the time-out period. Reviewing a number of studies, Griffin and Gross (2000) suggested that although there is no standard of time-out period, it may be determined by the age of the individual; upto five years of age, the period of time-out should be not more than 1 to 5-minutes whereas for older clients it may be extended upto 20 minutes. The rule of thumb is to require 1-minute time-out period for each age.

Schedules of Time-out

Pendergrass (1972) investigated the effectiveness of different schedules of time-out and observed that time-out following each episode of inappropriate behaviour is more effective than intermittent time-out. However, this finding was not fully supported. Calhoun and Matherne (1974) examined the effects of three schedules of reinforcement on disruptive aggressive behaviour of another 7-year old retarded girl attending a day care centre and a special school. The class was attended by 10 moderately retarded children in the age group of 5–8 years. The target behaviours included hitting, kicking, spitting on the teachers and other children, leaving the classroom frequently, cursing, snatching toys and edibles, out-of-seat behaviour, and throwing tantrums when disciplined. Apart from that, she had serious attention seeking behaviour, calling names and threatening the teachers. After baseline observation, time-out was administered for three hours per day, between 9 a.m. to 12 noon. A time-out room was constructed out of a four-sided plywood structure located in a storeroom adjoining to the classroom. There were three conditions of time-out. The child was placed in time-out room either after each fifth (FR5), second (FR2) or every aggressive response (CRF). Except aggressive responses, all other responses were handled by the teacher. Handling aggressive responses was the sole responsibility of the experimenter. Altogether, 12 one-hour sessions for treatment I and II, and 20 for III were required to reduce the behaviour to a stable level.

The experimenter recorded the behaviour and during the treatment period, when the critical response was emitted, the client was led to the time-out room. The client was instructed saying, 'When you hit (kick, spit, throw) you go in the time-out room'. If she spent the time quietly in the time-out room, after two minutes of continuous silence the child was taken out of it saying, 'You have been perfectly quiet, so you may come out now'. If she showed any undesirable behaviour (e.g. removing clothes or urinating) during the time-out period, it was extended by another two minutes. The FR2 time-out schedule demonstrated better effects in reducing disruptive behaviour than FR5 schedule. The best effect was obtained from a continuous (CRF) schedule. FR5 schedule had no effect on the critical response. Clark et al. (1973: 454) who worked with a mongoloid child, however reported, 'some schedules of punishment may be as effective as continuous punishment, at least in the case of the continued suppression of a response that has already been reduced to a low frequency.'

Intermittent time-out is equally effective as the continuous schedule and that is an inverse, nonlinear relationship between the percentages of response put under time-out and the frequency of response. These inconsistencies in current research have failed to specify the most effective parameter of time-out, although it has been proved an effective technique of response elimination of much inappropriate behaviour of children maintained by social reinforcement (Patterson et al. 1967; Patterson et al. 1973).

While using time-out procedure, the therapists should examine and compare the reinforcing potential of the time-out environment with that of time-in environment. As a rule of thumb, the time-in environment must be more reinforcing than the time-out environment. While using time-out procedures, particularly while removing the client from one environment and placing in another, the therapist should carefully see that the latter is not more reinforcing than the previous environment. For example, when the classroom environment is taxing and teaching is monotonous, removal from this kind of aversive environment may itself prove to be reinforcing. This may serve as negative reinforcement for the critical responses. Thus, the effectiveness of time-out depends on the nature of 'time-in' setting (Solnick et al. 1977).

Particularly while working with severely and profoundly retarded individuals, one may find that their natural environment is often impoverished. Therefore, removal from such an environment to another that is less reinforcing may hamper the learning process itself, and would therefore be unethical. Hence, logically the learning environment should be enriched with alternative and new modes of reinforcement before their contingent withdrawal. In order to reduce self-abusive behaviour Nunes et al. (1977) used vibratory stimulation as an alternative source of stimulation (reinforcement for quiet responding) for profoundly retarded individuals. It was withdrawn when self-abusive behaviour occurred. The technique was found to be effective in elimination of the above behaviour. Under normal circumstances, chair time-out is often recommended in place of any form of social isolation, as it provides opportunity for learning.

There are fundamental differences between chair time-out (e.g. contingent observation) and social isolation (e.g. room time out) procedures. Social isolation procedures not only remove the client from the reinforcing environment but also deprive him of the opportunities to learn and may therefore be considered as unethical. Apart from that, social isolation requires additional staff to implement the programme. Similarly, when time-out is conducted on continuous schedules, a lot of time is spent on it. Instructor's involvement in it would affect the smooth classroom activity. Therefore, time-out should be maintained on an intermittent schedule. Other methods of response deceleration such as reprimands, paced instruction or response cost, which are less time-consuming, may be used.

When children and adults exhibit severe disruptive behaviour, the time-out period is likely to be prolonged much more than required. Under these conditions, exclusionary time-out is sometimes maintained as a passive-avoidance response on the part of the caring personnel. Removal of the individual from the environment reduces their responsibility; therefore, it acts as a negative reinforcement.

Response Cost

Sherman and Baer (1969) defined two types of punishment contingencies: response cost and punishment. Response contingent withdrawal of acquired positive reinforcers following undesirable or problematic behaviour is known as response cost. Loss of some reinforcers (positive consequence) after problematic behaviour is in fact, an alternative to verbal or physical punishment. Penalty for misbehaviour, late fee for late payment of bills, or fines for rash driving are some of the examples of response cost. However, scientific use of the technique should be restricted to those costs that are clearly defined and systematically applied, contingent on some client behaviour (Nay 1976). It must be differentiated from naturally occurring consequences, for instance a financial loss following a business transaction.

Response cost may be put under two categories: (i) removal of reinforcers that naturally occur for the client prior to the intervention, and (ii) removal of those reinforcers that are withdrawn in response to certain undesirable behaviour (Nay 1976). The first group of events may be labelled as Type I response cost and the second as Type II response cost. Although, it is closely related to time-out, subtle differences exist between the two. Time-out is a period during which a person is prevented from acquisition of future reinforcement. Reinforcers are no longer available during time-out period, whereas in response cost, there is no necessary temporal restriction for earning further reinforcers (Kazdin 1972c) which means response cost time does not prevent the client to earn reinforcers for good behaviour, whereas time-out does. Consequently, the response cost procedure presupposes the existence of a system in which the individual has earned or possessed some quantity of reinforcers. From these reinforcers, a portion is subtracted or access may be restricted.

In order to make response cost effective, Nay (1976) suggested the following guidelines:

(1) The reinforcer to be withdrawn must possess some incentive properties. In order to ascertain it, one must carefully assess and identify an effective reinforcer.
(2) The client himself/herself must participate in deciding which reinforcer will be withdrawn, and thus should not be viewed as 'unfair'.
(3) The behaviour for which response cost will be used must be informed before its use.

(4) The reinforcers to be withdrawn must be occurring with sufficient frequency, so that it can be easily withdrawn on occurrence of undesirable behaviour.

(5) Response cost must be directly related to the problem behaviour. For instance, while playing a group game, removing the client's opportunity to play another game following undesirable behaviour will be more meaningful with reference to the target behaviour. It provides a more direct communication to the client.

(6) Response cost must be clearly specified prior to the occurrence of maladaptive behaviour. This can avoid the response cost being used inconsistently across the treatment. It should not be imposed for a longer period, since the purpose is to sensitise about the mistakes. 'When left a free hand, many direct agents impose excessive costs for some targeted behaviour, because the coat decision is made while emotions are flaring and judgment may be impaired' (Nay 1976: 51).

   Although longer response cost produces greater suppression of behaviour in adolescents (Burchard and Barrera 1972), removal of reinforcers or privileges should not be imposed for a very long time. Even a very low amount of response cost, including the imagined ones can cause significant change in behaviour (Weiner 1962). The amount of response cost is not as important as the feedback a client receives. The informational feedback plays an important role in suppressing behaviour.

(7) In order to make the application of response cost effective, the therapist must teach the client to self-impose the response cost. It requires a good deal of encouragement and reinforcement. Initially cues may be used to signal the application of response cost. Finally, the behaviour must come under self-mediated regulation.

   Discussing the limitations of the technique of response cost procedure, Millan and Kolko (1985) reported that reliance on removal of an effective reinforcer poses procedural difficulty in situations where reinforcers cannot be easily withdrawn, or in conditions where multiple reinforcers control inappropriate behaviour. In these conditions, alternative procedures may be selected for use. In order to examine the long-term effects of response cost, Kazdin (1971) conducted a 10-year long follow-up study after lifting response cost and found no relapse of the targeted behaviour. Azrin and Holz (1966) found it to be as effective as mild electric shock. Whereas, Winkler (1970) found a relapse in the target behaviour after the response cost contingency was removed. Response cost can serve as a viable component of comprehensive contingency management systems.

OVERCORRECTION

Overcorrection is considered as an alternative to the use of punishment as well as differential reinforcement procedures. The goal of reducing undesirable behaviour is to enhance the possibility of obtaining positive reinforcement, reduce aversive consequences like criticism, or disapproval, and allow the individual to engage in meaningful behaviour. Through this process, the client acquires new adaptive behaviours while eliminating the undesirable ones. Overcorrection combines both suppressive as well as educative components. As a behaviour therapy procedure, it was introduced by Foxx and Azrin (1972). Overcorrection is generally used in the situations in which extinction, response cost, differential reinforcement, and time-out have little chance of succeeding. While punishing an undesirable behaviour, an alternative adaptive behaviour is simultaneously reinforced. A number of elements may be involved in it, such as restitution, positive practice, avoidance, time-out and punishment. Thus, it is a package approach involving more than one learning principle. Contingent on an inappropriate behaviour, the client is first asked to cease the responding. Then the overcorrection starts. Restitution and positive practice are the two main components of overcorrection (Foxx and Azrin 1972; Foxx and Bechtel 1983). Restitution or restitutional overcorrection requires the disrupter to correct the sequences of his misbehaviour and restore the situation to a state vastly improved from what existed before the disruption (Foxx and Azrin 1973). Positive practice requires the disrupter to practice thoroughly the overly corrected forms of appropriate behaviour. The therapist may use modelling and graduated guidance in order to improve the quality of performance. It is intended to develop a sense of personal responsibility for the act in the client. Little, if any, reinforcement is provided during positive practice (Cooper et al. 1987).

In order to manage disruptive behaviour in a special classroom, Azrin and Powers (1975) used overcorrection and compared it with other methods of behavioural intervention. The entire treatment programme involved three components: (i) an explicit statement of rules regarding disruptive behaviour, (ii) a response contingent reprimand to the child whenever such behaviour occurred, and (iii) loss of forthcoming recess period whenever the disruptive behaviour occurred. The participants were boys aged 7–11 years. They were jointly identified by the class teacher and the school principal as deficient in academic skills and exhibiting highly disturbing disruptive behaviour, hyperactivity and aggressive behaviour. The disruptive behaviour involved talking-out and out-of-seat behaviour without permission.

Under a warning, reminder and reprimand condition, the teacher reminded the boys that they were not allowed to talk or leave their seats without permission of the class teacher. If they did so, the teacher called them by name and reminded the rules. In the second condition, they were informed at the beginning about the rules and on each occasion when the rule was transgressed. In addition to that, the disruptive child was prevented from going outside during the 10-minutes recess time. They were refrained from talking-out during that time, and were not allowed to engage in any recreational activities. In the third condition, a delayed positive practice method was used. The classroom rules were announced at the beginning. Whenever there was any violation of the rules, the child was instructed to remain in the classroom during the recess. During this period, they were engaged in positive practice procedure, which involved the following components: (i) Teacher reminding the child about the correct procedure for talking out and leaving the seat; (ii) Students reciting the correct procedure to the teacher; (iii) Students raising their hands and wait until the teacher acknowledged them by names, and (iv) When he asks the teacher for permission, (v) Teacher acknowledged his correct performance, asking him to practice. (vi) Finally, the subject repeats the same for some time. In the fourth condition, that is, immediate positive practice, the procedure was almost identical with the third condition, except that the student began positive practice immediately after the transgression of rules and completed it later. In the next recess, they practiced, asking for permission for five minutes. Results revealed that positive practice was more effective than other methods of intervention.

Foxx and Azrin (1972) used overcorrection successfully to reduce aggressive behaviour (i.e. physical assault, property damage and tantrums) in brain-damaged retarded children. Overcorrection was used effectively by Martin and Matson (1978) to reduce disruptive vocalisation in retarded adults. Azrin et al. (1973, 1974) used it as a component in dry bed training of children with enuresis. If the bed was wet, the child was made to engage in cleanliness training (changing of clothes) and positive practice (behaviour rehearsal). If he remained dry through out the night, he was reinforced. Overcorrection was used extensively to reduce stereotyped behaviour. Comparing the effects of positive overcorrection with other behavioural procedures (such as punishment by slap, differential reinforcement of other behaviours (i.e. for not engaging in stereotyped behaviour), Foxx and Azrin (1973a) concluded that it was the only procedure that maintained the stereotyped behaviour. Verbal reprimand in conjunction with an intermittent application of overcorrection procedure maintained the behaviour at reduced levels. These findings were confirmed by other investigators (e.g. Azrin et al. 1973; Epstein et al. 1974; Harris and Wolchik 1979; Herendeen et al. 1974). This procedure was used to eliminate a wide range of other behaviours such as encopresis (Butler 1977), coprophagy (Foxx and Martin 1975), self-injury (Azrin et al. 1975; Freeman et al. 1975; Harris and Romanczyk 1976; Kelley and Drabman 1977a), vomiting (Azrin and Wesolowski 1975a; Ducker and Sey 1977; Marholin et al. 1980), public disrobing (Foxx 1976b), nervous habits and tics (Azrin and Nunn 1973).

Reviewing the research literature on overcorrection, Axelord et al. (1978) concluded that its side effects are yet to be critically examined. The importance of maintaining the topographies, that is the similarities between the responses and their consequences in overcorrection, is unclear. Similarly, the parameters of administering maximum effective overcorrection procedures, as for instance, the duration of overcorrection is not yet known. While conducting positive practice training, the therapist is required to be vigilant to see that the rehearsal to success does not acquire a noxious valence due to either its undue repetition or elaboration. It should occur spontaneously whenever an undesirable behaviour occurs. In future, the procedure may serve to explicitly relate to punishment. Although it is an effective procedure, its use may be restricted because of the demand on the therapist's time and energy. In spite of its effectiveness, several researchers have started questioning the rationale and procedural components of overcorrection (Doke and Epstein 1975; Forehand and Baumeister 1976). Overcorrection is a robust package that can be very effective in elimination of behaviour. At the same time, its acceptability for the individual client has to be carefully assessed. In some cases, clients have resisted overcorrection to such an extent that it had to be abandoned (e.g. Kelley and Drabman 1977; Webster and Azrin 1973). There is need of careful training of the practitioners too in administration of this technique to prevent its abuse.

11

Exposure Procedures

E xposure procedures are used to reduce undesirable behaviours, particularly conditioned avoidance responses such as phobias, obsessions, and compulsions by exposing the client to the stimuli that provoke such responses. Three principal procedures of exposure are used by behaviour therapists such as: (i) flooding, (ii) implosion, and (iii) aversion relief. These are also called anxiety-induction procedures. Systematic desensitisation is considered as a variant of exposure technique, although it does not fit entirely into the approach. Relaxation training is used as a major component in the systematic desensitisation procedure. Anxiety-inducing component, if any, is minimal.

FLOODING

The term 'flooding' was first used by Polin (1959) while reporting on the effects of exposure to anxiety-provoking stimuli and physical suppression of anxiety-motivated locomotor response on avoidance behaviour in animals. The method is also called response prevention. It involves therapist-controlled prolonged exposure to anxiety-provoking conditioned stimuli (CS) simultaneously blocking the individual's chance of escape and avoidance. It helps him to habituate to the anxiety-provoking conditioned stimuli. In a natural setting, instrumental responses such as running away from the situation help in relieving the individual from the stress. The responses that occur prior to it may include instrumental and autonomic responses such as crying, increased palpitation, sweating, fainting, repetitive washing, cleaning, checking and so on. When these responses are frequently associated with a feeling of relief, they are negatively reinforced. This is how many phobic, anxious, obsessive or compulsive responses are maintained over time. Literally, 'We are afraid as we run away from the situation.' In order to eliminate fear, we must encounter the fear-provoking stimulus. Lack of opportunity to do so 'incubates' the 'neurotic' response. The response continues to be negatively reinforced.

During flooding, the therapist presents a conditioned stimulus (e.g. dog) that usually elicits a strongly conditioned emotional response (fear) without being followed by the unconditional stimuli (e.g. physical injury or pain due to dog bite). Prolonged exposure to the stimulus (dog) extinguishes the avoidance response (fear). By preventing avoidance behaviour in presence of the anxiety-provoking stimulus, extinction is allowed to occur at a faster rate. Flooding may involve actual exposure to the real-life situations (flooding *in vivo*) through films, or computer-generated images (virtual reality therapy) or they could even be imaginary.

Flooding and Systematic Desensitisation

Although both systematic desensitisation and flooding procedures are classified under exposure-based treatment methods (Kazdin 2001), in the former method, the client is trained to be deeply relaxed, then the acquired relaxation is paired with the anxiety-provoking stimulus gradually and step by step; whereas in flooding, the client is 'flooded' with the anxiety-provoking stimulus until the avoidance response habituates. There is considerable evidence that response blocking is an effective method of speeding up the extinction of avoidance response (e.g. Baum 1966, 1970; Black 1958). Thus, slow extinction of avoidance response (as it is done in systematic desensitisation), is not seen in flooding. However, reviewing a number of studies comparing flooding and systematic desensitisation, Morganstern (1973) observed that both the procedures are equally effective. Occasionally when systematic desensitisation is not effective, flooding may successfully reduce avoidance response.

Yule et al. (1974) demonstrated the case of an 11-year-old boy who was afraid of a number of events such as loud noise of a balloon bursting, guns, motorcycles and so on. Several weeks of systematic desensitisation could not bring a change in the behaviour. At last, flooding was used. The procedure was as follows: In the first session, the child along with the therapist entered into a room full of balloons. The mere sight of balloon made the child anxious and he started crying when the therapist started breaking them one after another. He then persuaded the child, too, to break the balloons with his legs, and then with his hands. Initially, the therapist covered his (child's) ears with hands. Like this, the child was made to burst several dozens of balloons. At the beginning of the second session, he was still anxious, but after bursting another hundreds of balloons, he seemed to enjoy it. Finally, he had no fear of loud noises. A 25-months follow-up study revealed complete extinction of fear of loud noise.

Meyer et al. (1975) reported the case of an obsessive woman who used to engage in elaborate washing rituals after the death of her husband. She used to wash all objects 'contaminated' with death. The *in vivo* flooding technique used to treat this case included touching a dead body in the hospital mortuary in presence of the therapist. Turner et al. (1994) successfully used a combination of *in vivo* flooding in treatment of social phobias. People suffering from social phobia often report physiological symptoms like increased heartbeat, trembling or sweating in social situations that others do not find disturbing. The authors compared the effects of three treatment conditions: (i) flooding therapy, (ii) drug (atenol) therapy, and (iii) placebo (where the clients consumed tablets thought to be atenol). All were exposed to three months each of these treatments. The clients were assessed through psychological tests measuring anxiety and through verbal interaction, where they were asked to speak to an audience of three persons. Flooding was found to be more effective than drug or placebo conditions. The gain from the treatment was maintained in six months follow-up.

Operationally, there is a subtle difference between *in vivo* flooding and *in vivo* exposure. They are similar except that the *in vivo* exposure can be conducted on a graduated or hierarchical basis and not desired to maximise the fear/anxiety reaction, whereas flooding always aims at maximising these responses in order to extinguish them faster.

Conducting a long series of studies on confronting real life exposures in phobic and obsessive compulsive disorders, Marks (1981) suggested that anxiety disorders are not necessarily caused by conditioning. Instead, he described the fear situation as an 'evoking stimulus' (ES) and the avoidance behaviour that follows (e.g. phobic or compulsive response) as 'evoking response' (ER). In flooding exposure *in vivo*, the therapist's task is to identify the ES and present it until the ER is reduced. Stronger the evoking stimulus, longer would be the required duration of exposure to extinguish the response. The relationship between stimulus intensity and stimulus duration in flooding will determine whether it will be sensitising or desensitising (Reiss, 1980). However, Yule and his associates cautioned that if the flooding session is terminated prematurely, it might even increase the phobic response. Indeed Staub (1968) reported some similar cases where fears worsened after a short duration of flooding. Systematic desensitisation is considered as a rather pleasant procedure; therefore, it is more popular. It does not allow the person to experience high degree of anxiety/fear, whereas flooding does. Therefore, Mazur (1986) even stated that there is little justification for using flooding. This may be an over generalised view of the technique. In many situations, flooding is found to be more effective than imaginary desensitisation (Marshall et al. 1977). On the other hand, there are real life situations (e.g. natural disaster, accidents, rape or a terrorist attack) that cannot be simulated to create a situation for flooding *in vivo*. Thus, there are limitations and advantages of both the procedures.

Regardless of which theory best explains this phenomenon, flooding and exposure *in vivo* have been used by behaviour therapists successfully for treatment of a number of disorders including phobias (Jones 1924; Kandel et al. 1977; Kolko 1984; Yule et al. 1974), anxiety disorders (Girodo 1974), obsessive-compulsive disorder (Hackmann and McLean 1975; Levy and Meyer 1971; Meyer et al. 1975; Rachman et al. 1873; Rainey 1972), children's agitated depression (Hannie and Adams 1974); somatic complaints (Stambaugh 1977) and psychogenic urinary retention (Glasgow 1975; Lamontagne and Marks 1973).

Flooding is not a fixed technique but there are different parameters involved it. When a client is not able to tolerate extremely intense stimulation, the therapist is required to present the stimuli in a graded manner. This method is called graded exposure. One has to proceed in short hierarchies, depicting smaller level of anxiety (Borden 1992). Failure to modify the procedure by downgrading the level of anxiety through limited or graded exposure may lead the client to drop out. The therapist should also be careful to see that the threatening stimulus (CS) is not accompanied by unpleasant stimuli (US) like pain or injury.

Flooding may also involve a wide range of allied procedures. Sinha and Jalan (2001) successfully used a combined method that included relaxation, exposure and cognitive restructuring in the treatment of social phobia. Recently, Abramowitz et al. (2002) treated obsessive-compulsive disorders in 14 males and 14 females using exposure and ritual prevention. The therapists were asked to rate the treatment compliance of these clients. Results showed that understanding of the treatment rationale and compliance with in-session and homework exposure instruction were more closely linked with the treatment outcome, than with ritual prevention and self-monitoring.

Is flooding a safe method of response elimination? This is an important question. For that matter, acceptability of any form of therapy depends on the safety of the client under treatment. Exposure to the fearful situations in real life may have serious side effects. This may perhaps even worsen the client's condition. However, a survey conducted by Shipley and Boudewyns (1980), negative outcomes were only in nine out of 3500 cases. Thus, most therapists consider the procedure to be quite safe. The second question, which is often asked is that whether it is necessary for a therapist to accompany the client. Research findings reveal that presence of the therapist during flooding does not enhance its effectiveness (Al-Khubaisy et al. 1992). In spite of controversies, flooding has been used successfully in many clinical conditions.

IMPLOSION

Implosion or implosive therapy is a variant of flooding but it takes place at the imaginary level. The technique was developed by Thomas Stampfl (Hogan 1968; Stampfl 1966, 1970; Stampfl and Levis 1967). It involves prolonged exposure of the client to relevant negative fantasies connected with an anxiety-provoking event. The therapist's task is to describe the scenes in an involved and dramatic manner repeatedly with variation in order to arouse maximal anxiety, maintaining it almost at an intolerable level, so that the stress/anxiety caused by it dissipates. The scenes are usually unrealistic, exaggerated or physically damaging events, that are unlikely to happen in real life (Morganstern 1973; Stampfl and Levis 1967). For instance, a snake phobic client is asked to imagine a snake coiling around his body and starting to bite his finger. He is trying to put his finger out, feeling the fangs going right down into the finger. The terrible pain is spreading throughout the shoulder and the body, and blood dripping out of his finger. At the next stage, the animal begins to attack his face and other vital organs of the body. The therapist may also assist the client in doing so, instead of directly being engaged in description of the scenes. It is based on the hypothesis that neurotic and avoidance responses are perpetuated because they reduce anxiety. Stampfl theorised that the cues from early traumatic experiences caused by punishment, rejection, deprivation, or humiliation are retained throughout the lifetime of an individual. Everything associated with these events tends to elicit anxiety. These 'neurotic' behaviours can be treated by re-creating the original trauma, or something quite similar to it in the absence of real punishment, deprivation or rejection. If intense emotional reactions are made to occur in absence of primary reinforcement, extinction of neurotic behaviour perpetuated by anxiety would occur (Hogan 1968). While explaining implosion, Stampfl combined psychodynamic principles with behaviour therapy. The unique aspect of this therapy is that the client avoids not only the real situations or objects but also the thoughts and ideas concerning the event. Implosion is useful in changing the catastrophic ideas concerning an anxiety-provoking stimulus directly.

Implosion differs from flooding in that in flooding, the client is exposed to the fear-provoking stimuli either in real life or in imagination, whereas in implosion these scenes are presented verbally in an exaggerated and dramatic manner. The descriptions are rather unrealistic. The length of imagining anxiety-provoking scenes may be upto two or more hours, although 40 to 60 minutes sessions are more common (Marks 1972).

Research does not indicate that implosion therapy is better than systematic desensitisation (Morganstern 1973, 1974). Inclusion of implosion like material in flooding either has no effect or the outcome of it is poor (Wilson 1982). Looking at these findings, some authors do not recommend the use of implosive therapy in clinical practice (e.g. Martin and Pear 1992).

AVERSION RELIEF

Aversion relief is an avoidance learning method in which the individual is required to perform a response to avoid punishment. The response is generally the one which is desirable. For instance, in laboratory setting, an individual is continuously exposed to aversive stimulation like a mild electric shock or painful imagery until he/she actively engages in some response to avoid it. A 'deviant stimulus' may occur prior to either the aversive stimulation or following such stimulation. In order to terminate it, he switches on to a 'relief stimulus'. For instance, an alcoholic may be administered a low-level shock in presence of a preferred brand of alcohol (deviant stimulus), until he/she chooses to switch over to a relief stimulus such as pleasant slides of nutritious food, a soft drink or a relaxing scene. In case of a homosexual client, he is administered the deviant stimuli consisting of those homosexual stimuli, which elicit sexual arousal. The aversive stimulation terminates as soon as the client switches over to either a neutral or heterosexual stimulus. Kazdin (1978) viewed aversion relief as a special case of escape training in which escape is associated with a particular stimulus.

In one of the earliest studies, Thorpe et al. (1964) provided a detailed description of the use of aversion relief method in case of homosexuals. The treatment combined both aversion therapy and aversion relief methods (i.e. relief from electric shock). One client reported that his reaction to homosexuals changed from pleasure to 'aggression and disgust'. This method also brought substantial cognitive changes in the clients. Attitude towards women, which was assessed through the 'Osgood Semantic Differential Test', also changed. The client started considering women as desirable 'sexual partners'. Another potent homosexual reported that his thoughts of homosexuality had become 'frightening and sickening'. He preferred to spend more time on heterosexual fantasies. Still another client reported about disappearance of motorcycle fetish too. Apart from aversion therapy and aversion relief, the authors also asked the clients to masturbate to heterosexual fantasies to enhance the treatment effect. Although the treatment was successful, it was difficult to establish which aspect of this treatment programme was effective in behaviour change.

12

Relaxation and Systematic Desensitisation

RELAXATION

A wide range of distressing behaviours such as anxiety, fears, phobias, aggression and psychosomatic disorders are caused by maladaptive learning that triggers undesirable autonomic arousal. These responses can be unlearned effectively through acquisition of antagonistic responses generally labelled as relaxation response. Relaxation training is a self-control procedure that requires the client to develop a set of responses to modify autonomic arousal. Apart from mental and physical relaxation, the individual develops a feeling of control and starts assuming responsibility for management of his life and health (Beech et al. 1982). Different forms of relaxation techniques have been used by behaviour therapists. Edmund Jacobson's progressive muscle relaxation (JPMR) technique is one of the most commonly used techniques.

In his classic book *Progressive Relaxation,* Jacobson (1938) explained that an individual experiences anxiety when there is a marked degree of muscular tension. Conversely, exercises that reduce muscular tension would reduce anxiety. This technique involves successive flexing and relaxing of voluntary muscles. The individual experiences a very marked reduction in anxiety. The progressive relaxation technique begins with alternately flexing and relaxing the muscles to appreciate the difference between relaxed and tense muscles. Next, the client is asked to shake his arms and let them flop beside the body; then to relax the shoulders, he is asked to slowly roll them up and down. Then it proceeds to the neck, forehead, eyes, mouth, chest, abdomen, thighs, calf muscles, feet, toes, and at last, the entire body until the client is completely relaxed.

Cue-controlled relaxation is an anxiety reduction technique based on self-control. It involves two components: (i) deep muscle relaxation training, and (ii) establishing a conditioned stimulus as a cue for relaxation. This can be accomplished by repeated use of a cue word like 'relax', 'quiet' or any word associated with deep relaxing experience.

Guided somato-psychic relaxation was another technique of relaxation, which was developed by Sreedhar (1996). The method consisted of a brief rehearsal of physical relaxation and mental relaxation. The total duration of the session is about 30 minutes. It was found to be effective in reducing blood pressure, both systolic and diastolic pulse rate, improving the quality of sleep, anxiety, depression mania, inferiority feelings and paranoia (Anjana and Sreedhar 2000).

Vipassana is one of the most ancient techniques of relaxation. It is a concentrative form of meditation. Purohit and Chowdhary (1999) used it in a group setting with 106 subjects. Pre- and post-Vipassana measures included co-dependence and self-rated anxiety. Co-dependence means the extent to which the individuals organise their lives, decision-making, perception, beliefs and values around something (Brown 1988). Comparison of scores revealed that both Indian as well as foreign clients benefited from Vipassana. However, there was very little change in the co-dependence scores of the foreign participants. This was attributed to differences in cultural beliefs.

Rangaswami's (1990) deep relaxation training as an adjunct to Anger Control Training (Feindler and Ecton 1986; Feindler et al. 1984) was used for a child who exhibited uncontrolled aggression, quarrelling with children in school and neighbourhood. The client was treated in 15 sessions spread over four weeks time, each session lasting for about an hour. The post-treatment assessment indicated a significant decrease in self-destructive tendencies, conflict with parents, regressive anxiety, and fighting and isolation behaviour. Jacobson's progressive relaxation technique was also used along with lifestyle modifications such as, developing positive attitude and thinking, cessation of brooding, morning exercise, deep breathing and break from monotonous work for 20 students suffering from various stress-related problems (e.g. obsessive brooding, insomnia, stammering and somatoform disorders). The therapy could decrease these problems significantly along with a decrease in the GSR activity. Follow-up did not reveal any relapse.

Singh and Kaushik (2000) taking an across-subject design attempted to compare the effects of the shortened version of deep muscle relaxation (Phillips and Judd 1978), mindfulness meditation technique used by Kabat-Zinn (1990), and cognitive therapy that focused on corrective self-talk method (Meichenbaum and Cameron 1973) in enhancing coping skills of three middle-aged women at the risk of depression. Results revealed that relaxation and cognitive therapy reduced their problems to some extent but meditation was found to be the most effective among all techniques. In order to examine the cognitive effects of relaxation and other related techniques, Nathawat and Kumar (1999) exposed 40 subjects, 10 in each group, to one of these treatments: JPMR and transcendental meditation. All subjects were assessed on their perceptions of life situations, satisfaction with life, positive and negative affects, depression, hostility and aggression. After exposure to 10 sessions of therapy, post-treatment evaluation revealed that there were significant cognitive changes. Negative mental health measures such as negative affect, depression, hostility and aggressive tendency declined, whereas positive mental health measures increased significantly in all the experimental groups as compared to a control group. The psychobiological change that takes place under Jacobson's progressive muscle relaxation was studied by Chinnian et al. (1975) on 11 subjects. The results revealed significant reduction in pulse pressure and rate of respiration.

In one of the early applications of relaxation technique, Kaliapan and Murthy (1970) demonstrated its effects in tension headache. In a study of Jacobson's progressive relaxation technique with 21 psychogenic headache cases, Kumaraiah and Murthy (1975a) reported improvement in 19 cases. Kaliappan and Murthy (1973) used a modification of Yate's procedure and standard procedure of JPMR in the treatment of a case with tics and headache. Three and half years of follow-up revealed maintenance of the treatment effects. Mishra (1974) used JPMR for controlling reflex epileptic seizure such as hot water epilepsy and acoustic epilepsy. With other techniques, like assertive training and aversion, relaxation training was used for the treatment of addiction (Kumaraiah 1979b). Relaxation technique was used along with (electromyograph) EMG biofeedback for treatment of tension headache (Kumaraiah 1980). Bhargava (1983) also successfully used JPMR along with assertive training in case of headache in a 25-year-old male. In obstetrical and gynaecological problems also, behaviour therapy has been used. Mathur, Sharma and Likhari (1983) studied 60 cases of spasmodic dysamenorrhea. 30 of them were administered progressive muscle relaxation and 30 acted as the control group. Pre- and post-treatment measures revealed significant reduction of pain in the experimental group. Effects of relaxation on premenstrual psychological variables were studied by Mohan and Chopra (1985). The investigators observed significant reduction in neuroticism and anxiety scores. Singh (1986, 1989) treated a case of abdominal pain and functional fit using behaviour therapy techniques. Prasad and Sitholey (1988) also reported successful use of behaviour therapy in treatment of conduct disorder of a retarded child. Cognitive-behaviour therapy started appearing in 1990s. Rangaswami (1995) conducted one of the earliest intervention studies on panic disorder. After that, there has been an upsurge of interest in the application of cognitive-behaviour therapy for various conditions. Suvadarshani (1994) used JPMR and cognitive restructuring in order to reduce premenstrual tension. There is an extensive use of relaxation either as an independent technique or as an adjunct in a wide variety of other behavioural disorders like insomnia (Reynolds et al. 1984), duodenal ulcer (Thankachan 1993), anxiety, insomnia, fear, pain, and indigestion in HIV patients (Prachi 1996), and writer's cramp (Rangaswami 1982).

SYSTEMATIC DESENSITISATION

Many maladaptive responses learned due to prior conditioning with aversive events can be effectively eliminated by developing antagonistic responses. The process is termed as counter-conditioning or reciprocal inhibition. Wolpe (1958) names this technique as systematic desensitisation. In 1924, Watson explicitly endorsed the idea that, for decreasing the maladaptive response (e.g. fear), the individual should be brought into contact with the fear-provoking stimulus and associated with a 'rival' stimulus that does not elicit fearful response. During the same year, Jones (1924a and 1924b) demonstrated the usefulness of this procedure with a 3-year-old boy, Peter, who was afraid of rabbits. The laboratory procedure included the following steps:

1. Rabbit anywhere in the room in a cage causes fear reaction
2. Rabbit 12 feet away in cage tolerated
3. Rabbit 4 feet away in cage tolerated
4. Rabbit 3 feet away in cage tolerate
5. Rabbit close in the cage tolerated

6. Rabbit free in the room tolerated
7. Rabbit touched when experimenter holds it
8. Rabbit touched when free in the room
9. Rabbit defied by spitting at it, throwing things at it, imitating it
10. Rabbit allowed to tray on high chair
11. Squats in defenseless position beside rabbit
12. Helps experimenter to carry rabbit to its cage
13. Holds rabbit on the lap
14. Stays alone in the room with rabbit
15. Allows rabbit in play-pen with him
16. Fondles rabbit affectionately
17. Lets rabbit nibble his fingers (Jones 1924b, 310–11).

However, this procedure could not be fully adopted with Peter as he discontinued the treatment for about two months and perhaps encountered a large dog in the mean time. The procedure was made more direct and objective by using food as a rival stimulus to reduce fear. Jones stated, 'Through presence of pleasant stimulus, whenever the rabbit was shown, the fear was eliminated in favour of positive practice' (Jones 1924b: 313).

In 1958, Joseph Wolpe developed it more systematically as a clinical technique of counter-conditioning to use it for treating anxiety. He called it systematic desensitisation (SD). Counter-conditioning was the basic operational concept underlying SD. It is defined as the use of learning procedure to substitute one type of response for another. Systematic desensitisation attempts to substitute relaxation for anxiety. Although anxiety is one of the numerous reactions to experimental neurosis and a major component, there are other reactions, too, like aggression, inactivity, stupor, stereotyped movement, psychosomatic disorder, or displacement of existing conditioned response. Wolpe considered behaviour as neurotic when it is maladaptive and acquired through learning. Over excitation of the nervous system can produce maladaptive behaviour. In systematic desensitisation, the therapist attempts to present one element of stimulus to fear under conditions where an alternative response to fear is being evoked. This is what roughly resembles 'transference' in psychoanalytic approach.

THEORETICAL BASIS

Reciprocal Inhibition Theory

Wolpe explained SD through the concept of reciprocal inhibition. The term was first introduced by Charles Sherrington (1906) who intended the inhibition of one spinal reflex by another. Wolpe extended this concept to clinical conditions and beyond its original definitions. He stated the general principles of reciprocal inhibition in the following words, 'if a response antagonistic to anxiety can be made to occur in presence of anxiety-provoking stimuli, so that it is accompanied by a complete or partial suppression of the anxiety responses, the bond between these stimuli and the anxiety responses will be weakened' (Wolpe 1958: 71). He assumed that most neurotic patterns are fundamentally conditioned anxiety responses and attempted to train the clients to remain calm and relaxed in situations that formerly produced anxiety. Thus neurotic responses declined, as the autonomic effects that accompanied deep relaxation were diametrically opposed to those characteristics of anxiety (Wolpe 1969: 96). In laboratory setting, Wolpe produced neurotic responses in cats either by presenting shock alone or in conjunction with presence of food, while the cat approached the food. The neurotic responses included symptoms like resistance to be placed in the cage, refusal to eat even after 1–3 days of starvation. Thereafter, he attempted to reduce these anxiety responses by feeding the animal in rooms resembling the original room in which the neurotic behaviours were introduced. Once the animal ate in the given room it was given several opportunities to eat until all signs of anxiety decreased in that room. Then it was successively placed in more similar rooms until the anxiety was eliminated. This was continued until the neurotic responses were fully eliminated in the original room that included the same. In human subjects, the relaxation component of systematic desensitisation produces muscular relaxation, which is incompatible with the state of anxiety triggered by anxiety or fear provoking stimulus. The reinforcement due to reciprocal inhibition leads to conditioned inhibition.

Habituation Theory

The response decrement in systematic desensitisation was explained by Lader and Wing (1966) through a habituation theory. This was subsequently elaborated by Lader and Mathew (1968) and reformulated by Watts (1971, 1973 and 1979). Habituation is defined as the waning of a response to a stimulus due to its repeated presentation. It applies only to unconditional responses. The decremental processes of anxiety that operate in desensitisation are more closely analogous to those found in habituation, because both the novel stimuli that elicit orienting responses and the stimuli that have been paired with aversive stimuli and arouse anxiety, activate the 'behavioural inhibition system' (Gray 1975, 1976). This system produces an inhibition of ongoing behaviour and increases arousal. This system is particularly active in neurotic introverts (Nicholson and Gray 1972). Reformulation of this theory by Lader and Mathew (1968), and Lader and Wing (1966) is called the 'maximal habituation theory'. It postulated that the rate of observed reduction in the magnitude of fear or anxiety response to aversive stimulus is a habituation process. Thus, habituation process is maximised by aspects of the procedure (notably relaxation) that lowers the central arousal. This can be experimentally measured by galvanic skin response (GSR) changes. Lader and Mathew (1968) viewed that relaxation is instrumental in lowering the central arousal that increases the rate of response decrement. Physiologically, deep muscle relaxation excites the parasympathetic division of the autonomic nervous system, whereas the sympathetic division of the nervous system is involved in anxiety and phobic responses. Thus, excitation of parasympathetic nervous system has automatic inhibitory effect on the sympathetic division. This state of anxiety inhibition is conditioned to each step of the hierarchy scenes in graded manner, so that the client learns to relax instead of getting anxious. In this sense, it is a form of 'counter-conditioning'. The 'dual-process habituation theory' was proposed by some authors (Groves and Thompson 1970; Thompson et al. 1973). They stated that the observed response decrement is the summation of two inferred processes: habituation and sensitisation. Watts (1979) stated that during the imagery and actual exposure phase of systematic desensitisation, there is initial sensitisation (i.e. incremental response) to specific phobic stimuli in the hierarchy, which is accompanied by habituation. The combination of short presentation of low intensity stimuli and relaxation can apparently prevent the development of sensitisation and therefore appear to facilitate response decrement.

Cognitive Theory

Ellis (1962) stated that systematic desensitisation discourages the client from engaging in self-verbalisations that lead to anxiety. Bandura (1977) however, observed that lowering of physiological arousal in presence of anxiety-provoking stimulus enhances the client's belief that he/she can cope with the phobic situation. Weitzman (1967) reinterpreted the process in which SD presumably achieves its effects. He explained that during the course of SD, the aversive scenes presented by the therapist get transformed and elaborated by the clients into imaginal content not in line with the usual fearful or anxiety-provoking ones, leading to newer forms of adaptive responses. Thus the changes are derived primarily from the associative material that are aroused and eventually integrated into the 'ego complex' ego. Thus, active cognitive restructuring is involved in the process of desensitisation. However, researches have revealed that when clients modify presented scenes by either transforming them into less threatening events or by introducing unintended anxiety-provoking elements, they are least likely to benefit from desensitisation (Lazovik and Lang 1960; Weinberg and Zaslove 1963). The above findings suggest that the associative process invoked by Weitzman can better account for failures of desensitisation therapy than its success (Bandura 1971). On the other hand, experiments conducted by Strahley (1966) indicated that much better outcomes were shown when the method was based on real life exposures to aversive stimuli.

METHOD

Systematic desensitisation involves three phases of training: (a) relaxation training, (b) construction of hierarchies, and (c) desensitisation procedure.

a. Relaxation Training

During relaxation training, the client is trained to learn to relax himself by using any of the relaxation procedures. Various methods of relaxation training are used, depending on the suitability for the client and expertise of the therapist. However, JPMR technique is generally used. The other relaxation techniques include meditation, yoga, hypnosis and drugs (Bandura 1969; Brady 1967). This is done in about the first six sessions.

b. Construction of Hierarchy

With relaxation training, the client is given 'home-work' to prepare a hierarchy of scenes in descending order, at the top of which remains the most anxiety arousing scene and at the bottom, the least anxiety-provoking (neutral) scene. Here, hierarchy of scenes refers to a graded series of events or situations that a client has to imagine during relaxation. Therefore, the scenes must be as realistic as possible, with vivid details of the scene which are relevant to the concrete situations that the client either has experienced or expects to experience. The extent to which a scene or an actual event evokes distress to a client is called subjective unit of distress (SUD). The hierarchy of events or scenes is marked according to the level of distress they generate in the client. A hierarchy of events can be prepared by asking the clients to rate each item. When a client experiences a wide range of phobias for different things, each of them can also be graded sequentially as per the degree of distress involved.

The typical 'home-work' assignment requires the client to: (i) prepare index cards depicting the situation, (ii) arrange them initially in terms of the levels of distress under broad categories like 'mild', 'moderate', 'severe' or 'profound' levels of anxiety, and (iii) rearrange them in terms of the subjective units of distress. The therapist assists the client to provide all necessary details about each event, so that he can clearly visualise them while relaxing. The total number of scenes will depend on the intensity of the problem. Marquis and Morgan (1969) suggested that in most cases 10 items are sufficient. Additional items may be introduced during the desensitisation phase if the hierarchy fails to cover the entire spectrum of the phobia. There may be possible inconsistencies in the construction of hierarchy. The client may be again asked to re-rate the same anxiety arousing event(s) in the hierarchy by being independent of the previous rating. Paul (1969b) made a distinction between thematic and spatial-temporal hierarchies. The client may be asked to visualise themes of similar events. For example, if one has irrational fear for spiders, then he/she may be asked to visualise other insects also that cause anxiety and construct a hierarchy with common themes.

c. Desensitisation Procedure

Desensitisation training is introduced only after the client has mastered the act of relaxation. While the client relaxes completely in a comfortable chair or couch with his eyes closed, the therapist directs him to imagine and experience each situation in the hierarchy from the pleasant or neutral to the most anxiety-provoking one in a graded manner. Initially, the lowest scene in the hierarchy is presented; if the client relaxes well, the therapist moves progressively up to the next item. The scene at which the client experiences anxiety is indicated by raising his index finger and the treatment is discontinued and restarted with the next below item. It continues until the client remains relaxed and vividly imagines the scene.

Lal et al. (1976) treated a 35-year-old stuttering client with 22 sessions of desen-sitisation. The patient showed 75 per cent improvement in the symptoms. The reciprocal inhibition technique was used by Majumder (1975) for treatment of pedagophobia in a 14-year-old adolescent. Rangaswami (1982) used the technique in treatment of writer's cramp. The hierarchy included steps like (i) drawing with a brush, (ii) writing alphabets using a chalk, (iii) writing on the writer's cramp apparatus, (iv) writing on a blackboard, (v) writing on a paper with felt pen, and finally, (vi) writing with the usual pen. The method was successful in controlling writer's cramp. The same author (Rangaswami 1983) also used three weeks systematic desensitisation programme *in vivo* to treat school phobia of an 8-year-old child. Mishra et al. (1970); Shantha et al. (1972), and Kumaraiah and Murthy (1975c) reported successful use of systematic desensitisation in phobias. In a case of washing compulsion in a female, Kumaraiah and Murthy (1975) used systematic desensitisation both *in vivo* and *in vitro* to eliminate anxiety for contamination. After 27 sessions, the duration of washing compulsion reduced from 90 to four minutes. Four months of follow-up study revealed maintenance of the treatment gains. In another study, Chopra (1974) used the technique successfully in four cases with obsessive-compulsive neurosis. The group included one male and three females. Their ages were 20, 26, 49 and 41 years. He also used thought-stopping in three out of the four cases and suggested that in acute cases of recent onset where anxiety is still dominant, the technique was effective. However, in cases with long standing obsessive compulsive symptoms, direct intervention in target behaviour could be more effective than those of anxiety-reduction techniques alone. The obsessive behaviour was viewed largely as a conditioned avoidance response. After the 1970s, the progress in behaviour therapy in India was quite remarkable. Relaxation techniques were used successfully to cure drug addiction (Kumaraiah 1979). Mehta and Chawla (1985) used the technique in the successful treatment of asthma.

13

Restricted Environmental Stimulation Technique

For treatment of psychological problems as well as enhancement of mental abilities, restricting environmental stimulation methods have been practised for ages in various forms, especially as a part of religious rituals. Practice of self-isolation, self-induced social detachment and *samadhi* are some of the examples. However, these procedures of self-control through sensory and cognitive isolation have attracted scientific attention very recently. Restricted environmental stimulation technique (REST) is one such method, which was introduced to the scientific community by Suedfeld in 1980. Now, its application has expanded remarkably as a method of treatment of a variety of behavioural disorders. REST is a technique that requires the client to place himself in an environment of greatly reduced stimulation for a specified time, varying between two days to two weeks.

THE TECHNIQUE

REST is performed in a number of ways. A few of them are: (i) being left alone in a room, sitting alone facing a blank wall, lying on a soft bed, sitting on a couch in isolation, observing complete social isolation in a semi-furnished room, or (ii) floating the body in a tank of buoyant water kept at skin surface temperature, to the consistency of a gel, alone in a dark and soundproof room. The second variety of REST is called 'floatation REST'. The fundamental procedure of all REST techniques involves development of a stimulus hunger by placing a subject in a chamber where the sound is attenuated, tactile stimulation is reduced, and visual stimulation is eliminated. The subject is instructed to limit his movement to that required for maintaining comfort. Barabasz et al. (1985) used an isolation tank specially made for REST. The subjects were seated in a fixed recliner with eyes closed and sound attenuated. Low-level white noise was produced through padded earphones to prevent other distracting sounds.

The floatation REST environment is created usually in a closed dark tank that can hold about 450 litres of filtered water kept at skin temperature (94° F). The tank and room air temperature is kept at 86° F. It is saturated with 850 pounds of magnesium sulphate. It allows the subject to float one-third of his body and most of the face above the water. The tank is placed in a quiet dark room. An earplug is used by the subject to prevent water from entering the ears. The duration for initial floatation is usually longer (about 150 minutes) than the subsequent sessions (60 minutes) (Fine, Bruno and Nestor 1985). Turner and Fine (1985) used an egg-shaped fibreglass high enclosure chamber with 8' × 4' × 4' dimensions. The chamber contained a 12" deep solution of saturated Epsom salt (sp. gr. 1.28). The temperature of the solution was maintained within 94°, plus or minus 0.5° F. A waterbed heater was used for the same. Light was eliminated and the sound level was less than 10 decibels. The participants floated nude in a supine position with arms at their sides. Now-a-days ready-made floatation environments are available commercially for relaxation training.

THE RATIONALE

REST requires an environment in which excessive stimulation and information load is severely reduced in order to develop more adaptive ways of behaviour. Until the 1960s, most sensory deprivation studies were focused on the long-term effects of deprivation, which included negative cognitive and affective consequences. Systematic studies on isolation and its therapeutic use started in the late 1960s and the 1970s. Lilly (1977) suggested that people can thoroughly relax in a floatation environment, and therefore it can be used for therapeutic purposes.

Prolonged sensory deprivation creates a 'stimulus hunger' for the individual that makes him more receptive. This psychophysiological state makes him more suggestible than under normal conditions. Therefore, he is less defensive to the therapeutic intervention (Suedfeld 1982). In behavioural terms, it creates a drive state for acquisition of new and adaptive responses. Reduced physiological arousal for two to three hours creates a pleasant experience due to reduced blood pressure and pituitary-adrenal axis activity.

Behaviourally, the environment of REST may also be interpreted as a situation of learning where stimulus attenuation acts as a self- or therapist-administered punishment to eliminate maladaptive patterns of behaviour. The participant is placed under deprived stimulus situation for the behaviour that is considered inappropriate by some standard. Low general stimulation and lack of social interaction creates an unpleasant experience, making REST as a situation of punishment. It is considered as a form of non-contingent time-out from positive reinforcement. This supposedly aversive condition is deliberately chosen by people, as it is more tolerable than the distress caused by the normal environment in which they live. For some individuals, it is a reinforcing and relaxing experience that restores calmness and self-control.

For psychoanalysts, REST simulates early childhood experience (Azima et al. 1961). A similar approach is followed in 'anaclitic therapy' that attempts to facilitate a return to childhood experiences. Thus, it fosters regression. Janov (1970) provided a somewhat similar description of primal therapy too. A day or more of isolation and sensory restriction, sometimes coupled with sleeplessness and food deprivation, is a stressful experience that lets down cognitive controls. Decreased cognitive control facilitates regression. Immersion in water in a restricted environment for sometime and return to the natural environment is considered as a symbolic act of being re-born or regressive experience of return to early childhood. The situation is made to eliminate the after effects of birth trauma; REST is in a way similar to this. REST may involve dissociation or detachment from the immediate environment and reality (Hilgard 1977, 1979). Therefore, it enhances the subjects' hypnotic responsiveness (Barabasz 1980a, 1980b, 1982). When REST was used as an adjunct with behavioural self-management and smoking behaviour of the subjects were assessed after a follow-up period of six months, abstinence rate was 80 per cent.

From the angle of information processing approach, this technique has a special significance. The stimulus level that is encountered in modern society is too much to handle for some people. REST actually creates a situation where the individual is removed from such uncontrollable environmental conditions that trigger clinical symptoms. Reduction of stimulus overload helps the individual to process information in a normal way, thus eliminating many symptoms that are caused by information overload.

Restricted environmental stimulation technique can be interpreted physiologically based on 'rest principle'. It states that neural pathways that rest after firing develop stronger internal connections (Sinclair 1981). Therefore, learning gets impaired. An optimal rate of firing is required for producing the greatest increase in the strength of the pathways facilitating learning. The post-REST condition prepares the body for better responding.

Physiologically, the buoyancy of the gel-like solution used for REST provides a more supportive environment than a cushion, reclining chair or even a soft bed, and thus allows deeper muscle relaxation. The client can attend to the muscle tension better than before.

RESEARCH

Many laboratory research programmes originally conducted in the area of stimulus deprivation are now considered as the fundamental research in REST. Two such experiments were conducted by Lichstein and his associates. The first experiment (Salis and Lichstein 1979) was designed to find out if any relaxation effect would occur if the setting conditions for relaxation were created but no conventional relaxation technique was introduced. 14 volunteers were engaged in this study. They were instructed to close their eyes and refrain from body movement while reclining comfortably in a quiet and dimly lit room for 15 minutes at a stretch (a REST-like condition). The only dependent measure studied was the frontalis muscle tension. Significant reduction in muscle tension was observed during this short period.

In a second study, Lichstein, Salis, Hills and Young (1981) replicated the first study increasing the length of the session to 30 minutes. Some other measures like heart rate, skin resistance were also taken into consideration along with muscle tension. Global parasympathetic effects were levelled off in 15 minutes. The findings were in contrast to a similar experiment conducted by Meyers and Craighead (1978). It failed to reveal any such changes. The negative findings of the latter study may be attributed to the length of the session; for instance, the electrode placement in the reclining chair for a longer time.

Lichstein, from his studies concluded that optimal relaxation benefits are obtained in about 15 minutes. Possibly, some points beyond this lead to reversal of the autonomic effects. Such critical period phenomena in sensory deprivation studies were also reported by Zubek (1937). Many studies reporting idiosyncratic patterns of responses may be interpreted in the light of time of exposure to REST and the individual's history of related experience.

In a controlled study, Jacobs, Heilbronner and Stanley (1984) compared a relaxation package including progressive relaxation, breathing regulation and imagery practiced in conventional setting, and under floatation REST. Physiological indicators revealed that the relaxation in REST setting could induce better relaxation in comparison to the conventional setting, although it was presumed that the multiple sources of emotional expectancy and limited home relaxation practice had contributed to this difference.

Belinson and Forgays (1985) attempted to examine the relaxation potential of floatation isolation technique, taking both subjective and objective measures of 40 subjects (20 males and 20 females). A floatation tank placed in a dark, soundproof room was used for the purpose. The subjects were floated in the tank for up to 150 minutes, three sessions per week. Heart rates of the subjects were monitored before, during, and after floatation. In most subjects, heart rate increased before the floatation, lower during the therapy and again increased after the therapy. While the experience was generally relaxing, it was related to the individual differences in personality.

Although considerable amount of research has been conducted on REST, in attempting to identify the subject characteristics such as age, sex, occupation, hearing capacity, anxiety level, as well as introversion-extraversion that correlate with response to REST, no strong and consistent results—except a few—were found to correlate any of these variables with REST (Suedfeld 1980).

APPLICATIONS

Since the 1950s, REST has been used for treatment of different types of disorders. Prolonged periods of stimulus reduction and partial social isolation have dramatic positive effects on schizophrenics, autistic (Schechter et al. 1969), retarded, and learning disabled children (Cohen 1963; Glynn 1975; Janz 1978; Suedfeld 1980). Harris (1959) exposed some inpatient schizophrenics to a brief period of restricted stimulation over two successive days and found reduction in some of the core symptoms. Similar findings were reported by Smith, Thakurdas and Lawes (1961) and Luby et al. (1962). Luisada (1978) studied the effects of REST on phencyclidine (PCP) induced psychosis. The treatment components included darkness, silence, and social isolation. The method was found to be successful in treatment of this condition. In another case, Adams (1980) successfully used REST for treating a case of LSD induced psychosis.

Two systematic studies were conducted by Suedfeld and his associates on smoking cessation (Suedfeld et al. 1972; Suedfeld and Ikard 1974). Their research design included three conditions: REST without messages, messages without REST, and a no treatment control group. Significant reduction in smoking was found in individuals who had spent 24 hours in stimulus reduction chamber, without receiving any persuasive informational inputs about smoking. There was no significant difference between the REST–message and REST–no message groups, although both groups showed substantial decrease in smoking rate over two years of follow-up period. REST was used as an effective method of intervention in cigarette smoking by other investigators (e.g. Best and Suedfeld 1982; Christensen and DiGiusto 1982;

Suedfeld 1977; Suedfeld, Landon, Pargment and Epstein 1972). Best and Suedfeld (1982) introduced messages to the subjects in the REST environment. The messages were pertaining to smoking cessation, general heath attitudes and behaviour. Follow-up conducted after an year of this treatment indicated that 53 per cent clients were abstinent.

Suedfeld and Hare (1977) used a five hours REST for the snake phobic clients. After the session, they were asked to press a button in order to view slides of snakes. The hypothesis was that stimulus hunger would induce the subjects to expose themselves to the fear arousing stimuli instead of avoiding it. Therefore, it would be less frightening for them after REST. As observed in the clients' self-report and actual approach responses, the treatment was successful. This procedure was used to reduce blood pressure in patients suffering from hypertension (Suedfeld et al. 1982).

The role of REST in enhancing positive mental health has been reported in many studies. For instance, Antista and Jones (1975) found that university students undergoing only 45 minutes of REST sessions became less anxious and showed less discrepancy between actual and ideal selves. Many participants using floatation tanks report experiences of self-actualisation, increased creativity, improved self-esteem, and deeper and better understanding of personal problems (Lilly 1977).

In 1985, Fine and Turner used floatation REST with other modalities of training such as relaxation (with autogenic phrases and/or progressive relaxation), EMG and/or thermal biofeedback and stress-oriented psychotherapy with 15 patients (10 males and 5 females) suffering from chronic pain (eight of them were treated as outpatients and seven as inpatients). The duration of their illness ranged from three months to 16 years (mean 7.3 years). Eight of them had daily chronic low back pain, three had chronic shoulder pain, and two had chronic headache. Prior to treatment, the baseline measures of frontal/neck EMG and peripheral temperature were taken. The biofeedback sessions ranged from 6 to 36 sessions (mean 13), one hour each (the first 25 minutes of which was for EMG biofeedback and the rest for psychotherapy). These sessions were followed by floatation REST. The authors used it for two reasons; one, to enhance the relaxation experience, and second, to increase subjective sense of pain reduction. Initially, after a period of silence, ranging 10–25 minutes, tapes of autogenic phrases were played while relaxing. With the progress of therapy, audiotapes were replaced with self-recitation of autogenic phrases. Some of the clients were provided imagery to enhance the effects of relaxation. For floatation REST, the clients were required to float themselves in the artificially designed tank either nude or in bathing suits. The period of floatation was 40–60 minutes. All subjects were asked to rate the depth of their pain on a 0–6 point scale and relaxation on a scale of 0–10. Results revealed that floatation REST was more relaxing and effective in relieving chronic pain than other modalities of treatment. Eight rated themselves to be pain-free after REST; one after biofeedback and two did not become free from pain at all. The same authors (Turner and Fine 1983) and others (Jacobs, Heilbronner and Stanley 1984) have also observed that REST is physiologically as well as psychologically more relaxing than relaxation training. The lack of environmental stimulation disrupts the cognitive processes required for pain perception. In a recent study, Turner and Fine (1984) demonstrated that REST either increases the endogenous opoid production or heightens sensitivity to existing opoid levels. It brings a substantial change in the perception of pain.

CONCLUSION

REST is considered as a special form of relaxation technique by many investigators (e.g. Lichstein 1988; Borrie and Suedfeld 1980; Jacobs, Heilbronner and Stanley 1984; Suedfeld, Roy and Landon 1982) as there are many commonalities with the general relaxation procedures. In therapeutic practice, even other techniques of relaxation can be enriched by using REST as an adjunct. It has added a new dimension to our knowledge of the mechanism of relaxation. However, it will be wrong to conceptualise REST as a variant of relaxation technique alone. Its interpretation as a self-administered punishment for maladaptive responding or as a self-control technique yields fertile ground for more therapeutic research.

Psychological and physiological evidence for REST appears to be growing rapidly. However, one should not speculate therapeutic effects of stimulus deprivation alone. There are individual differences in response to therapy. It may not be a cure for certain people but certainly a valuable experience for them. Some may have to practice it throughout their lives for better mental hygiene. There is substantial literature to suggest that the environment influences our well-being and, thus, psychopathology (Forgays 1983). Light, noise, temperature, density, privacy, predictability and control are just some of them. From this perspective, REST only represents some of them (Reisenberg 1985). Enrichment of sensory experience is at another dimension in the same continuum. Many people do not require reduction in environmental stimulation in order to function at an optimal level. There are individuals who are poorly aroused in spite of adequate stimulation, due to the state of the nervous system or neurological disorders. Depression, dementia, retardation and narcolepsy are some clinical conditions in which higher levels of stimulation yield better results. For instance, morning exposure to bright light has been established as an effective therapy for seasonal and non-seasonal affective disorders (particularly depression) in mentally handicapped people (Altabet et al. 2002) and geriatric patients (Ancoli–Israel et al. 2003), including ante partum depression (Oren et al. 2002) and sleep cycle disturbance.

Reduction of environmental stimulation is the key assumption behind REST. Thus, we presume that this therapeutic procedure will be more helpful for individuals who suffer from disorders caused by over-stimulation rather than under-stimulation.

Therefore, while drawing a conclusion about the beneficial effects of REST, it is necessary to examine the opposite poles of psychopathology, too. Perhaps a unifying theory of 'environmental stimulation management' therapy can be advanced and empirically examined. This will clarify some of the conceptual issues linked with diagnosis as well as treatment by manipulating the sensory environment. This will provide a broader framework for understanding the role of sensory environment in the treatment of mental disorders.

14

Eye Movement Desensitisation Reprocessing: EMDR

E ye movement desensitisation reprocessing (EMDR) is a technique that has been used extensively and successfully in the treatment of post-traumatic stress disorders (PTSD). Although it has a therapeutic basis, both in psychodynamic and behavioural approaches, it involves cognitive reattribution and incorporates a variety of techniques, thus considered as a self-contained eclectic or multi-modal approach as well. Pioneering work on the technique was conducted by Shapiro (1989a, 1989b and 1991). Initially the technique was labelled as 'Eye movement desensitisation (EMD) only. Later on, she refined the technique and renamed it as EMDR. Shapiro's method was introduced to the behaviour therapists by Joseph Wolpe in the annual meeting of the Association for Advancement of Behaviour Therapy in 1990.

The study of therapeutic role of eye movement although has a long history, it has been put into empirical analysis very recently. Earlier, in an ingenious experiment, Antrobus and associates (Antrobus, Antrobus and Singer 1964: 251) demonstrated that spontaneous eye movements were associated with suppression of thought. They stated, '…attempt to break up a thought sequence when it is unpleasant or anxiety provoking may very well lead to a series of almost desperate rapid shifts in cognitive activity with consequent ocular motility.' The statement conversely meant that saccadic eye movements would enable the clients to break up unpleasant thoughts.

Shapiro (1998a, 1998b) proposed that in order to get relief from the traumatic memories, the client must be aware of one or more of the following: (i) an image of the memory, (ii) a negative self-statement, and (iii) the physical anxiety response. The effect is best when all these three conditions are fulfilled; although presence of any one of them would be sufficient for eye movement induced desensitisation to occur. Shapiro (2001) detailed the EMDR procedure in eight steps that include the following phases:

1. *Comprehensive history-taking and treatment planning*: In the history-taking phase, the therapist focuses on presenting complaints, history of substance abuse, family violence, legal and forensic concerns,

ego-strength, dissociative phenomena, current life situations, quality of support, secondary gains, irrational beliefs, impulse control, severity of torture and other traumatic experiences. The three essential steps involved in history-taking are identification of (i) past memories, (ii) the present stimuli that trigger disturbance, and (iii) skills and behaviours required for optimal functioning.

2. *Preparation*: In the second phase, the client is prepared for therapy. During this stage, he/she is explained the mechanism by which EMDR works. For instance, the therapist explains that traumatic events are 'locked in' in the brain in a dysfunctional manner without being processed adequately. This is due to the associated emotional states. Any reminder activates these old experiences: the memories of images, sounds, and feelings. Shapiro (1995: 120) used the following model explanation for introducing the technique:

> Often when something traumatic happens it seems to get locked in the nervous system with the original picture, sound, thoughts, feelings and so on. Since the experience is locked there, it continues to be triggered whenever a reminder comes up. It can be the basis for a lot of discomfort and sometimes a lot of negative emotions such as fear and helplessness that we cannot seem to control. These are really the emotions connected with the old experience that are being triggered. The eye-movement that we use in EMDR seems to unlock the nervous system and allows your brain to process the experience. That may be what is happening in REM or dream sleep: The eye movement may be involved in processing unconscious materials. The important thing to remember is that it is your own brain that will be doing the healing and that you are the one in control.

3. *Assessment*: At this stage, the therapist identifies the traumatic incident to be reprocessed. The basic procedural elements may include selection of images, negative and positive cognitions, emotions, and physical sensations. The anxiety level concerning the incident is assessed by using Wolpe's (1990) scale of subjective units of distress (SUDs) and a validity of cognition (VOC) scale. The former is a 10-point scale of anxiety in which '0' equals to no anxiety and '10' is the highest anxiety. The latter is a 7-point scale used to measure negative self-cognitions. It was developed by Shapiro (1989a) in order to assess the shift in self-cognition due to traumatic events and to asses the effects of therapy. On this scale, '1' means that the cognition is completely untrue and '7' means that it is completely true. The rating shows how a client feels emotionally.

Negative cognitions (NC) of the client are represented by the client's irrational, dysfunctional or maladaptive self-assessment. He is asked to say what words go best with the incident that describes the position. The client often states, 'I felt helpless', 'I was foolish' or 'I was stupid'. Some of these self-statements could be very genuine also. Like the NCs, the client may have positive cognitions as well (PC). PCs are explored by asking questions like 'What would you believe about yourself'. The PCs which reveal strong positive self-appraisal and an internal locus of control are selected. The goal is to explore the statements that instil feelings of self-worth in the client. It is assumed that appropriate validity of cognition (VOC) would enhance information processing and inappropriate ones would reduce it.

For an assessment, the client is usually asked to focus on the traumatic memory and isolate the most traumatic point; then visualise and rate himself/herself on the SUDs and VOC. He may indicate the physical locus of the symptoms as well.

4. *Desensitisation*: The treatment is conducted in a place, which should be free from distraction. The therapist ensures confidentiality of the information provided by the client. Metaphors are regularly used for developing skill of dual attention. For example, the client is told to imagine riding a train and watching the scenery go by. Such metaphors help the client in distancing him/herself from the painful

emotional experience. At the initial stage, the client is asked how he/she would like to feel and generate a new positive self-statement that reflects the desired feelings, and then asked as to how true the new statement is. Before the desensitisation starts, the therapist gathers the above materials concerning the traumatic event. Before the therapy begins the client is instructed as follows:

> What we will be doing is often a physiology check. I need to know from you exactly what is going on, with as clear feedback as possible. Sometimes things will change and sometimes they won't. I may ask you if the picture changes—sometimes it will and sometimes it won't. I may ask if something else comes up—sometimes it will and sometimes it won't. There are no 'supposed to's' in this process. So just give as accurate feedback as you can as to what is happening, without judging whether it should be happening or not. Just let whatever happens, happen (Shapiro 1989a: 213), must notice whatever type of internal material may emerge (Shapiro, Snyker and Maxfield 2002).

The client is generally asked to generate and visualise the actual scene of trauma. When there are multiple traumatic events, they are clustered around the person involved or a specific situation. Several sets of dual stimulation are provided by guiding the client to attend to the present stimuli (eye movement, tones, clinician's reassurance, present safety, etc.) while focusing on the target event.

For desensitisation, the client is asked to follow the therapist's finger movement visually, while generating the specific traumatic event. The therapist moves his/her finger back and forth, rapidly, and rhythmically within the visual field, approximately at one-foot distance from the face, for at least 24 cycles at the rate of one cycle per second across the visual field. Other stimuli like taps and tones may also be used for stimulating dual attention. For the clients who have trouble in following this approach, Shapiro suggested that the therapist's fingers may be kept to the side of the client's field of vision and be alternatively moved up and down. The movement is repeated for 12 to 24 times for one set of saccade (Gilliland and James 1998). After each set of saccade, the client is asked to blank out the scene and take a deep breath. Thereafter, he/she is again asked to bring up the noxious image and assign SUDs level to it. After two sets of saccades, if the image does not change, the therapist should enquire if anything new has emerged. In that case, the new image has to be desensitised first before tackling the old one. Periodic assessment of the image, cognition and memory are conducted to assess the degree of change induced by the therapy. Dual attention helps in improving the capacity for observation, reflecting on internal states, and insight increases the sense of self-efficacy. Reprocessing the traumatic materials, which are stored in dysfunctional manner, becomes easier.

Sometimes there may be a mismatch or incongruence between the image and its cognition; therefore, the cognition fails to change even after two sets of saccades. In this case, one or the other needs to be replaced. If the SUDs level remains high, the client may have to be asked to identify the physical location of anxiety. When the physical discomfort subsides, standard EMDR may be resumed (Shapiro 1989a, 1989b). At times, as part of free association, new memories and experiences may emerge. In order to ascertain the client's response to the question 'What do you get now?', certain things are discouraged during the sessions: (a) repeating client's statements, (b) offering interpretations, (c) engaging in conversation to elicit other information, and (d) distracting from the client's current focus. During therapy, the nature of images, feelings and emotions associated with the traumatic event may change. The impression may become less prominent, feelings may be less intense, or the quality of memory would change.

Shapiro (1995) developed an additional procedure, called 'cognitive interweavers' for clients, whose progress have been blocked due to complicated psychopathologies. The blocked pre-processing is 'jump started' by introducing certain cognitive materials.

5. *Installation*: When the SUDs level declines to 1 or 0, the client is asked to self-assess the validity of the original cognition by assigning a VOC rating. This is the stage at which positive cognitions (PCs) are paired with original noxious events in order to replace them with positive cognitions. Thus, regardless of the rating, the client is asked to visualise the original image along with the positive self-assessment and another set of saccades is introduced. When no new distressing image emerges and the VOC rating reaches 7, EMDR is discontinued.

6. *The Body Scan*: The treatment is incomplete until the physical residues associated with the original event continue. In order to assess such residues, the client is instructed to close his/her eyes, concentrate on the incident and the PCs and mentally scan the entire body. He/she is asked to report if he/she feels anything, anywhere. If such sensations are reported, another set of eye movement is introduced as it is assumed that negative sensations are linked with other ancillary targets that require reprocessing. It continues till VOC reaches up to 7 and SUDs level come down to 0.

7. *Closure*: At the end of the body scan session, the client usually expresses a sense of relaxation by saying that he/she feels very different, lighter and can do it on his/her own or that he/she is no more afraid of the incident. The therapist assures the client that the reprocessing exercise may continue after the session, in case of new thoughts, images, memories or dreams. In case he reports such events, the therapist may employ relaxation, guided imagery and see that the client goes back to his natural activities after the treatment.

8. *Re-evaluation*: This is the final stage of EMDR, where the previously targeted material is reassessed to determine whether the client needs further processing of these unpleasant memories. This decision is made by asking the client to keep a log that is maintained for recording his/her feelings. Accordingly, new targets of intervention are determined.

The standard EMDR procedure involves the past, present and future of the client. At the initial stage, the therapist deals with the past trauma, then moves on to the present fears and anxieties and finally to future activities. Teaching parenting and social skills, assertiveness training and referral for vocational evaluation are the elements of this therapy. Finally, it may deal with anticipatory anxieties, fears of failure, rejection and so on. The therapist may focus on a single traumatic event in one to three sessions each of 90 minutes duration or may deal multiple traumas in multiple sessions, clustering the similar ones.

THE PROCESS

The verbal instructions given to the client in the initial stage of treatment focuses on the traumatic memory (Foa and Kozak 1986). With clarity of visualisation and vividness of the traumatic memory, anxiety also increases until hand tracking starts. Once hand tracking continues along with eye movement, it becomes increasingly difficult to visualise and memorise the traumatic event. Moreover, cognitive appraisal shifts from negative to positive and realistic one. During hand tracking, about 20 per cent clients with PTSD show motor and verbal reactions. Some show emotional responses like crying or slapping themselves.

Speed of change in SUD that occurs during therapy is remarkably fast. Kleinknecht and Morgan (1992) reported that the SUD of 9.5 declined significantly in a single set of EMDR that was of approximately

15 seconds duration. In the second set it almost disappeared. Similarly, Vaughan et al. (1994) studied 210 clients; most of which were suffering from PTSD. They demonstrated that in 148 seconds of EMDR, the average SUD of 8.7 declined to 2.3. However, exposure to audiotape description alone takes hours to produce a comparable reduction in SUD. The marked decline in flashbacks and nightmares is reported to be the most remarkable. A stage of plateau may occur in some cases where no further reduction in anxiety may occur. One may proceed further but by focusing on the insight of the client or by providing new information about the client's response during the session.

There is a possibility that the client may misidentify some stimuli in the environment, especially when traumatic memories involve other persons; some of these feelings may be generalised to the therapist. His face may appear similar to the person involved. The environmental features considered as safe and reassuring may appear unsafe and threatening. The therapist's hand waving may be associated with the fear of attack. Headaches and other pains may be reported during the eye movement. It loses its severity as eye movement proceeds but becomes more severe, if the eye movement stops. Sensitivity to light may also increase during the session (Matthews 1992). Tracking eye movements may cause flickers and nystagmus-like motion. Slippiness may occur as a defense while working through traumatic memory, and when the client is relaxed.

THEORETICAL MODELS

Adaptive Information-processing Model

As stated earlier, Shapiro in her early writings (e.g. Shapiro 1989a) considered eye movement desen-sitisation as another method of desensitising anxiety arousing materials but after analysis of several cases, she came to the conclusion that desensitisation was simply a by-product of facilitating general information processing activity. The rationale is that there is a significant difference between the ways in which traumatic and non-traumatic stimuli are stored. Most people experiencing traumatic events are often emotionally disturbed and are therefore unable to assimilate the information and integrate the experience normally as other neutral events. The memory is stored in the state-dependent form, disturbing the affect, cognitions or somatic responses. As a result, they become resistant to further processing. The sensory elements of trauma may penetrate into awareness in the form of pathological symptoms like nightmares, flashbacks or phobias. Whereas, neutral events are routinely processed; therefore, they lose their distinctiveness in the course of time. EMDR helps the clients to focus on memories and images of traumatic events. Their processing is enhanced by eye movements. As the sessions continue, they become more adaptive, positive and realistic pieces of information.

Conditioning Model

Dyck (1993) offered the first experimentally tested and useful model of EMDR. He suggested that EMDR is a stimulus generalisation process in which the original contextual clues of the trauma are replaced by new elements (hand waving). It restricts the conditioned anxiety. Three outcomes of this generalisation process may be conceptualised: the first is extinction and the other two are equivalent to exposure paradigms. If the client completely focuses on the hand tracking and gets distracted from the unpleasant, trauma-relevant thoughts, the extinction process continues to occur through these trials (CS no-CS). Second, even if he is not completely distracted, either partially focuses on both the elements, that is, contextual cues of trauma and hand waving instead of engaging in alternative escape response that is negatively reinforcing. Third, during these treatment sessions, being preoccupied with traumatic memory, instead of focusing on hand movement, he may also try to focus on contextual cues of trauma alone. If the first possibility of focusing on hand movement alone may be interpreted as a classical extinction paradigm, the later two categories of alternative response may be interpreted as response prevention paradigms analogous to standard flooding procedure. The common outcome is diminution of trauma-related anxiety response.

Although Dyck's model is useful in explaining the processes involved in EMDR, it cannot account for the commonly observed phenomenon of EMDR. In order to examine the model, Armstrong and Vaughan (1996) stated that the major criticism of Dyck's model was that the desensitisation that occurs in EMDR is faster than the usual flooding process. Thus at least as far as the effects of EMDR are concerned, the latter two explanations of his model are not acceptable. Thus, extinction remained the only explanation of EMDR mechanism. Even if it is accepted, it does not fully explain the observed phenomena like verbal and motor responses, misidentification, or sleepiness that occur immediately following the desensitisation; even plateau is observed in clients. Looking at these phenomena and the habituation model's failure to explain them, Armstrong and Vaughan (1996) offered an alternative model.

Orienting Response Model

Armstrong and Vaughan (1996) suggested that the client who is exposed to EMDR sessions already has a cortical set or propensity to respond in a specific manner in response to traumatic stimuli. Therefore, he is highly vigilant to similar stimuli. Due to the presence of an already lowered threshold, autonomic reactions and flashbacks are readily triggered. Precisely speaking, there is a propensity to recognise trauma-related stimuli. Further, the instruction to focus on traumatic events and rate them according to their SUDs increases the chances of voluntary access to the fear structure. This might not have happened otherwise. It creates a 'preparatory set to respond' (Lang 1977).

During hand tracking, when a therapist waves his hand in the presence of trauma-related stimuli, it triggers an intense orienting response (OR). This is because the therapist's moving hand acts as a rapidly changing stimulus, which has biological significance. In addition to this, it acquires a 'signal value' for being presented in the context with trauma-related memories. The mismatch between the stimuli previously present during the trauma and those presented currently elicits intense orienting response. Such orienting responses have a tendency to activate central analysers, leading to misidentification of stimuli in the therapy room. This also triggers verbal and motor conditional responses as expected. Activation of peripheral analysers by orienting the response results in retinal (light) sensitivity (Sokolov 1963b) and/or papillary dilation. The orienting response also has a limiting effect on pain reaction; therefore, it decreases the level of aversive arousal related to painful memory.

EMDR modifies the neuronal model of trauma. In traumatic situations, the conditioned stimuli (objective as well as subjective feelings of trauma, 'Nothing I can do') are associated with conditioned responses (CRS) (e.g. autonomic and skeletal responses). EMDR puts the client in a contrasting situation, where the CS is replaced by the waving of therapist's hand and the accompanying feeling, 'Now you are here, safe and protected'. As the original CS is not reinforced (associated with avoidance/relief) anymore, the client becomes increasingly relaxed. This extinction model explains why relaxation occurs so quickly. Due to repetitive waving of the therapist's hand, habituation also occurs fast, causing a marked degree of sleepiness (i.e. tonic cortical inhibition) when hand-waving is continued past the point of extinction of OR. In summary, the basic difference between Dyck's conditioning model and the OR model is the significance of hand-waving. In the conditioning model, it has been conceptualised as distinct from the original traumatic memory whereas, in the OR model, it is viewed as an act to facilitate intense orienting response that helps in perceiving the true current situation. Because of which the client's neuronal model of trauma alters. Instead of trauma, it reflects more of his survival and current safety.

APPLICATIONS

EMDR has been used effectively in treatment of various disorders. A majority of them are post-traumatic stress disorders (PTSD) (e.g Marcus, Marquis and Sakai 1997; Rothbaum 1997; Wilson, Becker and Tinker 1995, 1997). These studies have indicated that 84–100 per cent cases reported no symptoms after at least three 90 minutes treatment sessions. Carlson et al. (1998) used EMDR with combat veterans and revealed that after 12 sessions, the treatment was effective in 77 per cent cases. The practice guidelines of the International Society for Traumatic Stress Studies have declared EMDR as an effective method of treating PTSD (Chemtob et al. 2000; Shalev et al. 2000).

Shapiro (1995, 2001) developed a specific protocol of 8 to 10 steps EMDR for treatment of phobias. This was found to be effective in a number of cases (e.g De Jongh et al. 1999; Fensterheim 1996; Lipke 1994, 1995; Marcus et al. 1991), although other studies were reported to be less positive (e.g. Acierno et al. 1994; Bates et al. 1996; Lohr et al. 1995, 1996; Muris et al. 1998; Muris et al. 1997; Sanderson and Carpenter 1992). This was attributed to lack of procedural fidelity and protocol adherence (inappropriately structured targets, inexact application, etc.) (Shapiro 1999).

Spates and Burnette (1995) reported three complex cases of PTSD in which EMDR was used successfully. The first client reported sustained psychological symptoms attributed to four separate traumatic events, including accidental killing of a woman while practicing shooting. The second traumatic experience was witnessing and narrowly escaping from being killed in a massacre in a foreign country. Another panic attack occurred during the lecture of a favourite professor who claimed that individuals who fail to forgive themselves sometimes commit suicide. The last traumatic experience occurred in a congregation when he looked at the eyes of some people. The second case was a 39-year-old professional woman who experienced extensive sexual abuse by both her parents from the pre-teen to early adulthood. The trauma led to sexual dysfunction. The third case was a 38-year-old police officer who was shot in the forehead while chasing a criminal in the woods and spent 25 hours in the woods before escaping in the nightfall. He reported frequent flashbacks, poor concentration, nightmares, spontaneous emotional flooding and occupational disability.

To date, most evidences addressing to the efficacy of EMDR as a treatment of PTSD and other disorders are based on uncontrolled case studies (e.g Klinknecht and Morgan 1992; Lipke and Botkin 1992;

Marquis 1991; McCann 1992; Puk 1991; Wolpe and Abrams 1991). Few controlled studies conducted on civilian population (e.g. Marcus et al. 1997; Rothbaum 1997; Scheck et al. 1998; Wilson et al. 1997) revealed that treatment programmes of three to five hours duration were effective in eliminating PTSD symptoms in 84 to 100 per cent clients. The treatment effects were maintained over 3–15 months period. The outcome of EMDR with combat veterans was mixed. Carlson et al. (1998) offered a 12 session full treatment regime. 77 per cent clients showed improvement, which was maintained over a 9-month period. Very few studies have been conducted to compare the effects of EMDR with other therapies in the same group of clients or in the same individuals across sessions. A meta-analysis of PTSD using EMDR and other therapies revealed that EMDR is more effective than other psychotherapies (van Etten and Taylor 1998) and exposure based cognitive behavioural treatments (Brom et al. 1989; Foa et al. 1999; Keane et al. 1989; Marks et al. 1998; Resick and Schnicke 1992; Tarrier et al. 1999).

EMPIRICAL STUDIES

Since the first publication (Shapiro 1989), EMDR has generated substantial clinical research and scholarly debates. Its application has been expanded to a wide range of disorders. Several detailed methodological reviews have been made (e.g. Herbert and Mueser 1992; Lohr et al. 1994). The reviews have been focused on the following principal issues: methodological concerns, including validity measures, diagnostic classification, reliance on case reports, procedural confounds, limiting internal validity and the experimental paradigm used for evaluating the effectiveness of the procedure. Most reviewers claimed that the empirical support of its efficacy is meagre.

Lohr et al. (1995) suggested that inclusion of trait-like characteristics such as MMPI-derived indices of PTSD may be insensitive to treatment effects. In order to evaluate the therapeutic change, diagnostic validity is required to be examined carefully. Magnitude of disturbance and generality of change are some of the important parameters.

Reviewing about 14 case studies, using EMDR, they concluded that only a small minority of them provided minimal procedural details and data to support their empirical validity. Comparing EMDR with other procedures like imagery, only Sanderson and Carpenter (1992) observed that EMDR is no more effective than imaginal techniques (imaginal exposure). There was no difference between SUD ratings during imaginal and *in vivo* exposure.

In most studies, the effects were more conspicuous on verbal reports than psychophysiological measures. Affective symptoms are more influenced than any other response. Not many studies have been reported on this subject. Systematic measurement of behavioural indices of fear has not been incorporated into any study except Acierno et al. (1994), nor are there sufficient number of studies to examine the treatment components.

Some investigators are of the opinion that eye movement is not an essential component of therapy. Even fixed gaze and image concentration process may bring a substantial change in the behaviour. Various forms of lateral stimulation techniques may execute the same function as eye movement. Treatment fidelity is another important issue. Moncher and Prinz (1991) argued that training and competence procedures for promoting fidelity assessment and fidelity validation are essential in our ability to evaluate the quality of therapeutic research.

FUTURE DIRECTION

Future research on EMDR requires addressing some of the very significant issues, which have not been studied adequately. Control of non-specific effects is one of them. So far, no study has compared EMDR with attention placebo or wait-listed controlled condition. Such studies may include other techniques like imagery or re-exposure. Similarly, there is a need to conduct separate studies on different kinds of disorders in order to isolate the treatment reactivity, attention/demand, or expectation variables. Study of the client, therapist and situational variables would help in predicting the outcome of therapy. There is always a need for applying new and yet to be validated techniques for treatment of extreme and intractable cases.

Despite methodological and professional cautions and criticisms, EMDR has been an internationally accepted as an effective procedure for treatment of post-traumatic stress disorder and other related disorders. Some therapists have reported its miraculous effects on clients in one or two sessions of EMDR (e.g Shapiro 1989b; Spates and Burnette 1995). About 14,000 therapists have been trained to use this procedure. However, most of the efficacy reports are obtained from case studies or uncontrolled studies. Controlled studies are very few (e.g. Boudewyns et al. 1993; Montgomery and Ayllon 1994: Sanderson and Carpenter 1992; Shapiro 1989b). Therefore, more research is required to examine its empirical basis. Controlled research would shed more light on its untouched dimensions.

15

Covert Conditioning Procedures

To varying degrees, most people control their behaviours by imagining the consequences. Based on this assumption, a number of behaviour therapy methods have been introduced. The underlying procedure is known as covert conditioning. It is a set of behaviour therapy techniques through which covert events (imagery, thinking or feeling) are associated with an imagined target behaviour in order to increase or decrease it. Precisely, the imagined target behaviours are associated with certain imagined consequences in order to either strengthen or weaken an actual behaviour. Cautela and Kearney (1990: 86) defined covert conditioning as

> a process through which private events such as thoughts, images, and feelings are manipulated in accordance with principles of learning, usually operant conditioning, to bring about changes in overt behaviour, covert psychological behaviour (i.e. thoughts, images, feelings) and/or covert physiological behaviour (e.g. glandular secretions).

The roots of this procedure can be traced out from the works of Skinner (1953), Thorndike (1911) and Tolman (1932). Homme, in 1965 provided an early account of covert conditioning while introducing the word 'coverant' or covert operant, referring to the unobservable responses. It is described as 'covert conditioning' method because a client is asked to imagine all components of the conditioning process, including antecedent, target activity and its consequence.

There are three fundamental assumptions of covert conditioning:

(1) The homogeneity assumption: All categories of behaviour whether overt or covert, obey the same laws.
(2) The interaction assumption: Covert psychological behaviour, physiological behaviour and overt behaviour interact with each other in predictable ways.
(3) The learning assumption: All behaviours are subject to the same laws of learning (Cautela and Kearney 1987).

A variety of covert conditioning methods have been described by Cautela (1972), such as covert positive reinforcement, covert negative reinforcement, covert modelling, covert response cost, covert sensitisation and covert extinction. These procedures are selected depending on whether the therapist attempts to increase or to decrease behaviour. Since the entire procedure depends on the client's capacity to imagine, the therapist must verify it with the client before using the covert conditioning procedures. Most covert conditioning procedures are analogous to their operant counterparts.

COVERT SENSITISATION

Covert sensitisation is one of the most widely used covert conditioning methods in which undesirable target behaviour is reduced by associating it with an imaginal aversive event (Cautela 1972). It is based on the assumption that imagined association of aversive events exert similar control over overt behaviour as the actual aversive events do. Therefore, logically overt behaviour can be changed by imagining various consequences for them. When administered by the therapist, it is termed as 'assisted covert sensitisation'. Standardised scripts are employed to guide the client through clinically relevant scenes in which ultimate imaginal aversive consequences are presented (Plaud 2002). The aversive images are usually anxiety inducing. Some of them cause aversive physiological changes (nausea, sweating, giddiness etc.). Although the therapist helps the client in preparing the script of aversive events and presents it in the initial sessions, it is self-administered by the client. Strength of the imagined stimulus and clarity of imagined response determine the extent of generalisation of the modified response from clinical setting to actual life situations. Covert sensitisation or aversive imagery is considered as a variant of covert aversion technique. As in Wolpe's (1958) systematic desensitisation, in this method also, the imagery of a deviant stimulus is followed by a symbolic (imagined) aversive event. The client is exposed to increasingly aversive events, as he engages in deviant behaviour, in order to establish a negative counter-conditioning.

Theory

Both classical as well as operant conditioning theories explain the underlying mechanism of its effect. The unpleasant unconditioned stimulus (imagery) normally leads to an unconditioned unpleasant overt or covert avoidance response (nausea, vomiting, shame, fear of criticism, or legal action). When these imageries (US) are paired with the conditioned stimuli (sight of homosexual partner, child, female's undergarments or smell of alcohol) that elicit undesirable conditioned approach response (CR) (such as sexual arousal or addictive behaviour) repeatedly, the client starts showing avoidance response (abstinence) or restores the natural and desirable response. At this stage, along with the negative counter-conditioning method, in some cases reinforcement may be used to stabilise the natural response. In the operant conditioning perspective, a maladaptive responding is weakened by following it up with responses with aversive imagery. The negative consequences of the client's deviant behaviour are symbolically presented to him as a possible consequence. Some authors begin with relaxation training and finally terminate it with an escape or relief scene (Cautela 1967). Mahoney (1974) stated that termination of a target behaviour (e.g. escape from aversive situations or scenes) provides relief.

Research and Application

A majority of research on covert conditioning is focused on modifying appetitive processes such as cigarette smoking, overeating, deviant sexual arousal such as exhibitionism and excessive masturbation (Hayes et al. 1978), or nail biting (Daniel 1974; Paquin 1977).

Sexual Deviance

Current literature on covert sensitisation reveals that its applications are mostly in the area of sexual deviance and disorders. An early description of the technique was given by Gold and Neufeld in 1965. Their client was a 16-year old convicted boy who was soliciting men for sexual contact at railway station toilets, cinemas, swimming pools and other places and often engaged in homosexual fantasies, associating them with masturbation. During the initial sessions of therapy, the client was relaxed. Then, he was asked to visualise himself in a toilet along side an old man. He was suggested that under no circumstance he would solicit the man for sexual contact. His visualisation and complete imagination of the scene was indicated by signalling to the therapist. When agreed, he was verbally rewarded, saying 'well done'. In the next phase, gradually the image of the old man was transformed into an attractive young man. At the same time, he was provided with added imagery of prohibitions like presence of a police officer in the scene. After some sessions, the client could learn to ignore handsome and attractive men. Later, imagery of attractive young women was presented along with sexually arousing pleasant experiences. When these images of young attractive men and women were compared in the context of pleasant experiential cues, the client preferred the alternative imagery of heterosexual events.

Kolvin (1967) used aversive imagery with a case of fetishist and another case of patrol sniffing addiction. With the first case, Kolvin initially presented a pleasant background story and asked the client to visualise the fetish act. The client was emotionally aroused with those scenes, as observed from his motor tension, change of breathing and expression. At this stage, a vividly described aversive imagery was introduced. This imagery was in contrast to the deviant erotic imagery, which was introduced earlier in association with the fetish. Eight sessions of this treatment coupled with reassurance and brief psychotherapy significantly reduced the deviant sexual orientation. A 17-month follow-up revealed no relapse of symptoms.

Hayes et al. (1978) treated an adult male who was admitted to a psychiatric hospital with history of attempted rape, multiple sadistic fantasies involving sadistic sexual acts (e.g. forced sexual acts with bound women, using pins and whips during intercourse) and exhibitionism. Covert sensitisation was used to treat this classic case. During treatment, the client was asked to imagine aversive consequences associated with the situations where the sadistic and exhibitionistic acts occurred. The client's erection (i.e. penile blood volume) was measured as he viewed the slides of sadistic, exhibitionistic and heterosexual scenes. The heterosexual slides depicted nudes of females and sadistic slides included females chained down in various provocative postures. The client was asked to sort the cards describing these pictures according to the levels of arousal. A multiple baseline design was used to evaluate the treatment effects. There was a significant decline in both physiological arousals as well as self-report of attraction to both sadistic and exhibitionistic stimuli after treatment. This positive effect was maintained up to eight weeks of follow-up period.

Thorpe and Olson (1990) described the use of social skills training and covert sensitisation to treat exhibitionism of a divorced man in his twenties. He used to derive sexual pleasure from exposing genitals to strangers, especially women, and after each episode he felt depressed, even contemplating suicide. The client was instructed to imagine himself driving a car, looking for a victim, a woman walking along the lonely road. He stops his car, loosens his clothes, and feels strongly sexually aroused. Suddenly a police car pulls up, with its lights flashing and siren ringing. The police officer handcuffs the man. At the same time, his work mate arrives in the scene. Now he realises that this will be big news. He would obviously lose his job and there will be adverse publicity in the local newspaper. He feels physically sick and apprehensive of the fact that he may be jailed as a sex offender. The client benefited from the treatment. Within few weeks, the strength of his urge to expose himself declined to zero on the self-rating scale.

Maletzky (1974) successfully used a method of 'assisted' covert sensitisation method in which the conventional method of covert sensitisation was altered by adding an aversive odour (valeric acid). He treated 10 exhibitionists using this procedure. A large number of measures were taken to ascertain the therapeutic effects. The measures included: (i) self-reported covert activities, including fantasies, urges, dreams and so on, (ii) self-reported occurrence of exhibitionism, (iii) arrests, and (iv) performance during the 'temptation test'. An attractive female was paid to tempt the client by passing seductively past his car. One-year follow-up study revealed total elimination of exhibitionism, arrests, and there was no temptation for the exhibitionistic act.

Barlow et al. (1969) successfully treated a case of paedophilia and homosexuality. The clients were asked to subjectively rate their arousal potential of deviant sexual scenes. The more arousing scenes received higher rating than the less arousing ones. They also self-recorded the frequency of deviant sexual urges between the therapy sessions. The GSR measures were taken during the therapy sessions. An A-B-A-B design was followed. Covert sensitisation procedure was used after five baseline sessions. Then the baseline was reinstated. This extinction phase was described to the clients as 'the best course of action at this time'. In the last phase, covert sensitisation phase was reinstated. The subjective arousal ratings and sexual-urge frequency correlated very well with the GSR measures. Similar phasic patterns were displayed. The data suggested that covert sensitisation was effective in reducing deviant sexual preference and arousal.

This technique was further refined and replicated by Barlow et al. (1972). They treated four homosexuals with a modified covert sensitisation procedure. In order to have a more direct assessment of the sexual arousal, the penile circumference of the clients were measured using a mechanical strain gauge. During the baseline phase, the clients were led to believe that they are going to learn a substitute relaxation response in place of their deviant sexual arousal. During the second (covert sensitisation) phase, they were instructed to associate negative imagery with sexual arousal. They were told 'to obtain the best effects, we are going to heighten the tension by pairing the sexually arousing scenes with images of vomiting.' In the third phase (extinction), the baseline phase was reinstated. During the fourth and final phase, the same scenes were presented with positive (pleasant) imagery. In spite of the counter therapeutic imagery, the sexual arousal was similar to the one seen during the covert sensitisation phase. The penile circumference declined during both the covert sensitisation phases.

Addictive Behaviour

Covert sensitisation has been used effectively in alcoholism. In the method, a client is first relaxed and instructed to imagine aversive scenes associated with each episode of drinking. It provides a detailed description of the onset of nausea and vomiting while drinking. Miller (1959) used a hypnotic procedure for inducing covert aversion in 24 treated alcoholics and was successful in maintaining abstinence during the post-treatment follow-up. Cautela (1966) treated a 29-year-old nurse who used alcohol to alleviate social anxiety. The client was trained initially to relax. Then he was required to imagine carrying out the compulsive drinking while imagining noxious and distressful feelings described in the suggestions. The client was required to imagine that when the glass of alcohol was about to touch his lips, he would begin to feel sick in his stomach and would start to vomit all over the bar, restaurant or home, or wherever he did it. In order to ascertain it, the client was asked to signal the feeling by raising his index fingers. He was asked to practice himself. In the next phase, the client was asked to imagine the experience of immediate calm when he puts the glass down. At the final stage, the client was asked to discriminate between the act of drinking and not drinking.

A similar method was used by Aschem and Donner (1968). They took a non-treatment control group to evaluate the forward and backward covert sensitisation procedures. In the backward procedure, an unpleasant imaginal event (e.g. nausea) is introduced prior to the imaginal rehearsal of problematic behaviours; whereas, in forward procedure, aversive events were introduced following the imaginal rehearsal. A follow-up study conducted after six months indicated that 47 per cent of the contacted clients showed improvement, that is, 6 out of 15 men receiving treatment for alcohol abuse abstained from alcohol and eight people who did not receive treatment did not abstain. Anant (1967) treated 26 institutionalised alcoholics using covert aversion. Follow-ups conducted at different intervals revealed good maintenance of its positive effects. However, the absence of control group in this study limits its contribution. Miller (1982) reported that covert sensitisation appears to be at least as effective as chemical aversion. High degree of procedural variability in these studies warrants suspension of judgment until more empirical evidence is available (Mahoney 1974).

Several investigators have attempted to evaluate the effects of covert conditioning on cigarette smoking. Many of them had deviated procedurally from the original treatment guidelines as suggested by Cautela (1972). Thus, the results do not exactly explain the efficacy of the classical covert sensitisation procedure. However, we would examine here some of the studies that employed covert sensitisation in some form or the other. Some authors had tried to pair external aversive stimulation (e.g. electric shock) with the imaginal performance of cigarette smoking (e.g. Steffy et al. 1970; Berecz 1972). Most of these studies claimed success of covert sensitisation procedure, although there is little controlled comparison of the procedure. Some investigators have tried to combine covert sensitisation with other treatment procedures for treatment of smoking. Tooley and Pratt (1967) combined it with coverant control and contingency contracting in treatment of a smoking couple. They observed that covert sensitisation was effective only in the initial phase of the treatment. The effect declined rapidly with time. In another study, Wagner and Bragge (1970) compared the effects of covert sensitisation, desensitisation, a combination of these, relaxation and counseling. The combined group received systematic desensitisation to a standardised hierarchy of cigarette deprivation. When the clients reported discomfort, they were asked to visualise a covert sensitisation scene. Although there was no difference in the treatment effects between the groups, after four weeks of treatment, the combined treatment group showed less relapse than the other groups. Interestingly, the covert sensitisation group demonstrated more relapse than other groups. Lawson and May (1970) compared the effects of covert sensitisation, coverant control, and contingency contracting and self-monitoring on 12 smokers. Although there was a decline in smoking behaviour, the post-treatment data did not reveal any significant difference between these four treatment methods. In absence of any follow-up data, the interpretation of the conclusion had limited scope. Utilising attention-placebo control group (self-monitoring) and covert sensitisation or self-control group, Sachs et al. (1972) found no treatment effect. One-month follow-up revealed that only the experimental group had reduced their smoking. High attrition rate was assumed to have inflated the treatment effect (Mahoney 1974).

Overeating

Cautela (1966) used this method successfully to treat obesity in a female client. He could achieve 66 pounds weight loss in her. This initial success of covert sensitisation encourages several investigators to use the technique for treatment of obesity and overeating. Janda and Rimm (1972) used covert sensitisation procedure in the treatment of obesity, and compared its effects with attention (relaxation) control and no-treatment conditions. After the first six weeks of treatment they failed to differentiate the three groups, but a subsequent six weeks follow-up revealed significant difference in weight loss. The covert sensitisation group lost 11.7 pounds as compared to a loss of 2.3 and a gain of 0.9 pounds by the attention and control clients, respectively. The authors also made an interesting observation that weight loss in covert sensitisation was highly correlated with their subjective discomfort reported during the aversive imagery phase. Manno and Marston (1972) employed two methods of covert conditioning: covert sensitisation and covert reinforcement for weight reduction and compared them with the control group performance. Clients exposed to covert conditioning procedures achieved significantly better weight reduction than the control group. However, there was no significant difference in weight loss between the covert conditioning groups. A three months follow up revealed maintenance of weight loss of 8. 9 pounds in each group.

There are some other studies that have failed to demonstrate the efficacy of covert sensitisation. Meynen (1970) conducted a comparative study of three treatment approaches: relaxation, covert sensitisation and modified version of systematic desensitisation with obese clients. After eight weeks of treatment, all three groups lost significant amount of weight; however there was no significant difference between these groups. Similar findings were obtained by Lick and Bootzin (1971) who studied 40 overweight females, assigning them to one of the four groups: no treatment control, covert sensitisations with relief (escape), covert sensitisation without relief and covert sensitisation with 'automatic immunisation' instructions. The treatments were conducted over a period of four weeks, followed by a follow-up period of five weeks. Results showed very little weight loss (10 pounds over 10 weeks), although there was a report of reduction in attraction for favourite food. There was no difference between the treatment groups.

In another weight management programme, Foreyt and Hagen (1973), 39 overweight females were assigned to one of the following three groups: covert sensitisation, attention-placebo and no-treatment control. Treatment was conducted for a period of nine weeks during which 18 sessions were conducted. During the covert sensitisation sessions, the clients were asked to visualise food approach scenes, simultaneously engaging in aversive nauseous imagery. For the attention-placebo group, the same scenes were followed by positive imagery. Assessment conducted after treatment showed no significant difference among these three groups. Attention-placebo clients lost 8.5 pounds whereas the covert sensitisation and control groups lost only 4.1 and 3.7 pounds respectively. Expectancy influence was attributed to be the cause of this change rather than the therapy itself. It lends further doubt on the efficacy of covert sensitisation. Similarly, Sachs and Ingram (1972) did not find any significant difference between forward and backward covert sensitisation procedures. The food intake of 10 clients who participated in the study declined significantly, regardless of the procedure. Wilson (1974b) in one study added covert sensitisation (aversive imagery) and relaxation to a behavioural programme that included stimulus control and self-monitoring. It did not produce any significant weight loss. In a second study, he utilised an indigenous and relatively unobtrusive 'taste test' to assess the effects of covert sensitisation. The clients were offered snacks and asked to evaluate their palatability. Covert sensitisation, in addition to a self-monitoring procedure, had no significant effect on the actual food consumption. These contradictory observations lead to the conclusion that covert sensitisation alone is relatively ineffective in controlling overeating. Procedural variations, subject variations and other non-specific variables require to be carefully studied before drawing any definite conclusion.

Covert sensitisation procedure enjoys certain advantages over the classical aversion therapy methods. This method can be used without the presence of undesirable behaviour and actual unpleasant consequences. This has practical and ethical advantage and ensures safety of the client too (Moore 2001). This procedure is, of course, not free from methodological problems. Paniagua (1993) identified the following problems: (i) The integrity of covert conditioning procedure is questionable because of the difficulty in assessing the procedural reliability; (ii) Failure in behaviour change cannot be clearly attributed to the inadequate instruction provided by the therapist or the client's difficulty in obtaining clear imagery; and (iii) Most supporting evidence of the procedure is based on studies of single cases, and technically what has been demonstrated is that the practitioner reinforces the self-report of the client. There is no way to ascertain whether the imagery is directly reinforced. Thus, a question arises whether it is conditioning of covert (e.g. imagery) or overt (verbal self-report) behaviour. The exact mechanism involved in the procedure has also been questioned. The role of suggestibility (Foreyt and Hagen 1973) and habituation processes (Plaud and Gaither 1997) have been implicated as alternative explanations for covert conditioning.

Although there are numerous case studies, there are very few case reports where experimental controls have been used. Thus, the differential efficacy of covert sensitisation has not been adequately demonstrated (Morris 2000). Reviewing a number of studies on covert sensitisation, Mahoney (1974) concluded that: (i) covert sensitisation has not shown any consistent result in suppression of alcohol consumption or smoking, (ii) it has shown variable success with obesity, and (iii) it has shown impressive and relatively consistent efficacy in preliminary application to sexual deviations.

THOUGHT-STOPPING

Thought stopping is a cognitive-behavioural method used for minimising the distress associated with intrusive unwanted thoughts by interrupting them using a self-generated strong and obtrusive stimulus (e.g. a command 'Stop'). The client is instructed to deliberately engage in ruminative thoughts, concentrate on it for sometime, and then signal the therapist about its occurrence. As soon as a signal is given, the therapist shouts, 'Stop!' The client usually shows a startled response. The therapist, at this stage points out how a distraction terminates his ruminative thinking. Then additional training sessions are conducted to train the client himself to use the technique and gradually sub-vocalises the loud 'Stop!'

In the typical therapeutic setting, the client is instructed to sit with his eyes closed, and asked to raise his index finger once the intrusive thoughts are deliberately brought into focus. When the client raises his finger, the therapist shouts loudly 'Stop!' Even aversive electric shock can also be used. Here, the therapist explains that these two things, namely, saying, 'Stop!' and the target thought cannot go together. The client is then encouraged to practice a sub-vocal yell 'Stop!' in order to control intrusive thoughts. This practice should continue for at least 10 minutes or 20 trials or until the specific thought disappears. Rehearsal makes the client skilled in using the command more effectively. The yell 'Stop' is now changed to more unobtrusive acts like snapping a rubber band on the wrist or visualising a stop scene and so on (O'Neil and Whittal 2002). They are encouraged to emit a sub-vocal 'Stop' whenever they come across such self-defeating thoughts. Gradually the locus of control is shifted from the therapist to the client. Thus, it is viewed as a self-control technique.

Theory

Different theories have been advanced to explain why thought-stopping modifies behaviour. The underlying process which is assumed to be involved in thought-stopping is an abrupt cognitive distraction. As a result, the client's attention is shifted from distressing maladaptive behaviour (e.g rumination) to a distracting stimulus (e.g. Stop!). This causes a temporary termination of the behaviour and the relief is reinforcing for the client, as it provides an opportunity for escape from the distressing ruminative thought process. Thus, a negative reinforcement hypothesis explains its behavioural effect.

Research and Application

The earliest use of thought stopping is found in Alexdander Bain's (1928) book *Thought Control in Everyday Life*. The technique was revived by Taylor, Wolpe and Lazarus in the 1950s and the 1960s (Taylor 1955, 1963; Wople 1958, 1969; Lazarus 1966). Earlier, thought-stopping technique was considered as a method of punishment for ruminative thoughts and used primarily for treatment of obsessions, in the same way as aversion therapy was used for compulsions. Now the usage has extended to treatment of other disorders also. Its role in modifying the mediational process has been recognised.

Obsession

The attentional distraction feature of thought-stopping was examined by Mahoney (1971). In his study, an obsessive client was asked to count backwards by '7' from a four-digit number when he experienced ruminations. Unfortunately, this distraction increased obsessive thinking. However, Campbell (1973) found a more positive result when he combined backward counting with positive imagery training.

Phobia

Rimm (1973) demonstrated the use of thought-stopping in a case of phobia. The case was a young female student who was extremely nervous to drive an automobile. The problem started after witnessing an automobile accident a few months earlier. Instead of using systematic desensitisation, Rimm used thought-stopping as an 'experimental' method. It was assumed that the anxiety was generated by self-defeating thoughts. In order to analyse the content of the thoughts, initially the client was asked to describe specific situation where she was afraid of driving. After reaching the stage of the situation, the client was asked to close her eyes and imagine the situation that actually happened earlier. The therapist assisted in giving details of the situation where it happened and as if she was in the same situation. She described as if the girl was running out onto the road and her husband driving the car did not see her. Then she screamed out. On probing, it appeared that the thoughts were unnecessary and self-defeating. Then the client was asked to loudly verbalise the thought to find out whether they are healthy (connected to the fear of driving) or not. Only the thoughts jointly agreed by the client and therapist as obsessive were interrupted.

Thought-stopping was achieved in four different stages. In the first stage, the therapist asked the client to describe her thoughts loudly and used a loud shout 'Stop' to interrupt them. In the second stage, the client was asked to think about it without speaking. Occurrences of such thoughts were indicated by the client by raising her finger. The therapist used a loud shout 'Stop' to block them. Then, the client was instructed to say, 'Stop' when such thoughts occurred. Finally, she was instructed to interrupt such thoughts sub-vocally, without any overt statement. She was encouraged to use this technique on her own. Thus, the thought-stopping technique involved four steps: (i) Therapist's interruption of overt thoughts, (ii) Therapist's interruption of covert thoughts, (iii) Client's overt interruption of covert thoughts, and (iv) Client's covert interruption of covert thought (Rimm and Masters 1979).

Empirical Status

Empirical evidence on the effectiveness of thought-stopping is quite meagre. Rimm, Saunders and Westel (1974) conducted a study in which thought-stopping and covert assertion techniques were combined to treat snake phobia in a group of clients. Covert assertion included symbolic rehearsal of assertive coping responses. Clients who were exposed to this combined treatment were more successful than individuals in attention-placebo control group. However, the specific effect of thought-stopping on snake phobia was not assessed.

In another study, Wisocki and Rooney (1974) examined the effectiveness of four conditions: thought stopping, covert sensitisation, attention-placebo and no-treatment on smoking behaviour of a group of smokers. The no-treatment group comprised of those clients who could not schedule their time to accommodate with the treatment programme. The study was methodologically poor. It did not reveal any significant positive effect of thought-stopping on smoking behaviour. A number of investigators have claimed successful use of thought-stopping in various disorders, like obsessions, phobias (Kumar and Wilkinson 1971), transvestism (Gershman 1970), impotence (Garfield et al. 1969), heroin addiction (Wisocki 1973b), self-injurious behaviour (Cautela and Baron 1973), and marital disharmony (Stern 1970; Yamagami 1972; Rosen and Schnapp 1974) combining it with a wide range of techniques including relaxation, systematic desensitisation, positive imagery and other procedures. Many of these studies have methodological problems. Poor operational definitions, the absence of within-subject control, and lack of adequate follow-up are some of the major problems (Mahoney 1974).

A number of investigators have identified the physiological correlates of gross thought processes such as vocal cord EMG and other physiological responses (Jacobson 1973; McGuigan 1970). These measures can be used as objective measures to examine the effects of thought-stopping on the individual client. At the moment, more systematic empirical exploration is required to establish its credibility as a therapeutic procedure.

16

Cognitive-Behaviour Therapy

Human cognition plays a vital role in causation as well as maintenance of maladaptive responding. Therefore, the recent expansion of behaviour therapy has included cognition as a legitimate area of study. In recent years, this has generated a great deal of interest among clinicians and researchers. The approach is generally labelled as cognitive-behaviour therapy (CBT). Now a variety of models of such therapies are available for treatment. Few examples are Rational Emotive Therapy (Ellis 1962), Cognitive Therapy (Beck 1976), Stress Inoculation (Meichenbaum and Cameron 1973) and Self-instructional Training (Meichenbaum 1974). Cognitive-behaviour therapies reflect an integration of internalism and behaviourism (Mahoney 1977). Many traditional approaches to psychopathology (psychoanalytic, Rogerian, humanistic-existential) primarily focus on internal causation of behaviour, whereas behaviourism focuses largely on external events as causes of maladaptive behaviour. Integration of both the approaches is seen as an example of interactionism (Rimm and Masters 1979). Many of these approaches attempt to change maladaptive behaviour by changing beliefs and providing training to clients in information-processing skills.

Cognitive variables used in behaviour therapy had grown steadily in the 1970s. Cognitive-behaviourism received inputs from a number of contributors including Tolman (1932), Rotter (1954), Kelley (1955), Bandura (1969), Mowrer (1960) and Mahoney (1974). The attributional cognitions are valued by most of these contributors as the key mediating variables in the acquisition and maintenance of behaviour. In the mid 1960s, behaviourists showed a renewed interest in self-control by behaviourists, while the terminology was largely behaviouristic (e.g. Goldiamond 1965; Stuart 1967). Skinner (1953) viewed self-control as a process or response sequence, which an individual makes to control other responses. The former is called 'controlling response' and the latter as 'controlled response'. In natural settings, controlling responses are maintained through self-reinforcement. Administration of rewards by the individual himself following controlling responses maintains them. It forms the basis of most self-control training programmes.

Aronfreed (1969) explained self-control in terms of internalisation. Internalisation of behaviour creates resistance against extinction. The behaviour persists in the absence of external reinforcing outcomes also. It becomes resistant to change due the fact that it is supported by outcomes of more established values. Precisely speaking, when behaviour sustains without external reinforcement, it presupposes that its reinforcing consequences are internal. Aronfreed also argues that much of the internalised control of the conduct (behaviour) is mediated by cognitive operations, what is called conscience. Emphasis is placed on training the clients in different cognitive and behavioural skills for coping and problem solving. The clients are taught 'what to think' and 'how to think' strategies in specific problem situations. Attempts are also made to facilitate generalisation of these skills from clinical setting to real life situations. The representative approaches included Rational Emotive Behaviour Therapy or REBT (Ellis 1962), Cognitive Therapy or CT (Beck 1976), Problem-Solving Training or PST (D'Zurrila and Goldfried 1971), Dialectic Behaviour Therapy or DBT (Linehan 1993), Self-Control Therapy or SCT (Rehm 1977), Stress Inoculation or SIT (Meichenbaum 1985) and Relapse Prevention or RP (Marlatte and Gordon 1985).

RATIONAL EMOTIVE BEHAVIOUR THERAPY

One of the most influential approaches to cognitive-behaviour therapy is Rational Emotive Behaviour Therapy (REBT). It employs cognitive (thinking), emotive (feeling) as well as behavioural (acting) techniques for the treatment of psychological problems. Albert Ellis initiated the development of REBT, earlier known as Rational Emotive Therapy (RET), as a separate system in 1955. He viewed that the major drawback of the then dominant psychoanalytic psychotherapy was that even if the clients developed insight by associating their present problems to their childhood experiences, they rarely gave up the symptoms; at times even developed new ones indoctrinating themselves with the irrationalities they had invented and learned in the early childhood (Ellis 1979). The 'historical insight' obtained on the couch is not essential for cure. The fundamental tenet of Ellis's approach was that men are disturbed not by the events that happen around them, but by the *view* they take of them. Psychological disorders arise from their own beliefs, philosophies and faulty or irrational patterns of thinking.

This was parallel to the Buddhist and Taoist idea that human emotions originate from human thinking and that in order to change emotions, one must change one's thinking (Ellis 1979). Earlier, in a similar vein, Alfred Adler suggested that an individual's emotional reactions are generated by his or her attitudes, beliefs and perceptions. They are 'created' by the individual himself. Therapy is a learning process through which a person acquires the ability to speak with himself in appropriate ways to control his own conduct (Shaffer 1947). Psychological disorders can be treated by making people learn how to make appropriate verbalisations to themselves.

The therapeutic goal of REBT is to develop necessary skills in the clients to identify their irrational beliefs, dispute them and replace them with rational ones. REBT attempts to teach the clients to examine the rationality of their beliefs empirically and change the irrational (self-defeating) beliefs. The socially sabotaging conduct is changed into self-healing. The client learns to solve his problems in a socially ef-fective manner (Ellis 2000).

The A-B-C Paradigm of REBT

The REBT is based on certain fundamental assumptions about human behaviour. One of these assumptions is that almost all people try to remain alive and try to achieve their basic goals. When these goals are thwarted, they encounter adversities A. In a general sense, A also stands for any activating event that has a recognisable consequence C, even if they are not adverse. The second component is the individual's belief system B. It refers to all the beliefs or chains of thoughts associated with A and that leads to a consequence C. The consequences C are emotions and behaviour that occur due to the beliefs B held by the individual. The interpretation of consequences is largely influenced by the belief systems. They either help or hinder satisfaction of the goals. Ellis (2000) stated that, although the activating events are important contributors to their emotional and behavioural consequences, they do not directly cause the consequences. A interacts with beliefs B to bring a consequence C. We may symbolically state, $A \times B = C$. People, largely 'construct' their consequences. The A-B-C of REBT explains Ellis's theory of emotional reactivity.

Wessler (1986) partitioned the A-B-C paradigm into smaller components. The A (activating event) includes three components: (a) objective stimulus, (b) awareness of the existence of the stimulus event, (c) its definition and description, and (d) interpretations , that is, inferences made about the unobservable and unknown aspects of the objective event which has the potential to lead to irrational thinking. B (beliefs) includes (a) evaluation of the event , that is, whether the event is positive, negative or neutral. There are at least four objects of evaluation; the action, its intent, the consequences of the action and the actor. Usually people do not make a distinction between these entities. The singular evaluation becomes all-inclusive and catastrophic when irrationality prevails. The consequences C incorporate affective arousal, behaviour, and reinforcing consequences. Here, it should be noted that not all overt behaviour might follow arousal. However, for emotionally disturbed individuals negative overt behaviour usually follows arousal. The reinforcing consequences maintain irrational thinking as well as behaviour. Therefore, it serves as an important entity in the sequence.

Ellis (1962) explained that irrational and self-defeating beliefs are quite common to our culture. For instance, people's beliefs that they will be loved by everybody, or that one will be competent in all spheres of life, although irrational, are shared by many. Similarly, most people do believe that they must or should behave in a particular manner. They have many such unconditional 'musts' and 'shoulds'. Ellis's observation is parallel to Karen Horney's hypothesis about the 'tyranny of the shoulds'. Such irrational beliefs upset the individual when the behaviour proves to be contrary to these beliefs. When they keep speaking to themselves with these words, (what Ellis called 'musterbate'). Musturbatory thinking leads to three irrational beliefs: (i) Awfulising, (ii) Self-damnation, and (iii) 'I can't stand it'. He explained that these three common irrationalities lead to innumerable irrational beliefs and cause disturbed emotional and behavioural consequences.

For example:

1. 'I absolutely *must* perform well at important tasks and be approved by significant others, or else I am an inadequate person'.
2. 'Other people absolutely *must* treat me kindly, considerately and fairly'.
3. 'Condition under which I live, absolutely *must* provide me with what I really want, or else the life is horrible, I can't stand it and the world is a rotten place!'

The rational emotive behaviour therapists believe that there are three types of conditions that explain cognitions: cold cognitions, warm cognitions and hot cognitions. Cold cognitions are generally observations, descriptions and non-evaluative inferences. Warm cognitions emphasise preferences and non-preferences, whereas hot cognitions are loaded with emotional-demand statements that often lead to disturbances in emotion and behaviour, such as depression, anxiety, aggression and so on. Hot cognitions appear in a variety of forms, such as overgeneralisations, catastrophising, magnification, personalisation and so on. These are unrealistic, all-or-none type of statements having no empirical basis (Ellis 1984).

The Techniques

Rational emotive therapists believe that people are innately constructivists. They acquire emotional problems. At childhood such disturbances are acquired though self-teaching, training and through the 'help' of others. As they continue to construct dysfunctional beliefs, dysfunctional thinking, feeling and behaviour become a habitual pattern. At this stage, people find it difficult to change them, although they have the power to change their self-defeating irrational thinking that causes undesirable emotions and behaviour. The crucial role that a therapist plays is to facilitate the process of change by using various cognitive, experiential (affective) and behavioural techniques. Thus, REBT is a multimodal approach.

Ellis extended the steps involved in REBT to A-B-C-D-E paradigm. Here, D generally refers to disputing, debating, redefining and making appropriate communication regarding events, feelings and behaviour of the individual client's by himself and/or by the therapists. E refers to the experience of the changes in feelings, emotions and behaviour caused by rational thinking. After active self-verbalisation, the client experiences a relief from the symptoms that kept disturbing him previously. Within the rubric of REBT, a number of cognitive, affective and behavioural techniques are used.

Cognitive Techniques

(1) *Disputing*: Active disputing of irrational beliefs is the core technique of REBT. Rational emotive therapists use three processes for disputing irrational beliefs: (a) debating, (b) discriminating, and (c) defining (Ellis and Grieger 1986) .

(2) *Coping self-statements*: Statements about philosophy of effective living and self-statement of alternative and rational forms of behaviour help the clients stabilise themselves. What people speak to themselves, influences their thoughts, behaviour and feelings. Therefore, the therapist attempts to modify these self-verbalisations. He trains his client to think empirically and rationally.

(3) *Modelling* is used to demonstrate skilful behaviour in various situations where the client feels inadequate. Models who have mastered similar or even worse situations are illustrated as examples of role models. It motivates the client to acquire skills of managing difficult situations.

(4) *Cost-benefit analysis*: It aims at sensitising the client about the behavioural and financial cost of his dysfunctional feelings and actions. He is explained how certain behaviour may be beneficial in short term but may cost him heavily in the long run.

(5) *Cognitive homework* is meant for practicing and maintaining the acquired skills of disputing dysfunctional beliefs in home setting.

(6) *Use of psycho-educational materials*: Various psycho-educational materials such as books, audio and videocassettes are used for promoting self-help skills.

(7) *Positive visualisation*: The client is trained to visualize self-efficacious behaviour and feelings.

(8) *Reframing*: This is a technique that requires the client to develop a fresh and rational realisation that the situation was not catastrophic as he thinks it was.

(9) *Resistance to overgeneralisation*: Overgeneralisation of feelings and actions from one stray situation to another is one of the common behaviour shared by many people who experience problems in life situations. Therefore, the therapist attempts to train the client how to resist the tendency to over-generalise their observations, feelings and actions and how to refrain from black and white (either/or) thinking.

(10) *Real-life application*: The therapist attempts to help the client in application of problem-solving skills in actual life situations, in order to generalise the skills.

Emotive–experiential Techniques

Disputing ones own irrational beliefs is done *in vivo* or on a tape recorder by the client himself. Experiencing a close and trusting relationship with the therapist, using visualisations to recognise positive as well as intense negative feelings are some additional emotive experiential techniques. Other techniques include role playing of the difficult emotional situations, and handling them, using 'shame-attacking' and exercises involving 'embarrassing' acts, help the client to get rid of performance anxiety. Another emotive-experiential method is to encourage the client not to denigrate oneself even while encountering disapproval.

Activity–oriented Behavioural Techniques

A wide range of behavioural techniques are used in REBT. They include exposure or *in vivo* desensitisation of various problem behaviours like phobias and compulsions. Taking deliberate risks, failing on an important work, refusing to upset, staying in uncomfortable situations and mastering it are some of the frequently used methods. Other activity-oriented methods are self-reinforcement and punishment for helping behaviour and self-defeating ones, respectively. Stimulus control technique is used against addictions and compulsions. Relapse prevention technique is used against sliding back to old feeling and irrational thinking. Skill training is often used to enhance assertiveness, communication, improve public speaking and other desired actions.

BECK'S COGNITIVE THERAPY

In many ways, Aaron Beck's approach is similar to that of Ellis, although it developed independently. The primary goal of Beck's cognitive learning approach is to modify the client's faulty assumptions that maintain maladaptive behaviour and emotions. Cognitive therapy was developed out of his earlier research on the psychopathology of depression (e.g. Beck 1963, 1964, 1967). The approach was influenced by other systems of psychotherapy such as psychoanalysis and behaviour therapy as well.

Beck's conceptualisation of psychological problems is reflected in his cognitive model of depression. It assumes that depression is created during the childhood and that the individual develops a 'negative self-schema'. The underlying cluster of rules which maintain the negative self-schema are cluster of rules like, 'The situation in which I was put, was highly irritating', 'I am good for nothing' or 'I will never succeed in my life'. By analysing these kinds of self-dialogues of people with depression, Beck found three fundamental themes: (i) The tendency to view the environment (events) negatively, (ii) Disliking oneself, and (iii) Interpretation of the future. He stated that these three themes together constituted the 'cognitive triad'. Once activated, the triad determines all other affective-behavioural and motivational features of depression.

Beck also suggested that depressive self-judgment affects information-processing skills leading to cognitive errors. Different types of cognitive errors are often encountered in decision-making:

(a) *Polarised thinking*: All-or-none, either/or kind of dichotomous thinking. For example, if there is something to be shared, the client says, 'I shall get the entire thing or not at all.' A slight disagreement with parents is treated as total rejection.

(b) *Personalisation*: Wrongly blaming oneself for negative things that happen in the environment. For example, for failure of electricity in the town, the client feels himself/herself responsible and guilty.

(c) *Selective abstraction*: The tendency to focus on a negative detail of the event and viewing the entire event and the whole experience in that light.

(d) *Magnification/Minimisation*: The tendency to over emphasise the negative events and under emphasise the positive ones.

(e) *Overgeneralisation*: Tendency to draw sweeping generalisations from limited observations.

(f) *Arbitrary inference*: Tendency to draw conclusions from absence of clear or insufficient evidence. These information-processing errors maintain 'depressionogenic' patterns of behaviour. The challenge of a cognitive therapist is to deal with these cognitive distortions.

The Techniques

Three core techniques are used in cognitive therapy to facilitate cognitive and behavioural changes in the client. The most popular one is collaborative empiricism; the other two are Socratic dialogue and guided discovery. These techniques help the client to recognise his erroneous assumptions, counteract them, and then reject the wrong or distorted cognitions.

Collaborative Empiricism

Beck's cognitive therapy is based on exploring the cognitive distortions and correcting them. In order to do so, collaborative work is required on part of the client as well as the therapist. They jointly and scientifically examine the evidence and, either support or reject the hypothesis held by the client. Collaborative relationship helps in determining the goal of therapy. Through this process, biased cognitions are corrected and adaptive alternatives are jointly developed.

Socratic Dialogue

Socratic dialogue refers to careful questioning by the therapist in order to promote new cognitive learning in the client. The therapist acts as a catalyst for the client to facilitate exploration of the problem, identification of assumptions, thoughts and images, their careful evaluation, and assessment of the consequences of these cognitions and behaviour.

Socratic method of asking questions and generating contradictions creates a situation for examining and refuting client's own constructs. For example, if the client puts forward a thesis, construct, belief or idea that loss of love makes the life meaningless and, consequently, it makes him depressed. The arguments may proceed somewhat like this:

Client: Nobody loves me, therefore, I feel depressed. Life appears meaningless for me.
Therapist: How do you know that people don't love you?
Client: Nobody around me in my family tells me that they love me, nor appreciate my work.
Therapist: Is it always necessary that their love be expressed in speech?
Client: Not of course.
Therapist: Do you love everybody?
Client: Not all.
Therapist: Then why do you think people will love you? and for that, you would feel depressed and even consider your life to be meaningless?
Client: Yes, I do understand... but...

The therapist engages the client in such Socratic dialogues to develop a clear definition of his personal constructs. If the client asserts a thesis p, the therapist says q and r arguing that q and r entails *not-p* (i.e. negation of the original assertion). These arguments and contradictions bring him closer to the truth.

Guided Discovery

Guided discovery is a technique by which a client is guided to develop new and alternative ways of thinking instead of falling into the trap of his 'cognitive triad'. In order to do so the client is helped to design and carry out new experiments to test his hypotheses. Discovery of new and adaptive ways of thinking helps him to have improved cognitive and behavioural alternatives.

While dealing with severely depressed clients, Beck noted that they make negative labelling of their behaviour. They see themselves as losers, unable to achieve anything. On the contrary, when they succeed, it hardly causes any mood-elevating effect. Therefore, the therapist asks the client to label his/her behaviour, and failures (and successes) properly. The therapist may demonstrate to the client how to do the same by taking few of such events in the client's life. Graduated tasks assignments are given as homework in order to have the experience of success. Then gradually the level of difficulty of the task assigned is increased. For instance, an adult depressed male who has lost interest in his regular work is asked to complete small tasks like arranging his belongings neatly at his home or jogging two kilometres every morning. Accomplishments in simple tasks and persistent encouragement by the therapist motivate the client to engage in other complex and elaborate activities. Homework assignments are also given to translate these skills into day-to-day problem solving. In order to enhance the effectiveness of these cognitive strategies, video and audiotapes are also used. Apart from listening and watching theses audio and videotapes about their conversation and behaviour with the therapists, they participate in other adjunct activities including relaxation and modelling.

There are many similarities between the approaches followed by Ellis and Beck, although these therapies developed independently. Rules or basic assumptions are likely to predispose people to depression (Beck 1976: 295). Some of these rules or assumptions are:

(1) In order to be happy, I have to be successful in whatever I undertake.
(2) To be happy, I must be accepted by all people at all times.
(3) If I make a mistake, it means that I am inept.
(4) I can't live without love.
(5) If somebody disagrees with me, it means he does not like me.
(6) My value as a person depends on what others think of me.

In the language of REBT (Ellis 1977), these basic rules are irrational beliefs that people hold, and consequently experience emotional and behavioural problems. Both the approaches use empirical and deductive methods for examining cognitive distortions and irrational beliefs. However, there are different levels of structure involved. Beck's treatment package is specifically designed for depressives for 20 hours, particularly for the reason that it is a time-limited, no-nonsense approach, and discourages both the therapist and the client from wasting time. The client develops the much-needed sense of order and discipline. The second reason is that such highly structured approach is easily researched (Rimm and Masters 1979).

STRESS INOCULATION

This approach was first proposed by Meichenbaum and Cameron (1973) for controlling anxiety problems in their clients. Thereafter, the technique has been used with variation for treatment of several other emotional and behavioural disorders. The medical metaphor 'inoculation' was used to explain its underlying process of exposing the clients to a tolerable dosage of stress in order to develop competence to cope with actual stressful events. Three basic phases are involved in the application of this technique: (i) Cognitive preparation, (ii) Skill acquisition, and (iii) Application and practice.

1. Cognitive Preparation

At the initial stage, the client is encouraged to discuss the stressors with the therapist. It familiarises the therapist with the client's perception and language pattern. Sharing his/her observations, the client is educated about the nature of stress, its function and individual patterns of reaction. The cognitive preparation aspect of stress inoculation consists of (i) identifying the stressors (e.g. events, situations, behaviours or people), (ii) distinguishing emotional responses (e.g. anxiety from fear, anger from aggression), (iii) distinguishing justified responses from unjustified ones, (iv) recognising the determinants of stress, (v) identifying the sequences of stress response, and (vi) introduction to stress-management techniques.

In order to introduce the treatment, explain its rationale, and acquaint the client with the treatment techniques, some therapists introduce a treatment manual also. This is how the therapeutic process is initiated.

2. Skill Acquisition

Apart from analysis of negative emotional states caused by stressful situations, the client is taught the required cognitive and behavioural skills to cope with the stress. He/she is trained to view the provoking events objectively and reduce the undue importance attached to it. Alternative appraisal of the event helps to improve flexibility of the cognitive structuring of the event. Singer (1968) suggested that humour might be used to neutralise negative emotions associated with stressful events. Relaxation techniques are often taught to the clients as a healthy response which facilitate coping. Self-regulated private speech (self-instruction) (Meichenbaum 1974) is taught to the client to alter the undesirable responses. This may be used at various stages: while preparing for a provocation ('I am aware that the event may be tough to deal with but I know how to deal with. I shall plan carefully to handle the situation, stick to the issues and shall not be emotional'), impact and confrontation ('I shall maintain my cool, no matter whatever provocation I face, and speak up the facts'), coping with arousal ('I am feeling uneasy, my muscles are tight. I must relax taking a deep breath and being in a comfortable posture on the chair') and subsequent reflections ('I could resolve the conflict successfully. This is a great achievement. I must keep it up'), or ('I could not handle the situation so effectively. I must try again. Prepare myself better to cope. I shall certainly succeed.'). Self-instruction helps to mediate human behaviour. Therefore, self-instructional training has a bearing on altering maladaptive responding too.

3. Application and Practice

The skill acquisition stage helps in developing competence in the client that has to be implemented in stressful situations. Therefore, it requires generalisation. Application and practice caters to these needs. Practice may be conducted in an actual setting or through role-play. While the skill acquisition phase involves introduction, modelling and rehearsal of coping techniques, application and practice involves application of these methods in real stressful situations. These situations may be graded from low intensity stressful situations to higher ones. This kind of exposure continues throughout the stress inoculation training. It helps the therapist to gauge the improvement.

APPLICATIONS OF CBT

Cognitive-behaviour therapy has been used effectively in treatment of a wide range of disorders. Constraint of space does not allow us to describe each area of its application; therefore, attempt has been made to illustrate some of the important areas of intervention.

CBT for mood disorders, particularly depression has been reported to be effective by a numbers of researchers. Training clients to identify distortions of thinking and modifying their thinking as well as behaviour patterns are the two principal components of CBT. In a systematic study, Rush et al. (1977) took 41 unipolar depressed outpatients with moderate to severe degree of depression. The mean duration of treatment was 8.8 years. The clients were randomly distributed into pharmacotherapy (n = 22) as well as CBT (n = 19). The clients in CBT were seen twice a week initially for 20 sessions in 12 weeks. The pharmacotherapy group was seen only once a week. Imipramine was administered in increasing dosage to a maximum of 250 grams per day for a maximum of 12 weeks.

Both cognitive therapy and pharmacotherapy cases had the same mean depression score at the beginning of the treatment on Beck's Depression Inventory (BDI), and similar rates of improvement were noticed during the first eight weeks of treatment. However, clients treated with cognitive therapy showed more rapid improvement than in pharmacotherapy during the initial sessions. Second, due to the adverse side effects of drugs, dropout rate was more than what was observed in cognitive therapy (eight versus one). Thirdly, using analysis of covariance, it was observed that the mean end of BDI score was significantly higher in the cognitive therapy group than the chemotherapy group when the dropouts were included in the computation of scores (7.3 versus 17.4, p<0.01). Similar results were obtained when the dropouts were excluded from computation also (5.9 versus 13.0). 75 per cent of the cognitive therapy group of clients showed marked or complete remission whereas only 23 per cent pharmacotherapy cases showed such amount of improvement. In both the treatment groups, there was significant reduction in the anxiety scores of the clients on Hamilton Anxiety Scores. When between-groups comparison was made, neither of the treatment was found to be superior to the other. Follow-ups conducted on 38 clients at three and six months intervals indicated that there were substantially fewer relapses in the cognitive therapy group. This experiment was one of the earliest ones to indicate that cognitive therapy can be effective in the treatment of mood disorders.

Depressed individuals tend to show increased memory for negative autobiographical events than positive events (Mineka and Nugent 1995). Such individuals dwell on rumination and regret pertaining to the current negative mood states and related past events. It generates alternative or counter-factual scenarios of what might have been (Gilovich and Medvec 1995; Roese 1994). Williams (1997) reported that depressed individuals are often plagued by the persistence of 'overgeneral' memories that represent the past in a non-specific and highly negative manner. Such memories often amplify and contribute to depression. Drawing the observations from these studies, Dixit et al. (1999) attempted to use brief cognitive therapy to treat depression. 60 participants in the age group of 32–38 years were studied. Depressive Experience Scale in Hindi developed by the first author was used for assessment of dependency, self-criticism and efficacy of the depressive subjects. The authors highlighted two important aspects of Cognitive-behaviour therapy: (i) self-evaluation, and (ii) time-orientation.

Self-evaluation process involves continuous noticing, monitoring, thinking about, and experiencing the affective consequences of one's enduring patterns of behaviour. Attention to internal events such as thoughts and feelings was also included as a part of self-evaluation. Time-orientation aspect of therapy helps the client focus on the present, that is, here-and-now events instead of the past or the future. The client is continually encouraged to experience and express the thoughts and feelings as they occur. They were also asked to describe their behaviours as they occur ('behavioural focus'). The therapy sessions lasted for about one and a half hours. The authors claimed clinically significant improvement in their negative memories. It was also observed that larger percentage of males had negative memories than females. It was attributed to the cultural difference in their attitude toward life as well as strategies of handling difficult life situations.

Cognitive Behavioural Analytic Systems of Psychotherapy (CBASP) is an interesting combination cognitive, behavioural, dynamic and interpersonal approaches. In a recent study Keller and his colleagues (Keller et al. 2000) studied the effects of Nefazdone and CBASP on depression, separately as well as in combination. The results revealed that although initially there were similar treatment gains in both the therapies, at the later stage the effects of CBASP was found to be more long-lasting than the effects of chemotherapy. Combination of different treatment modalities was more effective than any single modality. That means overall gain of combined treatment was better than single modality treatment.

The cognitive-behavioural approach to anger-control is based on the assumption that emotional arousal and the course of action that such arousal instigates are determined by one's cognitive structuring of the situation. The intervention programmes aim at handling the problem at cognitive, affective and behavioural levels. Ellis (1973) explained that it is not the events themselves, rather one's interpretations and internal dialogues about those events that shape the response pattern. The cognitive aspect of the situation determines how people label their emotion and to what extent they exhibit anger (Schachter and Singer 1962; Conn and Crowne 1964). The appraisal of provocation, amplification and attenuation of aggression are influenced by cognitive factors.

Novaco (1975) conducted some of the earliest studies on anger management to examine the comparative effectiveness of cognitive coping and relaxation training separately and in combination. Four treatment conditions were constructed: (1) combination of cognitive and relaxation control, (2) cognitive treatment, (3) relaxation training, and (4) attention control. The treatment effects were evaluated in pre- and post-treatment designs. A variety of assessment procedures was used. It included psychometric, physiological and situational tests. An 80 items self-report scale describing the provocation incident was used. The respondent was required to evaluate them on a 5-point scale. The physiological indices included measurement of changes in systolic and diastolic blood pressure and EMG. These measures were obtained under two provocation instances created for anger coping in the laboratory; one in imaginal and the other, in role-play mode. Apart from that, each subject was asked to maintain an anger diary that narrated real-life anger experiences and evaluate them on a 7-point scale. The assessment and treatment were conducted in 12 sessions of approximately 45 minutes each.

The findings revealed that combined treatment (cognitive and relaxation) had the most significant and generalised effect in reducing anger. Cognitive therapy was the next effective treatment method in the control of anger. Relaxation alone was the least effective method. Although relaxation training showed considerable improvement, it was restricted to imaginal provocations mode alone. Therefore, it was concluded that cognitive method alone was more effective than relaxation alone in control of anger.

A good deal of self-control programmes involve children. In an interesting study, Black (1970) used verbal self-control training for aggressive-disruptive children. The boys were asked to orally read, essays on their behaviour problems. It contained responses to four questions that the children were required to ask after each incident of disruptive behaviour. Camp et al. (1977) conducted a cognitive-behavioural programme with aggressive children for developing self-control. This work was primarily based on the earlier works of cognitive-behaviour therapists (e.g. Meichenbaum and Goodman 1971; Shure and Spivack 1974a). Transfer of the treatment effects to another non-target behaviour or setting is another meaning of generalisation. Rath (1995) in a verbal self-instruction (VSI) training for tribal and non-tribal children reported generalisation of treatment effects to various tasks and across settings.

Rational emotive therapy (RET) attempts to alter a person's belief system about himself and his environment and thereby reduces his worries and anxieties through cognitive appeals (Ellis 1962). The technique has been used effectively by investigators for treatment of various disorders. Helode (2002) used RET for treatment of occupational stress of a group of 13 Indian bank managers, who were in the age group of 35–45 years and were affected by occupational stress. Cognitive restructuring was one of the techniques used. Although, the details of treatment procedures were not reported, all the clients improved after treatment. The changes were measured through Occupational Stress Index (Srivastava and Singh 1981).

The number of symptoms manifested by the clients, the extent of psychological distress and disability, are largely maintained by interaction between the psychological and physiological processes. How a person interprets his bodily symptoms is a very important issue in the onset, maintenance, treatment as well as relapse of most disorders. It sets-in a vicious process when psychological factors are involved. When clients experience emotional distress, it causes further bodily sensations leading to increased attention to these. The type of behaviour which is used to cope with conditions, may be dysfunctional and act to exacerbate the problem. Individuals and treating clinicians may respond to the client in a way to intensify rather than alleviate their concern for disease. Bodily sensations and dysfunctional coping serve to self-perpetuate the disorder. Akoijam and Prasadarao (2002) used a multicomponent cognitive-behaviour therapy including Jacobson's progressive muscle relaxation, activity scheduling, somatic interview (to elicit the onset and nature of symptoms and their attribution), retribution, cognitive restructuring, behavioural and family counselling in the treatment of somatoform disorder in a 50-year-old female. The symptoms included complaints of multiple body aches and pains, associated anxiety and depressive symptoms occurring for 25 years. 31 sessions of cognitive-behaviour therapy incorporating the above components brought clinically significant change in the core symptoms such as somatic symptoms, depression, anxiety and negative thoughts.

Arun and Kaur (2002) used a cognitive-behavioural package comprising of relaxation training, distraction, differential reinforcement, self-control and diary maintenance in order to control impulsivity in four children in the age range of 3–12 years. The target behaviour included impulse to steal (kleptomania), pull hair (trichotillomania) and compulsive spitting (a culture-bound symptom, Bhatia 2000). Follow-up conducted over a period ranging between eight months to two years revealed maintenance of the positive behaviour change.

A number of methodologically sound studies have been conducted to examine the effects of cognitive-behaviour therapy on panic and anxiety disorders. Pathak (1999) attempted to use Beck's model (Beck et al. 1985) of cognitive therapy in the treatment of generalised anxiety disorder. Beck's cognitive model of psychopathology assumes that people experience pervasive anxiety because of their beliefs about themselves and the world. Such beliefs make them prone to interpret a wide range of situations in a threatening fashion. It is not the event per se but their interpretations that make them anxious. They gradually learn to overestimate the danger inherent in a given situation. It worsens and perpetuates the symptoms. The author studied 18 male and two female clients in the age range of 18–55 years. The cognitive techniques used in the therapy aimed at examining the client's specific misconceptions and maladaptive assumptions. It included monitoring negative automatic thoughts, recognising the connection between cognition, affect and behaviour, examining the evidences for and against distorted automatic thoughts, substitution of some reality-oriented interpretations for those biased cognitions, and learning to identify and alter dysfunctional beliefs which predispose the individual to distort his/her experience. The behavioural techniques included deep muscle relaxation, weekly activity schedule, rating of mastery and pleasure schedule. Out of 20 cases, 18 responded well to the treatment. One year follow-up revealed maintenance of therapeutic gains.

Agoraphobia is one of the most carefully studied disorders. Catastrophic cognitions play crucial role in this disorder. People show panic reactions when they interpret bodily sensations as signs of impending physical or mental catastrophe (Beck and Emery 1985; Clark 1986). Therefore, checking the accuracy of their beliefs is considered as an essential ingredient in CBT. Based on this model Barlow and Cerny (1988) developed a treatment programme for panic disorders called panic control treatment (PCT). A few years later Clark and Salkovskis (1991) used a cognitive therapy package that included disconfirmation of catastrophic beliefs and discouraging defensive strategies of the client that prompts safety behaviours. In spite of theoretical differences, both the approaches were equivalent.

In a review of the studies conducted in the 1990s, Barlow and Lehman (1996) reported that either panic control treatment or cognitive therapy eliminated panic in 80 per cent cases and were better than either no treatment or psychotherapy controls. CBT was better than other alternative treatments or minimal treatment controls (DeRubeis and Crits-Christoph 1998). Clark and his associates (1994) compared the effects of cognitive therapy focused on modification of catastrophic misinterpretations with two other treatments, namely, Imipramine chemotherapy and Applied Relaxation. All the above treatments were superior to wait-list controls. Nearly 90 per cent clients treated with cognitive therapy were symptom free after three months of treatment whereas only 50 per cent with other two treatments were symptom-free after intervention. Only five per cent clients treated with focused cognitive therapy relapsed during follow-up, as compared to 40 per cent treated with medication.

Taking a large sample of 312 clients with panic disorder, Barlow and his colleagues (2000) conducted a study on 312 clients with panic disorder. The clients were randomly assigned to either CBT or Imipramine, or combination of these two or placebo. All of them received three months of treatment. Each single modality of the treatment was found to be better than placebo. Imipramine produced better results, whereas effect of CBT was more enduring. Only four per cent relapsed as compared to 25 per cent in case of Imipramine chemotherapy. However, clients under combined treatment had highest rate of relapse.

Raj et al. (1999) used CBT for treatment of deliberate self-harm in three male and five female cases. The treatment package was a combination of Beck's Cognitive-behaviour therapy (Beck, Rush, Shaw and Emery 1979), Problem Solving Skill Training (D'Zurilla 1998), Jacobson's Progressive Muscle Relaxation (modified version; Mishra 1974) and Behavioural Counselling (Krumboltz 1969). Comparison of the pre- and post-test scores revealed clinically significant behavioural and cognitive changes in all cases. Follow-up interviews conducted at an interval of two years revealed maintenance of treatment gains.

Hallucinations is considered as an indication of thought disorder. It may be caused by deficits of meta-cognitive skills required for reality testing (Slade and Bentall 1988), anxiety and stress (Slade 1972) or unstimulating environmental conditions (Grassian 1983). Sometimes clients use coping strategies such as using earplugs or smoking to stop the ongoing hallucinations (Badley 1986). Various cognitive behavioural techniques to treat hallucinations include systematic desensitisation (Slade 1973), thought-stopping (Allen et al. 1985), aversion therapy (Weingartner 1971) and self-monitoring (Glaister 1985).

Jena (1999) used a multi-component behaviour therapy for treatment of recurrent auditory hallucination, stereotyped shoulder jerks and jumping, in a 44-year-old client diagnosed with schizophrenia. The treatment programme was developed after a detailed functional analysis. GSR biofeedback, cognitive restructuring and reciprocal inhibition were used as treatment techniques. The former technique was introduced for modifying irrational thinking, as the client viewed the condition to be 'uncontrollable' and falsely attributed to 'hearing of voices'. Cognitive restructuring was focused on distinguishing between hallucination and thought process, and explaining the situations that frequently triggered 'hallucinations' and consequent self-defeating actions. Apart from the projection of changes in biological indices, EMG was used as an instrument for masking the reported hallucinations. Competing mental and physical activities such as working on an ergograph, mental arithmetic reading served as stimuli for reciprocal inhibition. 15 sessions of intervention reduced hallucinations completely. A one month follow-up indicated maintenance of the treatment gains. Raj et al. (1999) used CBT comprising of two distinct phases of treatment. The first phase was focused on distraction techniques (Bentall et al. 1994). It comprised of doing mental activities, de-focusing, changing body postures, talking to others, listening to music, using sub-vocal activities such as humming, reading in a low voice and doing physical activities. The second phase of the treatment—cognitive restructuring—was aimed at analysing negative self-appraisals that made the client feel helpless and hopeless. At the second stage, the client's irrational beliefs were disputed. The treatment conducted in 12 sessions over two months. It showed significant improvement. Follow-up assessment conducted after a month revealed maintenance of the treatment gains.

Rath (1995) examined the effects of verbal-self instruction (VSI) training on reflective and impulsive reading disabled tribal and non-tribal children. The VSI training programme consisted of the following six steps: (i) the therapist modelled the performance while speaking aloud to himself, (ii) the child performed the tasks speaking aloud, (iii) the therapist modelled the performance while whispering to himself, (iv) the child performed the task in the same manner, (v) the therapist performed the task with covert self-instruction, with pauses and behavioural signs of covert thinking such as stroking the chin, looking at the ceiling, and the like, and, (vi) the child tried the next item in the task while speaking aloud. Two months of VSI training was found to be most effective for the non-tribal children who had non-reflective cognitive style but failed to yield desirable results for tribal impulsive children. There were clear generalisation effects of the learned skills on a variety of task situations and settings. The study also reveals the effects of culture in determining the effects of CBT.

Narayanan (1999) treated a 65-year-old sharebroker suffering from alcoholism and depression, with a package of CBT programme that included a wide range of 14 different techniques. The most important of them were rational emotive therapy, Jacobson's progressive muscle relaxation and systematic desensitisation of the anxiety provoking beliefs. Nine sessions of treatment conducted over two-and-a-half months improved the condition. However, the treatment effects were not examined empirically using any experimental or quasi-experimental design.

In one of the rare case reports, Garg (1999) reported the use of CBT in the treatment of a 27-year-old rape victim who suffered from dysthymia. The author analysed the irrational beliefs associated with the traumatic experience and the loss of virginity, were examined and explained to the client in a matter-of-fact way. Seven sessions of treatment improved her condition. She could handle her irrational thought effectively and managed to lead a happy conjugal life.

Khan (1999) studied 21 cases of tension headache in the age range of 15–45 years. The clients were assigned to one of the three treatment conditions, seven in each group: CBT, progressive muscle relaxation, and EMG biofeedback with minimal use of drugs. Use of biofeedback training and drugs was a basal factor in all therapy conditions. All cases were assigned to the treatment for eight sessions over a period of four weeks. CBT was found to be more effective than progressive muscular relaxation. The superior effects of CBT were attributed to the client's perception of increased life control with regard to the daily activities and problems.

Obsessive-compulsive disorder has been conceptualised by cognitive behaviour therapists from different perspectives. Inflated responsibility, deficits in decision-making, thought–action fusion, or perfectionist beliefs are some of the cognitive deficits found in these cases. Salkovskis (1989) and Salkovskis, Richards and Forrester (1995) explained that the occurrence of obsessions and intrusive thoughts (that they might be responsible for harming self or others) engage them in rituals, ruminations, checking and so on. These attempts are strategies to stop such obsessive ideas and neutralise the inflated risk-appraisals. Modification of dysfunctional appraisals, beliefs pertaining to the danger of fusion between thoughts and actions, and the beliefs about rituals and ruminations are the main targets of cognitive-behaviour modification. Rangaswami (1999) used CBT techniques that included verbal retributions to prevent thought-action diffusion and thought-event diffusion (Wells 1997), for treatment of 11 clients suffering from obsessive-compulsive disorder. All cases were diagnosed based on ICD-10 (WHO) criteria. For treatment, 31 different obsessions and compulsions, reported by the clients, were taken up. Modification of doubts and dysfunctional beliefs and associated affects were made by verbal retributions (Rangaswami 1997), modification of cognitive distortions and generating realistic thoughts (Burns 1989) were the main targets of intervention. The author attempted to restructure rules, assumptions and beliefs held by the clients. Post-treatment assessment and six months to three years follow-up indicated improvement in all symptoms except in obsessions like losing things, checking not to harm others, and contaminations and compulsions of cleaning and washing. This could be because they are associated with religious practices and values associated with them. Some of them might have been practiced or learned across generations (Clark and Purdon 1993; Salkovskis 1989). Religious and sexual compulsions are refractory to treatment (Rangaswami 1985; James and Blackburn 1995).

Datta and Broota (2000) treated 15 cases with obsessive-compulsive disorders with yoga and cognitive behavioural therapy. Five clients who participated in this treatment were assigned randomly to three treatment modalities. The first package of behaviour therapy and Jacobson's progressive relaxation included graded exposure to situations associated with obsessive thoughts or compulsions and the second included thought-stopping through yoga therapy. It included *Hatha yoga asanas* such as *sukhasana, vajrasana, dhanurasana, yogendra, nispanda bhava, yonimudra, makarasana, sabhasana,* and *suryanamaskar*. The third package was thought-stopping through both Jacobson's progressive relaxation and yoga therapy. Although the procedure of thought stopping was not described, the treatment was conducted for 10 sessions, one hour each over a period of three weeks. Combination of behaviour therapy, Jacobson's progressive relaxation and yoga therapy was more effective than any one of the other techniques described above. Yoga therapy alone was not found to be as effective as the other two methods in the management of obsessive-compulsive disorder.

RELIGIOSITY AND SPIRITUALITY

Spirituality is an important dimension of human behaviour. The spiritual pursuits recommended by religious scriptures have helped in preventing mental and physical disorders in people for ages. Spiritually based treatment procedures such as transcendental meditation, yoga, vipassana, and other religious therapies have been used for treatment of various disorders. Many people report considerable behaviour change after they are exposed to some kind of spiritual experience. Not only does it help in the treatment of behavioural disorders but also enhances quality of life. These techniques have now been examined empirically and are slowly getting incorporated into different treatment approaches. Association of Behaviour Therapy (ABT), USA in 1984 organised a special symposium on this subject. Bergin (1980, 1983) focused on the religious factors used in psychotherapy. Words and mantras used in prayer, meditation, or worship could be interpreted as the use of a 'second signalling system' that contains symbolic meaning. These words act as conditioned stimuli to easily induce relaxation or a trance-state. Spilka et al. (1985) considered religion from empirical perspective. He observed that 'shifting of theoretical structure has led to an intrusion of spiritual factors to go before even the cognitive ones'. It has high potential for self-control, coping and detachment from suffering (Rangaswami 1994).

CONCLUSION

Application of cognitive-behaviour therapy has been enormous in the last three decades. Now special volumes and journals devoted entirely to this subject reflect the bulk of researche conducted. Any attempt to describe the entire spectrum of CBT available today for treatment would require several volumes. Constraints of space press us to restrict ourselves to some of the fundamental dimensions of these representative approaches only. Therefore, readers are suggested to refer to the source materials cited in the references.

In a thoughtful article, Beck wrote that cognitive behaviourism in behaviour therapy has been characterised by far-reaching and challenging theoretical analyses on the basis of behaviour therapy and mushrooming of cognitive and behavioural therapies. This cognitive revolution has been resisted vehemently. Radical behaviourists strongly criticised the approach and viewed it as dilution of behaviourism.

However, in spite of its mismatch with radical behaviourism, cognitive-behavioural approach fills a conspicuous gap in our understanding of human behaviour. Perhaps this is one of the most crucial reasons for which the approach has been used in a wide range of disorders. Even the religious rituals practiced by people for ages for treatment of mental and behavioural disorders need fresh examination. It may provide new insights into our current understanding of behaviour therapy. However, it requires systematic analysis. Need of empirical methods of analysis would help us in discovering new laws of behaviour. The next chapter deals with research designs in behaviour therapy.

PART III
RESEARCH AND PRACTISE

17

Research Designs

The empirical status of behaviour therapy has been remarkably enhanced by application of experimental designs. In a broader sense, research design could be compared with an architect's plan for a building, a lay out or a blueprint for carrying out research (Winer 1971). Adoption of experimental designs provides a rational basis for collection and analysis of the data. The therapist attempts to schedule treatments for optimal statistical efficiency, so that valid conclusions can be drawn about them. The effects of intervention can be evaluated more objectively by using such designs. Technically speaking, the most important function of experimental design is to control variance (Broota 1989). A wide range of activities are involved in behaviour therapy such as conducting baseline observations of the selected target behaviour to intervention, follow-up and finally, statistical analysis of the obtained data. Although many behaviour therapists do not adhere to the classical statistical tradition of data analysis, and prefer to be more descriptive and qualitative in their approach, experimental designs add an additional dimension to the interpretation of observations. It makes the conclusions more meaningful. Applied behaviour analysis can be conducted using a group of individuals or a single individual, observing them over a period and putting them under one or more treatments. The former is generally called group design and the latter as single-case design.

GROUP DESIGNS

Studies using group designs remain the primary means of assessing whether a behavioural intervention is effective on a group of clients or not. The deductive process involved in it helps in distinguishing the independent variables from a wide range of other coexisting variables which influence therapy, such as motivational, biological, socio-cultural and environmental variables. From this perspective, group designs are considered the strongest approach to draw valid inferences from observations. This approach has both pragmatic and theoretical goals. The pragmatic interest is to device more efficient and helpful behaviour-change strategies. The theoretical interest is focused on deriving general behavioural laws. It clearly demonstrates the cause-and-effect relationship by ruling out the artifacts or rival hypotheses. Group designs provide basis for making strong inferences about the techniques used. The experimenter constructs a scientifically testable hypothesis to examine it statistically for either rejecting or accepting the alternative ones, although hypothesis testing is not confined to the group designs alone. Here, the experimenter assigns the clients into various experimental (intervention) or control (no-intervention) groups. The former being the condition where the independent variable (intervention) is introduced and manipulated, and the latter, where it is withdrawn in the control group or not introduced at all. It may also involve more than two groups or conditions. The experimenter systematically varies the conditions. The variations in the dependent measures of the clients exposed to such manipulated conditions are compared with those in the control condition where the independent variable is not manipulated.

Randomisation

Random assignment of clients to experimental and control groups is perhaps the signature characteristic of any true experiment. At times random assignment is confused with random selection. Random selection is used in the context of survey or demographic research, wherein an attempt is made to make the sample adequately representative of the population, so that the findings can be generalised. The purpose is to ensure that all clients in the population have equal chances of selection for the experiment. It enhances the external validity of the experiment.

Whereas, random assignment refers to allocation of clients to groups in such a way that the probability of each client's appearing in any of the groups is equal. The clients are randomly selected and assigned to the experimental conditions in such a manner that each of them will have an equal opportunity to be included in these groups (Kazdin 1998). It provides greater certainty that the outcome of this research is due to the treatment. This is linked with the internal validity, which is critical to intervention research. In order to make random assignment, the table of random numbers may be used. For instance, if there are three groups designated as 1, 2, and 3, the clients are selected in the order these numbers appear in the random number table, ignoring other numbers. (e.g 2, 3, 1, 1, 1). Even if the samples are selected randomly, it does not ensure that there will be equal distribution of samples for each condition. Some clients will have a higher chance to be included in one condition or the other.

For conducting powerful statistical analysis and for the convenience of handling data, it is advisable to have equal number of clients in each condition. In order to do that, while maintaining a random order of assignment, these are grouped into blocks and assigned to different treatment or no-treatment conditions randomly by picking up the numbers of each condition (e.g. 1–3) in random order.

Matching is another procedure of random assignment. Pairs of clients are matched on a variable that is salient to the outcomes in the study. Based on random assignment, one member of the pair is assigned to the control group and the other to the experimental group (Cook and Campbell 1979). Another procedure of random assignment is stratification of the clients on a salient variable (e.g. anxiety); then assigning each of them to each stratum (e.g. mild, moderate and severe). In order to ensure that the groups are equivalent in important client characteristics (age, sex, motivation, length of hospitalisation, severity), they can be equally distributed by making smaller groups or blocks of equal number of clients. When random assignment is impossible, quasi-experimental designs may be the only suitable alternative. Random assignment of subjects to experimental and control groups is the key characteristic of experimental design. However, this is not possible in all cases, particularly in field studies. Due to practical constraints, clients are administered post-test treatment alone. However, the validity of inferences drawn from such design is always subject to question (ibid.).

Limitations of Group Designs

In spite of the fact that group designs have been used extensively in research for generating theories of human behaviour, these have a number of pitfalls. Particularly in therapeutic research, this pattern of research has been questioned on several grounds. Criticisms have been primarily levelled against generalisation and ethical issues. Group outcome researches do not permit conclusions as to particular individual's characteristics that are correlated with improvement or deterioration of behaviour (Chassan 1967). A large part of the individual variation in the group are 'masked' or 'washed-out' by group averages. This 'summation of incompatibles' (Eysenck 1976) affects the results adversely.

Second, sometimes the observed differences in results could be due to larger changes in behaviour in a smaller proportion of the group. Therefore, it becomes difficult to correlate the specific treatment effects to specific characteristics of individual client(s). Such outcome researches may be important in basic research for different reasons. However, they are statistically significant but clinically useless.

Third, though the principles of learning are applicable to all individuals, the idiosyncratic learning histories preclude the assumption of commonality in response of the manifested symptoms. Thus, the idea of true control across individuals is debatable. Apart from these generality issues, group designs were also questioned on ethical grounds. The idea of no-treatment (placebo) group clearly deprives the client's from the right for treatment. Such deprivation is unethical. In order to overcome these problems, single-case designs are suggested as an alternative. The other justification is that in these designs one can continuously monitor the responses throughout the experiment. It reflects real concern for the client, which is difficult to exercise in traditional group designs.

While choosing group designs, the presumption is that the findings will have better generality. Its methodological pre-eminence of comparing treatment effectiveness is another attraction for researchers. However, these assumptions require careful analysis. Most behaviour therapists would acknowledge the virtual impossibility of meeting all the criteria of group research described in textbooks. Commenting on the myths and realities of group designs in behavioural research, Kiesler (1966) remarked, 'we incorrectly began with the philosophy of science offered by physics while ignoring the models offered by biology and astronomy, emphasising on nomothetic research. It pulled us out from ecological-naturalistic approaches and away from single-cases.' However, we believe that, it was neither a mistake to begin with nor a wrong model of approach. New methodology of research has always been incorporated in order to expand the horizon of research. The philosophy of science and methodology of proof has never remained a static phenomenon. Enshrinement to any single theoretical formulation is an obstacle to research progress (Strupp 1978). On the other hand, the declining status of psychoanalysis has also taught us the lessons of what to do and not to do. Comparing on the scientific validity of single-case designs, Skinner (1966: 21) wrote 'instead of studying a thousand rats one hour each, or a hundred rats for ten hour each, the investigator is likely to study one rat for thousand hours.' Practical problems of control, ethical objections on use of no-treatment groups as controls, inter-client variability and poor generality of findings are the four major limitations of group designs. Here the goal is not to present an exhaustive treatise; rather an overview is offered for the readers to make them conversant with the philosophy of the experimental designs in applied research.

SINGLE-CASE DESIGNS

Single-case design is described in various names such as, N=1, same-client, intra-client replication, own-control, intensive time-series designs or time-series experimentation. The term, 'time-series experimentation' is sometimes confused with time-series analysis, which is a statistical technique used for time-series data. However, for all practical purposes, we shall use the term single-case design throughout the text. Single-case design is essentially exploratory in nature and one of the most sensitive approaches to research in behaviour therapy. It is closely tied with the philosophy of behaviour analysis itself. Controlled investigation of individual cases is required to verify whether the change in behaviour is really a function of the therapeutic procedures applied to the individual case (Leitenberg 1973). Although used for a long time, it was scientifically understood as a method of proof very recently. Historically, many innovations in the field of neurology, psychology and psychiatry have been attained through single-case studies. The findings obtained from these studies have led to the formation of many scientific laws of human behaviour. However, there is an overwhelming emphasis on research involving a large number of clients. In spite of the fact that single-case studies have significant contribution in the field of applied behaviour analysis, use of group designs undoubtedly remains the primary means and the most powerful method of assessing intervention effectiveness (Cook and Campbell 1979; Slavin 1999). Single-case strategy in this connection facilitates the transformation of operant conditioning principles from laboratory to the clinic. Skinner (1973) regarded it as an exemplification of demonstrated experimental control, in which the problems are to be tackled by means of a hypothetico-deductive method. Single-case designs emphasise on individual cases to investigate the effects of an independent variable (treatment) on the dependent variable (behaviour) of a client. The treatment is continued until the behaviour is predictable, that is, until a steady state is attained. Single-case designs have achieved a legitimate place in confirmatory aspect of scientific activity (Kessler 1971) for the reason that the design is always tentative, amenable to change if significant questions arise on the way and it is an assumption-free approach. In addition to its scientific contribution as a distinct methodology of science, it has important functions in detecting more exactly as to what happens during the interventions. Making further distinction between a case study in natural environment and laboratory experiments, Gelso (1979: 28) observed and he quotes, 'in laboratory situations, we inevitably attain internal validity at the expense of generalisability, by pressing one bubble, we create another ... for ... bubbles cannot be eliminated.' Therefore, case studies and experiments fall at two different levels of a continuum on which scientifically adequate inference can be drawn (Kazdin 1980). Some authors have even viewed behaviour modification itself as application of single-case study to psychotherapy (Yates 1970).

Independent Variables

The variable, which an investigator can control or manipulate directly is an independent variable. The research in which this control or manipulation of variables is possible to be performed is described as an experimental research. In order to do that effectively, an accurate and precise definition of the independent variable is crucial. In behaviour therapy research, independent variables are often the treatment methods. The task is quite intricate in single-case experimental research because the same variables have to be applied for the same client on a number of occasions. Thus, one has to provide operational details, as the intervention labels can be quite misleading. For instance, simply a change in the contingency and schedule of treatment can have a substantial change in behaviour. Therefore, fine-grained detailing is necessary.

Baseline

In most single-case designs, baseline is the period of observation during which the natural occurrence of target behaviour is studied. It serves as a standard against which the treatment phases are compared. Most clinicians look for a stable baseline in which variability of behaviour is very low. Sidman (1960) defined stability as a five per cent or less range of variability. However, applied researchers often work with time constraints, and therefore find it difficult to maintain a sufficiently long period of baseline study for a treatment. Therefore, it may be suggested that the clinician should carefully evaluate the source of extreme variability in response.

Hersen and Barlow (1976) have stated eight different types of baselines such as (i) stable baseline, (ii) increasing baseline (target behaviour worsening), (iii) decreasing baseline (target behaviour improving), (iv) variable baseline, (v) variable-stable baseline, (vi) increasing-decreasing baseline, (vii) decreasing-increasing baseline, and (viii) unstable baseline. There can be many permutations and combinations of these too. How many minimum data points (observations) are to be obtained to evaluate the data? Barlow and Hersen (1973: 320) stated, 'a minimum of three separate observation points, plotted on the graph during the baseline phase are required to establish a trend in the data.' However, there are situations in which the nature of behaviour under study (e.g. self-injurious behaviour, or aggressive acting-out) compels the clinician to start the treatment immediately. Although we believe that longer baseline data would provide better data for analysis of the treatment effects, in many clinical settings it is not possible due to ethical and practical reasons. It is also suggested that the investigator should attempt to secure a relatively equal number of data points per phase, otherwise if the treatment phase were substantially longer than the preceding baseline, the effects could be attributed to the extended time factor rather than the treatment (Hersen and Barlow 1976).

While studying behaviour change in clinical setting, one may come across different patterns of variability. These can be classified under three groups: (i) spontaneous variation in behaviour without intervention, (ii) deterioration in behaviour, and (iii) improvement in behaviour following treatment. In order to ascertain the source of variability, under the first two conditions, the investigator should use improved research design to identify the source. Researchers have developed a wide range of single-case designs to study whether an intervention really 'works' or not, whether the behaviour improves, declines or the intervention has no effect at all. Some principal forms of single-case designs are discussed here.

B Design

This is the crudest and simplest form of time-series analysis (Glass, Wilson and Gottman 1974). Since there is complete absence of control it can hardly be called an 'experimental' design. In this condition, only a single treatment condition is introduced and the baseline measure is omitted. The investigator may take one or more target behaviours and focus on the changes in behaviour during the treatment period. He assumes that any change in behaviour is a function of treatment only. He may refer to previous cases or a theoretical assumption as the basis of interpretation of data. In many cases, pre-treatment baseline data is either difficult to obtain or it is unethical to gather (e.g. aggression, self-injurious behaviour). Under these circumstances, the clinician has to depend on the effects of intervention during the treatment sessions only. Figure 17.1 demonstrates a hypothetical case of responding positively to a behavioural treatment during 10 sessions of behavioural intervention. Until the fourth session, the rate of change was low. However, after this session the rate of acceleration was more perceptible. It indicates that the treatment was effective.

FIGURE 17.1
B Treatment Design

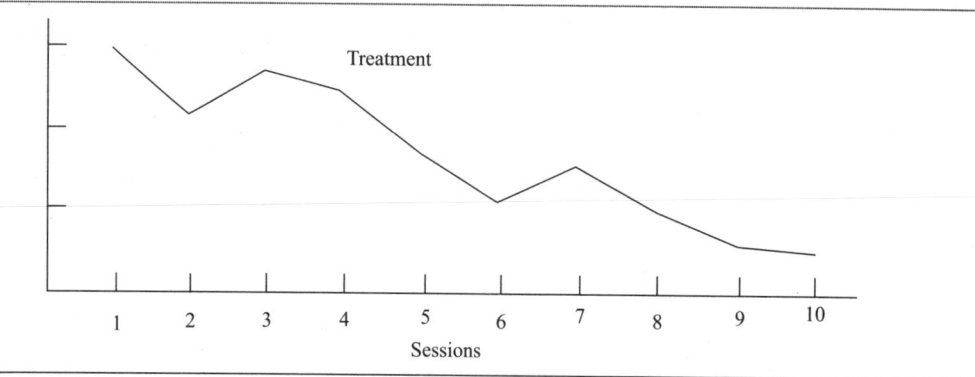

The major drawback of this design is that it does not promote new hypotheses, which can be confirmed by data. This design can only demonstrate the acceleration and deceleration effects associated with treatment procedure (that may demonstrate the trend of change) but cannot establish cause-and-effect relationship adequately as there is no true control phase. The inferential errors committed in B design are comparable with that of the case study method. Inferences are made based on the previous experiences of the clinician with similar cases. However, in spite of the disadvantages of the B design, it is gaining popularity for the reason that it is easy to administer and inexpensive. To some extent, it is comparable to the traditional psychotherapeutic intervention. Therefore, the practitioners making a transition from psychotherapy to behaviour therapy procedures can conveniently make use of it.

B-C Design

The B-C design is an extension of B design. It attempts to examine the differential acceleration or deceleration of behaviour between two successively administered techniques of treatment. The investigator may administer a varied schedule of the same technique or a different technique to study their differential effects. A hypothetical case of B-C design is illustrated in Figure 17.2.

FIGURE 17.2
B-C Treatment Design

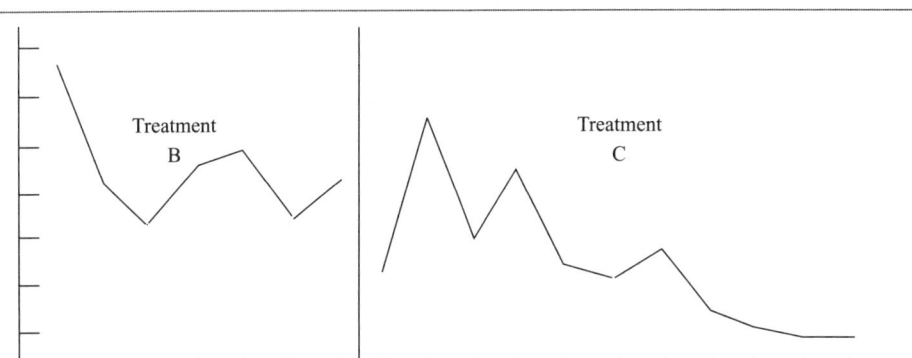

There are some advantages of B-C design. Counterbalance designs in behaviour therapy are often expensive and to some extent unethical, because these designs require the target behaviour to be observed at least for some time without intervention. At times, the no-treatment condition complicates the intervention, triggering new undesirable patterns of behaviour.

In order to avoid such complicacies, B or B-C designs are best suited. However, these are not free from weaknesses. As there is no pre-treatment baseline to evaluate the 'pure' treatment effects, it has poor empirical value for evaluating the treatment effects. It may reflect the difference treatment effects. One is uncertain as to whether the treatment effect during the second treatment phase is a continuing trend of the previous change. These drawbacks require treatment designs, which have at least one no-treatment phase for comparison. The factors, which control the dependent measure, are not completely documented unless the treatment is withdrawn after its introduction in a specific phase. Thus, it has poor potentiality for inferring causality, although it is better than a B design.

A-B Design

This is the simplest and crudest of all single-case experimental designs in terms of interpreting the cause and effect relationship. Inference about the effectiveness of a treatment is drawn upon the difference between the base rate of behaviour that occurred during no-treatment and treatment phases. A sample A-B design for a hypothetical case is illustrated in Figure 17.3.

FIGURE 17.3
A-B Treatment Design

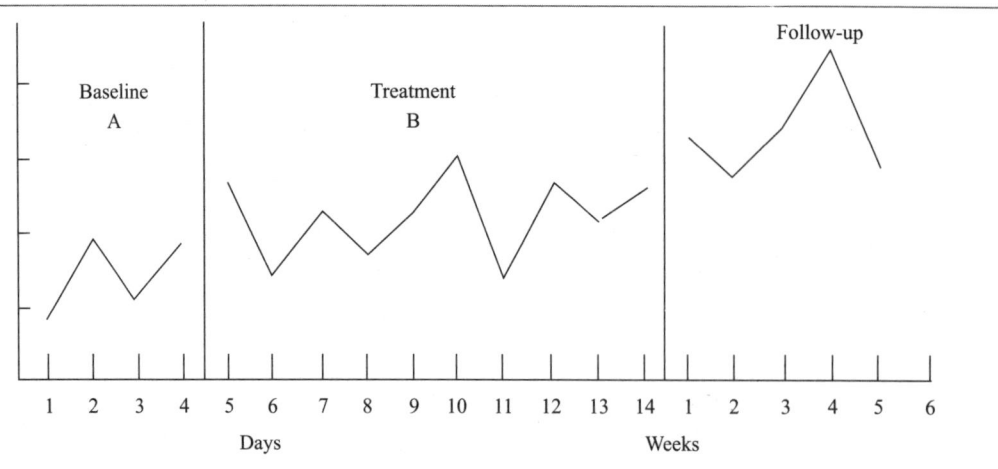

This design provides an opportunity to know the condition under which the baseline is obtained and whether a stable rate of behaviour was witnessed during this period; although by this design it is not possible to infer unequivocally that the intervention applied is the sole responsible agent of change. Effects of treatment that control the outcome are not completely documented because there is no scope for comparing the behaviour after the treatment is withdrawn. The A-B design is better than simple B design because it provides a chance of comparison between the behavioural baseline and the treatment baseline. However, it does not facilitate an evaluation of the generality of treatment beyond the therapeutic condition, that whether the change induced by the treatment persists after the treatment is withdrawn.

A-B-C Design

When the therapist wants to make a comparison between two interventions and a baseline condition, this design is the simplest one to use. After making a baseline observation, the client is exposed to two different treatments successively. Although this is an economical design, the order effect remains uncontrolled when one compares the earlier treatment with the later one. As there may be an accumulation effect of the former on the latter treatment, A-B-C design is considered a weak design. Of course, the same problem is observed in any design that compares the treatment effects of consecutive treatments. This type of design is most appropriately used when the first treatment (B) fails to yield desired effect; therefore, a modified treatment (C). A hypothetical A-B-C design is depicted in Figure 17.4.

A-B-A Design

The A-B-A design adds a return-to-baseline phase or a reversal phase to the A-B design. This removal of treatment in the second A phase introduces experimental control to the existing design. It facilitates demonstrable control and firm conclusions regarding the effect of the variables administered

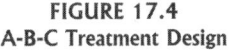

FIGURE 17.4
A-B-C Treatment Design

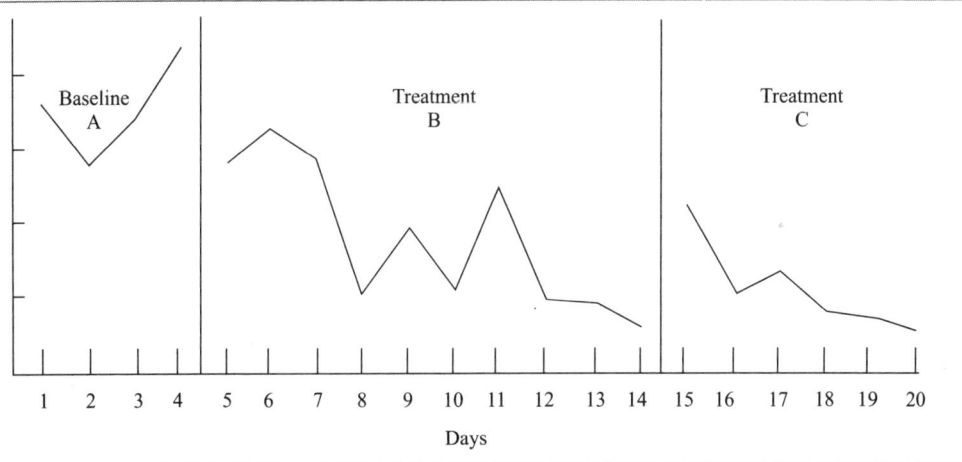

during treatment. Thus, it confirms that the changes obtained were a direct function of the institution and removal of the treatment variables (Barlow et al. 1973). Although in many ways A-B-A design (Figure 17.5) is superior to the A-B design, it has certain weaknesses too. The treatment ends in a no-treatment phase of the study, which is unethical. Most clients require either continuation of the treatment or thinning of the schedule of treatment before discharge. This problem is taken care of by another improved design like A-B-A-B, where there is a complete reversal of the entire sequence of treatment, and baseline is incorporated or by A-B-A-B-A-B. These designs are extensions of A-B-A design. There are various other extensions of the basic A-B-A design, such as A-B-A-C-A or A-B-C-A designs.

A-B-A-C-D Design

In some cases, while replicating the baseline after treatment, an investigator may see either negligible or no effect of treatment. Under these circumstances, one has to alter the design and test other methods of treatment successively. Here, a comparison of the successive treatment techniques is made against a replicated baseline. This may be viewed as a modification of the basic A-B-A-B design after failure of a single treatment. This successive treatment designs examine the differential effectiveness of the treatment programmes instituted under C and D phases (Figure 17.6).

SUCCESSIVE AND SIMULTANEOUS DESIGNS

What we discussed above were successive designs, where a single treatment method was applied at a time. When a single treatment is not effective in a given case, it is suggested that a new treatment technique should be introduced. This kind of design is closer to the realities of normal environment, where

FIGURE 17.5
A-B-A Treatment Design

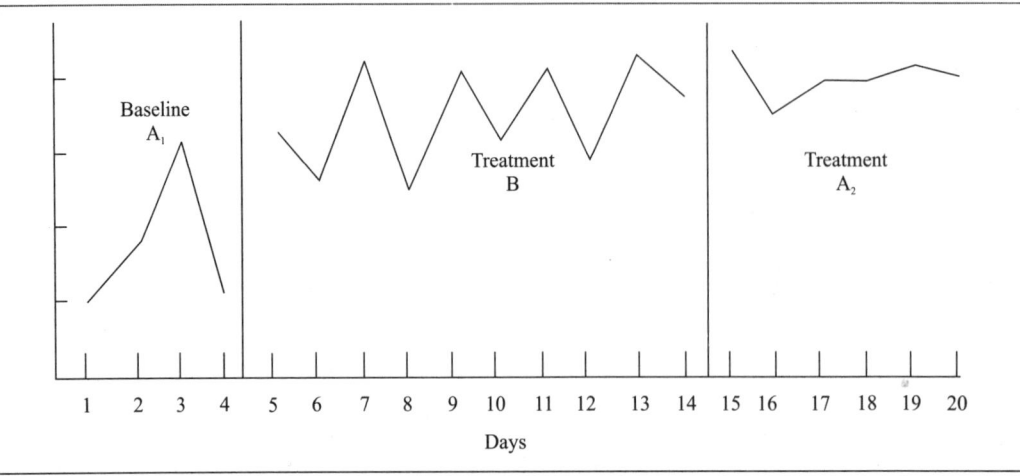

FIGURE 17.6
A-B-A-C-D Treatment Design

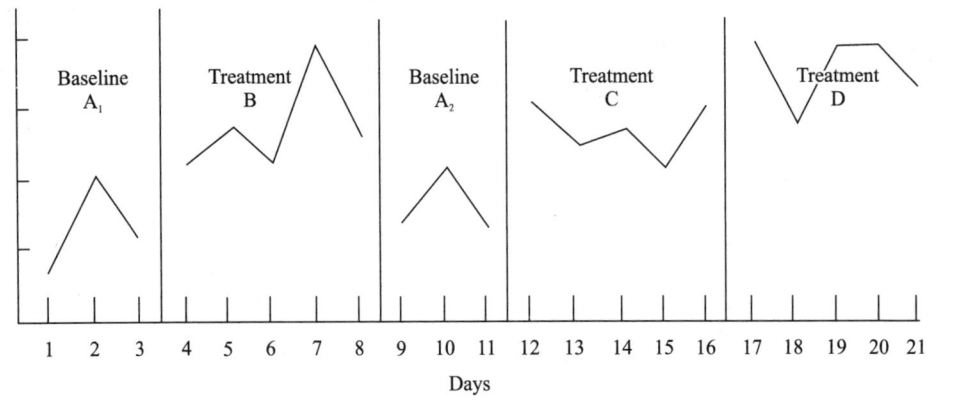

a client is given different modalities of treatment one after another. A-B-A-C-D and A-B-A-A-C-D are two such designs. It may be suggested that such designs should have at least one or two return to baseline conditions between successive treatments.

The term simultaneous treatment design was used by Browning (1867). This is also known as alternating treatment design (ATD). The concurrent or simultaneous application of two or more treatment techniques for the same target behaviour in a single case is its fundamental characteristics.

COMBINED OR INTERACTION DESIGNS

In most situations, therapy contains a combination of different techniques. Therefore, behaviour analysts often try to find out which component of therapy was more effective. When different elements of treatments are combined, the effects are different from the single component. Interaction or combined designs help to study these additive effects systematically. The interaction effects are contrasted with the individual effects of various therapeutic components. For instance, in B-BC-B-A-B-BC-B design the clinician attempts to examine effects of two therapeutic components in combination or either of the two, separately. In some cases, three, more than three, or more components are used sequentially and in combination, such as A-B-BC-B-BC and A-B-BCD-BC-BCD. A number of researchers have used combined single-case research designs such as B-BCB-BC-BCD (e.g. Agras et al. 1974), A-B-BC-B-BC (Kallman et al. 1975). The relative advantages of one such design A-BC-B-BC are discussed in the next section.

A-BC-B-BC Design

For controlling specific components of treatment techniques, this design is considered as the design of choice. The first phase of this design is the pre-treatment baseline. Second phase involves combination of two treatment components for controlling the same set of target behaviours. In the third phase, the second treatment component is withdrawn and only one treatment (B) is instituted in order to find out the differential effect of a single treatment component. In the last phase, once again the previous treatment condition is reinstituted. This design provides ample scope for comparing efficacy of individual treatment components in a therapeutic programme, demonstrating the single and combined treatment effects on the background of a pre-treatment baseline. Changing one variable at a time across conditions is considered as an important rule of the thumb in carrying out all types of experimental single-case researches (Barlow, Hersen and Jackson 1973). The present design adheres to this principle through systematic institution and withdrawal of treatment components to study their differential effects.

MULTIPLE BASELINE DESIGNS

In multiple baseline designs, the treatment effects are demonstrated by introducing the intervention to different baselines across behaviours, individuals, or settings at different points of time. A basic assumption is that the targeted behaviours should be independent from each other. The treatment variable is not introduced until a stable baseline is obtained. The changes that occur after introduction of intervention only are considered to be due to this intervention and not for the extraneous factors. The repeated demonstration that the target behaviours change significantly after intervention, indicate a causal relationship between intervention and behaviour change. In this design, at one time the clinician can examine the effects of a single intervention programme on a number of behaviours. This can also be examined in different settings and with different people exhibiting the same behavioural disorders. This is the unique aspect of this research design. When a number of behaviours of the same client are taken for intervention, this experimental design can establish which behaviours respond best to a given treatment.

WITHIN-SUBJECT VARIABILITY

The time-series methodology that is the core of this design requires a continuous record of the behaviour, including thoughts and feelings. Repeated measurement of the target behaviour provides an estimation of the degree of variability about the level as well as trend of behaviour. It facilitates prediction about the future course of behaviour. The probable effects of intervention can be studied through the anticipated variation of behaviour across time. If the variations were large, it would be difficult to assess the effects of therapy. In view of this, and to maximise the treatment effects, the clinician has to be prepared to alter the treatment method in course of the intervention programme. One cannot plan beforehand and proceed according to this pre-determined plan. He should be guided in response to the new information. The chances of rejection hypotheses are quite high. In fact, the term 'variable' itself means the factor or treatment that can be varied or altered. Thus, the approach is more realistic and pragmatic than group designs.

Single-case experimental design is hardly a newcomer in the methodological scene of behaviour therapy. However, its use has been quite limited for several reasons:

(1)   The training opportunity in experimental design is restricted because in most universities and institutions, the subject is taught by non-clinicians, who themselves have little commitment or expertise in the field of applied behaviour analysis. Thus, the approach is rather theoretical.

(2)   The funding agencies and institutions, consider single-case experimental designs less 'scientific' as the reports are confined to a small number of cases. Thus, there exists a tendency to provide little funding for such researches. Studies conducted on large samples are often considered as more scientific. It shapes the researcher's preference.

(3)   Single-case design is often theory-free. The course of treatment is determined by the effects of treatment on the behaviour.

(4)   Researchers, on the other hand commit the mistake of approaching the single-case study like group comparison research, predetermining the phases of treatment and their lengths. In spite of certain inherent drawbacks and prevailing misconception about this methodology, single-case design is the most pragmatic, dynamic, and interactive enterprise. The design is tentative; therefore ready to incorporate any change in the course of research, if significant questions arise on the way.

18

The Evidence-based Approach

The amount of research which is conducted in behaviour therapy every year is quite remarkable. However, the publication trend in behaviour therapy journals indicates that there is a significant decrease in the articles referring to fundamental research. Aguilar and Peyre (1985) were of the opinion that behaviour therapy will remain a mere curative technology if the basic research is lost. Deitz (1978) also noted that in behaviour therapy, a potential problem is the premature transfer of analysis into technology. The researchers are neglecting its theoretical underpinnings. It would confine us only to those, which have already been known to us (discovered), and would block innovation. Research is now influenced more by techniques and not necessarily by the principles or analytic methods (Aguilar and Peyre 1985).

Recently, applied behaviour analysts have been focusing on outcome research (Azrin 1977). Behavioural analysis is done superficially (Michael 1980; Ribes 1980) and is getting diluted with the influence of cognitive tendencies, distorting it (Branch and Malagodi 1980). Even established journals such as *Applied Behaviour Analysis* reject articles, which are more analytical instead of applied (Baer 1981). Thus, applied behaviour analysis is truly like an endangered species. Use of research methods that allow direct, sensitive and continuous assessment of behavioural change would rescue behaviour analysis (Kelley 1977; Springer et al. 1981). Conducting a content analysis of articles published in behaviour therapy journals, Aguilar and Peyre (1985) concluded that these are the products of contingencies in the scientific milieu (grants, editorial policies, etc.). Therefore, they constitute something that can be analysed as the product of behaviour of scientists with regard to certain antecedent conditions, such as previous articles in the field, grants and editorial policies. Review of 241 articles in six major journals published during 1983 was performed by these investigators. It was noted that unlike the previous studies conducted mostly on university students, the present one showed that 70 per cent studies were conducted on clinical population. This was perhaps the main reason why emphasis was placed on curative approach at the expense of analytical work.

Many practicing behaviour therapists differ on the issue of theory-driven practice and theoretical approach to behaviour change. Many of them disregard that a theoretical framework would make them more effective as clinicians while others are of the opinion that in order to develop an effective technology of behaviour change, a systematic theoretical approach is required. It will provide foundations for future research (Hake 1982; Ribes 1980). In order to enhance theoretical orientation in behaviour therapists, Aguilar and Peyre (1985) suggested several steps. The first was a change of contingencies of re-inforcement for theoretical research by providing better funding for theory-driven, that is, analytical applied research (Hayes et al. 1980). The second step involves termination of the conditions that have occasioned the behaviour therapists' behaviour to be less analytical and more applied. Third, change of editorial policy for publication of research work in behaviour therapy to encourage theory-driven work and focusing more on 'doing' than 'saying'.

Behaviour therapy has emerged as a powerful movement in conceptualising the treatment of behaviour pathology. The applications have expanded enormously from clinic and laboratories to a wide variety of natural settings. Apart from therapeutic practices in clinical psychology, psychiatry, paediatrics, rehabilitation and education, it has influenced our current understanding of human behaviour quite immensely. Along with clinical problems, behaviour therapy has focused on socially relevant behaviour. The voluminous body of research has exemplified its rapid development in the last few decades.

Many critics of behaviour therapy have questioned the extrapolation of animal laboratory data to complex human problems like thinking, attitude, social behaviour and so on. However, such criticism should not be taken at face value. The experimental research has contributed to this approach in a significant way demonstrating scientific methodology, providing basic principles of understanding behaviour so that behaviour therapists can develop better models for approximation for human behaviour. A second criticism is that behaviour therapy is restricted to a limited number of techniques. In fact, the techniques are not determined by the variety of behaviours, but by their nature. The techniques of behaviour therapy are tailored according to the individual's choice, environmental support, as well as the feasibility of application in a given setting. Therefore, the variations are immense.

THEORY-DRIVEN VS DIAGNOSIS-BASED PROTOCOL APPROACH

Behaviour therapy is known for its individually tailored treatments, which are based on functional analysis. The treatment is guided mostly by behavioural theories. Recently, for treatment of some common behaviour disorders, many treatment manuals have been developed. These manuals have provided session-by-session details of treatment. Some of them have been designed as per the diagnostic criteria of DSM-IV (APA, 1994). A list of such manuals is available with Sanderson and Woody (1995). This approach of developing manuals for streamlining the therapy process is known as the protocol approach. Publication of such literature, a 'cook-book' approach is gradually emerging in the field of behaviour therapy. This approach seems to conform to the medical model, which was resented by behaviour therapists (e.g. Ullman and Krasner 1975). Neither ICD nor DSM classification of behaviour disorders is based on the understanding of the mechanism of the underlying processes of the dysfunction.

Therefore, there is a danger of misuse of the techniques of behaviour change. Eifert (1996) discussed the relative advantages and disadvantages of this method. Treatment based on protocol approach, although not sufficient, it fulfils the needs of many clients. It makes sense of the complex information on the disorder. Categorisation and systematisation of information save a good deal of time.

EVIDENCE-BASED BEHAVIOUR THERAPY

In present times, behaviour therapists are increasingly focusing on those treatment techniques which have strong empirical footing. This approach is called 'evidence-based' behaviour therapy. Different terminologies are being used to describe it, such as 'empirically supported treatment', 'treatments that work' or 'evidence-based practice' in behaviour therapy. It includes use of those selected intervention techniques or programmes that would be exemplary and where palpable progress has been achieved. It includes those techniques, which are established in controlled trials. In order to build up evidence-based database on behaviour therapy, the authors are now encouraged to (i) describe the intervention, (ii) discuss how it is implemented, (iii) who served as the therapist, (iv) how he/she is trained, and (v) who served as mediators to carry out the programme. In journal articles, it is increasingly stressed to make the contributor write the nature or characteristics of the clients on whom the treatment was used and the evidence in support of the work as it helps the therapist to identify valid treatments.

Consumers of mental health services show preferences for the most promising and effective methods of treatment. In order to facilitate their choice of therapy, the treatment modality has to be presented to the potential consumers in the most credible manner. This will reduce the gap between the consumer expectation and actual practice. This is true even for the seasoned health professionals to facilitate referrals. Through publications in popular and professional journals, public lectures, or placing the material on websites, this dissemination of information can be done in the most effective manner. Supervisors who train behaviour therapists have primary influence on its practice. The therapist's adherence to protocol is largely determined by evidence-based training (Weisz and Hawley 1998).

Outcome research has an important bearing on the credibility of any kind of therapy. For that matter, it is doubly important for behaviour therapy, as it is influenced by a galaxy of situational, behavioural and therapeutic components. An outcome research reveals that a particular practice element should lead to positive effects. Chorpita (2003) suggested four types of research that facilitate evidence-based practice: (i) Type I: Efficacy, (ii) Type II: Transportability, (iii) Type III: Dissemination, and (iv) Type IV: System.

Type I: Efficacy Research

Efficacy research is the first level of research that helps to establish the fact that there is a connection between laboratory or clinic-based research practice and outcome. It is in some way controlled by the screening of clients, therapists and supervisors. For example, the clients and their families are thoroughly screened before the treatment; strict inclusion and exclusion criteria are maintained in their selection and the therapists are usually highly trained and sometimes supervised by experts. Such outcome research would permit us to say whether a treatment programme is effective for a particular disorder or not.

Type II: Transportability

The real life conditions are addressed by Type II kind of research. It involves the study of interventions in laboratory (or clinical) conditions without the exclusionary criteria, which is typical in most Type I research. This type of effectiveness research was termed as 'transportability' by Schoenwald and Hoagwood (2001). It examines whether a particular intervention might be promising for delivery into true practice setting. It helps us to find out whether a particular approach is useful in real-world cases.

Type III: Dissemination

The next level of outcome research aims at examining whether the system employees, such as counsellors, teachers, nurses or other staff can make use of the approach in their own settings. This is termed as 'dissemination' (Schoenwald and Hoagwood 2001). In this kind of research, the supervision is still provided to the system employees and examined whether the approach can be maintained even after withdrawal of the supervisors.

Type IV: System Evaluation

When a particular approach is used in a particular social system, it is important to see that the system stands on its own and does not require to be monitored by the expert supervisor. Thus, the system to be evaluated and the investigator team should be fully independent. This kind of research demonstrates the substantive difference between the client outcomes. It also specifies not only the supervision and case management practice but also specific intervention to be used by the therapist for a given client.

In the international scenario, evidence-based practice is skewed to Type I research whereas Type II, III and IV research is rare to find. Persons (1991) commented that the evidence that exists may not be considered fully relevant to systems that seek to use such evidence to shape practice. In behaviour therapy, although a number of good researches appear in scholarly journal, many of them will have little meaning for a given community or client population, until Type II, III and IV variety of researches are conducted.

19

Ethical Issues in Behaviour Therapy

Behaviour therapists have a fundamental moral commitment to the advancement of human welfare by introducing new methods of treatment and using the existing ones for the betterment of their clients. For achieving these goals, they are required to follow certain ethical principles. Ethics refer to the application of value judgment to human action. Plainly speaking, these are the certain 'dos' and 'don'ts' of professional behaviour. Although moral theories do not explain the effectiveness of the techniques of behaviour therapy, behaviour therapists are required to adhere to certain ethical principles while studying or treating their clients and subjecting them to research.

What will happen if the therapist simply applies the treatment methods which he has learned, or what has been proved to be effective? Do they have the right to change the free choices, orientation and preferences of people? Such intriguing questions are sometimes posed by the therapists themselves (e.g. Erwin 1978). Therefore, it is important to discuss the issues here. Adherence to ethical standards of practice helps in protecting the dignity of the participants. Apart from preventing abuse of the behavioural technology, it enhances the acceptability of this treatment modality. It determines largely, whether a client will continue to seek such services or not. Thus, adherence to ethical standards is not only a moral requirement but also an important determinant in progress of behaviour therapy.

Distinguishing the nature of science and the nature of ethics, Skinner (1971) stated that science is concerned with facts, that is, what we *can* do, whereas ethics is concerned about what we *ought* to do. It entails value judgments, which are out of the reach of science. Science seeks knowledge; others decide where and how to apply it. Decisions about the use of this knowledge seem to demand a kind of additional knowledge, which for some curious reason is denied to scientists. In this respect, the behavioural scientists have a different position. How people feel about the facts and how they react to them, are questions that behavioural scientists can answer in a better way.

HUMANISM AND BEHAVIOUR THERAPY

Some authors have argued that behaviour therapy tends to dehumanise man (Carrea and Adams 1970). Some humanists are concerned at the rapid development in behaviour therapy in the last few decades. They are afraid that it may be creating a potential danger of controlling human choices, although such apprehensions and statements do not reflect the true character of behaviour therapy. Contrary to this view, the technology of behaviour therapy has been used extensively in the alleviation of human distress, making people more humane and providing them better ways of living. It demonstrates and tells us how to change human behaviour, whereas the therapist and the client decide what changes to be made in the behaviour. The changes that a therapist ought to make are the things that society values or feels good about. In a sense, all good and pleasant things are positive reinforcers. To be good to a person (client) professionally means reinforcing him by providing effective treatment, and responding to his needs. This may include a number of things that respect his dignity as an individual. In doing so, one has to carefully judge and make choices, because even with the best intentions, one tends to make mistakes. What is good for one individual may not be good for others. Therefore, one has to carefully weigh the alternatives available within the behavioural techniques and between other treatment approaches. Thompson (1975: 444) stated, 'behavioural science is safe as long as it remains innocuously impotent; but when it bears practical fruit, it becomes to many a frightening menace.' People start questioning as it has the potential to affect their lives at workplace, home, educational and correctional institutions and so on. Such questions are natural and necessary to provide a direction. Now we are more concerned with the justifications for applications of behavioural technology than before as we get more enlightened and informed, and question, challenge and compare the risks and benefits. On the other hand, even if a client asks for a particular type of treatment, it may not be permissible or obligatory to offer. Similarly, even if a treatment is proved to be effective, it cannot be given without consent. Marks (1976: 255) bluntly states, 'Behavioural treatment can only be given to adult neurotics if they are cooperative, successful treatment cannot be forced on patients against their will.' Although the entire behavioural treatment is not confined to treatment of neurotic disorders, no treatment can be forced on clients. The therapist has to decide which kind of therapy fits to his client best and will be acceptable by him.

ACCEPTABILITY OF TREATMENT

The extent to which a treatment is considered as reasonable and justified by an individual client is called acceptability of that treatment. Till recently, acceptability measures were not taken so seriously. Now, accumulating research data indicate that treatments that are more acceptable may be more frequently sought out or adhered to than those which are not. How well a therapist carries out a treatment is also a function of the extent to which he/she views the treatment as acceptable (Allinder and Oats 1997). The decision to remain under treatment seeing it as demanding or irrelevant, contributes directly to the dropouts too (Kazdin et al. 1997). Since acceptability is an important independent variable for developing effective treatment programmes, it will be useful to understand what can be done to improve their acceptability. For example, Foxx et al. (1996) used video programmes to improve acceptability of treatments. Conversely, there may be treatment modalities that are highly acceptable for the clients, even though they have little or no demonstrated efficacy. In this situation, evidence-based approach would be more useful in treatment decision.

INFORMED CONSENT

Accountability of the therapist to his client is a pivotal issue. The behaviour therapist must inform the client about the nature of intervention or research in which the client is going to participate and obtain written consent from him. He must fairly explain the procedure, the possible discomfort and risks involved in it, and disclose other alternative methods available. He should be explained the significance of the experiment for the advancement of knowledge and human welfare. The client should also be informed that he can freely enquire about any aspect of the therapy and may withdraw his consent and discontinue his participation. This should be done so that the client can make an adequate choice as to which procedure is he capable of agreeing or refusing to become a volunteer (Guttentag 1968). It enhances mutual trust and concern for human dignity. Many clients such as chronic schizophrenics, severely or profoundly retarded individuals or even children for that matter, are not in a position to give consent. In these cases, consent must be obtained from the guardian of the client.

CONFIDENTIALITY

Confidentiality includes anonymity, in which the identity of the client is selectively suppressed so that no identification is possible. If video or audiotapes are to be made it should be clear, who will have access to it. If the case report is sent for publication, the personal identity must be suppressed. Sometimes secure research codes are provided for case records. In spite of the best caution on part of the therapist, these case records are vulnerable to theft or legal scrutiny. The consent form should specify who would have access to the data. The kinds of changes, which may arise due to breaches of confidentiality may also be informed. A sample Treatment Consent Form is provided in Appendix–4.

BALANCING HARMS AND BENEFITS

Therapy helps to alleviate pain or discomfort of the individual. It involves harms like pain, discomfort and other negative side-effects and benefits like relief from pain of discomfort caused by the disorder being treated. There are some methods which are painful. At times, such treatment methods are more effective than those which conspicuously do not involve pain or discomfort. A therapist has to carefully balance these effects in the welfare of his client. Analysis of these two components is critical to maintain ethical standards. In a favourable harm-benefit balance, the anticipated benefits outweigh the harm; therefore, it helps to make the therapy more acceptable. An unfavourable balance increases the chance of the client dropping out. Whatever harm is involved in a therapeutic procedure, it must have ethical justification. While undergoing treatment, a client must not be subjected to unnecessary risks of harm. Biological treatment procedures like administering intravenous injection, conducting surgery even under anaesthesia, or exposure to radiotherapy involve some risk but the expected positive outcome outweighs the risk. Therefore, they are accepted by the client. Similar is the case of using aversion therapy procedures in behaviour therapy. Mild aversive procedures may be used in the interest of the client, for his future benefits. Such risks may be considered as minimal for the client to benefit from the treatment.

RESPECT FOR HUMAN DIGNITY

At the outset, a behaviour therapist must adequately respect the dignity of the client. In behaviour therapy, he is not used as an object to achieve certain goals, but as a collaborator. His welfare remains a paramount issue in therapy. One must strive to understand the views of the client.

Respect for human dignity also entails ethical obligation towards vulnerable people including those who have diminished competence for understanding the treatment methods. Children, institutionalised people, and those who suffer from incapacitating mental disorders like schizophrenia fall in this group. Due to their diminished capacity to make decisions, they should be given special protection against abuse, exploitation and discrimination. The therapist is required to adopt adequate ethical guidelines, before subjecting such clients to intervention.

Bibliography

A

Abramowitz, J. S., M. E. Franklin, L. A. Zoellner and C. L. DiBernardo. (2002). 'Treatment compliance and outcome of obsessive compulsive disorder', *Behaviour Modification*, 26 (4): 447–63.

Acierno, R., G. Tremont, C. Last and D. Montgomery. (1994). 'Tripartite assessment of the efficacy of eye movement desensitization in a multi-phobic patient', *Journal of Anxiety Disorders*, 8: 259–76.

Adams, H. B. (1980). 'Effects of reduced stimulation on institutionalized adult patients', in P. Suedfeld (ed.), *Restricted Environmental Stimulation: Research and Clinical Applications*. New York: Wiley.

Agarwal, S. (1990). 'Behaviour modification through 'contracts': Two cases', *Indian Journal of Clinical Psychology*, 17 (1): 52–55.

Agras, W. S., D. H. Barlow, H. N. Chaplin, G. G. Abel and H. Leitenberg. (1974). 'Behaviour modification of anorexia nervosa', *Archives of General Psychiatry*, 30: 279–86.

Aguilar, G. and C. Peyre. (1985). 'Current trends in applied behaviour analysis', in J. J. Sanchez-Sosa (ed.), *Health and Clinical Psychology, Selected/revised papers, Vol. 4*, pp. 597–621, XIII, International Congress of Psychology, Amsterdam, North-Holland.

Ahmed, S., V. D. Swaminathan, and K. V. Kaliappan. (2000). 'Efficacy of Jacobson's deep relaxation on interpersonal relationship among women volley-ball player', *Social Science International*, 10: 1–2, 34–41.

Akoijam, L. and P. S. D. V. Prasadarao. (2002). 'Cognitive Disorder in Somatoform Disorder', *Indian Journal of Clinical Psychology*, 29 (1): 49–53.

Al-Khubaisy, T., I. M. Marks, S. Logsdail, M. P. Marks, K. Lovell, M. Sungus, and R. Arya. (1992). 'Role of exposure homework in phobia reduction: A controlled study', *Behaviour Therapy*, 23 (4): 599–621.

Allen, H. A., J. Halperin, and R. Friend. (1985). 'Removal and diversion tactics and the control of auditory hallucinations', *Psychological Bulletin*, 107: 82–85.

Allinder, R. M. and R. G. Oats. (1997). 'Effects of acceptability on teachers' implementation of curriculum-based measurement and student achievement in mathematics computation', *Remedial and Special Education*, 18: 113–20.

Altabet, S., J. K. Neumann, and S. Watson-Johnston. (2002). 'Light therapy as a treatment of sleep cycle problems and depression', *Mental Health Aspects of Intellectual Disabilities*, 5: 1–6.

Altman, J. (1974). 'Observational study of behaviour sampling methods', *Behaviour*, 49: 227–67.

American Psychiatric Association. (1993). *DSM-IV draft criteria*. Washington DC.

———. (1994). *Diagnostic and statistical manual of mental disorders-IV*. Washington DC.

Anant, S. S. (1966). 'Effects of prior discussion about traumatic situations on desensitization', *Psychological Studies*, 11 (2): 89–98.

———. (1967). 'A note on the treatment of alcoholics by a verbal aversion technique', *Canadian Psychologist*, 8 (1): 19–22.

———. (1968a). 'Behaviour therapy or behaviour therapies', *Psychological Studies*, 13 (1): 21–28.

———. (1968b). 'The use of verbal aversion (negative conditioning) with an alcoholic: A Case Report', *Behaviour Research and Therapy*, 6: 695–96.

———. (1969a). (ed.), *Readings in behaviour therapy*. New York: MSS Educational Publishing Co.

Anant, S. S. (1969b). 'The use of operant conditioning with the mentally retarded: A report of a pilot experiment', *Indian Journal of Applied Psychology*, 6 (1): 15–21.

———. (1970). 'An experiment on group relaxation, sex, marital and other differences', *Psychological Studies*, 15 (1): 17–22.

Ancoli-Israel, S., P. Gehrman, and T. Shochat. (2003). 'Effects of light on agitation in institutionalized patients with severe Alzheimer's disease', *American Journal of Geriatric Psychiatry*, 11 (2): 194–203.

Anjana, R. and K. P. Sreedhar. (2000). 'Effect of guided somato-psychic relaxation on elderly persons', *Indian Journal of Clinical Psychology*, 27 (1): 80–88.

Antista, B. and A. Jones. (1975). '*Some beneficial consequences of brief sensory deprivation*', Paper presented at the meeting of the Western Psychological Association, Sacramento, California.

Antrobus, J. S., T. S. Antrobus, and J. L. Singer. (1964). 'Eye movement accompanying day dreaming, visual imagery and thought suppression', *Journal of Abnormal Social Psychology*, 69 (3): 244–52.

Armstrong, M. S. and K. Vaughan. (1996). 'An orienting response model of eye movement desensitization', *Journal of Behaviour Therapy and Experimental Psychiatry*, 27 (1): 21–32.

Aronfreed, J. (1969). 'The concept of internalization', in D. A. Goslin (ed.), *Handbook of socialization: Theory and Research*, pp. 263–323. Chicago: Rand McNally.

Arora, M., S. Murthy, and V. K. Verma. (1975). 'Operant conditioning in symbiotic infantile psychosis', *Indian Journal of Clinical Psychology*, 2 (2): 105–12.

Arun, P. and H. Kaur. (2002). 'Psychological treatment of impulse control disorders of childhood', *Indian Journal of Clinical Psychology*, 29 (1): 54–59

Ash, D. W. and D. H. Holding. (1990). 'Backward versus forward chaining in the acquisition of a keyboard skill', *Human Factors*, 32 (2): 139–46.

Aschem, B. and L. Donner. (1968). 'Covert sensitization with alcoholics: A controlled replication', *Behaviour Research and Therapy*, 6: 7–12.

Axelord, S., J. P. Brantner, and T. D. Meddock. (1978). 'Overcorrection: A review and critical analysis', *The Journal of Special Education*, 12: 367–91.

Ayllon, T. and N. H. Azrin. (1968). *The token economy: A motivational system for therapy and rehabilitation*. New York: Appleton-Century Crofts.

Azima, H. and F. J. Cramer-Azima. (1961). 'Observations on anaclitic therapy during sensory deprivation', in P. Solomon, P. E. Kubazansky, P. H. Leiderman, J. S. Mandelson, R. Turnbull, and D. Wexler (eds), *Sensory deprivation*, pp. 143–60. Cambridge: Harvard University Press.

Azrin, N. H. (1956). 'Some effects of two intermittent schedules of immediate and non-immediate punishment', *Journal of Psychology*, 42: 3–21.

———. (1977). 'Strategies for applied research: Learning-based but outcome oriented', *American Psychologist*, 32: 140–49.

Azrin, N. H., L. Gottlieb, L. Hughart, M. D. Wesolowski, and T. Rahn. (1975). 'Eliminating self-injurious behaviour by educative procedures', *Behaviour Research and Therapy*, 13 (2/3): 101–11.

Azrin, N. H. and M. A. Powers. (1975). 'Eliminating classroom disturbance of emotionally disturbed children by positive practice procedures', *Behaviour Therapy*, 6 (4): 525–34.

Azrin, N. H. and M. D. Wesolowski. (1975). 'Elimination of habitual vomiting in a retarded adult by positive practice and self-correction', *Journal of Behaviour Therapy and Experimental Psychiatry*, 6 (2): 145–48.

Azrin, N. H. and R. G. Nunn. (1973). 'Habit reversal: A method of eliminating nervous habits and tics', *Behaviour Research and Therapy*, 11: 619–28.

Azrin, N. H., S. J. Kaplan, and R. M. Foxx. (1973). 'Autism reversal: Eliminating stereotyped self-stimulation of retarded individuals', *American Journal of Mental Deficiency*, 78 (3): 241–48.

Azrin, N. H. , T. J. Sneed, and R. M. Foxx. (1973). 'A rapid method of eliminating bed wetting (enuresis) of the retarded', *Behaviour Research and Therapy*, 11: 427–34.

———. (1974). 'Dry bed: Rapid elimination of childhood enuresis', *Behaviour Research and Therapy*, 12: 147–56.

Azrin, N. H. and W. C. Holz. (1966). 'Punishment', in W. K. Honig (ed.), *Operant behaviour areas of research and application*, pp. 380–447. New York: Appleton-Century.

B

Badley, A. (1986). *Working Memory*. Oxford: Oxford University Press.

Baer, D. M. (1978). 'On the relation between basic and applied research', in A. C. Catania and T. A. Brigham (eds.), *Handbook of Applied Behaviour Analysis*, pp. 11–16. New York: Irving.

———. (1981). 'Flight of behaviour analysis', *The Behaviour Analysts*, 3: 31–38.

———. (1984). 'Review of single-case research designs: Methods for cinical and applied settings', *Behavioural Assessment*, 6: 191–93.

Baer, D. M., M. M. Wolf, and T. R. Risley. (1968). 'Some current dimension of applied behaviour analysis', *Journal of Applied Behaviour Analysis*, 1: 91–97.

Bailey, S. L., J. Pikrzywinski, and L. E. Bryant. (1983). 'Using water-mist to reduce self-injurious and stereotypic behaviour', *Applied Research in Mental Retardation*, 4: 229–41.

Bain, J. A. (1928). *Thought control in everyday life*. New York: Funk and Wagnalls.

Baker, J. C. and G. Whitehead. (1972). 'A portable recording apparatus for rating behaviours in Free-operant Situations', *Journal of Applied Behaviour Analysis*, 5: 191–92.

Baker, T. and T. H. Brandon. (1988). 'Behavioural treatment strategies', in *A Report of the Surgeon General: The Health Consequence of Smoking (Nicotine Addiction)*. US Department of Health and Human Services, Rockville, MD.

Balakrishn, S. and S. P. Mandanna. (1969). 'Progressive relaxation in treatment of involuntary knee jerk'. Paper presented at the Scientific Session of First All India Convention of Clinical Psychologists.

Bancroft, J., H. Gwynne, and B. Pullan. (1966). 'A simple transducer for measuring penile erection with comments on its use in treatment of sexual disorders', *Behaviour Research and Therapy*, 4 (2): 234–41.

Bandura, A. (1969). '*Principles of behaviour modification*', New York: Holt Rinehart and Winston.

———. (1971). 'Psychotherapy based on modelling principles', in A. E. Bergin and S. L. Garfield (eds.), *Psychotherapy and Behaviour Change*. New York: John Wiley and Sons.

———. (1977). *Social learning theory*. Englewood Cliff, New Jersey: Prentice-Hall.

Bandura, A., E. B. Blanchard, and B. Ritter. (1969). 'The relative efficacy of desensitization and modelling approaches for inducing behavioural, Affective and attitudinal changes', *Journal of Personality and Social Psychology*, 13: 173–99.

Bandura, A., J. E. Grusec, and F. L. Menlove. (1966). Observational learning as a function of symbolization. *Child Development*, 37: 499–506.

Bandura, A. and R. H. Walters. 1959. '*Adolescent Aggression*', New York: Ronald Press.

———. (1963). '*Social learning and personality development*', New York: Holt, Rinehart and Winston.

———. (1969). '*Social learning and personality development*', New York: Holt Rinehart and Winston.

Barabasz, A. F. (1980). 'EEG alpha, skin conductance, and hypnotizability in antarctica', *International Journal of Clinical and Experimental Hypnosis*, 28: 63–74.

———. (1982a). 'Restricted environmental stimulation and the enhancement of hypnotizability: Pain, EEG alpha, Skin Conductance and Temperature Responses', *International Journal of Clinical and Experimental Hypnosis*, 30: 147–66.

———. (1982b). 'Enhancement of Hypnotic susceptibility following perceptual deprivation: Pain tolerance, electrodermal and EEG correlates', in M. Pajntar, E. Raskar, and M. Larvric (eds.), *Hypnosis in Psychotherapy and Psychosomatic Medicine*, pp. 13–28, Ljubljana: Yugoslavia University Press.

Barabasz, A. F., L. Baer, D. K. Sheehan, and M. Barabasz. (1985). 'Effects of hypnosis and restricted environmental stimulation therapy (REST) on chronic smoking', in J. J. Sanchez-Sosa (ed.) *Health and Clinical Psychology*, selected/revised papers, Vol. 4, (pp. 237–50), XIII, International Congress of Psychology, Amsterdam: North-Holland.

Barer, A. M., T. Rowbury, and D. M. Baer. (1973). 'The Development of Instructional Control over Classroom Activities of Deviant Preschool Children', *Journal of Applied Behaviour Analysis*, 6: 289–98.

Barkley, R. A. (1997). *Defiant children: A clinician's manual for assessment and parent training (2nd Ed.)*. New York: Guilford Press.

Barkley, R. A. and C. E. Cunningham. (1978). 'Do stimulant drugs improve the academic performance of hyperactive children?', *Clinical Paediatrics*, 17: 85–92.

Barlow, D. H. (1980). 'Behaviour therapy, the next decade', *Behaviour Therapy*, 11 (3): 315–28.

Barlow, D. H. and C. L. Lehman. (1996). 'Advances in psychosocial treatment of anxiety disorders', *Archives of General Psychiatry*, 53: 727–35.

Barlow, D. H., H. Leitenberg, and W. S. Agras. (1969). 'Experimental control of sexual deviation through manipulation of the noxious scene in covert sensation', *Journal of Abnormal Psychology*, 74: 596–601.

Barlow, D. H. and J. A. Cerny. (1988). *'Psychological treatment of panic'*, New York: Guilford Press.

Barlow, D. H., J. M. Gormann, M. K. Shear, and S. W. Woods. (2000). 'Cognitive behaviour therapy, imipramine or their combination for panic disorder: A randomized control trial', *Journal of the American Medical Association*, 283: 2529–36.

Barlow, D. H. and M. Hersen. (1973). 'Single-case experimental designs: use in applied clinical research', *Archives of General Psychiatry*, 29: 319–425.

Barlow, D. H., M. Hersen, and M. Jackson. (1973). 'Single-case experimental designs: uses in applied clinical research', *Archives of General Psychiatry*, 29: 319–25.

Barlow, D. H., W. S. Agras, H. Leitenberg, E. J. Callahan, and R. C. Moore. (1972). 'The contribution of therapeutic instruction to covert sensitization', *Behaviour Research and Therapy*, 10: 411–15.

Barrish, H. H., M. Saunders, and M. M. Wolf. (1969). 'Good behaviour game: effects of individual contingencies on disruptive behaviour in the classroom', *Journal of Applied Behaviour Analysis*, 2: 119–24.

Bash, M. A. and B. W. Camp. (1980). 'Training teachers in the think aloud classroom programme', in Cart ledge and J. Milburn (eds), *Teaching Social Skills to Children: Innovative Approaches*, New York: Pergamon Press.

Bates, L., D. McGlynn, E. Montgomery, and T. Mattke. (1996). 'Effects of eye movement desensitization versus no treatment on repeated measures of fear of spiders', *Journal of Anxiety Disorders*, 10: 555–69.

Baum, M. (1966). 'Rapid extinction of an avoidance response following a period of response prevention in the avoidance apparatus', *Psychological Reports*, 18: 59–64.

———. (1970). 'Extinction of avoidance responding through response prevention (flooding)', *Psychological Bulletin*, 74 (4): 276–84.

Baumeister, A. A. and R. Forehand. (1972). 'Effects of contingent shock and verbal command on body-rocking of retardates', *Journal of Clinical Psychology*, 28: 586–90.

Baumeister, A. A. (1978). 'Origin and control of stereotyped movements', in C. E. Myers (ed.), *Quality of Life in Severely and Profoundly Retarded People: Research Foundation for Improvement* (pp. 353–84), Washington DC: American Association on Mental Deficiency.

Beck, A. T. (1963). 'Thinking and depression I: Idiosyncratic content and cognitive distortions', *Archives of General Psychiatry*, 9: 324–33.

———. (1964). 'Thinking and depression II: Theory and therapy', *Archives of General Psychiatry*, 10: 561–71.

———. (1967). *Depression: Clinical experimental and theoretical aspects*. New York: Hoeber.

———. (1976). *Cognitive therapy and the emotional disorders*. New York: International University Press.

Beck, A. T. and G. Emery. (1985). *Anxiety disorders and phobia—A cognitive perspective*. New York: Basic Books.

Beck, A. T., A. J. Rush, B. F. Shaw, and G. Emergy. (1979). *Cognitive therapy of depression*. New York: The Guilford Press.

Becker, J. V., S. M. Turner, and T. Sajwaj. (1978). 'Multiple behavioural effects of the use of lemon-juice with a ruminating toddler-age child', *Behaviour Modification,* 2 (2): 267–78.

Becker, W. C., S. Engelmann, and D. R. Thomas. (1975). *Teaching 2: cognitive learning and instruction.* Chicago: SRA.

Becker, W. C., C. H. Madsen Jr., C. R. Arnold, and D. R. Thomas. (1967). 'The contingent use of teacher attention and praise in reducing classroom behaviour problems', *Journal of Special Education,* 1: 287–307.

Beech, H. R., L. E. Burns, and B. F. Sheffield. (1982). *A behavioural approach to management of stress: Practical guide to techniques.* New York: Wiley.

Begelman, S. A. (1976). 'Ethical and legal issues of behaviour modification', in M. H. Hersen, R. M., Eisler, and P. H. Miller (eds.), *Progress in Behaviour Modification, Vol.1,* pp. 23–34. New York: Academic Press.

Bekhterew, V. M. (1912). 'Die Anwendung der Methode der motorischen Assoziatuons reflexe zur aufdeckung der Stimualtion, *Zeitschrift fur Die Gesamte Neurologie und Psychiatrie,* 13: 183–91.

Belinson, M. J. and D. G. Forgays. (1985). 'Floatation isolation as a relaxation environment', in J. J. Sanchez-Soza (ed.) *Health and Clinical Psychology, Selected/Revised papers, Vol. 4,* pp. 467–76. XIII. Amsterdam, North-Holland: International Congress of Psychology.

Bentall, R. P., G. Haddock, and P. D. Slade. (1994). 'Cognitive-behaviour therapy for persistent hallucinations: From theory to therapy', *Behaviour Therapy,* 25: 31–33.

Berecz, J. (1972). 'Modification of smoking behaviour through self administered punishment of imagined behaviour: A new approach to aversion therapy', *Journal of Consulting and Clinical Psychology,* 38 (2): 244–50.

Berger, S. M. (1962). 'Conditioning through vicarious instigation', *Psychological Review,* 69: 450–66.

Bergin, A.E. (1980). 'Psychotherpy and religious values', *Journal of Consulting and Clinical Psychology,* 48: 295–304.

———. (1983). 'Religiousity and mental health: A critical evaluation and meta-analysis', *Professional Psychology Research and Practice,* 14: 170–84.

Berkley, R. A. and C. E. Cunningham. (1978). 'Do stimulant drugs improve the academic performance of hyperactive children?', *Clinical Paediatrics,* 17: 85–92.

Berkson, G. (1983). 'Repetitive stereotyped behaviour', *American Journal of Mental Deficiency,* 88: 239–46.

Berlyne, D. E. (1960). *Conflict and arousal curiosity.* New York: McGraw-Hill.

Best, T. A. and P. Suedfeld. (1982). 'Restricted environmental stimulation therapy and behavioural self-management in smoking cessation', *Journal of Applied Social Psychology,* 12: 408–19.

Bharathraj, J. (1975). 'Control of stuttering behaviour thoughts response contingent shocks', *Journal of All India Institute of Speech and Hearing,* 5 (6): 10–16.

Bhargava, S. C. (1983). 'Progressive muscle relaxation and assertive training in case of tension headache', *Indian Journal of Clinical Psychology,* 10 (1): 23–25.

Bhatia, M. S. (2000). Compulsive spitting: A culture-bound symptom', *Indian Journal of Medical Sciences,* 54 (4): 145–48.

Bhattacharya, D. D. and R. Singh. (1971). 'Behaviour therapy in hysterical fits', *American Journal of Psychiatry,* 128 (5): 602.

Bhattacharya, D. D. and J. N. Vyas. (1975). 'Aversion therapy in hysterical vomiting', *Indian Journal of Psychiatry,* 17: 123–28.

Bijou, S. W. (1963). 'Theory and research in mental (developmental) retardation', *Psychological Record,* 13: 95–110.

Bijou, S. W. and J. A. Grimm. (1975). 'Behavioural diagnosis and assessment in teaching young handicapped children', in T. Thompson and W. S. Dokens III (eds.), *Application of Behaviour Modification,* pp. 161–80. New York: Academic Press.

Billingsley, F. F. and L. T. Romer. (1983). 'Response prompting and transfer of stimulus control: Methods of research and conceptual framework', *The Journal of Association for the Severely Handicapped,* 8 (2): 3–12.

Birch, D. (1966). 'Verbal control of non-verbal behaviour', *Journal of Abnormal Child Psychology*, 4: 266–75.

Biswas, A. (1995). 'Cognitive-behaviour therapy in GAD', *Indian Journal of Clinical Psychology*, 22: 1–10.

Bitensky, S. H. (1998). 'Spare the rod, embrace our humanity: Towards a new legal regime prohibiting corporal punishment of children', University of Michigan, *Journal of Law Reform*, 31: 353–447.

Black, A. H. (1958). 'Extinction of avoidance responses under curare', *Journal of Comparative and Physiological Psychology*, 51: 519–24.

Blackmore, C. B., J. G. Thorpe, J. C. Barker, C. G. Conway, and N. I. Lavin. (1963). Follow-up note to: The application of faradic aversion conditioning in a case of transvestism, *Behaviour Research and Therapy*, 1 (2–3): 191–220.

Black, W. (1970). 'The operant conditioning of verbally mediated self-control in the classroom', *Journal of School Psychology*, 8: 257–58.

Bootzin, R. (1972). 'Stimulus control treatment for insomnia', *Proceedings of the 80th Annual Convention of the American Psychological Association*, 7: 395–96.

Bootzin, R. and P. M. Nicassio. (1978). 'Behavioural treatment of insomnia', in M. Hersen, R. M. Eisler and P. M. Miller (eds.), *Progress in Behaviour Modification, Vol. 6*, pp. 1–45. New York: Academic Press.

Borden, J. W. (1992). 'Behavioural assessment of simple phobias', in S.M. Turner, K. S. Calhoun, and H. E. Adams (eds.), *Handbook of Clinical Behaviour Therapy*, 2nd ed. New York: Wiley.

Borden, K. A., R. T. Brown, M. E. Wynne,. and R. Schleser (1987). 'Piagetian conservation and response to cognitive therapy in attention deficit disorder children', *Journal of Child Psychology and Psychiatry and Allied Disciplines*, 28: 755–64.

Borrie, R. A. and P. Suedfeld. (1980). 'Restricted environmental stimulation therapy in a weight reduction programme', *Journal of Behavioural Medicine*, 3: 147–61.

Bostow, D. E. and J. B. Bailey. (1969). 'Modification of severe disruptive and aggressive behaviour using brief time-out and reinforcement procedures', *Journal of Applied Behaviour Analysis*, 2: 31–38.

Boudewyns, P. A., S. A. Stwertka, L. A. Hyer, J. W. Albrecht, and E. V. Sperr. (1993). 'Eye movement desensitization for PTSD for combat: A treatment outcome pilot study', *The Behaviour Therapist*, 16: 29–32.

Brackbill, Y. (1958). 'Extinction of the smiling response in infants as a function of reinforcement schedule', *Child Development*, 29: 115–24.

Brady, J. P. (1967). *Drugs in behaviour therapy*. Paper presented at the Sixth Annual Meeting of the American College of Neuropsychopharmacology, December, San Juan Puertorico.

Branch, M. N. and E. F. Malagodi. (1980). 'Where have all behaviourists gone?', *The Behaviour Analyst*, 3: 31–38.

Brantner, J. P. and M. A. Doherty. (1983). 'A review of time-out: A conceptual and methodological analysis', in S. Axelord and J. Apsche (eds.), *The Effects of Punishment on Human Behaviour*, pp. 87–132. New York: Academic Press.

Bricker, W. A. and D. D. Bricker. (1970). 'Programme of language training for the severely language handicapped child', *Exceptional Children*, 37: 101–11.

Broden, M., M. Bruce, M. Mitchell, V. Carter, and R. V. Hall. (1970). 'Effects of teacher attention on attending behaviour of two boys at adjacent desks', *Journal of Applied Behaviour Analysis*, 3: 199–203.

Broden, M., R. V. Hall, A. Dunlap, and R. Clark. (1970). 'Effects of teacher attention and token reinforcement system in a junior high school special education class', *Exceptional Children*, 36: 341–49.

Brodzinsky, D. M., C. Pappas, L. M. Singer, and A. M. Braff. (1981). 'Children's conception of adoption: A preliminary investigation', *Journal of Paediatric Psychology*, 6: 177–89.

Brom, D., R. J. Kleber, and P. B. Defares. (1989). 'Brief Psychotherapy for Posttraumatic Stress Disorder', *Journal of Consulting and Clinical Psychology*, 57: 607–12.

Brook, F. S. and D. L. Snow. (1972). 'Two case illustrations of the use of behaviour modification techniques in the school setting', *Behaviour Therapy*, 3 (1): 100–03.

Broota, K. D. (1989). *Experimental Design in Behavioural Research*. New Delhi: Wiley Eastern.

Brown, J. D. (1988). 'Dependency, self-criticism and depression attributional style', *Journal of Abnormal Psychology*, 98 (2): 187–88.

Brown, J. S. (1965). 'Generalization and discrimination', in D. I. Mostofsky (ed.), *Stimulus Generalization*, pp. 7–23. Stanford: Stanford University Press.

Brown, P. and R. Elliot. (1965). 'Controlling aggression in nursery school class', *Journal of Exceptional Child Psychology*, 2: 103–07.

Brown, P. L. and H. M. Jenkins. (1968). 'Autoshaping of the pigeon's key peck', *Journal of Experimental Analysis of Behaviour*, 11 (1): 1–8.

Browning, R. M. (1967). 'The same-subject design for simultaneous comparison of three reinforcement contingencies', *Behaviour Research and Therapy*, 5: 237–43.

Bucher, B. and O. I. Lovaas. (1968). 'Use of aversive stimulation in behaviour modification', in R. M. Jones (ed.), Miami Symposium on the Prediction of Behaviour, 1967: Aversive Stimulation. Coral Gables, University of Miami Press: Fla.

Burchard, J. D. and F. Barrera. (1972). 'An analysis of time-out and response cost in a programmed environment', *Journal of Applied Behaviour Analysis*, 5: 271–82.

Burchard, J. D. and V. O. Tyler. (1965). 'The modification of delinquent behaviour through operant conditioning', *Behaviour Research and Therapy*, 2: 245–50.

Burns, D. D. (1989). *Feel good handbook: Using the new mood therapy in everyday life*. New York: Morrow.

Butler, J. F. (1977). 'Treatment of encopresis by overcorrection', *Psychological Reports*, 40: 639–49.

C

Calhoun, K. S. and P. Matherne. (1974). *An investigation of the effects of varying schedules of time-out on aggressive behaviour*. Unpublished manuscript. Georgia: University of Georgia.

Camp, B., G. Bloom, F. Herbert, and W. J. Van Door Nick. (1977). ' "Think aloud": A programme for developing self-control in young aggressive boys', *Journal of Abnormal Child Psychology*, 5: 157–69.

Campbell, A. and B. Sulzer. (1971). *Naturally available reinforcers as motivators towards reading and spelling achievement by educable mentally retarded handicapped students*. Paper presented at the meeting of the American Educational Research Association, February, New York.

Campbell, L. M. (1973). 'A variation of thought stopping in a twelve-year-old boy: A case report', *Journal of Behaviour Therapy and Experimental Psychiatry*, 4 (1): 69–70.

Campbell, S. B. (1973). 'Mother-child interaction in reflective, impulsive, hyperactive children', *Developmental Psychology*, 8: 341–49.

Cannon, D. S., T. B. Baker, A. Gino, and P. E. Nathan. (1986). 'Alcohol-aversion therapy: Relation between strength of aversion and abstinence', *Journal of Consulting and Clinical Psychology*, 54 (6): 825–30.

Carlson, J. G., C. M. Chemtob, K. Rusnak, N. L. Hedlund, and M. Y. Muraoka. (1998). 'Eye movement desensitization reprocessing (EMDR) treatment for combat-related post traumatic stress disorder', *Journal of Traumatic Stress*, 11: 3–16.

Carr, E. G., C. D. Newsom, and J. A. Binkoff. (1980). 'Escape as a factor in the aggressive behaviour of two retarded children', *Journal of Applied Behaviour Analysis*, 13: 101–07.

Carrea, F., and P. L. Adams. (1970). 'Ethical perspective on operant conditioning', *Journal of American Academy of Child Psychiatry*, 9 (4): 607–23.

Cataldo, M. F. and J. Harris. (1982). 'The biological basis of self-injury in the mentally retarded', *Analysis and Intervention in Developmental Disabilities*, 2: 21–39.

Catania, A. C. (1968). *Contemporary research in operant behaviour*. Illinois: Scott, Foresman, Glenview.

——. (1971). 'Elicitation, reinforcement, and stimulus Control, in R. Glaser (ed.) *The nature of reinforcement*, pp. 196–200 New York: Academic Press.

——. (1992). *Learning*, 4th Ed. New Jersey: Elglewood Cliffs, Prentice-Hall.

Cattell, R. B. (1957). *Personality and motivation, structure and measurement*. Brace Lovanovich : Harcourt.

Cautela, J. R. (1966). 'Treatment of compulsive behaviour by covert sensitization', *Psychological Record*, 16: 33–42.

———. (1967). 'Covert sensitization', *Psychological Reports*, 20: 459–63.

———. (1968). *The Covert Conditioning Handbook*. New York: Springer.

———. (1972a). 'Rationale and procedures for covert conditioning', in R. D. Rubin, H. Fensterheim, J. D. Henderson and L. P. Ullman (eds.), *Advances in Behaviour Therapy, Vol. 4*, pp. 115–19. New York: Academic Press.

———. (1972b). 'Reinforcement schedule: Evaluation and current applications', *Psychological Reports*, 30: 683–90.

———. (1973). *Cues for tension and anxiety scale*, Unpublished manuscript, cited in Cautela, J. R. and Upper, D. (1975) 'Process of Individual behaviour therapy', in R. M. Eisler and P. M. Miller (eds.), *Progress in Behaviour Modification, Vol. 1*, pp. 276–304. New York: Academic Press.

Cautela, J. R. and M. G. Baron. (1973). 'Multifaceted behaviour therapy of self-injurious behaviour', *Journal of Behaviour Therapy and Experimental Psychiatry*, 4 (2): 125–31.

Cautela, J. R. and A. J. Kearney. (1987). 'Covert conditioning', in R. J. Corsini (ed.), *Corsini's consise encyclopaedia of psychology*, pp. 262–63. New York: Wiley Interscience.

———. (1990). 'Behaviour analysis, cognitive therapy and covert conditioning', *Journal of Behaviour Therapy and Experimental Psychiatry*, 21 (2): 83–90.

Chadwick, B. A. and R. C. Day. (1971). 'Systematic reinforcement: Academic performance of undergraduate students', *Journal of Applied Behaviour Analysis*, 4: 311–19.

Chassan, J. B. (1967). *Research design in clinical psychology and psychiatry*. New York: Appleton-Century-Crofts.

Chemtob, C. M., D. F. Tolin, B. A. van der Kolk, and R. K. Pitman. (2000). *Eye movement desensitization reprocessing*. New York: Guilford Press.

Chesser, E. (1970). 'Behaviour therapy', *The Practitioner*, 205, 1227, 269–306.

Chinnian, R., N. N. Rawlin, and A. V. Rao. (1975). 'Physiological changes during progressive relaxation', *Indian Journal of Clinical Psychology*, 2 (2): 188–90.

Chopra, H. D. (1974). 'Obsessive-compulsive neurosis and behaviour therapy', *Indian Journal of Clinical Psychology*, 1: 19–22.

———. (1975). 'Systematic desensitization therapy', *Indian Journal of Psychiatry*, 17: 63–72.

Chorpita, B. F. (2003). 'The frontier of evidence-based practice', in A. E. Kazdin and J. R. Weisz (eds), *Evidence-based psychotherapies for children and adolescents*, pp. 42–59. New York: Guilford.

Christensen, A. L., C. Caetano, and G. Rasmussen. (1969). 'Psychosocial outcome after an intensive neuropsychologically-oriented day-care programme: contributing programme variable', in B. P. Uzzell and H. H. Stonington (eds), *Recovery after traumatic brain injury*, pp. 235–46. New Jersey: Lawrence Erlbaum Associates.

Christensen, H. and E. DiGiusto. (1982). 'The effects of sensory deprivation on cigarette craving and smoking behaviour', *Addictive Behaviour*, 7: 281–84.

Cicchetti, D. and F. A. Rogosch. (2002). 'A developmental psychopathology perspective on adolescence', *Journal of consulting and clinical psychology*, 70: 6–20.

Clark, D. A. and C. Purdon. (1994). 'New perspectives of a cognitive therapy of obsessions', *Australian Psychologist*, 28: 161–67.

Clark, D. M. (1986). 'A cognitive approach to panic', *Behaviour Research and Therapy*, 24 (4): 461–70.

Clark, D. M. and P. M. Salkovskis. (1991). *Cognitive therapy with panic and hypochondriasis*. New York: Pergamon Press.

Clark, D. M., P. M. Salkovskis, A. Hackmann, H. Middleton, P. Anastasiades, and M. Geldere. (1994). 'A comparison of cognitive therapy, applied relaxation and imipramine in the treatment of panic disorder', *British Journal of Psychiatry*, 164: 759–69.

Clark, H. B., T. Rowbury, A. M. Baer, and D. M. Baer. (1973). 'Time-out as a punishment stimulus in continuous and intermittent schedules', *Journal of Applied Behaviour Analysis*, 6: 448–55.

Cohen, R. L. (1963). 'Developments in the use of isolation therapy of behaviour disorders of children', in J. H. Masserman (ed.), *Current Psychiatric Therapies, Vol. 3*. New York: Grune and Stratton.

Colby, K. M. (1967). 'Computer-aided language development in non-speaking mentally disturbed children', Technical Report, No. CS85, Stanford University.

Coleman, J. C. (1975). *Abnormal Psychology and Modern Life*. Bombay: Taraporevel and Sons.

Cone, J. D., J. A. Anderson, F. C. Harris, D. K. Goff, and S. R. Foxx. (1978). 'Developing and maintaining social interaction in profoundly retarded young males', *Journal of Abnormal Child Psychology*, 6: 351–60.

Conger, J. L. and S. P. Keane. (1981). 'Social skill intervention in the treatment of isolated withdrawn children', *Psychological Bulletin*, 90 (3): 478–93.

Conn, L. and D. P. Crowne. (1964). 'Instigation to aggression, emotional arousal and defensive emulation', *Journal of Personality*, 32: 163–79.

Conover, W. J. (1971). *Practical nonparametric statistics*. New York: Wiley.

Cook, T. D. and D. T. Campbell. (1979). *Quasi-experimentation design and analysis issues for field setting*. Chicago: Rand McNally.

Cooper, O. J., T. E. Heron, and W. L. Heward. (1987). *Applied Behaviour Analysis*. Columbus, Ohio: Merrill Pub. Co.

Corsisni, R. J. and L. J. Putzey. (1987). *Bibliography of group psychotherapy*. New York: Beacon.

Corte, H. E., M. M. Wolf, and B. G. Locke. (1971). 'A comparison of procedures for eliminating self-injurious behaviour of retarded adolescents', *Journal of Applied Behaviour Analysis*, 4: 201–13.

Curtiss, S. 1977. *Genie: Psycholinguistic study of a modern day 'Wild Child'*. New York: Academic Press.

D

Dandy, M. C., S. E. Oliver, and E. A. Eprowy. (1976). *Using differential reinforcement of other behaviour to reduce and maintain low levels of disruptive work behaviour of a severely retarded adolescent*. Paper presented at Annual Meeting of the Mid Western Association of Behaviour Analysis, Chicago, Illinois.

Datta, J. and A. Broota. (2000). 'Managing obsessive compulsive disorder (OCD) with yoga and cognitive-behaviour therapy', *Journal of Research and Application in Clinical Psychology*, 3: 41–50.

Daniels, L. K. (1974). 'Rapid extinction of nail-biting by covert sensitization: A case study', *Journal of Behaviour Therapy and Experimental Psychiatry*, 5 (1): 91–92.

Das, J. P. (1958a). 'Pavlovian theory of hypnosis', *Journal of Mental Science*, 104: 82–90.

———. (1958b). 'Conditioning and hypnosis', *Journal of Experimental Psychology*, 56 (2): 110–13.

———. (1959). 'A theory of hypnosis', *International Journal of Clinical and Experimental Hypnosis*, 7: 69–77.

———. (1962). 'Learning under conditions of hypnotically induced anxiety and non-anxiety', *International Journal of Clinical and Experimental Hypnosis*, 10 (3): 163–68.

Dave, G. (1981). 'Editor's introduction', in G. Dave (ed.), *Applications of conditioning theory*. New York: Metheun.

Davison, G. C. and R. B. Stuart. (1975). 'Behaviour therapy for civil liberties', *American Psychologist*, 30: 755–63.

De Jongh, A., E. Ten Broeke, and M. Renssen. (1999). 'Treatment of chocking phobia by targeting traumatic memories with EMDR: A case study', *Clinical Psychology and Psychotherapy*, 5: 1–5.

De Silva, P. (1984). 'Buddhism and behaviour modification', *Behaviour Research and Therapy*, 22: 661–78.

Deitz, S. M. (1978). 'Current status of applied behaviour analysis: Science versus technology', *American Psychologist*, 33: 805–14.

Deitz, S. M. and A. C. Repp. (1973). 'Decreasing classroom misbehaviour through the DRL schedules of reinforcement', *Journal of Applied Behaviour Analysis*, 6: 457–63.

Deitz, S. M., A. C. Repp, and D. E. D. Deitz. (1976). 'Reducing inappropriate classroom behaviour of retarded students through three procedures of differential reinforcement', *Journal of Mental Deficiency Research*, 20: 155–70.

Demchak, M. A. (1990). 'Response prompting and fading methods: A review', *American Journal of Mental Retardation*, 94 (6): 603–15.

Denny, M. (1980). 'Reducing self-stimulatory behaviour of mentally retarded persons by alternative positive practice', *American Journal of Mental Deficiency*, 84: 610–15.

DeRubeis, R. J. and P. Crits-Christoph. (1998). 'Empirically supported individual and group psychological treatments for adult mental disorders', *Journal of Consulting and Clinical Psychology*, 66 (1): 37–52.

DeVilliers, P. A. (1977). 'Choice in concurrent schedules and quantitative formulation of the law of effect', in W. K. Honig, and J. E. R. Stadon (eds), *Handbook of Operant Behaviour*, pp. 233–87. New Jersey: Englewood-Cliffs, Prentice-Hall.

———. (1980). 'Towards a quantitative theory of punishment', *Journal of the Experimental Analysis of Behaviour*, 33: 15–25.

Dinsmoor, J. A. (1954). 'Punishment: I. The avoidance hypothesis', *Psychological Review*, 61: 34–46.

———. (1955). 'Punishment: II. An interpretation of empirical findings', *Psychological Review*, 62: 96–105.

———. (1977). 'Escape, avoidance and punishment: Where do we stand ?', *Journal of the Experimental Analysis of Behaviour*, 28: 83–95.

Dishion, T. J. and G. R. Patterson. (1999). 'Model building in developmental psychopathology: A pragmatic approach to understanding and intervention', *Journal of Clinical Child Psychology*, 28: 502–12.

Dixit, R. C., A. K. Malik, and R. P. Singh. (1999). 'Self evaluation and time orientation in Cognitive-behaviour therapy for depression', *Indian Journal of Clinical Psychology*, 26 (1): 66–69.

Dodge, K. A., G. S. Pettit, C. L. McClaskey, and M. M. Brown. (1986). 'Social competence in children', *Monographs for Research in Child Development*, 51 (Serial No. 213): 1–85.

Doke, L. A. and L. H. Epstein. (1975). 'Oral overcorrection: Side effects and extended applications', *Journal of Experimental Child Psychology*, 20: 496–511.

Doke, L. A. and T. R. Risley. (1972). 'The organization of day care environments: Required vs. optional activities', *Journal of Applied Behaviour Analysis*, 5: 405–20.

Dollard, J. and N. E. Miller. (1950). *Personality and psychotherapy*. New York: McGraw-Hill.

Dollard, J., I. Doob, N. E. Miller, O. H. Mowrer, and R. R. Sears. (1939). *Frustration and aggression*. New Haven: Yale University Press.

Drabman, R. and R. Spitalnik. (1973). 'Training a retarded child as a behavioural teaching assistant', *Journal of Behaviour Therapy and Experimental Psychiatry*, 4 (3): 269–72.

Dua, J. K. (1977). 'Relaxation and hierarchy in anxiety reduction', *Indian Journal of Psychology*, 52 (3): 210–21.

Ducker, P. C. and D. M. Sey. (1977). 'Elimination of vomiting in a retarded female using restitutional overcorrection', *Behaviour Therapy*, 8: 255–257.

Dunlap, K. (1932). *Habits: Their making and unmaking*. New York: Livingstone.

Dyck, M. J. (1993). 'A proposal for a conditioning model of eye movement desensitization treatment for Post-Traumatic Stress Disorder', *Journal of Behaviour Therapy and Experimental Psychiatry*, 24 (3): 201–10.

D'Zurilla, T. J. (1998). 'Problem-solving therapies', in K. S. Dobson (ed.), *Handbook of Cognitive Behavioural Therapies*, pp. 85–135. New York: Guilford Press.

D'Zurilla, T. J. and M. R. Goldfried. (1971). 'Problem-solving and behaviour Modification', *Journal of Abnormal Psychology*, 78: 107–26.

E

Eifert, G. H. (1996). 'More theory-driven and less diagnosis-based behaviour therapy', *Journal of Behaviour Therapy and Experimental Psychiatry*, 27 (2): 75–86.

Ellis, A. (1955). 'New Approaches to Psychotherapy', *Journal of Clinical Psychology Monograph, Supplement*, 11: 207–60.

Ellis, A. (1957). 'Outcome of employing three techniques of psychotherapy', *Journal of Clinical Psychology*, 13: 344–50.

———. (1962). *Reason and emotion in psychotherapy*. New York: Lyle Stuart.

———. (1973). *Humanistic psychotherapy: The rational emotive approach*. New York: Julian Press.

———. (1977). 'Can we change thoughts by reinforcement? A reply to Howard Rachlin', *Behaviour Therapy*, 8: 666–72.

———. (1979). *New developments in rational emotive therapy*. Pacific Grove, California: Brooks/Cole.

———. (1984). *Rational emotive therapy and cognitive-behaviour therapy*. New York: Springer.

Ellis, A. and R. M. Grieger (eds). (1986). *Handbook of rational emotive therapy*. New York: Springer.

English, H. B. (1929). 'Three cases of the conditioned fear response', *Journal of Abnormal and Social Psychology*, 24: 221–25.

Epstein, L. H., L. A. Doke, T. Sajwaj, S. Sorrell, and B. Rimmer. (1974). 'Generality and side-effects of overcorrection', *Journal of Applied Behaviour Analysis*, 7: 385–90.

Erikson, E. H. (1963). *Childhood and society*, (2nd ed.). New York: W. W. Norton.

Eron, L. D., L. O. Walder, and M. M. Lefkowitz. (1971). *Learning of aggression in children*. Boston: Brown.

Erwin, E. (1978). *Behaviour therapy: Scientific, philosophical and moral foundations*. Cambridge: Cambridge University Press.

Etzel, B. C. and J. L. Gewirtz. (1967). 'Experimental modification of caretaker-maintained high-rate operant crying in a 6- and a 20-weeks old Infant (infants tyrannotearus): Extinction of crying with reinforcement of eye-contact and smiling', *Journal of Experimental Child Psychology*, 5: 303–17.

Everett, P. B. (1981). 'Reinforcement theory strategies for modifying transit ridership', in I. Altman, J. E. Wohlwill, and P. B. Everett (eds), *Transportation and behaviour: Human behaviour and environment, Vol. 5*, pp. 63–84. New York: Plenum Press.

Eyberg, S., E. Schuhmann, and J. Rey. (1998). 'Psychosocial treatment research with children and adolescents: Developmental issues', *Journal of Abnormal Child Psychology*, 26: 71–81.

Eysenck, H. J. (1955). 'Cortical inhibition, figural after effect and theory of personality', *Journal of Applied Psychology*, 15: 94–106.

———. (1958). 'A short questionnaire for the measurement of two dimensions of personality', *Journal of Applied Psychology*, 42: 14–17.

———. (1959). 'Learning theory and behaviour therapy', *Journal of Mental Science*, 105: 67.

———. (1971). 'Behaviour therapy as a scientific discipline', *Journal of Consulting and Clinical Psychology*, 36: 314–19.

———. (1972). 'Behaviour therapy is behaviouristic', *Behaviour Therapy*, 3 (4): 609–613.

———. (1976). *Case-studies in behaviour therapy*. New York: Rutledge Kagan Paul.

Eysenck, H. J. and G. D. Wilson. (1979). 'Psychology as a bio-social science', in H. J. Eysenck (ed.), *A text book of human psychology*. Lancaster: MTP Press Ltd.

F

Fantino, E. and C. A. Logan. (1979). *The experimental analysis of behaviour: A biological perspective*. San Fransisco: W. H. Freeman.

Farley, J. (1980). 'Reinforcement and punishment effects in concurrent schedules: A test of two models', *Journal of the Experimental Analysis of Behaviour*, 33: 311–26.

Favell, J. E. (1973). 'Reduction of stereotypies by reinforcement of toy play', *Mental Retardation*, 11: 21–23.

Favell, J. E., J. F. McGimsey, and M. Jones. (1978). 'The use of physical restraint in the treatment of self-injury and as positive reinforcement', *Journal of Applied Behaviour Analysis*, 11: 225–41.

Favell, J. E., J. F. McGimsey, and R. M. Schell. (1982). 'Treatment of self-injury by providing alternative sensory activities', *Analysis and Intervention in Developmental Disabilities*, 2: 83–104.

Feighner, J. P., E. Robbins, S. B. Guze, R. N. Woodruff, G. Winoker, and R. Munoz. (1972). 'Diagnostic criteria for use in psychiatric research', *Archives of General Psychiatry*, 26: 57–73.

Feindler, E. and R. Ecton. (1986). *Anger training.* New York: Pergamon Press.

Feindler, E., S. A. Merriott, and M. Iwata. (1984). 'Group control training for junior high school delinquents', *Cognitive Therapy and Research*, 8: 299–311.

Fensterheim, H. (1996). 'Eye movement desensitization and reprocessing with complex personality pathology: An integrative therapy', *Journal of Psychotherapy Integration*, 6: 27–38.

Ferster, C. B. and M. K. DeMyer. (1961). 'The development of performances in autistic children in controlled environment', *Journal of Chronic Diseases*, 13: 312–45.

Fine, T. H., J. Bruno, and M. Nestor. (1985). 'Floatation REST and smoking cessation: A preliminary report', in J. J. Sanchez-Sosa (ed.), *Health and clinical psychology, selected/revised papers, Vol. 4*, pp. 261–64. Amsterdam, North-Holland: XIII International Congress of Psychology.

Fine, T. H. and J. W. Turner Jr. (1982). 'The effects of brief restricted environmental stimulation in treatment of essential hypertension', *Behaviour Research and Therapy*, 20 (6): 567–70.

———. (1985). 'REST-assisted relaxation and chronic pain', in J. J. Sanchez-Sosa (ed.), *Health and clinical psychology, selected/revised papers, Vol. 4*, pp. 511–18. North-Holland, Amsterdam: XIII International Congress of Psychology.

Flavell, J. H., D. R. Beach, and J. M. Chinsky. (1966). 'Spontaneous verbal rehearsal in a memory task as a function of age,' *Child Development*, 37: 284–99.

Fleece, L., A. Gross, T. O'Brien, J. Kistner, E. Rothblaum, and R. Drabman. (1981). 'Elevation of voice volume in young developmentally delayed children via an operant shaping procedure', *Journal of Applied Behaviour Analysis*, 14: 351–55.

Foa, E. B., C. V. Dancu, E. A. Hembree, L. H. Jaycox, E. A. Meadows, and O. P. Sreet. (1999). 'A comparison of exposure therapy, stress inoculation training, and their combination in reducing Post Traumatic Stress Disorder in female assault victims', *Journal of Consulting and Clinical Psychology*, 67: 194–200.

Foa, E. B. and M. J. Kozak. (1986). 'Emotional processing of fear: Exposure to corrective information', *Psychological Bulletin*, 99 (1): 20–35.

Follingstad, D. R., J. Sullivann, and S. N. Haynes. (1978). 'Behavioural assessment of dissatisfied marital couple', in S. N. Haynes (ed.), *Principles of behavioural assessment*, pp. 122–440. New York: Gardner Press Inc.

Forehand, R. and A. A. Baumeister. (1971). 'Rate of stereotyped body-rocking of severe retardates as a function of frustration of a goal directed behaviour', *Journal of Abnormal Psychology*, 78 (1): 35–42.

———. (1976). 'Deceleration of aberrant behaviour among retarded individuals', in M. Hersen R. M. Eisler and P. M. Miller (eds.), *Progress in Behaviour Modification, Vol. 2*, pp. 223–78. New York: Academic Press.

Forehand, R., H. E. King, and S. P. Peed. (1975). 'Mother-child interactions: comparisons of a non-compliant clinic group', *Behaviour Research and Therapy*, 13 (2/3): 79–84.

Forehand, R. and M. Eierson (1993). 'The role of developmental factors in planning behavioural interventions for children: Disruptive behaviour as an example', *Behaviour Therapy*, 24: 117–41.

Foreyt, J. P. and R. L. Hagen. (1973). 'Covert sensitization: conditioning or suggestion', *Journal of Abnormal Psychology*, 82: 17–23.

Forgays, D. F. (1983). *Primary prevention of psychopathology.* New York: Appleton-Centuy-Crofts.

Fox, L. (1962). 'Effecting the use of efficient study habits', *Journal of Mathematics*, 1: 75–86.

Fox, R. G., R. E. Copeland, J. Harris, W. Rieth, and R. V. Hall. (1975). 'A computerized system for selecting responsive research studies, catalogued along twenty-eight important dimensions', in E. Ramp and G. Semb (eds), *Behaviour Analysis: Areas of research and application*, pp. 124–58. New York: Prentice-Hall.

Foxx, R. M. (1976). 'The use of overcorrection to eliminate public disrobing (stripping) of retarded women', *Behaviour Research and Therapy*, 14 (1): 53–61.

———. (1982). *Increasing behaviours of severely retarded and autistic persons.* Champaign, Illinois: Research Press.

Foxx, R. M. and D. R. Bechtel. (1983). 'Overcorrection: A review and analysis', in S. Axelord and J. Apsche (eds), *The effects of punishment on human behaviour*, pp. 285–316. New York: Academic Press.

Foxx, R. M. and E. D. Martin. (1975). 'Treatment of scavenging behaviour (coprophagy and pica) by overcorrection', *Behaviour Research and Therapy*, 13 (2/3): 153–62.

Foxx, R. M. and N. H. Azrin. (1972). 'Restitution: A method of eliminating aggressive-disruptive behaviour of retarded and brain-damaged patients', *Behaviour Research and Therapy*, 10: 15–20.

———. (1973a). 'The elimination of autistic self-stimulatory behaviour by overcorrection', *Journal of Applied Behaviour Analysis*, 6: 1–14.

———. (1973b). *Toilet-training the retarded: A rapid programme for day and night time independent toileting.* Champaign: III Research Press.

Foxx, R. M., B. A. Bremer, C. Schultz, J. Valdez, and C. Johndrow. (1996). 'Increasing acceptability through video', *Behavioural Intervention*, 11: 171–80.

Foxx, R. M. and S. T. Shapiro. (1978). 'The time-out ribbon: A non-exclusionary time-out procedure', *Journal of Applied Behaviour Analysis*, 11: 125–36.

Freeman, B. J. T. Somerset, and E. R. Ritvo. (1976). 'Effects of duration of time-out in suppressing disruptive behaviour of a severely autistic child', *Psychological Reports*, 38: 124–26.

Freeman, B. J., V. Graham, and E. R. Ritvo. (1975). 'Reduction of self-destructive behaviour by overcorrection', *Psychological Reports*, 37: 446.

Fuller, P. R. (1949). 'Operant conditioning of vegetative human organism', *American Journal of Psychology*, 62: 587–90.

G

Gada, M. (1987). 'A study of prevalence and pattern of attention deficit disorder with hyperactivity in primary school children', *Indian Journal of Psychiatry*, 29 (2): 113–18.

Ganesan, V. (1983). *Genital muscle relaxation technique and its uses.* Unpublished paper, Department of Psychology, Bharathiar University, Coimbatore.

Ganeshan, V. and J. S. Michael. (1988). 'Late-pubescence: Psychogenic causes and their treatment: A case report', *Indian Journal of Clinical Psychology*, 15 (2): 64–66.

Gardner, J. E., D. T. Pearson, A. N. Berocovici, and D. C. Bricker. (1968). 'Measurement, evaluation and modification of selected social interactions between a schizophrenic child, his parents and his therapist', *Journal of Consulting and Clinical Psychology*, 32 (5, part 1): 537–42.

Gardner, W. I. (1971). 'Use of behaviour therapy with the mentally retarded', in F. J. Menolascino (ed.), *Psychiatric approaches of mental retardation.* New York: Basic Books.

Garfield, Z. H., J. F. McBrearty, and M. A. Dichter. (1969). 'A case of impotence treated with desensitization, combined with in vivo operant training and thought substitution', in R. D. Rubin and C. M. Franks (eds), *Advances in behaviour therapy.* New York: Academic Press.

Garg, P. (1999). 'Myth of virginity: A case report', *Journal of Research and Applications in Clinical Psychology*, 2: 1–2, 79–82.

Geer, J. H. (1965). 'The development of a scale to measure fear', *Behaviour Research and Therapy*, 3: 45–53.

Gelfand, D. M. and D. P. Hartman. (1968). 'Behaviour therapy with children: A review of research methodology', *Psychological Bulletin*, 69 (3): 204–15.

———. (1975). *Child Behaviour: Analysis and therapy.* New York: Pergamon.

Gellert, E. (1955). 'Systematic observation: A method in child study', *Harvard Educational Review*, 25 (1): 179–97.

Gelso, C. J. (1979). 'Research in counselling methodological and professional issues', *Counselling Psychology*, 8 (7): 7–36.

Gershman, L. (1970). 'Case conference: A transvestite fantasy treated by thought stopping, covert sensitization and aversive shock', *Journal of Behaviour Therapy and Experimental Psychiatry*, 1: 153–61.

Gerst, M. S. (1969). *Symbolic coding operations in observational learning*. Unpublished doctoral dissertation. Stanford: Stanford University.

Gilliland, B. E. and R. K. James. (1998). *Theories and strategies in counseling and psychotherapy*. New York: Allyn & Bacon.

Gilovich, T. and V. Medvec. (1995). 'The experience of regret: what, when and why', *Psychological Review*, 102: 379–95.

Girodo, M. 1974. 'Yoga, meditation and flooding in treatment of anxiety neurosis', *Journal of Behaviour Therapy and Experimental Psychiatry*, 5 (2): 157–60.

Gittleman, R., H. Abicoff, E. Pollack, D. F. Klein, S. Katz, and J. A. Matters. (1980). 'Controlled trial of behaviour modification and methylphenidate in hyperactive children', in Wahlen, C. and B. Hencker (eds), *Hyperactive Children: The social ecology of identification and treatment*. New York: Academic Press.

Glaister, B. (1985). 'A case study with auditory hallucination treated by satiation', *Behaviour Research and Therapy*, 23 (2): 213–15.

Glasgow, R. E. (1975). 'In vivo prolonged exposure in the treatment of urinary retention', *Behaviour Therapy*. 6 (5): 701–02.

Glass, G. V., V. L. Wilson, and J. M. Gottman. (1974). *Design and analysis of time-series experiments*. Boulder: Colorado Associated University Press.

Glynn, E. (1975). 'The therapeutic use of seclusion in an adolescent pavilion', *Journal of Hillside Hospital*, 6: 156–59.

Gold, S. and I. L. Neufeld. (1965). 'A learning approach to the treatment of homosexuality', *Behaviour Research and Therapy*, 3: 201–304.

Goldfried, M. R. and R. N. Kent. (1972). 'Traditional versus behavioural personality assessment: A comparison between methodological and theoretical assumptions', *Psychological Bulletin*, 77 (6): 409–20.

Goldiamond, I. (1965). 'Self-control procedures in personal behaviour problems', *Psychological Reports*, 17: 851–61.

Goss, A. E. (1961). 'Verbal mediating responses and concept formation', *Psychological Review*, 68: 248–74.

Grandy, G. W., C. H. Jr. Madsen, and L. De Masserman. 1973. 'The effects of individual and interdependent contingencies on inappropriate classroom behaviour', *Psychology in School*, 10: 488–92.

Grashchenkov. (1914). In Luria, A. R., Nanydin, V. L. Tsvetkova and Vinarskaya, E. N. 'Restoration of higher mental function following local brain damage', pp. 368–433. In Vinken, P. J. and G. W. Bruyn (eds) (1969), *Handbook of neurology*. New Holland: Amsterdam.

Grassian, G. (1983). 'Psychotherapy of solitary confinement', *American Journal of Psychiatry*, 140 (11): 1450–54.

Gray, J. A. (1975). *Element of a two-process theory of learning*. London: Academic press.

———. (1976). 'The behavioural inhibition system: A possible substrate for anxiety', in M. P. Feldman and A. M. Broadhurst (eds), *Theoretical experimental bases of the behaviour modification*. London: Wiley.

Graziano, A. M. and K. C. Mooney. (1984). *Children and behaviour therapy*. New York: Aldine.

Green, C. W., D. H. Reid, McCarn, M. M. Schepis, J. F. Phillips, and M. B. Parson. (1986). 'Naturalistic observations of classrooms serving severely handicapped persons: establishing evaluative norms', *Applied research in mental retardation*, 7: 37–50.

Greene, R. J. and D. L. Hoats. (1971). 'Aversive tickling: A simple conditioning procedure', *Behaviour Therapy*, 2: 389–93.

Greene, R. J., D. L. Hoats, and A. J. Hornick. (1970). 'Music distortion: A new technique for behaviour modification', *Psychological record*, 20: 107–09.

Gregman, E. O. (1934). 'An attempt to modify the emotional attitudes of the infants by conditioned response techniques', *Journal of Genetic Psychology*, 45: 169–98.

Griffin, R. S. and A. M. Gross. (2002). 'Time-out', in M. Hersen and W. Sledge (eds), *Encyclopedia of psychotherapy, Vol II*, pp. 815–19. Amsterdam: Academic Press:.

Grolnick, W. S., E. L. Deci, and R. M. Ryan. (1997). 'Internalization within the Family: The self-determination theory perspective', in J. E. Grusec and L. Kukzynski (eds), *Parent and children's internalization of values: A handbook of contemporary theories*, pp. 135–61. New York: Wiley.

Grover, N., K. Thennarasu, G. D'Souza, and V. Kumaraiah. (2004). 'Psychological management of bronchial asthma', *Indian Journal of Clinical Psychology*, 31 (2): 135–40.

Groves, P. M. and R. F. Thompson. (1970). 'Habituation: A dual process theory', *Psychological Review*, 77: 419–59.

Gruber, B., R. Reeser, D. H. Reid. (1979). 'Providing a less restrictive environment for profoundly retarded persons by teaching independent walking skills', *Journal of Applied Behaviour Analysis*, 12: 285–97.

Grusec, J. E. and J. J. Goodnow. (1994). 'Impact of parental discipline method on child's internalization of values: A reconceptualization of current points of view', *Developmental Psychology*, 30: 4–22.

Guess, D., W. Sailor, and D. M. Baer. (1974). 'To teach language to retarded children', in R. L. Schiefelbusch and G. Lloyd (eds), *Language: Perspectives, acquisition, retardation and intervention*. Baltimore: University Park Press.

Guess, D., E. Helmstetter, H. R. Turnbull, and S. Knowlton. (1986). *Use of aversive procedures with persons who are disabled: A historical review and clinical review and critical analysis*. Seattle: The Association of Persons with Severe Handicaps.

Gupta, P. and L. Pinto. (1977). 'The effects of punishment on behaviour change', *Indian Journal of Psychology*, 52 (3): 256–61.

Guttentag, O. (1953). 'The problem of experimentation on human beings: The physician's point of view', *Science*, 117: 205.

H

Hackmann, A. and C. McLean. (1975). 'A comparison of flooding and thought-stopping in the treatment of obsessional neurosis', *Behaviour Research and Therapy*, 13 (2/3): 263–269.

Hagopian, L. P., D. A. Farrell, and A. Amari. (1996). 'Treating total liquid refusal with backward chaining and fading', *Journal of Applied Behaviour Analysis*, 29: 573–75.

Hake, D. F. and N. H. Azrin. (1963). 'An apparatus for delivering pain-shock to monkeys', *Journal of Experimental Animal Behaviour*, 6: 122, 297–98.

Hake, D. F. (1982). 'The basic applied continuum and possible evolution of human operant, social and verbal research', *The Behaviour Analyst*, 5: 21–28.

Hall, K. R. L. (1963). 'Observational learning in monkeys and apes', *British Journal of Psychology*, 54: 201–26.

Hall, R. V., D. Lund, and J. Jackson. (1968). 'Effects of teacher attention on study behaviour', *Journal of Applied Behaviour Analysis*, 14: 89–96.

Hall, R. V., M. Panyan, D. Rabon, and M. Borden. (1968). 'Instructing beginning teachers in reinforcement procedures which improve classroom control', *Journal of Applied Behaviour Analysis*, 1: 315–22.

Halder, S., A. R. Singh, and J. Prakash. (2005). 'Efficacy of cognitive-behaviour therapy for the treatment of OCD: A case report', *Indian Journal of Clinical Psychology*, 32 (2): 133–36.

Hamilton, J. W., L. Y. Stephens, and P. Allen. (1967). 'Controlling aggressive and destructive behaviour in severely retarded institutionalized residents', *American Journal of Mental Deficiency*, 71: 852–56.

Hanf, C. (1973). *Modifying problem behaviours in mother-child interaction: Standardized lab situation*. Paper presented at the meetings of the association of behaviour therapies, Washinngton.

Hannie, T. J. Jr. and H. E. Adams. (1974). 'Modification of agitated depression by flooding: A preliminary study', *Journal of Behaviour Therapy and Experimental Psychiatry*, 5 (2): 161–66.

Harris, A. (1959). 'Sensory deprivation and schizophrenia', *Journal of Mental Science*, 105: 235–37.

Harris, F. C. and B. B. Lahey. (1978). 'A method of combining occurrence and nonoccurence inter-observer agreement scores', *Journal of Applied Behaviour Analysis*, 11: 523–27.

Harris, G. M. and S. B. Johnson. (1983). 'Coping imagery and relaxation in covert modelling treatment for test anxiety', *Behaviour Therapy*, 14: 144–57.

Harris, S. L. and M. Ferrari. (1983). 'Developmental factors in child behaviour therapy', *Behaviour Therapy*, 5: 54–72.

Harris, S. L., R. E. Hershfield, L. C. Kaffashan, and R. G. Romanczyk. (1974). 'The portable time-out room', *Behaviour Research and Therapy*, 5: 687–88.

Harris, S. L. and R. G. Romanczyk. (1976). 'Treating self-injurious behaviour of a retarded child by overcorrection', *Behaviour Therapy*, 7 (2): 235–39.

Harris, S. L. and S. A. Wolchik. (1979). 'Suppression of self-stimulation: Three alternative strategies', *Journal of Applied Behaviour Analysis*, 12: 185–98.

Harris, V. W. and J. A. Sherman. (1973). 'Use and analysis of the "Good Behaviour Game" to reduce distinctive classroom behaviour', *Journal of Applied Behaviour Analysis*, 6: 405–17.

Hartmann, D. P. and R. V. Hall. (1976). 'The changing criterion design', *Journal of Applied Behaviour Analysis*, 9: 527–32.

Hatzenbuehler, L. C. and H. E. Scroeder. (1978). 'Desensitization procedures in treatment of childhood disorders', *Psychological Bulletin*, 85 (4): 831–44.

Hawkins, R. P., R. F. Peterson, and E. Schweid. (1966). 'Behaviour therapy in home: Amelioration of problem parent-child relations with the parent in a therapeutic role', *Journal of Experimental Child Psychology*, 4: 99–107.

Hawkins, R. P. and V. A. Dotson. (1975). 'Reliability scores that delude: An Alice in the wonderland trip through the misleading characteristics of inter-observer agreement scores in interval recording', in E. Ramp and G. Semp (eds), *Behaviour analysis: Areas of research and application*, pp. 359–76. California: Englewood Cliffs.

Hayes, S. C., K. D. Brownwell, and D. H. Barlow. (1978). 'The use of self-administered covert sensitization in a poorly motivated client', *Journal of Behaviour Therapy and Experimental Psychiatry*, 8: 181–83.

Hayes, S. C., A. Rincover, and J. V. Solnick. (1980). 'The technical draft in applied behaviour analysis', *Journal of Applied Behaviour Analysis*, 13: 275–85.

Haynes, S. N. (1978). *Principles of behavioural assessment.* New York: Gardner Press.

Heimstra, N. W. and R. T. Davis. (1962). 'A simple recording system for the direct observation techniques', *Animal Behaviour*, 10: 208–10.

Helode, R. D. (2002). 'Occupational stress and rational emotive therapy', *Indian Journal of Clinical Psychology*, 29 (1): 36–37.

Henggler, S. W., S. K. Schoenwald, C. M. Borduin, M. D. Rowland, and P. B. Cunningham. (1998). *Multisystem treatment of antisocial behaviour in children and adolescents.* New York: Guilford Press.

Herbert, J. D. and K. T. Mueser. (1992). 'Eye movement desensitization: A critique of evidence', *Journal of Behaviour Therapy and Experimental Psychiatry*, 23 (3): 169–74.

Herendeen, D. L. and M. C. Graham. (1974). *Reduction of self-stimulation in institutionalized children: Overcorrection and reinforcement for non-responding.* Paper presented at the eighth annual meeting of the Association for Advancement of Behaviour Therapy, Chicago.

Hersen, M. and D. H. Barlow. (1976). *Single-case experimental designs: Strategies for studying behaviour change.* New York: Pergamon Press.

Hilgard, E. R. (1977). *Divided consciousness: Multiple controls in human thought and action.* New York: John Wiley & Sons.

———. (1979). 'Consciousness and control: Lessons from hypnosis', *Australian Journal of Clinical and Experimental Hypnosis*, 7: 103–15.

Hobbs, S. A., R. Forehand, and R. G. Murray. (1978). 'Effects of various duration of time out on the non-compliant behaviour of children', *Behaviour Therapy*, 9 (4): 652–56.

Hochberg, J. E., W. Triebel, and G. Seaman. (1951). 'Colour adaptation under conditions of homogeneous visual stimulation (Ganzfeld)', *Journal of Experimental Psychology*, 41: 153–59.

Hoffman, M. L. (1983). 'Affective and cognitive processes in moral internalization', in E. T. Higgins, D. N. Rubbles, and W. W. Hartup (eds), *Social cognition and social development*, pp. 137–274. New York: Cambridge University Press.

Hogan, R. A. (1968). 'The implosive technique', *Behaviour research and therapy*, 6: 423–32.

Hollandsworth, J. G. Jr. (1986). *Behaviour therapy and physiology*. New York: Plenum.

Holmes, F. B. (1939). 'An experimental investigation of a method of overcoming children's fears', *Child Development*, 7: 630.

Holz, W. C. and N. H. Azrin. (1963). 'A comparison of several procedures for eliminating behaviour', *Journal of Experimental Analysis of Behaviour*, 6 (6): 399–406.

Holz, W. C., N. H. Azrin, and T. Ayllon. (1963). 'Elimination of behaviour of mental patients by response-produced extinction', *Journal of Experimental Analysis of Behaviour*, 6: 407–12.

Homme, L. E. (1965). 'Perspectives in psychology, XXIV, Control of covenants, the operants of the mind', *Psychological Record*, 15: 501–11.

Homme, L. E., P. C. de Baca, J. V. Devine, R. Steinhorst, and E. J. Rickert. (1963). 'Use of the premack principles in controlling the behaviour of nursery school children', *Journal of Experimental Analysis of Behaviour*, 6 (4): 444.

Horner, R. D. (1971). 'Establishing use of crutches by mentally retarded spina bifida child', *Journal of Applied Behaviour Analysis*, 4: 163–89.

Hospers, J. (1961). *Human conduct: An introduction to problem of ethics*. New York: Harcourt, Brace & World.

Huhuenin, N. H., L. E. Weidenman, and J. E. Mulick. (1983). 'Programmed instruction', in J. L. Matson and J. E. Mulick (eds), *Handbook of mental retardation*, pp. 451–67. New York: Pergamon Press.

Hull, C. L. (1943). *Principles of behaviour*. New York: Appleton-Century Crofts.

———. (1952). *A behaviour system*. New Haven, CT: Yale University Press.

Hulse, S. H., J. Deese, and H. Egeth. (1952). *The psychology of learning*. Tokyo: McGraw-Hill.

———. (1975). *The psychology of learning*. Tokyo: McGraw-Hill.

I

Indian Council of Medical Research. (1981). *National mental health programme strategies for research on mental health*. New Delhi.

Isaacs, W., I. Thomas, and I. Goldiamond. (1960). 'Application of operant conditioning to reinstate verbal behaviour in psychotics', *Journal of Speech and Hearing Disorders*, 25: 8–12.

Iwata, B. A., M. F. Dorsey, K. J. Slifer, K. E. Bauman, and G. Richman. (1982). 'Toward a functional analysis of self-injury', *Analysis and Intervention in Developmental Disabilities*, 2: 3–20.

Iwata, B. A., G. M. Pace, M. F. Dorsey, J. R. Zarcone, T. R. Vollmer, R. G. Smith, T. A. Rodgers, D. C. Lerman, B. A. Shore, J. L. Mazaleski, H. Goh, G. E. Cowdery, M. J. Kalsher, K. C. McCosh, and K. D. Willish. (1994). 'The functions of self-injurious behaviour: An experimental epidemiological analysis', *Journal of Applied Behaviour Analysis*, 27: 215–40.

Iwata, B. A., G. M. Pace, M. J. Kalsher, G. E. Cowdery, and M. E. Cataldo. (1990). 'Experimental analysis and extinction of self-injurious escape behaviour', *Journal of Applied Analysis*, 23: 11–27.

J

Jacobs, G. D., R. L. Heilbronner, and J. M. Stanley. (1984). 'Effects of short-term floatation REST on relaxation: A controlled study', *Health Psychology*, 3: 99–112.

Jacobs, J. (1970). *A comparison of group and individual rewards in teaching reading to slow learners*. Project No. 9–0257, Grant No. OEG-4-9-109257-0045-010. Southern Illinois University, Carbondale, Illinois, U. S. Department of health, Education and Welfare, Office of Education, Bureau of Research.

Jacobson, E. (1938). *Progressive relaxation*. Chicago: Chicago University Press

Jacobson, E. (1973). 'Electro physiology of mental activities, an introduction to the psychological process of thinking', in F. M. McGuigan and R. A. Schoonover (eds), *The psychophysiology of thinking*, pp. 3–31. New York: Academic Press.

James, I. A. and I. M. Blackburn. (1995). 'Cognitive therapy with obsessive compulsive disorders', *British Journal of Psychiatry*, 166: 444–50.

Janda, L. M. and D. C. Rimm. (1972). 'Covert sensitization in the treatment of obesity', *Journal of Abnormal Psychology*, 80: 37–42.

Janov, A. (1960). *The primal scream*. New York: Dell.

———. (1970). *The primal scream, primal therapy: The cure for neurosis*. London: Abacus.

Janz, G. (1978). 'Functional relaxation therapy applied to children suffering from disturbance of concentration', *Praxix der kinderpsychologie und kinderpsychiatrie*, 27: 201–05.

Jena, R., M. Sharma, and R. Kumar. (2004). 'Enhancing nicotine cessation amongst inpatient substance abusers through cognitive-behaviour therapy', *Indian Journal of Clinical Psychology*, 31 (2): 117–20.

Jena, S. P. K. (1995). 'Effects of differential reinforcement, physical restraint, and verbal reprimand on stereotyped body-rocking', *International Journal of Rehabilitation Research*, 18: 70–75.

———. (1998). 'Effects of differential reinforcement of alternative behaviour on disruptive noise making of a retarded child', *Indian Journal of Clinical Psychology*, 25 (1): 77–91.

———. (1999a). 'Treatment of self-injurious behaviour by differential reinforcement and physical restraint', *International Journal of Rehabilitation Research*, 22: 243–47.

———. (1999b). 'Use of GSR biofeedback, cognitive restructuring and reciprocal inhibition in treatment of hallucination induced stereotypes', *Behavioural Medicine Journal*, 2 (1): 48–53.

———. (2002). 'Manshik vikrition mein vyavahar chikitsa', *Dainik Jagaran*, 2, April, Sanjhi 1. Bareilly.

———. (2004). 'Parent-mediated behavioural intervention in physical aggression of a retarded child', *Indian Journal of Clinical Psychology*, 31 (1): 78–81.

Johnson, J. M. and H. S. Pennypecker. (1980). *Strategies and tactics of human behavioural research*. Hillsdale, New Jersey: Lawrence.

Johnson, S. M. and O. D. Bolstad. (1973). 'Methodological issues in naturalistic observation: Some problems and solutions for field research', in L. A. Hamerlynck, L. C. Handy, and E. J. Mash (eds), *Behaviour change: methodology, concept and practice*, pp. 7–64. New York: Campaign III, Research Press.

Johnson, W. L. and A. A. Baumeister. (1981). 'Behavioural techniques for decreasing aberrant behaviour of retarded and autistic persons', in *Progress in behaviour modification, Vol. 12*, pp. 119–60. New York: Academic Press.

Jones, M. C. (1924a). 'A laboratory study of fear: The case of peter', *Pedagogical Seminary*, 31: 308–15.

———. (1924b). 'The elimination of children's fear', *Journal of Experimental Psychology*, 7: 382–90.

K

Kabat-Zinn, J. (1990). *Full catastrophe living: The programme of the stress clinic at the University of Massachusetts Medical Centre*. New York: Dell Publications.

Kagan, J. (1971). *Change and continuity in infancy*. New York: Wiley.

Kakkar, S. B. (1972). 'Experimental extinction of tantrum behaviour', *Indian Journal of Experimental Psychology*, 6: 76–77.

Kaliappan, K. V. and H. N. Murthy. (1970). *A case of tension headache: Role of relaxation in treatment*, Proceedings, III Regional Conference of Indian Psychiatric Society, Bangalore, (Abstract).

———. (1973). *A case of tics: Behaviour therapy*. Proceedings, IV All India Convention of Clinical Psychologists, Madras (Abstract).

Kallman, W. M., M. Hersen, and D. H. O'Tooley. (1975). 'The use of social reinforcement in a case of conversion reaction', *Behaviour Therapy*, 6 (3): 411–13.

Kandel, H. J., T. Ayllon, and M. S. Rosenbaum. (1877). 'Flooding and systematic exposure in the treatment of extreme social withdrawal in children', *Journal of Behaviour Therapy and Experimental Psychiatry*, 8 (1): 75–81.

Kanfer, F. H. and G. Saslow. (1965). 'Behaviour analysis: An alternative to diagnostic classification', *Archives of General Psychiatry*, 12: 529–38.

———. (1969). 'Behavioural diagnosis', in C. M. Franks (ed.), *Behaviour therapy: Appraisal and status*, pp. 417–44. New York: McGraw-Hill.

Kapur, M. and I. Cariappa. (1979). 'An orientation course of school teacher', *Indian Journal of Clinical Psychology*, 6 (1): 75–80.

Kaushik, S. S. (1983a). 'Techniques to help in management and training of mentally retarded children', Hyderabad: Associated Press.

———. (1983b). *Parents as Teachers*. New Delhi: Northern Book Centre.

———. (2002). 'Behaviour analysis and modification of parenting training techniques in improving study and home work behaviour of academically backward children', NCERT funded Research project, NCERT, New Delhi.

Kazdin, A. E. (1971). 'The effects of response cost in suppressing behaviour in a prepsychotic retardate', *Journal of Behaviour Therapy and Experimental Psychiatry*, 2: 137–40.

———. (1972). 'Response cost: The removal of conditioned reinforcers for therapeutic change', *Behaviour Therapy*, 4: 73–82.

———. (1973). 'Methodological and assessment considerations in evaluating reinforcement programme in applied setting', *Journal of Applied Behaviour Analysis*, 6: 517–31.

———. (1975a). *Behaviour modification in applied settings*. Illinois: Homewood, Dorsey Press.

———. (1975b). 'Recent advances in token economy research', in M. Hersen, R. M. Eisler, and P. M. Miller (eds.), *Progress in Behaviour Modification, Vol. 1*, pp. 233–74. New York: Academic Press.

———. (1977). *The token economy: A review of evaluation*. New York: Plenum Press.

———. (1978). *History of behaviour modification: Experimental foundations of contemporary research*. Baltimore: University Park Press.

———. (1979). 'A model for developing effective treatments: Progression and interplay of theory, research and practice', *Journal of Clinical Child Psychology*, 26: 114–29.

———. (1980). *Research designs in clinical psychology*. New York: Harper & Row.

———. (1982a). 'Behaviour modification in retardation', in J. T. Neisworth (ed.), *Retardation: Issues, assessment and intervention*, pp. 299–340. New York: Mc-Graw-Hill.

———. (1982b). *Single-case research designs: Methods for clinical and applied settings*. New York: Oxford.

———. (1983). 'Psychiatric diagnosis, dimensions of dysfunction and child behaviour Therapy', *Behaviour Therapy*, 14: 73–79.

———. (1998). *Research designs in clinical psychology*. Boston: Allyn & Bacon.

———. (2001). *Behaviour modification in applied settings* (6th Ed.). California: Wadsworth.

Kazdin, A. E., L. Holland, and M. Crowley. (1997). 'Family experience of barriers to treatment and premature termination from child therapy', *Journal of Consulting and Clinical Psychology*, 65 (3): 453–63.

Kazdin, A. E. and J. Klock. (1973). 'The effects of non-verbal teacher approval on student alternative behaviour', *Journal of Applied Behaviour Analysis*, 6: 643–54.

Kazdin, A. E. and J. R. Weisz. (2003). 'Introduction: Context and background of evidence-based psychotherapies for children and adolescents', in A. E. Kazdin, and J. R. Weisz (eds), *Evidence-based psychotherapies for children and adolescents*, pp. 3–20. New York: Guilford.

Keane, T. M., J. A. Fairbank, J. M. Caddel, and R. T. Zimering. (1989). 'Implosive (flooding) therapy reduces symptoms of PTSD in Vietnam combat veterans', *Behaviour Therapy*, 20 (2): 245–60.

Keller, F. S., and W. N. Schoenfeld. (1950). *Principles of psychology*. New York: Apleton-Century Crofts.

Keller, M. B., J. P. McCullough, D. N. Klein, B. Arrow, D. L. Dunner, A. J. Gelenberg, J. C. Markowitz, C. B. Nemeroff, J. M. Russell, M. E. Thase, M. H. Trivedi, and J. Jazeka. (2000). 'A comparision of nefazodone, the cognitive behavioural analysis system of psychotherapy and their combination for the treatment of depression', *New England Journal of Medicine*, 342: 1462–70.

Kelley, B. M. (1977). 'A review of observational data collection and reliability procedures reported in journal of Applied Behaviour Analysis', *Journal of Applied Behaviour Analysis*, 10: 97–101.

Kelley, J. A. and R. S. Drabman. (1977). 'Generalizing response suppression of self-injurious behaviour through an overcorrection punishment procedure', *Behaviour Therapy*, 8 (3): 468–72.

Kelly, G. A. (1955). *The psychology of personal constructs, Vol. II. Clinical diagnosis and psychotherapy.* New York: Norton.

Kendall, P. C. and L. E. Wilcox. (1979). 'Self-control in children: Development of a rating scale', *Journal of Consulting and Clinical Psychology*, 47 (6): 1020–29.

———. (1980). 'A cognitive-behavioural treatment for impulsivity: Concrete versus conceptual training non-self controlled problem children', *Journal of Consulting and Clinical Psychology*, 48 (1): 80–91.

Kendall, P. C., W. R. Nay, and J. Jeffers. (1975). 'Time-out duration and contrast effects: A systematic evaluation of a successive treatment design', *Behaviour Therapy*, 6 (5): 609–15.

Kendler, T. S. (1962). 'Development of mediating responses in children', in J. C. Wright and J. Kagan (eds), *Basic cognitive processes in children: Monographs for the Society for Research in Child Development*, 28 (2): 33–52.

Khan, L. (1999). 'An evaluation of the effectiveness of cognitive-behavioural therapy and progressive relaxation in the treatment of tension headaches', *Journal of Research and Applications in Clinical Psychology*, 2: 1–2, 35–43.

Kiesler, D. J. (1966). 'Some myths of psychotherapy research and search for a paradigm', *Psychological Bulletin*, 65 (2): 110–36.

———. (1971). 'Experimental designs in psychotherapy research', in A. E. Bergin and S. L. Garfield (eds), *Handbook of psychotherapy and behaviour change: An empirical analysis* (2nd ed.), pp. 36–74. New York: Wiley.

Kirk, R. E. (1968). *Experimental design: Procedure for behavioural sciences.* Glenmont, California: Brooks/Cole.

Kleinknecht, R. A. and M. P. Morgan. (1992). 'Treatment of post traumatic stress disorder with eye movement desensitization', *Journal of Behaviour Therapy and Experimental Psychiatry*, 23 (1): 43–49.

Kneedler, R. D. and D. P. Hallihan. (1981). 'Self-monitoring of on-task behaviour with learning disabled children: Current studies and directions', *Exceptional Education Quarterly*, 2: 73–82.

Knight, M. F. and H. S. McKenzie. (1974). 'Elimination of bed time thumb-sucking in home-settings through contingent reading', *Journal of Applied Behaviour Analysis*, 7: 33–38.

Koch, L. and N. L. Breyer. (1974). 'A token economy for the teachers', *Psychology in Schools*, 11: 193–200.

Koegel, R. L. and A. Covert. (1972). 'The relationship of self-stimulation to learning in autistic children', *Journal of Applied Behaviour Analysis*, 5: 381–87.

Kohlberg, L. (1969). 'Stage and sequence: The cognitive-developmental approach to socialization', in D. A. Goslin (ed.), *Socialization theory and research*, pp. 347–480. Chicago: Rand McNally.

Kolko, D. J. (1984). 'Paradoxical instruction in elimination of avoidance behaviour in an agoraphobic girl', *Journal of Behaviour Therapy and Experimental Psychiatry*, 15 (1): 51–58.

Kolvin, I. (1967). 'Aversive imagery treatment in adolescents', *Behaviour Research and Therapy*, 5: 245–48.

Konorski, J. and S. Miller. (1937). 'On two types of conditioned reflex', *Journal of General Psychology*, 16: 246–72.

Krasner, L. (1963). 'Reinforcement, verbal behaviour, and psychotherapy', *American Journal of Orthopsychiatry*, 33: 601–13.

———. (1971). 'Behaviour Therapy', in P. H. Mussen (ed.), *Annual Review of Psychology, Vol 22*, pp. 483–532. California: Palo Alto.

Kratochwill, T. R. (1982). 'Advances in behavioural assessment', in C. R. Reynolds and T. B. Gutkin (eds), *The Handbook of School Psychology*, pp. 314–50. New York: Wiley.

Kropla, W. C., D. Yu, and R. Ward. (1994). 'Stereotyped human behaviour: A nonlinear dynamical analysis', *Journal of Behaviour Therapy and Experimental Psychiatry*, 25 (1): 1–14.

Krumboltz, J. D. (1969). *Behavioural counselling: Case and techniques*. New York: Holt, Rinehart and Winston.

Kuhn, T. S. (1962). *The structure of scientific evaluation*. Chicago: Chicago University Press.

———. (1970). *The structure of scientific evaluation*, (2nd ed.) Chicago: Chicago University Press.

Kumar, K. and J. C. M. Wilkinson. (1971). 'Thought stopping: A useful treatment for phobias of "Internal Stimuli"', *British Journal of Psychiatry*, 119: 305–07.

Kumaraiah, V. (1979a). 'Behavioural treatment of depression', *Indian Journal of Psychiatry*, 21 (1): 70–76.

———. (1979b). 'Behavioural treatment of drug addiction: A multiple approach', *Indian Journal of Clinical Psychology*, 6 (1): 43–46.

———. (1980). 'EMG biofeedback and progressive muscle relaxation in treatment of tension headache', *Indian Journal of Clinical Psychology*, 7 (1): 1–5.

Kumaraiah, V. and H. N. Murthy. (1975a). *Muscle relaxation treatment of psychogenic headache*. Proceedings, VI All India Convention of Clinical Psychologists, Banaras (Abstract).

———. (1975b). *A washing compulsion overcome by systematic desensitization to dirt contamination using both imaginary and real stimuli*. Proceedings, VI All India Convention of Clinical Psychologists, Banaras (Abstract).

———. (1975c). *Treatment of examination phobia through systematic desensitization*, VI All India Convention of Clinical Psychologists, Banaras (Abstract).

Kuruvilla, K. (1975). 'Usefulness of behaviour therapy in the treatment of psychogenic impotence', *Indian Journal of Psychiatry*, 17: 260–64.

Kushner, M. (1965). 'The reduction of a long standing fetish by means of aversive conditioning', in L. P. Ullman and L. Krasner (eds), *Case studies in behaviour modification*. New York: Holt-Rinehart & Winston.

Kuypers, D. S., W. C. Becker, and K. D. O'Leary. (1968). 'How to make a token system fail', *Exceptional Child*, 35 (2): 101–09.

L

Label, E. E. and D. A. Williamson. (1984). 'Behavioural treatment of elective mutism: A review of literature', *Clinical Psychology Review*, 4: 275–92.

Lader, M. H. and A. M. A. Mathew. (1968). 'Physiological model of phobic anxiety and desensitization', *Behaviour Research and Therapy*, 6: 411–21.

Lader, M. H. and L. Wing. (1966). *Physiological measures, sedative drugs and morbid anxiety*. London: Oxford University Press.

LaGrow, S. J. and A. C. Repp. (1982). *Stereotypic responding: A review of intervention research*. Paper presented at the Gatlinburg Conference on Research in Mental Retardation/Developmental Disabilities, Gatlinburg, Tennessee.

Lal, K. K. (1988). 'Relaxation therapy in a case of Spastic Dysphonia', *Indian Journal of Clinical Psychology*, 15 (1): 67–68.

Lal, K. K., G. A. Latte, and J. Bharathraj. (1976). 'Case report: Treatment of stuttering with systematic desensitization', *Indian Journal of Clinical Psychology*, 3 (2): 219–21.

Lamontagne, Y. and I. M. Marks. (1973). 'Psychogenic urinary retention: Treatment by prolonged exposure', *Behaviour Therapy*, 4: 581–85.

Lang, P. J. (1977). 'Imagery in therapy: An information processing analysis of fear', *Behaviour Therapy*, 8 (5): 862–86.

Lang, P. J. and A. D. Lazovik. (1963). 'Experimental desensitization of phobia', *Journal of Abnormal and Social Psychology*, 66 (6): 519–25.

LaVigna, G. W. and A. M. Donnellan. (1986). *Alternatives to punishment: Solving behaviour problems with non-aversive strategies*. New York: Irvington Publications.

Lawson, D. M. and R. B. May. (1970). 'Three procedures of extinction of smoking behaviour', *Psychological Record*, 20: 151–57.

Lazarus, A. A. (1958). 'New methods in psychotherapy: A case study', *South African Medical Journal*, 32: 660–64.

———. (1966). 'Behaviour rehearsal vs. non-directive therapy vs. advice in effecting behaviour change', *Behaviour Research and Therapy*, 4: 209–12.

———. (1971). *Behaviour therapy and beyond.* New York: McGraw-Hill.

———. (1977). 'Has behaviour therapy outlived its usefulness?', *American Psychologist*, 32: 550–54.

———. (1980). *Multimodal life history questionnaire.* New Jersey: Multimodal Therapy Institute.

———. (1981). *The practice of multimodal therapy: Systematic, comprehensive, and effective psychotherapy.* New York: McGraw-Hill.

Lazovik, A. D. and P. J. Lang. (1960). 'A laboratory demonstration of systematic desensitization psychotherapy', *Journal of Psychological Studies*, 11: 238–47.

LeBlanc, J. M., K. H. Busby, and C. Thomson. (1973). 'Function of Time-out for Changing Aggressive Behaviour of a Pre-school Child', in R. E. Ulrich, T. S. Stachnik, and J. E. Mabry (eds), *Control of human behaviour in education, Vol. 3.* Illinois: Scott, Foresman.

LeBlanc, L. A., M. R. Patel, and J. E. Carr. (2000). 'Recent advances in assessment of aberrant behaviour maintained by automatic reinforcement in individuals with developmental disabilities', *Journal of Behaviour Therapy and Experimental Psychiatry*, 31: 137–54.

Leiberman, R. P. (1978). 'Behaviour therapy in psychiatry: New learning principles for old problems', in J. F. Brady and H. K. H. Brodie (eds), *Controversy in psychiatry.* Philadelphia: Saunders.

Leitenberg, H. (1965). 'Is time-out from positive reinforcement an aversive event? A review of experimental evidence', *Psychological Bulletin*, 64 (6): 428–41.

———. (1973). 'The use of single-case methodology in psychotherapy research', *Journal of Abnormal Psychology*, 82: 87–101.

Lemere, F. and W. Vogtlin. (1950). 'An evaluation of the aversion treatment of alcoholism', *Quarterly Journal of Alcoholism*, 11: 99–204.

Lepper, M. R. (1973). 'Dissonance, self-perception and honesty in children', *Journal of Personality and Social Psychology*, 25: 65–74.

LeShan, L. (1977). *You can fight for your life: Emotional factors in causation of cancer.* New York: Evans.

Lewis, J.D. and C.P. Duncan. (1958). 'Expectation and resistance to extinction of a lever pulling response as a function of percentage of reinforcement and number of acquisition trials', *Journal of Experimental Psychology*, 15: 121–28.

Levy, R. and V. Meyers. (1971). 'Ritual prevention in obsessive patients', *Proceedings of the Royal Society of Medicine*, 64: 1115–18.

Lichstein, K. L., J. F. Salis, D. Hill, and M. C Young. (1981). 'Psychophysiological adaptation: An investigation of multiple parameters', *Journal of Behavioural Assessment*, 3: 111–21.

Lick, J. and R. Bootzin. (1971). *Covert sensitization for the treatment of obesity.* Paper presented to the Midwestern Psychological Association, Detroit.

Lighten, K. L. (1988). *Clinical Relaxation Strategies.* New York: John Wiley & Sons Inc.

Lilly, J. C. (1977). 'Mental effects of ordinary levels of physical stimuli on intact healthy persons', *Psychiatric Research Reports*, 5: 1–9, American Psychiatric Association, Washington DC.

Lindsley, D. R., B. F. Skinner, and H. C. Solomon. (1953). *Studies in behaviour therapy: Status Report-I.* Massachusetts: Waltham Metropolitan State Hospital.

Linehan, M. M. (1993). *Cognitive-behavioural treatment of borderline personality disorder.* New York: Guilford Press.

Lipke, H. J. (1994). 'Survey of practitioners trained in eye movement desensitization reprocessing'. Paper presented at the 102nd Annual Meeting of American Psychological Association, Los Angeles. Washington DC: American Psychological Association.

Lipke, H. J. (1995). 'EMDR clinician survey', in F. Shapiro (ed.), *Eye movement desensitization and reprocessing: Basic principles, protocols and procedures*, pp. 376–86. New York: Guilford Press.

Lipke, H. J. and A. L. Botkin. (1992). 'Brief case studies of EMDR with chronic PTSD', *Psychotherapy*, 29 (4).

Lobitz, G. K. and S. M. Johnson. (1975). 'Normal versus deviant children: A multi-method comparison', *Journal of Abnormal Child Psychology*, 3: 353–74.

Locke, E. (1971). 'Is behaviour therapy behaviouristic?', *Psychological Bulletin*, 76 (5): 318–27.

Lohr, J. M., R. A. Kleinknecht, and D. F. Tolin. (1994). *Procedural controls in treatment evaluation of imagery exposure procedures with application of single case designs.* Paper presented to the EMDR Special Interest Group at the 28 Convention of the Association for Advancement of Behaviour Therapy, Sandiego, California.

———. (1995). 'Eye movement desensitization for medical phobias: Two case studies', *Journal of Behaviour Therapy and Experimental Psychiatry*, 26 (2):141–51.

———. (1996). 'An intensive investigation of eye movement desensitization of claustrophobia', *Journal of Anxiety Disorders*, 10: 73–88.

Loney, J., F. E. Weissenberger, R. F. Woolson, and E. C. Lichty. (1979). 'Comparing psychological and pharmacological treatment for hyperactive boys and their classmates', *Psychopharmacologly Bulletin*, 31: 83–91.

Long, J. D. and R. L. Williams. (1973). 'The comparative effectiveness of group and individually contingent free time with inner city junior high school students', *Journal of Applied Behaviour Analysis*, 6: 465–74.

Lovaas, O. I. (1966). *Reinforcement Therapy*, (16 mm. sound film), Smith Kline French Laboratories, Philadelphia.

———. (1968). 'A programme for establishment of the establishment of speech in psychotic children', in N. H. Jr. Sloane and D. B. MacAulay (eds), *Operant procedure in remedial speech and language training*. Boston: Houghton Mifflin.

———. (1969). (producer) *Behaviour modification: Teaching language to psychotic children*. New York: Appleton-Century-Crofts.

———. (1977). *The Autistic Child: Language Development through Behaviour Modification*. New York: Irvington.

Lovaas, O. I., J. P. Berberich, B. F. Perloff, and B. Schaefer. (1966). 'Acquisition of imitative speech by schizophrenic children', *Science*, 151: 705–07.

Lovaas, O. I., G. Freitag, V. J. Gold, and I. C. Kassorla. (1965). 'Experimental studies in childhood schizophrenia: Analysis of self-destructive behaviour', *Journal of Experimental Child Psychology*, 2: 67–84.

Lovaas, O. I., C. D. Newsom, and C. Hickman. (1987). 'Self-stimulatory behaviour and perceptual reinforcement', *Journal of Applied Behaviour Analysis*, 20: 45–68.

Lovaas, O. I. and C.D. Newsom. (1976). 'Behaviour modification with psychiatric children', in H. Leitenberg (ed.) *Handbook of behaviour modification and behaviour therapy*. Englewood Cliffs, NJ: Prentice-Hall.

Lovaas, O. I., B. Schaefer, and J. O. Simmons. (1965). 'Building social behaviour in autistic children by use of electric shock', *Journal of Experimental Studies in Personality*, 1: 99–109.

Lovaas, O. I. and J. O. Simmons. (1969). 'Manipulation of self-destruction in three retarded children', *Journal of Applied Behaviour Analysis*, 2: 143–57.

Luby, E. D., J. S. Gottlieb, B. C. Cohen, G. Rosenbaum, and E. F. Domino. (1962). 'Model psychoses and schizophrenia', *American Journal of Psychiatry*, 119 (1) 61–67.

Luisada, P. V. (1978). 'The pencyclilidine psychosis: Phenomenology and treatment', in Petersen, R.C. and R. C. Stillman. (eds), *Pencyclidine (PCP) Abuse: An appraisal*. NIDA Research Monograph, 21. US Government Printing Office, Washington.

Luria, A. R. (1961). *The role of speech in regulation of normal and abnormal behaviour*. New York: Liveright.

———. (1963). *Restoration of function after brain trauma*. London: Pergamon Press.

———. (1969). 'Speech development and formation of mental processes', in M. C. Corle and I. Maltzman (eds), *A handbook of Soviet Psychology*. New York: Basic Books.

———. (1980). *Higher cortical functions in man*. New York: Basic Books.

Lutzker, J. R. (1978). 'Reducing self-injurious behaviour by facial screening', *American Journal of Mental Deficiency*, 82: 510–13.

Lyman, R. D. (1984). 'The effects of private and public goal setting on classroom on-task behaviour', *Behaviour Therapy*, 15: 395–402.

M

MacCulloch, M. J. and M. P. Feldman. (1967). 'Personality and treatment of homosexuality', *Acta Psychiatrica Scandinevica*, 43: 300–17.

MacFarlane, J., A. Allen, and M. Honzik. (1954). *A developmental study of the behaviour problems of normal children between twenty-one months and fourteen years*. Berkeley: University of California Press.

Madders, J. (1987). *Relax and be Happy: Techniques for 5–18 year olds*. London: Unwin.

Madsen, C., W. Becker, and D. Thomas. (1968). 'Rules, praise and ignoring: Elements of elementary classroom control', *Journal of Applied Behaviour Analysis*, 2: 49–53.

Madsen, C. H., W. C. Becker, L. Kosler, and E. Plager. (1970). 'Analysis of reinforcing function of "sit down" commands', in R. K. Parker (ed.), *Readings in educational psychology*. Boston: Allyn & Bacon.

Mahananda, P. (1970). 'A case of stuttering treated successfully with aversive noise technique', *Journal of All India Institute of Speech and Hearing*, 1: 132–33.

Mahoney, M. J. (1971). 'The self-management of covert behaviour: A case study', *Behaviour Therapy*, 2: 575–78.

———. (1974). *Cognition and behaviour modification*. Cambridge: Ballinger Pub. Co.

———. (1977). 'Reflections on the cognitive learning trend in psychotherapy', *American Psychologist*, 32: 5–13.

Majumdar, S. K. (1975). 'Psychotherapy of pedagophobia by reciprocal inhibition—A behavioural technique', *Indian Journal of Clinical Psychology*, 2 (2): 191–93.

Maletzky, B. M. (1974). 'Assisted covert sensitization for drug abuse', *International Journal of Addiction*, 9: 411–29.

Manno, B. and A. R. Marston. (1972). 'Weight reduction as a function of negative covert reinforcement (sensitization) versus positive reinforcement', *Behaviour Research and Therapy*, 10: 201–07.

Marcus, S. V., P. Marquis, and C. Sakai. (1997). 'Controlled study of treatment of PTSD using EMDR in HMO setting', *Psychotherapy*, 3: 307–15.

Marholin, D., J. K. Luiselli, M. Robinson, and I. T. Lott. (1980). 'Response contingent taste aversion in treating chronic ruminative vomiting in institutionalized profoundly retarded children', *Journal of Mental Deficiency*, 24 (1): 47–56.

Marquis, J. N. (1991). 'A report on seventy-eight cases treated by eye movement desensitization', *Journal of Behaviour Therapy and Experimental Psychiatry*, 22 (3): 187–92.

Marks, I. M. (1972). 'Flooding (implosion) and allied treatments', in W. S. Agras (ed.), *Behaviour modification: Principles and clinical Applications*. Boston: Little, Brown.

———. (1976). 'The current status of behavioural psychotherapy: Theory and practice', *American Journal of Psychiatry*, 133 (3): 253–61.

———. (1981). *Cures and care of neuroses: Theory and practice of behavioural psychotherapy*. New York: Wiley.

Marks, I. M. and M. G. Gelder. (1967). 'Transvestism and fetishism with masochism: Clinical and psychological changes', *British Journal of Psychiatry*, 119: 711–30.

Marks, I. M., K. Lovell, H. Noshirvani, M. Livanou, and S. Thrasher. (1998). 'Treatment of posttraumatic stress disorder by exposure and/or cognitive restructuring: A controlled study', *Archives of General Psychiatry*, 55: 317–25.

Marlatte, G. A. and J. R. Gordon (eds). (1985). *Relapse prevention*. New York: Guilford Press.

Marquis, J. N. and W. G. Morgan. (1969). *A guidebook for systematic desensitization*. California: Veteran Administration Hospital.

Marshall, W. L. (1985). 'Electrical aversion', in A. S. Bellack and M. Hersen (eds), *Dictionary of behaviour therapy techniques*, pp. 114–17. New York: Pergamon Press.

Marshall, W. L., J. Gauthier, M. M. Cristie, D. W. Currie, and A. Gordon. (1977). 'Flooding therapy: Effectiveness, stimulus characteristics and value of in vivo exposure', *Behaviour Research and Therapy*, 15 (1): 79–87.

Martin, G. and J. Pear. (1992). *Behaviour modification: What it is and how to do It*. Englewood Cliff, New Jersey: Prentice-Hall.

Martin, J. and J. L. Matson. (1978). 'Eliminating the inappropriate vocalization of a retarded adult by overcorrection', *Scandinavian Journal of Behaviour Research and Therapy*, 7: 203–09.

Masserman, J. H. (1943). *Behaviour and neurosis: An experimental psycho-analytic approach to psychobiologic principles*. Chicago: Chicago University Press.

Mathur, M. C., M. Sharma, and P. Likhari. (1983). 'A study of progressive muscle relaxation in the treatment of dysmenorrhea', *Indian Journal of Clinical Psychology*, 10 (2): 379–80.

Matthews, T. (1992). 'Intensity of visual stimulation from the environment during EMDR', *EMDR Network News Letter*, 2: 3–4.

Max, L. (1935). 'Breaking up a homosexual fixation by conditioned reaction technique', *Psychological Bulletin*, 32: 734.

Mayhew, G. and F. Harris. (1979). 'Decreasing self-injurious behaviour: Punishment with citric acid and reinforcement of alternative behaviour', *Behaviour Modification*, 3: 322–36.

Mazur, J. E. (1986). *Learning and behaviour*. New Delhi: Prentice-Hall.

McAllister, L. W., J. G. Stachowiak, D. M. Baer, and L. Conderman. (1969). 'The application of operant conditioning techniques in a secondary school classroom', *Journal of Applied Behaviour Analysis*, 2: 277–85.

McCann, D. L. (1992). 'Post-traumatic stress disorder due to devastating burns overcome by single session of eye movement desensitization', *Journal of Behaviour Therapy and Experimental Psychiatry*, 23 (4): 319–23.

McCommon, S. and S. Palotai. (1978). 'Behavioural assessment of a seven-year old girl with behaviour problems at school and at home', in S. N. Haynes (ed.), *Principles of behavioural assessment*, pp. 450–58 . New York: Gardner Press Inc.

McCullach, M. J. (1965). 'The application of anticipatory avoidance learning to the treatment of homosexuality: Theory, technique and preliminary results', *Behaviour Research and Therapy*, 2: 165.

McFall, R. M. and B. D. Lillesand. (1971). 'Behavioural rehearsal with modelling and coaching in assertive training', *Journal of Abnormal Psychology*, 77: 313–23.

McFall, R. M. and C. T. Twentyman. (1973). 'Four experiments on the relative contributions of rehearsal, modelling and coaching to assertive training', *Journal of Abnormal and Social Psychology*, 81: 199–218.

McFall, R. M. and A. R. Marston. (1970). 'An experimental investigation of behavioural rehearsal in assertive training', *Journal of Abnormal Psychology*, 76: 295–303.

McGee, J. J., F. J. Menolascino, D. C. Hobbs, and P. E. Menousek. (1987). *Gentle teaching: A non-aversive approach to helping persons with mental retardation*. New York: Human Sciences Press.

McGuigan, F. J. (1970). 'Covert oral behaviour during the silent performance of language task', *Psychological Bulletin*, 74 (5): 309–26.

McGuire, R. J. and M. Vallance. (1964). 'Aversion therapy by electric shock: A simple technique', *British Medical Journal*, 1: 151–53.

McLemore, C. W. and L. S. Benjamin. (1979). 'Whatever happened in interpersonal diagnosis: A psychosocial alternative to DSM-III', *American Psychologist*, 34: 17–34.

McReynolds, W. P. 1979. 'DSM-III and future applied social science', *Professional Psychology*, 10: 123–32.

Medland, M. B. and T. J. Stachnik. (1972). 'Good behaviour game: A replication and systematic analysis', *Journal of Applied Behaviour Analysis*, 5 (7): 45–51.

Mehta, M. and H. M. Chawla. (1985). 'Behavioural intervention in asthma: Report of a case', *Indian Journal of Clinical Psychology*, 12 (2): 75–78.

Meichenbaum, D. H. (1974). *Cognitive behaviour modification*. Moristown, New Jersey: General Learning Press.

———. (1975a). 'Toward a cognitive theory of self-control', in G. Schwartz and D. Shapiro (eds), *Consciousness and self-regulation: Advances in research*. New York: Plenum.

———. (1975b). 'Theoretical and treatment implications of developmental research on verbal control of behaviour', *Canadian Psychological Review*, 16: 22–27.

———. (1977). *Cognitive-behaviour modification: An integrative approach*. New York: Plenum.

———. (1985). *Stress inoculation training*. New York: Pergamon Press.

Meichenbaum, D. H. and J. Goodman. (1971). 'Training impulsive children to talk to themselves: A means of developing self-control', *Journal of Abnormal Psychology*, 77: 115–26.

Meichenbaum, D. H. and R. Cameron. (1973). 'Training schizophrenics to talk to themselves: A means of developing attentional controls', *Behaviour Therapy*, 4: 515–34.

Meyer, V., J. Robertson, and A. Tatlow. (1975). 'Home treatment of an obsessive compulsive disorder by response prevention', *Journal of Behaviour Therapy and Experimental Psychiatry*, 6 (1): 37–38.

Meyers, A. W. and W. E. Craighead. (1978). 'Adaptation period in clinical psychophysiological research: A recommendation', *Behaviour Therapy*, 9 (3): 355–61.

Meynen, G. E. (1970). *A comparative study of three treatment approaches with the obese: Relaxation, covert sensitization, and modified systematic desensitization*, Unpublished doctoral dissertation, Illinois Institute of Technology, Illinois.

Michael, J. (1975). 'Positive and negative reinforcement, a distinction that is no longer necessary: Or a better way to talk about bad things', in E. Ramp and E. Semb (eds), *Behaviour analysis: Areas of research and application*, pp. 31–44. New York: Prentice-Hall.

Michael, J. L. (1980). 'Flight from behaviour analysis', *The Behaviour Analyst*, 3: 1–22.

Millan, M. A. and D. J. Kolko. (1985). 'Social skills training and complementary strategies in anger control and the treatment of aggressive behaviour', in L. L. Abate and M. A. Millan (eds), *Handbook of social skills training and research*. New York: Wiley.

Miller, L. K. (1975). *Principles of everyday behaviour analysis*. California: Brooks/Cole.

Miller, M. M. (1959). 'Treatment of chronic alcoholism by hypnotic aversion', *Journal of the American medical Association*, 171: 1492–95.

Miller, N. E. and A. Carmona. (1967). 'Modification of a visceral response, salivation in thirsty dogs, by instrumental training with water reward', *Journal of Comparative and Physiological Psychology*, 63: 1–6.

Miller, N. E. and J. Dollard. (1941). *Social learning and imitation*. New Haven: Yale University Press.

Miller, W. R. (1982). 'Treating problem drinkers: What works?', *The Behaviour Therapist*, 5: 15–18.

Mineka, S. and K. Naugent. (1995). 'Mood-contingent memory bases in anxiety and depression', in D. L. Sachacter (ed.), *Memory distortion : How minds brains and societies construct the past*. Cambridge, Massachusetts: Harvard University Press.

Minge, M. R. and T. S. Ball. (1967). 'Teaching of self-help skills to profoundly retarded patients', *American Journal of Mental Deficiency*, 71 (5): 864–68.

Mishra, H. (1974). *Therapeutic procedures of behaviour modification*. Unpublished doctoral thesis, AIIMH, Bangalore University.

———. (1990). 'Behaviour therapy, biofeedback and behavioural medicine in India', *Journal of Behavioural Medicine*, 1: 3–10.

Mishra, H., H. N. Murthy, and P. M. Rao. (1970). 'An attempt to cure phobic reactions', *Proceedings, III Regional Conference of Indian Psychiatric Society*, Bangalore (Abstract).

Mishra, H., H. S. Narayan, C. R. Shantha, and H. N. Murthy. (1972). 'Alcoholism, its response to faradic aversion therapy', Proceedings of IIIrd All India Clinical Psychologists' Convention, Hyderabad (Abstract).

Mishra, H., C. R. Shantha, B. Mahapatra, and H. N. Murthy. (1972). 'Childhood psychoses and operant conditioning'. Proceedings of IIIrd All India Clinical Psychologists' Convention, Hyderabad (Abstract).

Mitchell, S. K. (1979). 'Inter-observer agreement, reliability, and generalizability of data collected in observational studies', *Psychological Bulletin*, 86 (2): 376–90.

Mohan, V. and R. Chopra. (1985). 'Effects of relaxation therapy on premenstrual variation in personality', *Indian Journal of Clinical Psychology*, 12 (2): 71–74.

Moncher, F. J. and R. J. Prinz. (1991). 'Treatment fidelity in outcome studies', *Clinical Psychology Review*, 11: 247–66.

Montgomery, R. and T. Ayllon. (1994). 'Eye movement desensitization across subject: subjective and psychological measures of treatment efficacy', *Journal of Behaviour Therapy and Experimental Psychiatry*, 25 (1): 217–30.

Moore, T. (2001). 'Covert sensitization', in B. Strickland (ed.), *Encyclopaedia of Psychology, 2nd Ed.*, pp. 157. Detroit: Gale Group.

Moore, W. E. (1938). 'A conditioned reflex study of stuttering', *Journal of Speech Disorders*, 3: 163–86.

Moreno, J. L. (1958). 'Fundamental rules and techniques of psychodrama', in J. H. Masserman and J. L. Moreno (eds), *Progress in Psychotherapy*, pp. 86–131. New York: Grune-Stratton.

Morgan, J. J. B. and F. J. Whitmer. (1939). 'The treatment for enuresis by conditioned reaction technique', *Journal of Genetic Psychology*, 55: 59–65.

Morganstein, K. P. (1973). 'Implosive therapy and flooding procedures: A critical review', *Psychological Bulletin*, 79 (5): 318–35.

———. (1974). 'Issues in implosive therapy: A reply to Levis', *Psychological Bulletin*, 81 (6): 380–82.

Morrell, F. (1960). 'Micro-electrodeeady potential studies suggesting a dendritic locus closure', *Electroencephalography and Clinical Physiology*, 13: 1553–93.

Morris, T. L. (2000). 'Covert conditioning', in A. E. Kazdin (ed.), *Encyclopaedia of Psychology, Vol 2*, pp. 336–37. New York: Oxford University Press.

Mowrer, C. H. and W. M. Mowrer. (1938). 'Enuresis: A method for its study and treatment', *American Journal of Orthopsychiatry*, 8: 436–59.

Mowrer, O. H. (1960). *Learning theory and symbolic processes*. New York: Wiley.

Mukhopadhyaya, P., A. Dutta, and N. Sanyal. (1998). 'Is conditionability a determinant of therapeutic responsivity? An investigation with dysthymic personality disorder', *Indian Journal of Clinical Psychology*, 28 (1): 82–87.

Mukhopadhyaya, P. and M. Chakrabarti. (1996). 'Token economy and cognitive modification in the treatment of study behaviour: A comparative study', *Indian Journal of Clinical Psychology*, 23 (2): 142–45.

Mulligan, W., R. D. Kaplan, and N. D. Repucci. (1973). 'Change in cognitive variables among behaviour problems of elementary school boys, treated in token economy special classroom', in R. D. Rubin, J. P. Brady, and J. D. Henderson (eds), *Advances in behaviour therapy, Vol. 4*. New York: Academic Press.

Muris, P., H. Merkelbach, I. Holdrinet, and M. Sijsenaar. (1998). 'Treating phobic children : Effects of EMDR versus exposure', *Journal of Consulting and Clinical Psychology*, 66: 193–98.

Muris, P., H. Merkelbach, H. van Haaften, and B. Nayer. (1997). 'Eye movement desensitization reprocessing versus exposure in vivo: A single session crossover study of spider-phobic children', *British Journal of Psychiatry*, 171: 82–86.

Murphy, G. (1973). 'Historical review', in B. B. Wolman (ed.), *Handbook of psychology*, pp. 3–7. New Delhi: Prentice-Hall.

Murthy, H. N. (1980). 'Counselling and therapy', in U. Pareek (ed.), *A survey of research in psychology, 1971–76*, pp. 333–71. New Delhi: ICSSR.

N

Nanda, B. (1999). 'Reducing self-stimulatory stereotyped body rocking of a retarded boy by differential reinforcement technique and environmental manipulation', *Indian Journal of Clinical Psychology*, 26 (2): 209–14.

Narayanan, G. (1999). 'Rational emotive therapy: A case of alcohol intoxication and major depressive disorder', *Journal of Research and Applications in Clinical Psychology*, 2: 65–78.

Nathan, P. E. (1984). 'Diagnostic and nosological issues in psychotherapy research', in M. Hersen, L. Michelson, and A. S. Bellack (eds), *Issues in psychotherapy research*. New York: Plenum.

Nathawat, S. S. and K. Gupta. (2000). 'Emotional factors in functional pain', *Indian Journal of Clinical Psychology*, 27 (1): 139–43.

Nathawat, S. S. and P. Kumar. (1999). 'Influence of meditational techniques and Jacobson's progressive muscular relaxation on measures of mental health', *Indian Journal of Clinical Psychology*, 26 (2): 192–99.

Nay, W. R. (1976). *Behavioural interventions: Contemporary strategies*. New York: Gardner Press.

Nekipelov, V. (1980). *Institute of fools: Notes from Serbsky*. London: Gollancz Ltd.

Newsom, C., J. E. Flavell, and A. Rincover. (1983). 'The side-effects of punishment', in S. A. Axelord and J. Apsche (eds), *Effects of punishment on human behaviour*, pp. 285–316. New York: Academic Press.

Nicholson, J. N. and J. A. Gray. (1972). 'Peak shift, behavioural contrast and stimulus generalization as related to personality and development in children', *British Journal of Psychology*, 63: 47–62.

Novaco, R. W. (1975). *Anger and its control: The development and evaluation of an experimental treatment*. Massachusetts: Lexington.

———. (1978). 'Anger and coping with stress: Cognitive-behavioural intervention', in J. Foreyt and D. Rathien (eds), *Cognitive-behaviour therapy: Research and applications*, pp. 135–73. New York: Plenum.

Novak, M. (1973). 'Is he really a grand inquisitor?', in H. Wheeler (ed.), *Beyond the punitive society: Operant conditioning: Social and political aspects*. San Fransisco: Freeman.

Nunes, D. L., R. J. Murphy, and M. L. Rpretcht. (1977). 'Reducing self-injurious behaviour of severely retarded individuals through withdrawal of reinforcement procedures', *Behaviour Modification*, 1: 499–516.

O

O'Leary, K. D. and W. C. Becker. (1967). 'Behaviour modification of an adjustment class: A token reinforcement programme', *Exceptional Children*, 33: 637–42.

O'Leary, K. D., K. F. Kaufman, R. E. Kass, and R. S. Drabman. (1970). 'The effects of loud and soft reprimands on the behaviour of disruptive students', *Exceptional Children*, 37: 145–55.

Olds, J. and P. Milner. (1954). 'Positive reinforcement produced by electrical stimulation of septal area and other regions of rat brain', *Journal of Comparative and Physiological Psychology*, 47: 419–27.

O'Neil, M. L. and M. L. Whittal. (2002). 'Thought stopping', in M. Hersen, and W. Sledge (eds), *Encyclopedia of psychotherapy, Vol II*, pp. 805–06. Amsterdam: Academic Press.

Oren, D. A., K. L. Wisner, M. Spinelli, and C. N. Epperson. (2002). 'An open trial of morning light therapy for treatment of antepartum depression', *American Journal of Psychiatry*, 194 (4): 666–69.

Ornitz, E. and E. R. Ritvo. (1976). 'The syndrome of autism: A critical review', *The American Journal of Psychiatry*, 133 (6): 609–92.

Osborne, J. G. (1969). 'Free time as a reinforcer in management of classroom behaviour', *Journal of Applied Behaviour Analysis*, 2: 113–18.

P

Packard, R. G. (1970). 'The control of "classroom attention": A group contingency for complex behaviour', *Journal of Applied Behaviour Analysis*, 3: 1–4.

Paniagua, E. A. and D. M. Baer. (1982). 'A procedural analysis of symbolic forms of behaviour therapy', *Behaviourism*, 9: 171–205.

Paniagua, E. A. (1993). 'Anomalies in covert conditioning', *Psychological Reports*, 73: 323–27.

Panyan, M. (1980). *How to use shaping*. Austin, Texas: Pro-Ed.

Paquin, M. J. (1977). 'The treatment of nail-biting compulsion by covert sensitization in a poorly motivated client', *Journal Behaviour Therapy and Experimental Psychiatry*, 8: 181–83.

Parameshwari, L. and I. J. Prakash. (2005). 'Behavioural management of anxiety during pregnancy', *Indian Journal of Clinical Psychology*, 32 (2): 103–09.

Parrish, J. M., M. F. Cataldo, D. J. Kolko, N. A. Neef, and A. L. Egel. (1986). 'Experimental analysis of response covariation among compliant and inappropriate behaviours', *Journal of Applied Behaviour Analysis*, 31: 165–89.

Pathak, B. N. (1999). 'Cognitive therapy in generalized anxiety disorder', *Indian Journal of Clinical Psychology*, 26 (2): 156–65.

Patterson, G. R. (1976). 'The aggressive child: Victim and architect of a coercive system', in A. Hammerlink, L. C. Handy, and E. J. Mash (eds), *Behaviour modification and families*. New York: Brunner/Mazel.

Patterson, G. R., J. A. Cobb, and R. Ray. (1973). 'A social engineering technique for training the families of aggressive boys', in H. Adam and I. Winikel (eds), *Issues and trends in behaviour therapy*. Illinois: Charles C. Thomas.

Patterson, G. R. and J. A. Cobb. (1971). 'A dyadic analysis of aggressive behaviour "aggressive" behaviours', in H. P. Hill (ed.), *Minnesota Symposium on Child Psychology, Vol 5*. Minneapolis: University of Minnesota Press.

Patterson, G. R., R. Littman, and W. Bricker. (1967). 'Assertive behaviour in children: A step toward a theory of aggressive behaviour', *Monograph of the Society for Research in Child Development*, 32: 1–38.

Patterson, G. R., R. S. Ray, and D. A. Shaw. (1968). 'Direct intervention in families of deviant children', *Oregon Research Institute Research Bulletin*, 8: 9.

Patterson, G. R., J. B. Reid, and T. J. Dishion. (1992). *Antisocial boys*. Eugene: Castalia.

Paul, G. L. (1969). 'Outcome of systematic desensitization I: Background, procedures and controlled reports of individual treatments', in C. M. Frank (ed.), *Behaviour therapy: Appraisal and status*. New York: McGraw-Hill.

Pavlov, I. P. (1927). *Conditioned reflex* (Translated by V. Arrep). London: Oxford.

———. (1928). *Lectures on conditioned reflexes*. Trans. W. H. Grants. New York: International Publishers.

———. (1949). *Lectures on the works of the cerebral hemispheres*. (Russian) Leningrad: Academy of Science Publishing House.

Pendergrass, V. E. (1972). 'Time-out from positive reinforcement following persistent high rate behaviour in retardates', *Journal of Applied Behaviour Analysis*, 5: 85–91.

Persons, J. B. (1991). 'Psychotherapy outcome studies do not accurately represent current models of psychotherapy: A proposed remedy', *American Psychologist*, 46: 99–106.

Pfaffmann, C. (1960). 'The pleasure of sensation', *Psychological Review*, 67: 253–68.

Phillips, D. and R. Judd. (1978). *How to fall out of love*. Boston: Houghton Miffin Co.

Phillips, L., J. G. Draguns, and D. P. Bartlett. (1975). 'Classification of behaviour disorders', in N. Hobbs (ed.), *Issues in the classification of children*. San Fransisco: Jossey-Bass.

Piacentini, J. and R. L. Bergman. (2001). 'Develomental issues in cognitive therapy for childhood anxiety disorders', *Journal of Cognitive Psychotherapy*, 15: 165–82.

Piaget, J. (1965). *The moral judgment of the child*. New York: Free Press (original work published in 1932).

Piazza, C. C., W. W. Fisher, G. P. Hanley, L. A. LeBlanc, A. S. Worsadell, S. T. Lindauer, and K. M. Keeney. (1998). 'Treatment of pica through multiple analyses of the reinforcing functions', *Journal of Applied Behaviour Analysis*, 31: 165–89.

Piere, D. W. and W. F. Epling. (1980). 'What happened to analysis in applied behaviour analysis?', *The Behaviour Analyst*, 3: 1–9.

Piggins, D., and D. Morgan. (1977). 'Note upon steady visual fixation in meditation and the laboratory', *Perceptual and Motor Skills*, 44: 357–58.

———. (1978). 'Perceptual phenomena resulting from steady visual fixation and repeated auditory input under experimental conditions and in meditation', *Journal of Altered States of Consciousness*, 3: 197–203.

Platanov, K. I. (1959). *The word as a physiological and therapeutic factor*. Moscow: Foreign Language Publishing House.

Plaud, J. J. (2002). 'Assisted covert sensitization', in M. Hersen and W. Sledge (eds), *Encyclopedia of psychotherapy, Vol. 1*, pp. 125–30. New York: Academic Press.

Plaud, J. J. and G. A. Gaither. (1997). 'A clinical investigation of the possible effects of long-term habituation of sexual arousal in assisted covert sensitization', *Journal of Behaviour Therapy and Experimental Psychiatry*, 28: 281–90.

Plummer, S., D. M. Baer, and J. M. LeBlanc. (1977). 'Functional considerations in the use of procedural time-out and an effective alternative', *Journal of Applied Behaviour Analysis*, 10: 689–706.

Plyushch, L. (1979). *History's carnival*. New York: Harcourt Brace Jovanovich.

Polin, A. T. (1959). 'The effects of flooding and physical suppression as extinction techniques on an anxiety motivated avoidance locomotor response', *Journal of Psychology*, 47: 235–45.

Poling, A., M. Picker, D. Grossett, E. Hall-Johnson, and M. Halbrook. (1981). 'The schism between experimental and applied behaviour analysis: Is it real and who cares?', *The Behaviour Analyst*, 4: 93–102.

Prabhu, G. G. (2004). 'Therapeutic role of the clinical psychologist: Progress and problems', *Indian Journal of Clinical Psychology*, 31 (1): 42–47.

Prachi. (1996). *Cognitive-behavioural intervention in HIV infected cases*. Unpublished M. Phil. dissertation submitted to NIMHANS, Bangalore, India.

Prakash, S. (1984). 'Patterns of child and adolescent psychiatric disorders in India', in V. Ramachandran, V. Palarippan, and L. P. Shah (eds), *Continuing Medical Education Programme, Vol.1*. Indian Psychiatric Society.

Prasad, M. and P. Sitholey. (1988). 'Behaviour therapy in a retarded adolescent with conduct disorder', *Indian Journal of Clinical Psychology*, 15 (2): 74–76.

Premack, D. (1959). 'Toward empirical behaviour laws-I: Positive reinforcement', *Psychological Review*, 66: 219–33.

———. (1965). 'Reinforcement theory', in D. Levine (ed.), *Nebraska symposium on motivation*, pp.123–80. Lincoln: Nebraska Press.

Prokasy, W. F. and J. F. Hall. (1963). 'Primary stimulus generalization', *Psychological Review*, 70: 310–22.

Puk, G. (1991). 'Treating traumatic memories: A case report on eye movement desensitization procedure', *Journal of Behaviour Therapy and Experimental Psychiatry*, 22 (2): 149–51.

Purkel, W. and M. H. Bornstein. (1980). 'Picture and imagery both enhance children's short-term and long-term Recall', *Developmental Psychology*, 16: 153–54.

Purohit, S. and R. Chowdhry. (1999). 'Effect of vipassana on correlates of mental health among adults', *Indian Journal of Clinical Psychology*, 26 (1): 51–54.

R

Rachlin, H. and R. J. Herrenstein. (1969). 'Hedonism revisited: On the negative law-of-effect', in B. A. Campbell and R. M. Church (eds), *Punishment and aversive behaviour*. New York: Appleton-Century-Crofts.

Rachman, S. (1961). 'Sexual disorders and behaviour therapy', *American Journal of Psychiatry*, 118 (3): 235–40.

———. (1966). 'Sexual fetishism: An experimental analogue', *Psychological Records*, 16: 293–96.

———. (1986). 'Forward', in J. G. Jr. Hollandsworth, *Behaviour therapy and physiology*. New York: Plenum.

———. (1993). 'Obsessions, responsibility and guilt', *Behaviour Research and Therapy*, 31 (2): 149–54.

Rachman, S. and G. T. Wilson. (1980). *The effects of psychological therapy* (2nd ed.). New York: Pergamon.

Rachman, S. and J. Tisdale. (1961). *'Behaviour therapy and behaviour disorder: An analysis*. Fla: Coral Gables, University of Miami Press.

———. (1969). *Aversion therapy and behaviour disorders: An analysis*. London: Routladge & Kegan Paul.

Rachman, S., I. M. Marks, and R. Hodgson. (1973). 'The treatment of obsessive compulsive neurotics by modelling and flooding in vivo', *Behaviour Research and Therapy*, 11: 463–71.

Rainey, C. A. (1972). 'An obsessive compulsive neurotic treated by flooding in vivo', *Journal of Behaviour Therapy and Experimental Psychiatry*, 3 (2): 117–21.

Raj, M., A. J., H. Mishra, S. Seshadri, and V. Kumaraiah. (1999). 'Cognitive-behavioural intervention in cases of self-harm', *Indian Journal of Clinical Psychology*, 26 (2): 172–82.

Raj, M., A. J., Prasadarao, P. S. D. V., and Kumaraiah, V. (1999). 'Cognitive-behaviour therapy in auditory hallucination', *Indian Journal of Clinical Psychology*, 26 (2): 183–87.

Raj, M., A. J., and Kumaraiah, V. (2000). 'Cognitive behavioural intervention in deliberate self-harm: A case study', *Indian Journal of Clinical Psychology*, 27 (1): 156–57.

Ramp, E., R. Ulrich, and S. Dulancy. (1971). 'Delayed time-out as a procedure for reducing disruptive classroom behaviour: A case study', *Journal of Applied Behaviour Analysis*, 4: 235–39.

Rangaswami, K. (1982). 'Behaviour therapy in writer's cramp: A case report', *Indian Journal of Clinical Psychology*, 9 (2): 157–61.

———. (1983). 'School phobia treated by desensitization: A case report', *Indian Journal of Clinical Psychology*, 10 (1): 47–49.

———. (1990). 'Anger management: A case report', *Indian Journal of Clinical Psychology*, 17: 49–51.

———. (1994). 'Spirituality and psychotherapy', editorial, *Indian Journal of Psychotherapy*, 21 (2): i–ii.

———. (1995). 'Cognitive-behavioural management of panic disorder', *Indian Journal of Clinical Psychology*, 22: 54–51.

———. (1997). *Modification of doubts and dysfunctional beliefs by verbal reattribution and socratic dialogue.* Unpublished manuscript. Mysore: Mysore University.

———. (1999). 'Treatment of obsessive-compulsive disorder with cognitive-behaviour therapy', *Indian Journal of Clinical Psychology*, 26 (1): 55–59.

Rao, V. N. (1986). 'Problems of children in india: Need for integrated approach', *Child Psychiatry Quarterly*, 8: 23, 108–12.

Rao, V. N., M. V. Moorthy, and R. Parthasarathy. (1984). 'Behavioural problems in school children: Implications for teachers training programme', *Experiments in Education*, 12 (3).

Rath, S. (1992). 'Cognitive-behavioural intervention with disadvantaged tribal children', *Indian Journal of Clinical Psychology*, 19 (1): 4–9.

———. (1995). 'Generalization and implications of verbal self-instruction training: An empirical evaluation', *Disabilities and Impairments*, 9 (2): 73–84.

Rathus, S. A. and J. S. Nevid. (1978). *Behaviour Therapy.* New Jersey: New American Library Publication.

Reese, H. W. (1962). 'Verbal mediation as a function of age level', *Psychological Bulletin*, 59: 502–09.

Reese, H. W. and L. P. Lipsitt (eds). (1970). *Experimental child psychology.* New York: Academic Press.

Reese, H. W. and S. W. Porges. (1976). 'Development of learning processes', in V. Hamilton and M. D. Vernon (eds), *The development of cognitive processes.* New York: Academic Press.

Rehfeldt, R. A. (2002). 'Chaining', in M. Hersen and W. Sledge (eds), *Encyclopaedia of psychotherapy, Vol. 1*, pp. 365–69. New York: Academic Press.

Rehm, L. P. (1977). 'A self-control model of depression', *Behaviour Therapy*, 8 (5): 787–804.

Reid, J. (1993). 'Prevention of conduct disorder before and after school rentry: Relating interventions to developmental findings', *Developmental Psychopathology*, 5: 243–62.

Reisenberg, R. D. (1985). 'The potential sociopsychological significance of restricted environmental stimulation', in J. J. Sanchez-Sosa (ed.), *Health and clinical psychology, selected/revised papers, Vol. 4*, Amsterdam: XIII International Congress of Psychology, North-Holland.

Reiss, S. (1980). 'Pavlovian conditioning and human Fear: An expectancy model', *Behaviour Therapy*, 11: 380–96.

Repp, A. C. (1983). *Teaching the mentally retarded.* New York: Prentice-Hall.

Repp, A. C., S. M. Deitz, and N. C. Speir. (1974a). 'Reducing stereotyped responding of retarded persons by differential reinforcement of other behaviour', *American Journal of Mental Deficiency*, 79: 279–84.

———. (1974b). 'Reducing aggressive and self-injurious behaviour of institutionalized retarded children through reinforcement of other behaviours', *Journal of Applied Behaviour Analysis*, 7: 313–25.

———. (1975). 'Reducing stereotyped responding through the differential reinforcement of other behaviour', *American Journal of Mental Deficiency*, 4: 57–71.

Resick, P. A. and M. K. Schnicke. (1992). 'Cognitive processing therapy for sexual assault victims', *Journal of Consulting and Clinical Psychology*, 60 (5): 748–56.

Reynolds, C. F., D. J. Kupfer, and D. E. Sewitch. (1984). 'Diagnosis and management of sleep disorders in the elderly', *Hospital and Community Psychiatry*, 35: 779–81.

Reynolds, G. S. (1968). *A primer of operant conditioning.* Illinois: Scott, Foresman.

Ribes, E. (1980). 'Considerations methodological y profesionales sobre el analisis conductual aplicado', *Revista mexicana de Analisis de la Conducta*, 6: 89–102.

Rimm, D. C. (1973). 'Thought stopping and covert assertion in the treatment of phobias', *Journal of Consulting and Clinical Psychology*, 41: 466–67.

Rimm, D. C. and J. C. Masters. (1979). *Behaviour therapy: Techniques and empirical findings (2nd ed.).* New York: Academic Press.

Rimm, D. C., W. D. Saunders, and W. Westel. (1974). *Thought stopping and covert assertion in treatment of snake phobics.* Unpublished manuscript. Illinois: Southern Illinois University.

Rincover, A. (1978). 'Sensory extinction: A procedure for eliminating self-stimulatory behaviour in developmentally disabled children', *Journal of Abnormal Child Psychology*, 6: 299–310.

Rincover, A. and R. Koegel. (1975). 'Setting generality and stimulus control in autistic children', *Journal of Applied Behaviour Analysis*, 8 (3): 235–46

Riopelle, A. J. (1967). *Animal problem-solving: Selected readings.* Baltimore: Penguin.

Risley, T. R. (1968). 'The effects and side-effects of punishing the autistic behaviour of a deviant child', *Journal of Applied Behaviour Analysis*, 1: 21–34.

Risley, T. R., B. Hart, and L. A. Doke. (1972). 'Operant language development: The outline of a therapeutic technology', in R. L. Schiefelbusch (ed.), *Language of the mentally retarded.* Baltimore: University Park Press.

Risley, T. R. and M. M. Wolf. (1967). 'Establishing functional speech in echolalic children', *Behaviour Research and Therapy*, 5:73–88.

Ritter, B. (1968). 'The group desensitization of children's snake phobias using vicarious and contact desensitization procedures', *Behaviour Research and Therapy*, 6: 1–6.

Roane, H. S., W. W. Fisher, and G. M. Sgro. (2001). 'Effects of fixed-time schedule on aberrant and adaptive behaviour', *Journal of Applied Behaviour Analysis*, 34: 333–36.

Roese, N. J. (1994). 'The functional basis of counterfactual thinking', *Journal of Personality and Social Psychology*, 66: 903–12.

Rogers, S. J., S. L. Hepburn, T. Stackhouse, and E. Wehner. (2003). 'Imitation performance in toddlers, with autism and those with other developmental disorders', *Journal of Child Psychology and Psychiatry*, 44 (5): 763–81.

Rojahn, J. and S. R. Schroeder. (1983). 'Behavioural assessment', in J. L. Matson and J. E. Mulick (eds), *Handbook of mental retardation*, pp. 227–43. New York: Pergamon Press.

Romanczyk, R. G., R. M. Kent, C. Diament, and K. D. O'Leary. (1973). 'Measuring the reliability of observational data: A reactive process', *Journal of Applied Behaviour Analysis*, 6: 175–84.

Rosen, L. A., S. G. O'Leary, S. A. Joyce, G. Conway, and L. J. Pfiffiner. (1984). 'The importance of prudent negative consequences for maintaining the appropriate behaviour of hyperactive students', *Journal of Abnormal Child Psychology*, 12 (4): 581–604.

Rosen, R. C. and B. J. Schnapp. (1974). 'The use of specific behavioural technique (thought stopping) in the context of conjoint couples therapy: A case report', *Behaviour Therapy*, 5 (2): 261–64.

Ross, L. L., D. Yu, and W. C. Kropla. (1993). *Stereotyped human behaviour: Rhythmic or non-rhythmic.* Manuscript submitted for publication.

Rothbaum, O. B. (1997). 'A controlled study of movement desensitization and reprocessing in the treatment of post traumatic stress disordered sexual assault victims', *Bulletin of Meninger Clinic*, 61: 317–34.

Rotter, J. B. (1954). *Social learning and clinical psychology.* Englewood & Cliffs, New Jersey: Prentice-Hall.

Rush, A. J., A. T. Beck, M. Kovacs, and S. D. Hollon. (1977). 'Comparative efficacy of cognitive therapy and pharmacotherapy in treatment of depressed outpatients', *Cognitive Therapy and Research*, 1:17–38.

S

Sachs, L. B., S. Bean, and J. E. Marrow. (1972). 'Comparison of smoking treatments', *Behaviour Therapy*, 1: 465–72.

Sachs, L. B. and G. L. Ingram. (1972). 'Covert sensitization as a treatment for weight control', *Psychological Reports*, 30: 971–74.

Sahoo, D., J. S. Gillis, and S. K. Mishra. (1999). 'Conditionability trait as a predictor of response to behaviour therapy in obsessive compulsive neurosis', *Social Science International*, 15 (2): 68–76.

———. (2002). 'The selected client variables as predictors of response to behaviour therapy', *Indian Journal of Clinical Psychology*, 29 (2): 110–17.

Sajwaj, T., J. Libet, and S. Agras. (1974). 'Lemon-juice therapy: The control of life-threatening rumination of a six-month-old infant', *Journal of Applied Behaviour Analysis*, 7: 557–66.

Sakthivel, L. M., K. Rangaswami, and T. N. Jayaraman. (1979). 'Treatment of homosexuality by anticipatory avoidance conditioning technique', *Indian Journal of Psychiatry*, 21: 146–48.

Salis, J. F. and K. L. Lichstein. (1979). 'The frontal electromyographic adaptation response: A potential source of confounding', *Biofeedback and Self-regulation*, 4: 337–39.

Salkovskis, P. M. (1989). 'Cognitive behavioural factors and the persistence of intrusive thoughts in obsessional problems', *Behaviour Research and Therapy*, 27 (6): 677–82.

Salkovskis, P. M., H. C. Richards, and E. C. Forrester. (1995). 'The relationship between obsessional problems and intrusive thoughts', *Behavioural and Psychotherapy*, 23: 282–301.

Salzinger, K., R. S. Feldman, and S. Salzinger. (1965). 'Operant conditioning of verbal behaviour of two young speech-deficient boys', in L. Krasner and L. P. Ullman (eds), *Research in Behaviour Modification: New Developments and implications*, pp. 82–105. New York: Holt, Rinehart and Winston, Inc.

Sanderson, A. and R. Carpenter. (1992). 'Eye movement desensitization versus image confrontation: A single session crossover study of 58 phobic subjects', *Journal of Behaviour Therapy and Experimental Psychiatry*, 23 (4): 269–75.

Sanderson, W. C. and S. Woody. (1995). *Manuals for empirically validated treatments: A project of the task force of psychological procedures*. Washington DC: Division of Clinical Psychology, Division of American Psychological Association.

Sandman, C. A., J. L. Barron, and H. Colman. (1990). 'An orally administered opiate-blocker, Naltrexone attenuates self-injurious behaviour', *American Journal of Mental Retardation*, 95: 84–92.

Sarason, I. G. and V. J. Ganzer. (1967). 'Social influence techniques in clinical and community psychology', in C. D. Spielberger (ed.), *Current topics in clinical and community psychology*. New York: Academic Press.

Saudargas, S. R. and K. Zanolli. (1990). 'Momentary time sampling as an estimate of percentage time: A field validation', *Journal of Applied Behaviour Analysis*, 23: 533–37.

Sawin, D. B. and R. D. Parke. (1979). 'Development of self-verbalized control of resistance to deviation', *Developmental Psychology*, 15: 129–27.

Schachter, S. and J. E. Singer. (1962). 'Cognitive, social and physiological determinants of emotional state', *Psychological Review*, 69: 379–99.

Schechter, M. D., J. T. Shurley, P. W. Toussieng, and W. J. Meier. (1969). 'Sensory isolation therapy of autistic children: A preliminary report', *Journal of Paediatrics*, 74: 564–69.

Scheck, M. M., J. A. Schaeffer, and C. Gillette. (1998). 'Brief psychological intervention with traumatized women: The efficacy of eye movement desensitization and reprocessing', *Journal of Traumatic Stress*, 11: 25–44.

Schepis, M. M., D. H. Reid, and J. R. Fitzerald. (1987). 'Group instruction with profoundly retarded persons: Acquisition, generalization, and maintenance of a remunerative work skill', *Journal of Applied Behaviour Analysis*, 20: 97–105.

Schleser, R., R. Cohen, A. Meyers, and J. D. Rodick. (1984). 'The Effects of Cognitive Level and Training Procedures on the Generalization of Self-instructions', *Cognitive Therapy and Research*, 8: 187–200.

Schleser, R., A. Meyers, and R. Cohen. (1981). 'Generalization of self-instructions: Effects of general versus specific content, active rehearsal and cognitive level', *Child Development*, 52: 335–40.

Schmidt, G. W. and K. E. Ulrich. (1969). 'Effects of group contingent events upon classroomn', *Journal of Applied Behaviour Analysis*, 2: 171–79.

Schneider, M. (1974). 'Turtle technique in the classroom', *Teaching Exceptional Children*, 7: 22–24.

Schoenwald, S. K. and K. Hoagwood. (2001). 'Effectiveness, transportability, and dimensions of intervention: What matters when', *Psychiatric Services*, 52: 1190–97.

Schoggen, P. (1963). 'Environmental forces in the everyday life of children', in R. G. Baker (ed.), *The stream of behaviour*. New York: Appleton-Centur-Crofts.

Schreibman, L. (1975). 'Effects of within-stimulus and extra-stimulus prompting on discrimination learning of autistic children', *Journal of Applied Behaviour Analysis*, 8: 91–112.

———. (1988). *Autism*. Newbury Park, CA: Sage Publication.

Schreibman, L., R. L. Koegel, M. H. Charlop, and E. L. Egel. (1982). 'Autism', in A. S. Bellack, M. Hersen, and A. E. Kazdin (eds), *International handbook of behaviour modification and therapy*, pp. 891–915. New York: Pergamon Press.

Schwartz, R. M. and J. M. Gottman. (1976). 'Toward a task analysis of assertive behaviour', *Journal of Consulting and Clinical Psychology*, 44: 910–20.

Scotti, J. R., I. M. Evans, L. H. Meyer, and P. Walker. (1991). 'A meta-analysis of intervention research with problem: Treatment validity and standards of practice', *American Journal of Mental Retardation*, 96: 233–56.

Seligman, M. E. P. (1970). 'On generality of the laws of learning', *Psychological Review*, 77: 406–18.

Sen, N. N. (1974). 'Behaviour therapy in depression I: Experimental analysis', *Indian Journal of Clinical Psychology*, 1 (1): 53–58.

———. (1975). 'Behaviour therapy in Depression II: Plan and procedure of case analysis and treatment', *Indian Journal of Clinical Psychology*, 2 (2): 53–58.

Shabani, D. B., D. A. Wilder, and W. A. Flood. (2001). 'Effects of differential reinforcement on stereotyped behaviour in autism', *Behavioural Interventions*, 16 (4): 279–86.

Shaffer, L. F. (1947). 'The problem of psychotherapy', *American Psychologist*, 2: 459–67.

Shalev, A. Y., T. Peri, D. Bandes, S. Freeman, S. Orr, and R. K. Pittman. (2000). 'Auditory startle response in trauma survivors with post traumatic stress disorder: A prospective study', *American Journal of Psychiatry*, 157 (2): 255–61.

Shantha, C. R., H. Mishra, and H. N. Murthy. (1972). *In-vivo desensitization of phobic reaction*. Hyderabad: Proceedings of III All India Convention of Clinical Psychologists (Abstract).

Shapiro, F. (1989a). 'Efficacy of eye-movement desensitization procedure in treatment of traumatic memories', *Journal of Traumatic Stress*, 2: 199–223.

———. (1989b). 'Eye movement desensitization: A new treatment for post-traumatic stress disorder', *Journal of Behaviour Therapy and Experimental Psychiatry*, 20 (3): 211–17.

———. (1991). 'Eye-movement desensitization and reprocessing procedure: From EMD to EMD/R: A new treatment model for anxiety and related trauma', *Behaviour Therapist*, 14: 133–35.

———. (1995). *Eye movement desensitization and reprocessing: Basic principles protocols and procedures*. New York: Guilford Press.

———. (1999). 'Eye movement desensitization and reprocessing (EMDR) and the anxiety disorders: Clinical and research implications of an integrated psychotherapy treatment', *Journal of Anxiety Disorders*, 13: 35–67.

———. (2001). *Eye movement desensitization reprocessing: Basic principles, protocols and procedures (2nd ed.)*. New York: Guilford Press.

Shapiro, F., E. Snyker, and L. Maxfield. (2002). 'EMDR: eye movement desensitization reprocessing', in F. M. Kaslow (ed.), *Comprehensive handbook of psychotherapy*, pp. 241–72. New York: John Wiley & Sons.

Sherman, J. and D. M. Baer. (1969). 'Appraisal of operant therapy techniques with children and adults', in C. M. Franks (ed.), *Behaviour therapy appraisal and research*. New York: McGraw-Hill.

Sherman, J. A. (1965). 'Use of reinforcement and imitation to reinstate verbal behaviour in mute psychotics', *Journal of Abnormal Psychology*, 70: 155–64.

Sherrington, C. S. (1906). *The integrative action of the nervous system*. New Heaven: Yale University Press.

Shipley, R. H. and A. P. Boudewyns. (1980). 'Flooding and implosive therapy: Are they harmful?', *Behaviour Therapy*, 11: 503–08.

Shirk, S. R., A. Talmi, and D. Olds. (2000). 'A developmental psychopathology perspective on child and adolescent treatment policy', *Development and Psychopathology*, 12: 835–55.

Shoben, E. J. (1949). 'Psychotherapy as a problem in learning theory', *Psychological Bulletin*, 46 (1): 366–92.

Shure, M. B. and G. Spivack. (1974). *A mental health programme for kindergarten children: A cognitive approach to solving interpersonal problem*. Department of Mental Health Sciences, Hahnemann Community Mental Health/Mental Retardation Centre.

Shvets, T. B. (1958). (Cited by Rusinov) *Conference of electrophysiology of higher nervous activity*, pp. 138–40. Abstracts, Moscow.

Sidman, M. (1960). *Tactics of scientific research: Evaluating scientific data in psychology*: New York: Basic books.

Sidman, M. and L. T. Stoddard. (1967). 'The effectiveness of fading in programming a simultaneous form discrimination for retarded children', *Journal of Experimental Analysis of Behaviour*, 10 (1): 3–16.

Siegel, B. S. (1988). *Love, medicine, and miracles*. UK: Arrow Books Ltd.

Siegel, S. (1956). *Nonparametric statistics for the behavioural sciences*. London: McGraw-Hill.

Silverstein, C. (1972). *Behaviour modification and the gay community*. Paper presented at the annual convention of the Association for Advancement of Behaviour Therapy, New York.

Simeonsson, R. J., L. Buckley, and L. Monson. (1979). 'Conceptions of illness causality in hospitalized children', *Journal of Paediatric Psychology*, 27: 445–47.

Simmel, E. C., R. A. Hoppe, and G. A. Milton. (eds). (1968). *Social facilitation and imitative behaviour: Outcome of the 1967 Miami University symposium on social behaviour*. Boston: Allyn & Bacon.

Simmons, F. T. and B. H. Washik. (1973). 'Small group contingencies and special activity times to manage behaviour in a first grade classroom', *Journal of School Psychology*, 11: 228–38.

Sinclair, J. D. (1981). *The rest principle: Neurophysiological theory of behaviour*. New Jersey: Lawrence Erlbaum Associates.

Singer, D. L. (1968). 'Aggression, arousal, hostility and catharsis', *Journal of Personality and Social Psychology*, *Monograph Supplement*, 8 (1): Part-2.

Singh, M. and S. S. Kaushik. (2000). 'Comparison of relaxation, meditation and cognitive therapy for enhancing stress-coping skills of depression at risk middle aged women', *Indian Journal of Clinical Psychology*, 27 (1): 89–96.

Singh, N. N., M. J. Dawson, and P. Manning. (1981). 'Effects of spaced responding DRL on the stereotyped behaviour of profoundly retarded persons', *Journal of Applied Behaviour Analysis*, 14: 521–26.

Singh, R. and I. Oberhummer. (1980). 'Behaviour therapy within a setting of karma yoga', *Journal of Behaviour Therapy and Experimental Psychiatry*, 11: 135–41.

Singh, S. B. (1986). 'Treating abdominal pain through behavioural approach', *Indian Journal of Clinical Psychology*, 13: 35–38.

———. (1989). 'Behavioural intervention in functional fit', *Indian Journal of Clinical Psychology*, 16: 93–95.

Sinha, U. K. and R. K. Jalan. (2001). 'Combining relaxation, exposure and cognitive restructuring in the out-patient treatment of chronic social phobia: A single case study', *Journal of Personality and Clinical Studies*, 17 (2): 75–83.

Skinner, B. F. (1938). *The behaviour of organisms*. New York: Appleton-Century-Crofts.

————. (1953). *Science and human behaviour*. New York: McMillan.

————. (1963). 'Behaviourism at fifty', *Science*, 140: 950–58.

————. (1966). 'Operant behaviour', in W. K. Konig (ed.), *Operant behaviour: Areas of research and application*. New York: Appleton-Century-Crofts.

————. (1968). *The technology of teaching*. New York: Appleton-Century-Crofts.

————. (1971). *Beyond freedom and dignity*. New York: Pelican.

————. (1973). 'Answers for my critics', in H. Wheeler (ed.), *Beyond the punitive society: Operant conditioning: Social and political Aspects*. San Francisco: Freeman.

————. (1979). 'Foreword', in P. Sjoden, S. Bates, and W. S. Doccens (eds), *Trends in Behaviour Therapy*. New York: Academic Press.

————. (1988). 'Comments', in A. C. Catania and S. Harnad (eds), *The selection of behaviour*, New York: Cambridge University Press.

Skinner, B. F. and S. A. Krakower. (1968). *Handwriting with write and see*. Chicago: Lyons & Carnahan.

Slade, P. D. (1972). 'The effects of systematic desensitization on auditory hallucinations', *Behaviour Research and Therapy*, 10: 85–91.

————. (1973). 'The psychological investigation and treatment of auditory hallucination: A second case report', *British Journal of Medical Psychology*, 46: 293–96.

————. (1974). 'Psychometric studies of obsessive illness and obsessional personality', in H. R. Beech (ed.), *Obsessional states*, pp. 95–109. New York: Metheun.

Slade, P. D. and R. P. Bentall. (1988). *Sensory deception: A scientific analysis of hallucination*. Baltimore: The John Hopkins University Press.

Slavin, R. E. (1999). 'Rejoinder: Yes control groups are essential in programme evaluation: A response to pogro', *Educational Researcher*, 28 (3): 36–38.

Sloane, H. N. Jr., M. K. Johnson, and F. R. Harris. (1968). 'Remedial procedure for teaching verbal behaviour to speech deficient or defective young children', in H. N. Sloane Jr. and B. D. MacAulay (eds), *Operant procedures in remedial speech and language training*: Boston: Houghton Mifflin.

Smith, S., H. Thakurdas, and T. G. G. Lawes. (1961). 'Perceptual isolation and schizophrenia', *Journal of Mental Science*, 107: 839–44.

Sohlberg, McM., and C. A. Mateer. (1989). *Introduction to cognitive rehabilitation: Theory and practice*. New York: Guilford Press.

Sokolov, E. N. (1963). 'Higher nervous functions: The orienting reflex', *Annual Review of Physiology*, 25: 545–580.

Solnick, J. V., A. Rincover, and C. R. Peterson. (1977). 'Determinants of reinforcing and punishing effects of time-out', *Journal of Applied Behaviour Analysis*, 10: 415–28.

Sowers-Hoag, K. M., B. A. Thyer, and J. S. Bailey. 1987. 'Promoting Automobile Safety Belt Use by Young Children', *Journal of Applied Behaviour Analysis*, 20: 133–138.

Spates, C. R. and M. M. Burnette. (1995). 'EMD/R treatment of post traumatic stress disorder: Three unusual cases', *Journal of Behaviour Therapy and Experimental Psychiatry*, 26 (1): 51–55.

Spilka, B., R. W. Hood, and R. L. Gorsuch. (1985). *The psychology of religion: An empirical approach*. Englewood Cliffs: Prentice-Hall.

Spinetta, J. J. (1974). 'The dying child's awareness of death: A review', *Psychological Bulletin*, 81 (4): 256–60.

Spitzer, R. L., J. Endicott, and E. Robbins. (1978). 'Research diagnostic criteria: Rationale and reliability', *Archives of General Psychiatry*, 35: 773–82.

Spooner, F. and D. Spooner. (1984). 'A review of chaining techniques: Implications for future research and practice', *Education and Training of the Mentally Retarded*, 19: 114–24.

Springer, B., T. Brown, and P. K. Dunkan. (1981). 'Current measurement in applied behaviour analysis', *The Behaviour Analysts*, 4: 19–31.

Sreedhar, K. P. (1996). *Guided somato-psychic relaxation.* Thiruvananthapuram: LIFE.

Srivastava, A. K. and A. P. Singh. (1981). 'Construction and standardization of an occupational stress index', *Indian Journal of Clinical Psychology*, 8: 133–36.

Stambaugh, E. E. II (1977). 'Audio-taped flooding in outpatient treatment of somatic complaints', *Journal of Behaviour Therapy and Experimental Psychiatry*, 8 (2): 173–74.

Stampfl, T. G. (1966). 'Implosive therapy: The theory, the subhuman analogue, The strategy, and the technique, Part I: The theory', in S. G. Armitage (ed.), *Behaviour modification techniques in treatment of emotional disorders.* Michigan: Battle Creek Veterans Hospital.

———. (1970). 'Implosive therapy: An emphasis on covert stimulation', in D. J. Levis (ed.), *Learning Approach in Therapeutic Behaviour Change.* Chicago: Aldine.

Stampfl, T. G. and D. J. Levis. (1967). 'Phobic patients: Treatment with learning theory approach of implosive therapy', *Voices: The Art and Science of Psychotherapy*, 3: 23–27.

Staub, E. (1968). 'Duration of stimulus exposure and determinant of flooding pin elimination of fear', *Behaviour Research and Therapy*, 6: 131–32.

Steffy, R. A., D. H. Meichenbaum, and J. A. Best. (1970). 'Aversive and cognitive Factors in modification of smoking behaviour', *Behaviour Research and Therapy*, 8: 115–25.

Stern, R. S. (1970). 'Treatment of a case of obsessional neurosis using thought stopping technique', *British Journal of Psychiatry*, 117: 441–42.

Stoddard, L. T. and B. J. Gerovac. (1981). 'A stimulus shaping method for teaching complex motor performance to severely and profoundly retarded individuals', *Applied Research in Mental Retardation*, 2: 218–95.

Strahley, D. F. (1966). 'Systematic desensitization and counterphobic treatment of an irrational fear of snakes', *Dissertation Abstracts*, 27: 973B.

Straus, M. A. and J. M. Stewart. (1999). 'Corporal punishment by american parents: national data on prevalence, chronicity, severity and duration in relation to child and family characteristics', *Clinical Child and Family Psychology Review*, 2: 5–70.

Strosahl, K. D. and J. C. Ascough. (1981). 'Clinical use of imagery: experimental foundation, theoretical misconceptions, and research issues', *Psychological Bulletin*, 89 (3): 422–38.

Strupp, L. W. (1978). 'Psychotherapy research and practice: An overview', in S. L. Garfield and A. E. Bergin (eds.), *Handbook of psychotherapy and behaviour change: An empirical analysis (2nd ed.)*, pp. 3–22. New York: Wiley.

Stuart, R. B. (1967). 'Operant interpersonal treatment for marital discord', *Journal of Consulting and Clinical Psychology*, 33: 675–82.

Sturmey, P. (1994). 'Assessing the functions of self-injurious behaviour: A case of assessment failure', *Journal of Behaviour Therapy and Experimental Psychiatry*, 25 (4): 331–36.

Suedfeld, P. (1977). 'Using environmental restriction to initiate long term behaviour change', in R. B. Stuart (ed.) *Behavioural self-management strategies techniques and outcomes*, pp. 230–57. Brunner/Mazel.

———. (1980). *Restricted environmental stimulation: Research and clinical applications.* New York: Wiley.

———. (1982). 'Behavioural applications of the restricted environmental stimulation technique', in J. R. Eiser (ed.), *Social psychology, and behavioural medicine*, pp. 393–412. Chichester: John Wiley & Sons.

Suedfeld, P. and F. F. Ikard. (1974). 'The use of sensory deprivation in reduction of cigarette smoking. *Journal of Clinical Psychology*, 42: 888–95.

Suedfeld, P. and J. A. Best. (1977). 'Satiation and sensory deprivation combined therapy smoking therapy', *International Journal of Addictions*, 12: 337–58.

Suedfeld, P. and R. A. Borrie. (1978). 'Altering states of consciousness through sensory deprivation', in A. A. Sugerman and R. E. Tarter (eds), *Expanding dimensions of consciousness*, pp. 226–52. New York: Springer.

Suedfeld, P. and R. D. Hare. (1977). 'Sensory deprivation in treatment of snake phobia: Behavioural self-report and physiological effects', *Behaviour Therapy*, 8 (2): 240–50.

Suedfeld, P., P. B. Landon, R. Pargment, and Y. M. Epstein. (1972). 'An experimental attack on smoking: Attitude manipulation in restricted environments III', *International Journal of Addiction*, 7: 721–33.

Suedfeld, P., C. Roy, and P. B. Landon. (1982). 'Restricted environmental stimulation therapy in treatment of essential hypertension', *Behaviour Research and Therapy*, 20: 553–59.

Sultana, M. (1999). 'Progressive muscle relaxation and life style in perspective of modern stress', *Indian Journal of Clinical Psychology*, 26 (1): 48–50.

Sultana, M., A. Q. Siddiqui, and R. K. Gaur. (1988). 'Progressive muscle relaxation and life style in perspective of modern stress', *Indian Journal of Clinical Psychology*, 15: 69–70.

Sulzer, B. and G. R. Mayers. (1972). *Behaviour modification procedures for school personnel.* Hinsdale: Dryden Press.

———. (1977). *Applying behaviour analysis procedures with children and youth.* New York: Holt Rinehart Winston.

Sulzer, B., A. Loving, and S. Hunt. (1973). *The contingent use of reinforcers usually available in the classroom.* Chicago: Paper presented at the meeting of the American Educational Research Association.

Suvadarshani, S. (1994). *Behavioural intervention in menstrual distress.* Bangalore: Unpublished Ph.D thesis submitted to NIMHANS, Deemed University. India.

T

Tanner, B. A. and M. D. Zeiler. (1975). 'Punishment of self-injurious behaviour using aromatic ammonia as the aversive stimulus', *Journal of Applied Behaviour Analysis*, 8: 53–57.

Tarrier, N., H. Pilgrim, C. Sommerfield, M. R. Faragher, E. Graham, and C. Barrowclough. (1999). 'A randomized trial of cognitive therapy and imaginal exposure in the treatment of chronic post traumatic stress disorder', *Journal of Consulting and Clinical Psychology*, 67: 13–18.

Tate, B. and G. Baroff. (1966). 'Aversive control of self-injurious behaviour in a psychotic boy', *Behaviour Research and Therapy*, 4: 281–87.

Tawney, J. and D. Gast. (1984). *Single-subject research in special education.* Ohio: Charles, E. Merrill.

Taylor, J. G. (1955). 'Personal communication', in J. Wolpe (ed.), (1958), *Psychotherapy by reciprocal inhibition.* Stanford: Stanford University Press.

———. (1963). 'A behavioural interpretation of obsessive-compulsive neuroses', *Behaviour Research and Therapy*, 1: 237–44.

Terrace, H. S. 1966. 'Stimulus Control', in W. K. Honig (ed.), *Operant Behaviour: Areas of Research and Application.* New York: Appleton-Century.

———. (1982). 'Can animals think?', *New Society*, 4: 339–42.

Thankachan, M. V. (1993). *Behavioural intervention in duodenal ulcer.* Bangalore: Unpublished Ph.D thesis submitted to NIMHANS, Deemed University.

Tharp, R. G. and R. J. Wetzel. (1969). *Behaviour modification in the natural environment.* New York: Academic Press.

Thomas, D. R., W. C. Becker, and M. Armstrong. (1968). 'Production and elimination of disruptive classroom behaviour', *Journal of Applied Behaviour Analysis*, 1: 35–45.

Thomas, D. R., L. J. Nielsen, D. S. Kuypers, and W. C. Becker. (1969). *Contributions of social reinforcement and remedial instruction in elimination of a classroom behaviour problem.* Illinois: Unpublished manuscript. University of Illinois.

Thompson, R. F., P. M. Groves, T. J. Teyler, and R. A. Roemer. (1973). 'A dual process theory of habituation: Theory and behaviour, in H. V. S. Peeke and M. J. Hertz (eds), *Habituation, Vol. 1*, pp. 239–71. New York: Academic Press.

Thompson, T. (1975). 'Humanism and applied behaviourism', in T. Thompson and W. S. Dockens, III (eds), *Applications of behaviour modification*, pp. 443–48. New York: Academic Press.

Thompson, T. J., S. J. Braam, and R. W. Fuqua. (1982). 'Training and generalization of laundry skills: A multiple probe evaluation with handicapped persons', *Journal of Applied behaviour Analysis*, 15: 177–82.

Thorndike, E. L. (1911). *Animal intelligence.* New York: McMillan.

Thorpe, G. L. (1975). 'Desensitization, behaviour rehearsal, self-instructional training and placebo effects on assertive refusal behaviour', *European Journal of Behavioural Analysis and Modification*, 1: 30–44.

Thorpe, G. L. and S. L. Olson. (1990). *Behaviour therapy: Concepts, procedures and applications.* Boston: Allyn & Bacon.

Thorpe, J. G., E. Schmidt, P. T. Brown, and D. Castell. (1964). 'Aversion-relief therapy: A new method of general application', *Behaviour Research and Therapy*, 2: 71–82.

Tinsley, H. A. E. and D. J. Weiss. (1975). 'Inter-rater reliability and agreement of subjective judgment', *Journal of Consulting and Clinical Psychology*, 22: 358–76.

Tolman, E. C. (1932). *Purposive behaviour in animals and men.* New York: Century.

Tooley, J. T. and S. Pratt. (1967). 'An experimental procedure for the extinction of smoking behaviour', *Psychological Record*, 17: 209–18.

Touchette, P. E. (1971). 'Transfer of stimulus control measuring the moment of transfer', *Journal of Experimental Analysis of Behaviour*, 15 (3): 347–54.

Turner, J. W. Jr. and T. H. Fine. (1983). 'Effects of relaxation associated with brief restricted environmental stimulation therapy (REST) on plasma cortisol, ACTH, and LH', *Biofeedback and Self-regulation*, 8: 115–26.

———. (1984). *Nalaxone and restricted environmental stimulation therapy.* Albuquerque: Paper presented at the 15th Meeting of Biofeedback Society of America.

———. (1985). 'Effects of physiological measures of restricted environmental stimulation therapy (REST) on self-control of heart rate', in J. J. Sanchez-Sosa (ed.), *Health and Clinical Psychology*, pp. 477–90. New York: North-Holland Amsterdam.

Turner, S.M., D.C. Beidel, and R.G. Jacob. (1994). 'Social phobia: A comparision of behaviour therapy and atenol', *Journal of Consulting and Clinical Psychology*, 52: 642–50.

Twardosz, S. and T. Sajwaj. (1972). 'Multiple effects of a procedure to increase sitting in a hyperactive retarded boy', *Journal of Applied Behaviour Analysis*, 5: 73–78.

U

Ullman, L. P. and L. Krasner. (1965). *Case studies in behaviour modification.* New York: Holt-Rinehart & Winston.

V

Valenstein, E. S. (1966). 'The anatomical locus of reinforcement', in *Progress in Physiological Psychology, Vol. 1*, pp. 149–90. New York: Academic Press.

Van Etten, M. L. and S. Taylor. (1998). 'Comparative efficacy of treatments for Post Traumatic Stress Disorder: A meta analysis', *Clinical Psychology and Psychotherapy*, 5: 126–44.

Van Houten, R. (1983). 'Punishment from animal laboratory to the applied setting', in S. Axelrod and J. Apsche (eds), *The effects of punishment on human behaviour*, pp. 13–44. New York: Academic Press.

Van Houten, R., S. Axelord, J. S. Bailey, J. E. Favell, R. M. Foxx, B. A. Iwata, and O. I. Lovaas. (1988). 'The rights to effective behavioural treatment', *Journal of Applied Behaviour Analysis*, 21: 381–84.

Van Houten, R., P. A. Nau, and Z. Marini. (1980). 'An analysis of public posting in reducing speeding behaviour on an urban highway', *Journal of Applied Behaviour Analysis*, 15: 36–83.

Vaughan, K., M. S. Armstrong, R. Gold, N. O'Conner, W. Jenneke, and N. Tarrier. (1994). 'A trial of eye movement desensitization compared to image habituation training and applied muscle relaxation in post traumatic stress disorder', *Journal of Behaviour Therapy and Experimental Psychiatry*, 25 (4): 283–91.

Vaughan, M. E. and J. L. Michael. (1982). 'Automatic reinforcement: An important but ignored concept', *Behaviourism*, 10: 217–28.

Verghese, A., A. Beig, S. A. Senseman, S. S. S. Rao, and V. Benjamin. (1973). 'A social and psychiatric study of a representative group of families at Vellore town', *Indian Journal of Medical Research*, 61: 609–20.

Verma, S. K. (1982). 'Critical analysis of research in clinical psychology in India', *Bombay Psychologist*, 4 (1), 75–82.

Verma, V. (1995). 'Exposure and response prevention in OCD', *Indian Journal of Clinical Psychology*, 22: 50–53.

Vollmer, T. R. (1994). 'The concept of automatic reinforcement: Implications for behavioural research in developmental disabilities', *Research in Developmental Disabilities*, 15: 187–207.

Vollmer, T. R. and B. A. Iwata. (1992). 'Differential reinforcement as treatment for behaviour disorders: Procedural and functional variables', *Research in Developmental Disabilities*, 13: 393–417.

Von Monakow, C. (1914). *Die localization im Großhirn un der Abau der Function durch kortikale Herde*. Weisbaden: Bergman.

Vygotsky, L. S. (1962). *Thought and language*. New York: Wiley.

W

Wagner, M. K. and R. A. Bragge. (1970). 'Comparing behaviour modification approaches to habit decrement-smoking', *Journal of Consulting and Clinical Psychology*, 34: 258–61.

Wahler, R. G. (1967). *Behaviour therapy with oppositional children: Attempt to increase their parents' reinforcement value*. Atlanta: Paper presented at the meeting of the South-Eastern Psychological Association.

———. (1976). 'Deviant child behaviour in the family development, speculations and behaviour change strategies', in L. Leitenberg (ed.), *Handbook of Behaviour modification and behaviour therapy*. Englewood Cliffs, New Jersey: Prentice-Hall.

Wahler, R. G. and W. N. Cormier. (1970). 'The ecological interview: A first step in out-patient child behaviour therapy', *Journal of Behaviour Therapy and Experimental Psychiatry*, 1: 279–89.

Walker, H. M. and N. K. Buckley. (1968). 'The use of positive reinforcement on conditioning attending behaviour', *Journal of Applied Behaviour Analysis*, 1: 245–50.

———. (1972). 'Programming generalization and maintenance of treatment effects across time and across settings', *Journal of Applied Behaviour Analysis*, 5: 209–24.

Walker, H. M. and H. Hops. (1976). 'Use of normative peer data on a standard for evaluating classroom treatment effects', *Journal of Applied Behaviour Analysis*, 9: 159–68.

Wallis, J. W., T. R. Hobbs, D. G. Kirkpatrick, and K. W. Maley. (1975). 'Training counselors as researchers in the natural environment', in E. Ramp and G. Semb (eds), *Behaviour analysis: Areas of research and application*, pp. 175–202. New York: Prentice-Hall.

Walters, G. C. and J. E. Grusec. (1977). *Punishment*. San Francisco: W. H. Freeman.

Walton, D. (1960). 'The application of learning theory to treatment of a case of neurodermatitis', in H. J. Eysenck (ed.) *Behaviour therapy and the neuroses*. New York: Pergamon Press.

Warren, A. B. and R. H. Brown. (1943). 'Conditioned operant response phenomena in children', *Journal of General Psychology*, 28: 181–207.

Watson, J. B. (1924). *Behaviourism*. Chicago: The People Institute.

Watson, J. B. and R. Rayner. (1920). 'Conditioned emotional reactions', *Journal of Experimental Psychology*, 3: 1–14.

Watts, F. M. (1971). 'Desensitization as a habituation phenomenon–I: Stimulus intensity as a determinant of the effects of stimulus lengths', *Behaviour Research and Therapy*, 9: 209–17.

———. (1973). 'Desensitization as a habituation phenomenon II: Studies of inter-stimulus interval lengths', *Psychological Reports*, 33: 715–16.

———. (1979). 'Habituation model of systematic desensitization', *Psychological Bulletin*, 86 (3): 627–37.

Webster, D. and N. H. Azrin. (1973). 'Required relaxation: A method of inhibiting agitated disruptive behaviour of retardates', *Behaviour Research and Therapy*, 11: 67–78.

Weeks, M. and R. Gaylord-Ross. (1981). 'Task difficulty and aberrant behaviour in severely handicapped students', *Journal of Applied Behaviour Analysis*, 14: 449–63.

Wehman, P., O. Karan, and C. Rettre. (1976). 'Developing independent play in three severely retarded women', *Psychological Reports*, 39: 995–98.

Weick, C. (1968). 'Systematic observational methods', in G. Lindsey and E. Aronson (eds), *Handbook of social psychology*, pp. 357–441. Adamson Wesely: Reading Mass.

Weinberg, N. H. and M. Zaslove. (1963). '"Resistance" to systematic desensitization of phobias', *Journal of Clinical Psychology*, 19: 179–81.

Weiner, H. (1962). 'Some effects of response cost upon human operant behaviour', *Journal of Experimental Analysis of Behaviour*, 5 (2): 201–08.

Weingaertner, A. H. (1971). 'Self-administered aversive stimulation with hallucinating hospitalized schizophrenics', *Journal of Consulting and Clinical Psychology*, 36 (3): 422–29.

Weisz, J. R. and K. M. Hawley. (1998). 'Finding, evaluating, refining and applying empirically supported treatment for children and adolescents', *Journal of Clinical Child Psychology*, 27: 206–16.

———. (2002). 'Developmental factors in treatment of adolescents', *Journal of Consulting and Clinical Psychology*, 70: 21–43.

Weitzman, B. (1967). 'Behaviour therapy and psychotherapy', *Psychological Review*, 74: 300–17.

Wells, A. (1997). *Cognitive therapy of anxiety disorders*. New York: John Wiley.

Wenar, C. (1982). 'Developmental psychopathology, its nature and models', *Journal of Child Psychology*, 11: 192–201.

Weniger, D., W. Huber, F. J. Stachowiack, and K. Poeck. (1980). 'Treatment of aphasia on a linguistic basis' in M. T. Sarno and O' Hook (eds), *Aphasia assessment and treatment*. Stolkholm: Almquist & Wiksell.

Wessler, R. A. (1986). 'Value judgements and self evaluation in rational-emotive therapy', in W. Dryden and P. Trower (eds), *Rational-emotive Therapy: Recent Developments in Theory and Practice*. Bristol, England: Institute of RET.

Wetzel, R. J., J. Baker, M. Roney, and M. Martin. (1966). 'Out-patient treatment of autistic behaviour', *Behaviour Research and Therapy*, 4: 169–77.

White, S. H. (1965). 'Evidence for a hierarchical arrangement of learning processes', in L. P. List and C. C. Spicer (eds), *Advances in child development and behaviour, Vol 2*. New York: Academic Press.

White, S. O. and M. A. Straus. (1981). 'The implications of family violence for rehabilitation strategy', in S. E. Martin, L. B. Sechrest, and R. Redner (eds), *New directions in the rehabilitation of criminal offenders*, pp. 255–88. Washington DC: National Academy Press.

Whitman, T. L., J. W. Scibak, and D. H. Reid. (1983). *Behaviour modification with the severely and profoundly retarded: Research and application*. New York: Academic Press.

Williams, C. D. (1959). 'The elimination of tantrum behaviour by extinction procedures', *Journal of Abnormal and Social Psychology*, 59: 269.

Williams, M. (1997). *Cry of pain*. London: Penguin.

Wilson, C. W. and B. L. Hopkins. (1973). 'The effects of contingent music on the intensity of noise in junior high home economics classes', *Journal of Applied Behaviour Analysis*, 6: 269–75.

Wilson, F. S. and R. H. Walters. (1966). 'Modification of speech output of near mute schizophrenic through social learning procedures', *Behaviour Research and Therapy*, 4: 59–67.

Wilson, G. T. (1974). *Behaviour therapy in adults*. Paper presented at the American psychopathological Association, Boston. March.

———. (1982). 'Psychotherapy process and procedures. The behavioural mandate', *Behaviour Therapy*, 13 (3): 291–312.

———. (1984). 'Adult disorders', in G. T. Wilson and C. M. Franks (eds), *Contemporary behaviour therapy: Conceptual and empirical foundations*. New York: Guilford Press.

Wilson, P. G., D. H. Reid, J. E. Phillips, and D. E. Burgio. (1984). 'Normalization of institutional mealtimes for profoundly retarded persons: Effects and non effects of teaching family style dining', *Journal of Applied Behaviour Analysis*, 17: 186–201.

Wilson, S. A., L. A. Becker, and R. H. Tinker. (1995). 'Eye movement desensitization and reprocessing (EMDR) treatment for psychologically traumatized individuals', *Journal of Consulting and Clinical Psychology*, 63 (6): 928–37.

———. (1997). 'Fifteen month follow-up of eye movement desensitization and reprocessing treatment for post traumatic stress disorder and psychological trauma', *Journal of Consulting and Clinical Psychology*, 65 (6): 1047–56.

Wilson, S. H. and R. L. Williams. (1973). 'The effects of group contingencies on first graders' academic and social behaviours', *Journal of School Psychology*, 11: 110–17.

Winer, B. J. (1971). *Statistical principles in experimental design.* New York: Mc Graw-Hill.

Winett, R. A. and E. M. Vachon. (1974). 'The effects of reinforcing academic performance on social behaviour: A brief report', *Psychological Reports*, 34: 1238–92.

Winkler, R. C. (1970). 'Management of chronic psychiatric patients by a token reinforcement system', *Journal of Applied Behaviour Analysis*, 3: 47–55.

Wisocki, P. A. (1973). 'The successful treatment of a heroin addict by covert conditioning techniques', *Journal of Behaviour Therapy and Experimental Psychiatry*, 4 (1): 55–61.

Wisocki, P. A. and J. E. Rooney. (1974). 'A comparison of thought stopping and covert sensitization techniques in treatment of smoking: A brief report', *Psychological Record*, 24; 191–92.

Wodarski, J. S., R. L. Hamblin, D. R. Buckholdt, and D. E. Ferritor. (1972). 'The effects of low performance group and individual contingency on co-operative play', *Psychological record.*

Wolf, M. M., T. R. Risley, and H. Mees. (1964). 'Application of operant conditioning procedures to the behaviour problems of an autistic child', *Behaviour Research and Therapy*, 1: 305–12.

Wolf, M. M., J. S. Birnbrauer, T. Williams, and J. Lawler. (1965). 'A note on apparent extinction of the vomiting behaviour of a retarded child', in L. P. Ulman and L. Krasner (eds), *Case studies in behaviour modification*, pp. 364–66. New York: Holt, Rinehart, & Winstton, Inc.

Wolfe, V. F. and A. J. Cuvo. (1978). 'Effects of within stimulus and extra stimulus prompting on letter discrimination of mentally retarded persons', *American Journal of Mental Deficiency*, 83: 297–303.

Wolpe, J. (1958). *Psychotherapy by reciprocal inhibition.* New York: Standard University Press.

———. (1965). 'Conditioned inhibition of craving in drug addiction', *Behaviour Research and Therapy*, 2: 185–87.

———. (1969). *The practice of behaviour therapy.* Oxford: Pergamon Press.

———. (1990). *The Practice of Behaviour Therapy (4th Ed.).* New York: Pergamon Press.

Wolpe, J. and A. A. Lazarus. (1966). *Behaviour therapy techniques.* New York: Pergamon Press.

Wolpe, J. and J. Abrams. (1991). 'Post Traumatic Stress Disorder overcome by eye movement desensitization: A case study', *Journal of Behaviour Therapy and Experimental Psychiatry*, 22 (1): 39–43.

Wolpe, J. and P. J. Lang. (1964). *A fear survey schedule for use in behaviour therapy.* Oxford: Pergamon.

Wong, S. E., D. Mark, M. D. Terranova, L. Bowen, R. Zarate, H. K. Massel, and R. P. Liberman. (1987). 'Providing independent recreational activities to reduce stereotypic vocalization in chronic schizophrenics', *Journal of Applied Behaviour Analysis*, 20: 27–30.

Woods, D.W. and E. J. Teng. (2002). 'Backward chaining', in M. Hersen and W. Sledge (eds) *Encyclopaedia of psychotherapy*, Vol.1, pp. 149–53. Sandiago, California: Academic Press.

Woods, T. S. (1980). 'On the alleged incompatibility of analysis: A response to Piere and Epling', *The Behaviour Analyst*, 3: 67–69.

Woodworth, R. S. and H. Schlosberg. (1954). *Experimental psychology.* New York: Holt.

World Health Organization. (1973). *The ICD-10 Classification of mental and behavioural disorders: Clinical descriptions and diagnostic guidelines.* Geneva: World health Organization.

Wyrwicks, W. (1967). 'An experimental approach to problem of mechanism of alimentary conditioned reflex type II', in G. A. Kumble (ed.), *Foundations of conditioning and learning*, pp. 260–68. New York: Appleton-Century Croft.

Y

Yamagami, T. (1972). 'The treatment of an obsession by thought stopping', *Journal of Behaviour Therapy and Experimental Psychiatry*, 2: 133–35.

Yates, A. J. (1970). *Behaviour therapy*. New York: Wiley.

Yeakel, M. H., L. L. Salisbury, S. L. Greer, and L. F. Marcus. (1970). 'An application of auto-induced adverse control of self-injurious behaviour', *Journal of Experimental Child Psychology*, 10: 159–64.

Young, P. T. (1948). 'Appetite palatability and feeding habit: A critical review', *Psychological Review*, 48: 289–320.

Yule, W., B. Sacks, and L. Hersov. (1974). 'Successful flooding treatment of a noise phobia in an eleven-year old', *Journal of Behaviour Therapy and Experimental Psychiatry*, 5 (2): 209–11.

Yulevich, L. and S. Axelord. (1983). 'Punishment: A concept that is no longer necessary', In M. Hersen, R. M. Eisler, ' and P. M. Peter (eds), *Progress in behaviour modification, Vol. 14*, pp. 355–82. New York: Academic Press.

Z

Zieler, M. D. and S. S. Zervey. (1968). 'Development of behaviour: Self-feeding', *Journal of Consulting and Clinical Psychology*, 32: 164–68.

Zimmerman, E. H. and J. Zimmerman. (1962). 'The alteration of behaviour in a classroom situation', *Journal of Applied Behaviour Analysis*, 5: 59–60.

Zivin, G. (1974). 'Removing common confusion about egocentric speech, private speech and self-regulation', in G. Zivin (ed.), *The development of self-regulation through innate speech*. New York: Wiley.

———. (1979). *Removing common confusions about egocentric speech, private speech, and self-regulation through private speech.* New York: Wiley.

Zlutnick, S., W. J. Mayville, and S. Moffat. (1975). 'Modification of seizure disorders: The interruption of behaviour chains', *Journal of Applied Behavior Analysis*, 8: 1–12.

Zubek, J. P. (1973). 'Behavioural and psychophysiological effects of prolonged deprivation: A review', in J. E. Rasmussen (ed.) *Man in isolation and confinement*, pp. 9–83. New York: Aldine.

Adult Behaviour History Form

I. Identifying Data

Source of Referral_____ Registration No._____ Date _____

Name_____ Age_____ Sex_____ Occupation_____

Address_____

Tel._____ Education_____ Income_____ Marital Status_____

Religion_____ Nationality_____ Place of Birth_____ Date of Birth_____

II. Present Complaints

1. _____

2. _____

3. _____

4. _____

5. _____

6. Client's causal attribution_____

7. Informant's causal attribution_____

III. Personal History

Significant reinforcers and punishers_____

Abilities/Coping skills of the client_____

Disabilities/Deficiencies_____

Physical and/or behavioural constraints_____

Clients likes and dislikes (people, activities & objects)_____

Dispensers of reinforcement and punishment_____

IV. Biological Analysis (Significant findings of physical examination, accident disease/disorder)

_____
_____
_____

V. Family & Social Environment

Relationship with family members_____

Family's response to the problem behaviour_____

_____

Relationship with other members (in workplace, community, and friends)_____

Others' response to the problem behaviour_____

Significant psychosocial events_____

_____

VI. Previous Treatment History

_____
_____

VII. Behaviour Analysis (Use Form for detailed analysis)

_____
_____

VIII. Behavioural Formulation

_____
_____
_____

IX. Intervention

_____

_____

_____

X. Home Assignment

_____

_____

_____

_____

XI. Evaluation & Termination Report

_____

_____

_____

_____

Date :   Behaviour Therapist

Appendix-2

Child Behaviour History Form

I. Identifying Data

Source of Referral_____Code_____Date_____

Name_____Age_____Sex _____

Guardian's Name_____Address_____

Tel. No.(s)_____Education & School_____Religion_____

Nationality_____

II. Presenting Problems

1._____

2._____

3._____

4._____

_____

Precipitating psychosocial stress (such as death of parents/divorce and others, specify the time) :

_____

_____

Informants' causal attribution_____

III. Personal History

Significant reinforcing and punishing events_____

Abilities/Behavioural Assets_____

Deficiencies/Disabilities_____

Constraints (Physical and/or Behavioural_____

Child's likes and dislikes (People, Activities and Objects)_____

Major dispensers of reinforcement and punishment_____

IV. Family Relationship

Present placement of the child (natural parent/step parent/foster parent/adoptive parent/institution/any other, specify)_____

_____

Relationship between: Child–parent_____

Parents_____

Child-siblings_____

Siblings_____

Child-significant others_____

Modes of reinforcement & punishment_____

Behaviour problems among adults_____

Behaviour problems among siblings_____

V. Biological Analysis (Significant findings of physical examination, accident/ disease/disorder)

_____

_____

_____

VI. Previous Treatment History

_____

_____

VII. Socio-cultural Analysis (Recent changes in the family, school or neighbourhood)

_____

_____

_____

VIII. Behaviour Analysis (Use separate form for detailed analysis)

_____ _____

_____

_____

IX. Intervention

_____

_____

_____

_____

X. Homework

_____

_____

_____

_____

XI. Evaluation and Termination Report

_____

_____

_____

_____

Date :   Behaviour Therapist

Appendix-3

Behaviour Analysis Form

Client's Name_____Age_____Sex_____Registration No._____

Date_____Source of Referral_____Informant_____

Sl. No.	Setting & Antecedents	Target Behaviour	Consequences
1.			
2.			
3.			
4.			
5.			
6.			

Summary :

Behaviour Therapist

Appendix-4

Treatment Consent Form

Name of the Subject_____Age_____Sex_____Education_____

Address_____

1. The purpose of this treatment is...

2. The following procedure will be used for treatment ....
   ....

3. There are other alternative treatment methods available in behaviour therapy also such as ....
   ....

4. The information given by the subject will be treated as confidential and will not be revealed to anyone without written consent of the subject (except under judicial instruction).

5. He/she (subject) will have the right to refuse the treatment at any stage.

6. The subject will clear his/her payments towards therapy (if any) in advance prior to the treatment session.

Subject's Declaration

I have been explained adequately about the above procedural details of behaviour therapy/research. I have also understood the foreseeable effects including discomforts, risks and benefits involved in it. I agree to volunteer and take responsibility for any medical care required as a result of injury or physical complications due to treatment.

I also understand that the information collected from the present treatment programme may be published or used for the purpose of dissemination of information to the public without revealing my identity. Every effort will be made to maintain the confidentiality.

Date _____   Signature of the Subject_____
                                                        Subjects' representative _____

Therapist's Declaration

I have explained to the above subject the nature and procedure of treatment, the foreseeable risks, discomfort, pain as well as benefits involved in the treatment and also assured about the confidentiality of information obtained from him/her. I have also considered that alternative treatments available for the client. All of the questioned raised by the client has been answered to the best of my ability.

Date_____   Therapist_____

Treatment Record Form

Client's Name_____Age_____Sex_____Registration No._____

Date_____Source of Referral_____Informant_____

Address_____Telephone_____

Date	Time	Details of the Session	Home Assignment	Next Session

Therapist

Appendix-6

Home Assignment Form

Name_____Age_____Sex_____Address_____

_____Phone_____FAX_____

Registration No._____Date_____Target Behaviours_____

Date	Time	Assignment	Next Appointment	Remark

Behaviour Therapist

Index

About the Author

S P K Jena is Reader in Applied Psychology at University of Delhi, South Campus. Being trained as a clinical psychologist at National Institute of Mental Health and Neurosciences, Bangalore, he specialised in behaviour therapy. He obtained a doctoral degree from Central Institute of Psychiatry, Ranchi, and served in teaching positions as a lecturer in Clinical Psychology at National Institute for the Mentally Handicapped, Secunderabad as a reader in Special Education at M. J. P. Rohilkhand University, Bareilly and Applied Psychology at Guru Jambheshwar University, Hisar. Prior to this, he wrote another book entitled *Perspective in Mental Retardation*, Anu Books, Meerut. His research articles have been published in national and international journals. Currently, he is a member of the editorial board of Indian Journal of Clinical Psychology.